CHURCH AND ESTATE

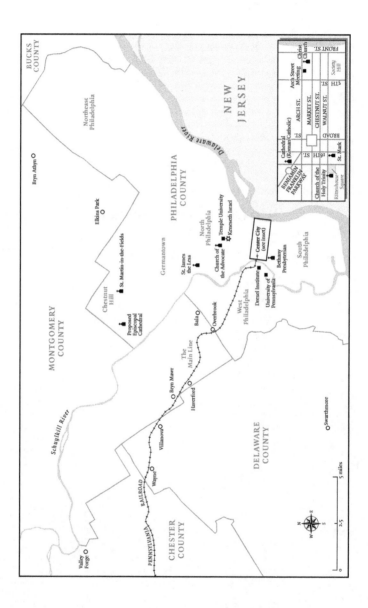

THOMAS F. RZEZNIK

CHURCH AND ESTATE

RELIGION AND WEALTH IN
INDUSTRIAL-ERA PHILADELPHIA

The Pennsylvania State University Press
University Park, Pennsylvania

Library of Congress Cataloging-in-Publication Data
Rzeznik, Thomas F., 1979–
Church and estate : religion and wealth in industrial-era Philadelphia / Thomas F. Rzeznik.
p.   cm.
Summary: "Examines the lives and religious commitments of the Philadelphia elite during the
period of industrial prosperity that extended from the late nineteenth century through the 1920s"—
Provided by publisher.
Includes bibliographical references and index.
ISBN 978-0-271-05967-9 (cloth)
ISBN 978-0-271-05968-6 (pbk.)
1. Upper class—Religious life—Pennsylvania—Philadelphia—History—19th century.
2. Upper class—Religious life—Pennsylvania—Philadelphia—History—20th century.
3. Upper class—Pennsylvania—Philadelphia—Social life and customs—19th century.
4. Upper class—Pennsylvania—Philadelphia—Social life and customs—20th century.
5. Wealth—Pennsylvania—Philadelphia—Religious aspects—Christianity.
6. Philadelphia (Pa.)—Church history—19th century.
7. Philadelphia (Pa.)—Church history—20th century.
I. Title.

BR560.P5R94 2013
305.5'2340974811—dc23
2012051317

To my parents

CONTENTS

ILLUSTRATIONS

ACKNOWLEDGMENTS

I have received a wealth of support in the course of researching and writing *Church and Estate*. It gives me great pleasure to recognize the many individuals to whom I owe debts of gratitude.

This work reflects the expert guidance of those who mentored me in graduate school. My advisor, John McGreevy, could not have been more gracious in his support or more generous with his time. His thoughtful reading and intelligent advice greatly helped me hone my arguments. Scott Appleby, Gail Bederman, and George Marsden rounded out an excellent committee. Thomas Slaughter was wise to encourage me to take up a project on Philadelphia. Kathleen Sprows Cummings shared my enthusiasm for our native city, and Robert Sullivan could always be trusted for wise counsel.

I am fortunate that Philadelphians and their religious communities have been such avid collectors and such dedicated custodians of their history. I am very much indebted to the archivists, librarians, and staff members who guided me though the collections at the following repositories: the Athenaeum of Philadelphia; the Architecture Archives of the University of Pennsylvania; the Archives of the Sisters of the Blessed Sacrament (with particular thanks to Stephanie Morris); the Bryn Athyn College Library, the Drexel University Archives; the Episcopal Divinity School Archives; the Free Library of Philadelphia; the Friends Historical Library at Swarthmore College; the Hagley Museum and Library; the Quaker and Special Collections of Haverford College; the Historical Society of Pennsylvania; the Lower Merion Historical Society (with particular thanks to Gerald Francis and Ted Goldsborough); the Philadelphia Jewish Archives Center, the Presbyterian Historical Society; the Philadelphia Archdiocesan Historical Research Center (with particular thanks to Shawn Weldon); the Temple University Archives; the Temple University Urban Archives; and the University of Pennsylvania Archives.

Several churches and congregations kindly opened their doors and private collections to me. For their hospitality, I wish to thank Church of St. Asaph, Bala Cynwyd; Church of the Holy Trinity, Philadelphia; St. Mark's Episcopal Church, Philadelphia; Cathedral of Our Saviour, Philadelphia; St. Thomas's Episcopal Church, Whitemarsh; Washington Memorial Chapel, Valley Forge;

Bryn Mawr Presbyterian Church; and Reform Congregation Keneseth Israel, Elkins Park, as well as Christ Church, Philadelphia, and St. Mary's Church, Roxborough, for generously allowing me to use images from their collections. My special thanks go to Nathanael Groton Jr. for sharing his father's diaries from his first two years as rector of St. Thomas's, Whitemarsh.

A number of scholars have been generous with both their time and advice. David Contosta, a wonderful supporter since the day I first sought his help in navigating the Philadelphia scene, was kind enough to bring me into a circle of scholars working on the history of the Episcopal Diocese of Pennsylvania. Anne Rose provided extensive feedback on conversion as dealt with in chapter 4, while Ken Fones-Wolf offered helpful comments on social reform as dealt with in chapter 6. Peter Williams both shared his research on Episcopalians and advised me on my own. David Bains provided information on national houses of worship. Jim McCartin and Vanessa May each read chapters and supplied helpful comments as the book neared completion. My colleagues in the history department at Seton Hall University offered me an intellectual home and supportive environment.

I also extend my appreciation and gratitude to those who have provided financial support at various stages of this project. A presidential fellowship from the University of Notre Dame and a three-year fellowship from the Dolores Zohrab Liebmann Foundation sustained my graduate studies. A Gest Fellowship from Haverford College funded my research in the college's Quaker and Special Collections. Seton Hall provided publication support through funding from the university core.

Kathryn Yahner and the staff of Penn State Press have been exceptionally helpful in guiding me and my book through the production process. I am grateful as well for earlier assistance from the editors of those journals where portions of this research first appeared. An earlier version of chapter 5 was published as "Representatives of All That Is Noble: The Rise of the Episcopal Establishment in Early-Twentieth-Century Philadelphia," *Religion and American Culture: A Journal of Interpretation* (Winter 2009). Portions of chapter 2 appeared in modified form in "The Parochial Enterprise: Financing Institutional Growth in the Brick-and-Mortar Era," *American Catholic Studies* (Fall 2010). I thank both journals for allowing me to use that material here.

Remarkable friends have offered encouragement and moral support throughout this project. Fellow graduate students at Notre Dame served as sounding boards for ideas, read through various portions of my research, and provided a remarkable community of fellowship. It has been an honor to count Meg Garnett, Timothy Gloege, Micaela Larkin, Stephen Molvarec, Justin Poché, and Charles Strauss among my friends and fellow historians. Tracey Billado, Howard Eissenstat, Maura Kenny, and Marianne Lloyd made my life in New Jersey all the more pleasurable. Across the Hudson, Mary Kate Blaine, Keira Dillon, Greg Eirich, Katie Kramer, and Stephanie Toti cheered me on; they have been true friends in every sense.

I owe my greatest debt of gratitude to my family, without whom none of this would have been possible. My brother, Stas, offered me support whenever I needed it, often in telephone conversations that lasted for hours. I am equally fortunate to have been blessed with loving parents, Felicia and Jozef, who fostered my intellectual curiosity and encouraged my academic pursuits, who welcomed me home on countless research trips to the Philadelphia area, and who humored me whenever I suggested that a family outing include a visit to some church in the region. They taught me the value of faith and love, those virtues beyond price. I dedicate this book to them.

In 1921, the board of the Provident Life and Trust Company of Philadelphia approved a reorganization plan that separated the firm's life insurance and trust divisions. Following its formal establishment in December 1922, the Provident Mutual Life Insurance Company of Philadelphia orchestrated an extensive advertising campaign to promote the new enterprise. Among the services it marketed were investment annuities, touted in one brochure as guaranteeing "relief from anxiety" and "comfortable income through life." To help potential clients visualize the benefits the firm's annuities could provide, the brochure included a series of drawings portraying the leisurely pursuits of the privileged class. In one, a golfer hits a long drive to a distant green as his caddie stands by. Another shows a transatlantic steamer carrying passengers to overseas adventures. A third portrays two women being chauffeured past a country estate in their luxurious touring sedan. For Philadelphians, these scenes of upper-class comfort evoked the idealized, carefree lifestyle of the "Main Line," the string of fashionable suburban communities that had grown up along the main east-west line of the Pennsylvania Railroad. If the illustrations were to be believed, annuities guaranteed their holders a share in this exclusive world of wealth and privilege.[1]

In and of itself, the brochure was hardly extraordinary. There was no shortage of depictions of the country club set in 1920s advertising. Nor was Provident marketing a new service; the company had been selling annuities since its inception in 1865. But for those familiar with the history of the firm, the brochure marked a radical departure from Provident's traditional attitude toward wealth. The company had been founded by members of the Religious Society of Friends (Quakers), who were guided by an ethic of "fiduciary responsibility." Provident's early advertising capitalized on public perceptions of Quaker trustworthiness and proudly spoke of the "strict economy with which affairs are managed." Unlike the brochures of the 1920s, which enticed readers with such alluring titles as "Saving and Success" and "Spend Your Money, and Have It . . . Too," the sober advertisements of earlier years stressed the responsibility that came with wealth rather than the pleasure and status it could provide.[2]

How should we interpret these new trends in Provident's advertising? On one level, they can be explained as part of the triumph of consumerism that had taken hold in American society by the 1920s. On another level, however, they reflected a distinct change in how money and its uses were understood within a religious community whose teachings traditionally cautioned against outward displays of wealth and warned of the corrupting influence of worldly desires. To use the lure of luxury to attract business, as Provident did in the 1920s, seemed contrary to the Quaker principles on which the firm had been founded. In his 1908 annual report, company president Asa S. Wing had reminded investors that selecting a firm for life insurance or the management of trusts should not be decided "by the liberality of promises made, but by the character of the company as evidenced by its past history and present standing, and by the character of the men who control its management." And, speaking at the company's fiftieth anniversary in 1915, Wing had reminded his colleagues that the "affairs of each patron have always been regarded as of a delicate and sacred nature, demanding the greatest integrity."[3] Yet, by the 1920s, the proper management of wealth, once seen as a spiritual exercise, came to be promoted as a pathway to conspicuous consumption. Although corporate expansion had by then diluted the Quaker presence within the firm, members of the Society of Friends remained well represented on the board of directors, who presumably had approved the new advertising initiative.[4]

This change in how Quakers within one firm understood the relationship between money and morality is just one small part of a much larger story of the interplay of religion and wealth in the United States during the late nineteenth and early twentieth centuries. At arguably no other time in American history were these two forces more intimately linked than during this period, which saw not only the creation of great industrial fortunes and the consolidation of a powerful capitalist class, but also the vast expansion of religious institutions and the strengthening of denominational identity across the religious spectrum. The temptation persists to segregate these spheres and draw stark dichotomies between the realms of God and Mammon, but such divisions obscure the considerable connections among the economic, social, and religious developments of the time and the transformations and tensions they engendered.

Provident's history provides one glimpse of how these developments worked in concert. Even as the tenor of its advertising changed, the company capitalized on the public trust it had accrued from the managers' strict adherence to Quaker principles. At least within the local sphere, the firm's religious heritage served as a marketable commodity, one that distinguished it from other investment houses. Known informally as "the Quaker bank," Provident made explicit references to its founding by Friends both in its early advertisements and in its later brochures.[5] Other Quaker concerns saw similar benefits in affirming their history. In 1911, Strawbridge and Clothier, one of the city's leading department stores, unveiled a company seal that depicted William Penn consummating a treaty with the leader of the local Indian tribe. The "Friendly handshake" that solemnized the agreement came to serve as the store's "seal of confidence," which was displayed prominently within the store and used extensively in advertising material.[6] As with Provident, Quakerism provided not only a guiding ethic, but also a corporate identity.

Provident's promotional strategies may not appear at first glance to offer much in return for the Quakers themselves, but they, too, gained from the relationship. Even though the Society of Friends, as a religious body, had no direct involvement in these company affairs, they nevertheless enjoyed the fruits of corporate success. Like other religious communities, the Society of Friends benefited from the increased wealth and upward social mobility of its members. Philanthropy and patronage sustained Quaker charitable initiatives and educational institutions. In a more indirect way, regular invocations of a firm's Quaker heritage and use of Quaker imagery in advertising helped keep the Society in the public eye at a time when its members had neither the numerical strength nor the degree of social influence they once enjoyed.

Yet alongside these symbiotic relationships, Provident's history also reveals the tensions and ambiguities inherent in this convergence of religion and wealth. The scenes of luxurious living that appeared in Provident's later advertising demonstrate all too clearly how financial success could cause individuals to succumb to worldly temptations. Without vigilance, Quakers had long taught, the same wealth that testified to an individual's hard work and honest dealing could lead to moral bankruptcy. The use of Quaker references and imagery in advertising held its own dangers, too. Those who publicly professed their Quaker identity invited religious scrutiny. Holding themselves to a higher moral standard, they needed to be mindful and protective of their reputations.[7] Unscrupulous business practices or risky economic behavior reflected poorly not only on the individuals who engaged in them, but also on the companies and religious communities to which those individuals belonged. Economic and spiritual imperatives continually vied for allegiance. How individuals and religious communities negotiated those competing impulses would shape the social and religious worlds of the industrial era.

The relationship between Provident Life and Trust Company and the Society of Friends points to a deeper set of dynamics working within American society during the transformative decades of the late nineteenth and early twentieth centuries. What could be framed as simply an episode in the history of corporate growth in the United States speaks just as powerfully to the influence religious belief and class aspirations had on individuals and communities alike during the industrial era, when those two forces were nothing short of pervasive. They lay at the core of personal identity and shaped the contours of social relations. They informed behavior and established boundaries. They were matters both intensely private and unavoidably public.

To gauge the social and religious transformations of these decades, *Church and Estate* sets its focus on Philadelphia, one of the nation's leading industrial centers throughout the period. The city's developmental trajectory serves as a representative example of how wealth transformed American society—creating value systems, reordering class relations, and structuring authority. In Philadelphia, as elsewhere, industrial prosperity not only reshaped the physical, social, and religious landscape, but it also enabled those who controlled economic resources to attain prominence and exercise considerable influence in economic, political, and civic affairs. Although the less affluent also sought to advance their own interests, those who possessed a disproportionate share of wealth ultimately possessed a disproportionate degree of power and authority. This was no less true in the religious sphere than it was in other areas of life.

The decision to focus on Philadelphia also stems from its rich religious history. Well before the industrial era, the city had secured a reputation for its religious diversity. The well-known Quaker legacy of religious toleration made Philadelphia, in the words of one work, "America's first plural society."[8] In addition to being a Quaker stronghold, Philadelphia was the seat of the mother diocese of the Episcopal Church, the site of the first Presbytery organized in the United States, home to one of the nation's oldest Jewish communities, the first place in the colonies where Catholics could worship openly, the cradle of American Methodism, the birthplace of the African Methodist Episcopal Church, and a haven for a number of persecuted religious minorities. On account of its deep religious roots, Philadelphia came to serve over time as an important administrative center for several denominations. The Philadelphia Yearly Meetings of Orthodox and Hicksite Friends were generally regarded as the most influential Quaker bodies in the United States. Many important boards and agencies for the Episcopal and Presbyterian churches were headquartered in the city. By the late nineteenth century, the strong Jewish institutional presence arguably made Philadelphia the "Capital of Jewish America."[9] Throughout the industrial era, the numerical strength of the city's various denominations further contributed to Philadelphia's importance as a religious center. The Episcopal Diocese of Pennsylvania, which covered the five-county Philadelphia region, was consistently the second largest and second wealthiest diocese in the nation at this time.[10] Presbyterian membership was equally impressive, with the Philadelphia Presbytery surpassed only by the Pittsburgh.[11] As Catholic numbers grew, the naming of Archbishop Dennis Dougherty to the College of Cardinals in 1921 signaled the city's importance within the Catholic Church. For all of these reasons, Philadelphians had the potential to extend their influence well beyond their local religious communities.

By examining the religious involvements of wealthy Philadelphians, *Church and Estate* draws attention to two complementary and interrelated processes. First, it examines how religious belief and denominational affiliation shaped individuals' class identity and informed their public actions. Although deeply personal, religious belief structured social relations, guided business decisions, and informed civic commitments; in doing so, it entered the public arena. Indeed, the elite themselves recognized that their status as a ruling class and their claims to social authority rested on moral foundations. Second, it explores the influence wealth and status afforded individuals within their local churches and broader denominations. It thereby traces how financial forces and class influence affected the development of religious communities and shaped the character of American religious life as it took its modern form. Though informed by the theological debates that emerged over the moral order and the nature of the capitalist system, this study concentrates instead on the everyday negotiations that occurred as Philadelphia's wealthy individuals and religious communities contended with competing moral and economic imperatives.

Exploring these dynamics contributes to our understanding of American social and religious history in two significant ways. First, it encourages historians to recognize the prevalence and power of religious belief among members of the social and financial elite, rather than simply regarding it as secondary to more material concerns.[12] The elite in Philadelphia and elsewhere in the United States had a need for moral satisfaction and spiritual security. For many, churchgoing and charitable work were not only important social rituals, but also sincere expressions of religious faith. Wealthy individuals drawn to religious expression cannot be reduced to Jackson Lears's aesthetes in search of authentic experience or Thorstein Veblen's conspicuous consumers of devout observances.[13] Even scholars who credit white Anglo-Saxon Protestants (WASPs) for providing the "integrating ethic of American life" have largely failed to examine the religious identity of their subjects or the religious roots of that ethic. Most offer only bittersweet laments for the loss of perceived cultural cohesiveness once provided by this group, and assume the existence of their cultural, political, and social power without describing its origins.[14] Although some recent biographies of Gilded Age greats have acknowledged the authenticity of their subjects' religious beliefs, it is striking how quickly religion drops out of the equation when wealthy individuals are aggregated as a class.[15] Too many accounts rely on an uncritical acceptance of a secularization thesis that views a decline of religious devotion as a corollary to increased education and affluence.

Second, it calls attention to the ways in which wealth and elite influence affected religious institutions and their mission. In the ecclesiastical realm, as in other areas, those who controlled financial resources enjoyed power and authority. Their wealth enabled members of the upper class to craft religious practices that conformed to both their theological and their social sensibilities. Yet, with the exception of several recent works that have deftly explored theological responses to market capitalism, historians of American religion have been largely silent on the issue of class—or money, for that matter.[16] Some scholars have employed rational choice models to describe the functioning of the American religious marketplace, but their works do not directly address the issue of class.[17] They fail to consider the issues of power and authority that characterize the broader history of class relations and the formation of class interests within and among groups. Furthermore, those who speak of the democratization of American religious life overlook the recurring influence of elites.[18] As with social and political institutions, wealth and elite interests have the potential to erode the democratic nature of religious bodies.[19] This caveat applies not only to elite assemblies but to all religious communities, since even the poorest congregation has its wealthiest member. By drawing attention to these forces, *Church and Estate* seeks to initiate a fuller and more open discussion of how class interests and financial forces shaped religious institutions, for better or for worse, and how they affected the social mission and theological message of the nation's churches.

Tracing the relationship between religion and wealth thus sheds new light on the process of class formation in the United States. Beyond a handful of older accounts, such as those of sociologist E. Digby Baltzell, scholars have paid only scant attention to religion's role in structuring class relations.[20] Even

Sven Beckert's masterful study of the rise of the American bourgeoisie in late nineteenth-century New York makes only passing references to the religious affiliation and faith commitments of its subjects.[21] Of the few studies that address the issue, most focus on the middle and working classes. Yet even here, religious identity is often perceived as transitional, fading once other social forces such as economic advancement, working-class consciousness, or Americanization have fostered a new group identity.[22] Too often religion is perceived as a difference to be overcome rather than as a force of social cohesion, with the inclusionary and exclusionary aspects of religious association helping to create and sustain class boundaries. Religion, among many other factors, contributed to how, in Beckert's words, "a group of people with often-divergent material interests forged themselves into a social class and how they were at times able to act collectively on this identity."[23]

More important, religious involvement and adherence to moral principles helped legitimize class authority. During the industrial era, wealth alone could not secure social respectability. To count among the ruling class, members of the social and financial elite were expected by their peers and the general public to abide by the teachings of their churches and to serve as exemplars of civic virtue. Only with the proper spiritual capital could members claim the moral authority they needed to exercise power. This is not to say, however, that religion served merely an instrumental function. Members of the upper class may not have been uniformly devout, but many were deeply religious and desired a sense of moral security that financial success alone could not provide. They weighed the ethical demands and wrestled with the social responsibilities that accompanied their economic and political power. Their religious beliefs and personal faith bound them to a particular cosmology and system of ethical standards that informed choices, conditioned behavior, and directed attention to ultimate ends. More than a source of status gained through nominal affiliation, religion served as a practical moral force and essential theological guide.

At the heart of these developments lay a complex system of economic and symbolic exchange. Just as churches depended on members of the social and financial elite for economic support, so these individuals relied on their churches for spiritual solace and moral approbation. They sought the spiritual and psychological comfort of knowing that they were justified, both in the eyes of God and their religious communities, in their use of wealth and exercise of power. They further recognized that religious affiliation conferred status, just as religious communities recognized the benefits of their association with members of the social and financial elite.

Throughout this study, I employ the metaphor "spiritual capital" as a conceptual tool to denote the benefits individuals derived from their religious involvements. Borrowing from recent research on "social capital" by Robert Putnam and others, "spiritual capital" helps convey the significance of religion in people's lives. It suggests that members of a religious community, like those who belong to other voluntary associations, derive certain benefits, both tangible and intangible, by virtue of their membership and participation in that group or social network.[24] The metaphor is particularly apt for the study of religion among the financial elite. Although it is important not to overrationalize religious choice, interpret spiritual motivation in purely functionalist ways, or crassly assume that the rich sought to buy their way into heaven, it is equally important to acknowledge that individuals "profit" from their religious participation. In return for their commitment to religious principles and their financial support for religious institutions, wealthy individuals obtained the spiritual capital they needed to secure their social status and strengthen their class authority.

The metaphor "spiritual capital" is also informed by the theoretical insights of Pierre Bourdieu, whose exploration of "cultural capital" reveals how social differentiation depends on the cultivation of shared tastes and aesthetic sensibilities. Bourdieu demonstrates that class identity is not simply the product of one's economic standing, but stems from one's habitus, a disposition that one shares with other members of a particular class or social group. Once internalized, the tastes and sensibilities of one's habitus serve as "structuring structures" by which individuals preconsciously order the social world and situate themselves within and among groups. These internalized subjectivities serve as the basis of social classification and facilitate the collective action upon which class formation depends.[25] In industrial-era Philadelphia, religious affiliation, modes of worship, and ecclesiastical tastes all served as classificatory devices and symbolic markers of class status. Drawing from Bourdieu, one can further argue that, like their cultural equivalents, these religious behaviors and attitudes are "predisposed, consciously and deliberately or not, to fulfill a social function of legitimating social difference."[26] Conforming to certain religious behaviors or expectations gave wealthy individuals moral sanction for their actions and conferred them with the religious authority needed to establish themselves as a ruling class.

Actual experience, however, was never this straightforward. Moving from the broad contours of social theory to the particulars of history, *Church and Estate* explores in more concrete terms the class dynamics at work within American religious life and religion's role in class formation. How did faith condition social behavior? What did wealthy individuals' quest for spiritual capital mean for their religious communities? Answering such questions deepens our understanding of the workings of two dominant forces—religion and wealth—that shaped American society during the transformative decades of the late nineteenth and early twentieth centuries.

In tracing these connections, particular attention needs to be given to the mechanisms that allowed wealthy individuals to use their economic resources to gain influence within their local religious communities and broader denominations. Theological beliefs, institutional structures, and denominational culture all governed the nature of the relationship. By looking closely at the lived religious experience of Philadelphia's elite and the inner workings of their religious communities, *Church and Estate* reveals both the range of their motivations and the limits of acceptable action. No one recognized the inherent complexity of their relationship better than wealthy benefactors and their religious leaders. As they were well aware, members of the social and financial elite were able to influence religious affairs in a variety of ways, whether through involvement in congregational formation and church governance or by their philanthropy and patronage. But given the nature of religious authority, they could not control their churches in the same way they could their businesses or the government. Those involved in religious affairs were subject to their churches' moral standards and ethical norms. Clergy possessed not only the ability to impart their blessing upon the wealthy and powerful, but also the power to withhold it, although doing so entailed considerable risk. Church leaders may have had the authority— and indeed the moral imperative—to place a check on overweening financial influence and to hold the wealthy morally accountable for their actions, but they could rarely afford to alienate prominent benefactors. The moral ambiguity of worldly wealth further complicated matters. Wealth could be an obstacle to personal salvation, of course, but members of the upper class also knew that, if used properly to promote the social good, it could also serve as a means to that end.[27]

So who were the Philadelphia elite? Social scientists have established a complex and technical vocabulary to describe the structuring of social relations, distinguishing between status groups, social classes, castes, elites, and other social groups. Though mindful of these important distinctions, I often employ "upper class" as a purely descriptive term used interchangeably with other classifiers such as the "financial elite" and "wealthy individuals" to identify the subjects of this study—those who controlled the great fortunes of the era. Speaking of the "upper class" as a singular term, though not meant to imply the existence of fixed social categories, also reflects the social outlook of the time, when individuals had a more objective sense of class and their own class identities. As Ira Katznelson has argued, social classes do, at some point, become "formed groups" with a shared outlook and disposition that makes collective action possible.[28] Admittedly, not all wealthy individuals were recognized as members of the upper class, nor did they choose to be. In Philadelphia, moreover, patterns of exclusion and self-segregation from "proper society" led to the creation of what might best be understood as parallel upper-class societies among certain groups, notably the Jewish and Quaker elite, each possessing their own unique markers of status.

Knowing who counted among the upper class, therefore, seemed to be at once instinctive and elusive. For outsiders, a search through *Who's Who* and the *Social Register* provided some sense of who qualified for recognition among the city's social elite. But as Nathaniel Burt once cautioned, these directories were a "handy but not always reliable index of upper-classness."[29] They relied on family pedigree, organizational membership, and place of residence to establish objective, quantifiable markers of upper-class status. Yet as anyone who was anyone would attest, these affiliations alone did not make an individual part of proper society. Class identity had as much to do with a shared mindset as it did with conformity to a set of criteria. As a result, the effort to define an upper-class mentality has long been a cottage industry among Philadelphia writers. Various social observers have attempted to distill the essence of the city's upper class into qualities like "privilege," "sense of position," or "family pedigree."[30] Writing in 1914, Elizabeth Robins Pennell, for instance, remarked that Philadelphia is a town "where it is important, if you belong at all, to have belonged from the beginning."[31] To her, no further explanation was needed.

If somewhat difficult to tally, members of the upper class were somewhat easier to locate. In Philadelphia, the upper class created and inhabited a unique social world, where their collective mentality found embodiment in place. As E. Digby Baltzell observed, elite enclaves, with their "distinctive architecture, fashionable churches, private schools, and sentimental traditions," were instrumental in the development of upper-class life.[32] Class identity depended on physical proximity to one's perceived social peers. One resident of fashionable Chestnut Hill described living with "Biddles to the north, Whartons to the south, Vauxes to the east, and Drexels to the west."[33] As his comment suggests, residential patterns also helped to reinforce the kinship networks so vital to the perpetuation of class status across generations. As members of the upper class themselves understood, knowing who counted among proper society required knowing where to look.

Over time, the city's social geography grew more pronounced as members of the upper class distanced themselves from those of lower rank. In the mid-nineteenth century, the migration of the elite from the old wards near what is today Society Hill helped make the area around Rittenhouse Square the city's premier Victorian neighborhood. With the expansion of rail networks in the late nineteenth century, Chestnut Hill, the Whitemarsh Valley, and the communities along the Main Line, which had first developed as seasonal escapes for the well-to-do, were transformed into fashionable commuter suburbs surrounded by great country estates. By the early twentieth century, the Main Line had assumed an almost mythical quality as the embodiment of the exclusive world of wealth and privilege.[34] Immortalized in works like Christopher Morley's *Kitty Foyle* and Philip Barry's *The Philadelphia Story*, the Main Line became a world unto itself.[35] Not surprisingly, this upper-class mobility and subsequent changes in the city's social geography had profound consequences for religious institutions, which would see their own fortunes rise and fall as members of the upper class extended or withdrew their financial support.

With these changes, social distinctions came to be patterned onto the religious landscape. Not only were members of Philadelphia's social and financial elite instrumental in supporting the broader institutional growth that defined religious life in America during the late nineteenth and early twentieth centuries, but within their own communities, they built and sustained churches that conformed to their religious and class sensibilities, knowing that the presence of fashionable churches would help attract others of their economic and social rank. These patterns of patronage also gave rise to distinct religious enclaves that reinforced religious bonds among segments of the upper class. Rittenhouse Square, Chestnut Hill, and the Main Line emerged as strongholds for wealthy Episcopalians and other prominent Protestants, while members of other religious communities established their own separate enclaves, whether as a result of social exclusion or self-segregation. Members of the Jewish elite, for instance, established a presence on North Broad Street and later in the region around suburban Elkins Park, while upper-class Quakers settled near their colleges at Haverford and Swarthmore or kept to their ancestral enclave in Germantown.

Given Philadelphia's religious and social diversity, a few additional comments need to be made about the selection of this study's subjects. I have not made a scientific sampling of Philadelphia's financial elite, but rather have selected individuals representative of their class who espoused religious belief, participated in church affairs, and contributed financially to their religious communities. Tracing the record of service and giving brought these individuals to the fore. Not all of these individuals have enjoyed enduring fame, but most were eminent figures in their day. Names like Drexel, Houston, Harrison, Pepper, Roberts, Wanamaker, and Wharton were recognized within religious circles and well regarded locally.

I have chosen the churches and religious institutions examined here with similar selectivity. To gauge upper-class financial influence within the religious sphere, I have focused on the city's elite congregations, which were recognized as such by virtue of their upper-class membership and location in fashionable neighborhoods. I have included as well a handful of less-affluent congregations for their noteworthy relationship with a particular donor, such as Bethany Presbyterian Church, whose fortunes depended on the generosity of department store magnate John Wanamaker. Since no single religious denomination claimed the undivided loyalties of the city's upper class, the churches under consideration reflect a cross section of the city's religious landscape. At the core of this study, though, are the Episcopal Church, Society of Friends, and Presbyterian Church, all three of which had long enjoyed close connections to the city's prominent citizens.

Although Catholics and Jews remained largely outsiders to Philadelphia's "proper society," there were members of these two communities who acquired sizable fortunes and gained social prominence. Drawing them into the discussion at critical junctions provides an opportunity not only to highlight broader differences in social outlook and religious practice among the city's elite, but also to demonstrate how different religious communities responded to the changes unleashed by industrial prosperity. Whereas Protestants tended to emphasize the authority of the individual donor, Catholics and Jews tended to be guided by a communal ethic in their giving to churches and synagogues. They also possessed a strong sense of internal solidarity, whether born of ethnic bonds or a shared sense of religious persecution, which helped them mediate internal class divisions in ways that Protestants could not. Philadelphia's industrial wealth may have remained concentrated in Protestant hands, and the ethos of the city's upper class may have remained rooted in Protestant values, but making comparisons with other groups draws attention to the fact that no religious community was immune to the social changes of the industrial era or free of elite influence.

No matter one's religious affiliation, personal faith and spiritual beliefs can be notoriously difficult to determine and evaluate. Many people were reticent to discuss their personal religious sentiments, let alone record and preserve them. Fortunately, many members of the Philadelphia elite penned autobiographies, memoirs, and other reminiscences of their family history and private social world. These introspective accounts, taken together with their personal papers and the record of their religious involvements, shed light on their religious worldview and help reveal the beliefs and principles that motivated them. Additional insights emerged from examining the spiritual practices individuals would likely have encountered within their local churches as well as from a close reading of the material elements to be found there. One should be careful not to assign religious devotion where none existed, but neither should one overlook such indirect forms of religious expression.

Determining the effects of financial influence and class authority within American religious life can be equally difficult. Although financial contributions can be quantified, the influence that donors derived from them cannot. It is similarly difficult to gauge the degree of influence members of the upper class gained from their personal involvement in church affairs. Therefore, in order to determine the nature and extent of upper-class influence within local religious communities and American religious life more broadly, I have focused primarily on official institutional records. One can speculate about backroom deals and the private influence enjoyed by wealthy donors, but it is more productive to focus on what can be substantiated, such as how members of the upper class fulfilled the responsibilities associated with board seats, committee appointments, and other positions of authority in their churches. As part of the historical record preserved in church annals, denominational publications, and institutional archives, these matters are open to public scrutiny.

Making sense of the social and religious transformations that suffused industrial-era Philadelphia requires coming to terms with the local terrain. Whatever their differences, members of the social and financial elite shared a common identification with the city. Those who mattered saw themselves first and foremost as "Philadelphians," a term that carried more than geographic connotations. For that reason, it is important to establish a sense of the city and its character. Despite its staid reputation, Philadelphia displayed a remarkable inner vitality. The economic prosperity of the era touched all areas of life. How Philadelphians came to terms with their industrial fortunes would shape the very essence of the city.

Philadelphia of the late nineteenth and early twentieth centuries was a paradoxical place. The city seemed at once reserved and vibrant. In the years and decades following the end of the Civil War, Philadelphia emerged as one of the nation's leading industrial centers. Among the events that marked its economic coming of age was the 1876 Centennial Exposition, which advertised the entrepreneurial spirit and industrial capacity of its host city like nothing else could. By the late 1920s, Philadelphia ranked as the third largest and third richest city in the nation, and "third too in the overall value of its products, with a billion dollars invested in 266 distinct lines of manufacturing, and a workforce of 670,865, almost evenly divided among persons in professional, industrial, and service categories."[36] Although rail, iron, steel, coal, and heavy manufacturing served as the foundation for industrial-era growth, the city's economy remained remarkably diverse. Not only did major Philadelphia firms excel in older segments of the economy, such as textile production, but they also contributed to developing fields, such as publishing and advertising, chemicals and pharmaceuticals, and consumer electronics. Philadelphia's industrial base, unlike that of other cities, included an impressive number of small and midsize firms that concentrated on specialized production and catered to niche segments of the market. Because its economy was not dominated by a handful of large companies, the city's wealth was spread more broadly among its citizens than elsewhere.[37]

Yet, even as Philadelphians embraced technological innovation and pursued economic progress, their collective ethos remained decidedly conservative. The exuberance of the era seemed not to have disturbed the city's traditional air of quiet contentment. Even as boosters spoke of what was to be, Philadelphians reflexively recalled earlier achievements. Indeed, the pervasive presence of the colonial past in the city's consciousness helps explain why Philadelphia's prominence as one of the nation's most productive industrial centers is often overlooked. Amid the social change of the period, Philadelphians affirmed traditional values as the bedrock of prosperity; they ascribed their city's economic success not to technological advances or protectionist policies, but to thrift, prudence, and integrity. Even as industrial prosperity reordered class relations, older notions of status became more entrenched; the patrician values of the past were embraced not only by the city's traditional elite but also by those who had more recently risen to social prominence. Though its power and influence extended nationally, Philadelphia was "isolated by custom antique," as writer Lafcadio Hearn observed in 1889;[38] its inhabitants remained decidedly parochial.

In seeking to explain this peculiar Philadelphia temperament, social observers both past and present have pointed to the city's Quaker heritage. They attribute the city's unique character and ethos to the vestigial influence of the Pennsylvania colony's religious founders, whose distinctive values became part of the city's cultural heritage. Writing in 1898, local essayist Agnes Repplier spoke poetically of how "the impress of the Quaker hand lingers still; not only in the simple, dignified old buildings to which time lends an added charm, but in the ineffaceable spirit of the town."[39] In a more scholarly vein, E. Digby Baltzell and David Hackett Fisher compelling demonstrate the formative influence of Quakerism on the city's social character and regional customs. The patterns of leadership and the ordering institutions established by the founding generation, they argue, left a lasting imprint on the city and its residents.[40]

This Quaker trope had a certain self-fulfilling effect. The more people spoke of Philadelphia as the "Quaker City," the more its inhabitants came to view themselves as heirs to its founders' legacy. They embraced the stereotype, seeing in the past what they valued in themselves. The latent Quaker ethos became the wellspring of civic virtue and the source of collective identity. For some, the glorification of the Quaker past also served as a way of registering concern about the unsettling social change of the industrial era. It provided a means to inveigh against foreign immigrants, the nouveaux riches, and other outsiders who threatened the established social order. Philadelphia's Quaker heritage thus served both as a readily accepted explanation for the city's peculiarities and a defense of the status quo in an era of immense flux.[41]

More than the Quaker heritage itself, the desire to preserve the established order helps explain the contradictory tendencies of industrial-era Philadelphia. Many who enjoyed the benefits of economic prosperity felt deeply ambivalent about the transformations unleashed. They desired the stability of an imagined past while gazing steadily toward the future. Calling Philadelphia "the staunchest city in America," a 1902 guidebook noted how "this quality of staunchness . . . has at times been designated as ultraconservatism," but in reality "the history of Philadelphia is one continuous story of more than two centuries of progress." The guidebook discerned no apparent contradiction between an unwavering commitment to established custom and an ardent faith in steady improvement.[42] Indeed, industrial-era Philadelphia would hold the countervailing tendencies of conservatism and progress together in productive tension.

Far from making it impassive or stolid, Philadelphia's staunchness provided the city with its own unique dynamism. Preserving prerogative and privilege required constant vigilance and active defense of one's interests. Within the economic sphere, Philadelphia's industrialists relied on a number of private forums, such as the Union League and the Manufacturers' Club, to develop strategies to that effect. They used their collective influence to promote a protectionist agenda and maintain their proprietary rights. They opposed government regulation and worked to weaken the power of labor unions and other groups that threatened employer prerogatives or managerial authority.[43] Indeed, the relative calm of labor relations in the city gave employers little reason to question their managerial decisions. "The antagonisms between labor and capital are few," the *Philadelphia Inquirer* reassured its readers in 1896, and the city did not experience a major strike until 1903, when some 100,000 textile workers seeking shorter hours walked off the job.[44] Overall, however, the general prosperity of the age left employers convinced of the essential soundness of their established economic and corporate policies.

Philadelphia's social character displayed similar retrenchment amid flux. As economic prosperity reshaped class relations, members of the city's elite vigilantly defended the social hierarchy and notions of class privilege. Those who belonged to "Old Philadelphia" families continued to view themselves as the true arbiters of proper society, even as their financial fortunes declined. Meanwhile, those of more recent wealth sought to claim that heritage for themselves. The region's great estates and elite residential communities, for instance, reflected their owners' efforts to convey a sense of established social position. By surrounding themselves with the trappings of the landed gentry, they sought to create a social world that transcended the industrial era and the recent provenance of their wealth. From a distance, class status may have seemed secure and absolute, but in reality it was as contrived and ephemeral as the laissez-faire economy and manufacturers' vision of industrial harmony.

Religious communities likewise found themselves searching for stability amid the dramatic transformations of the period. As population growth and urban expansion altered the city's social and physical landscape, established denominations sought to preserve their status and authority. Diversity of belief and sectarian competition added vitality to religious life but also fostered a need for self-differentiation and boundary maintenance. Sustained by industrial wealth and the benefactions of Philadelphia's elite, the vast program of church extension and institutional growth of the era tended to emphasize denominational distinctions and served as a catalyst for the hardening of denominational identity that came to define religious life in the United States during the second half of the nineteenth century.[45] The imposing churches built during these years provided a sense of spiritual security amid the disquiet of the industrial age. Much like the staunchness that characterized the city's economic and social affairs, religious life in Philadelphia acquired an air of institutional permanence that belied the period's dramatic transformations.

Philadelphia's distinctive staunchness, though often mistaken for provincial backwardness, in reality reflected the dynamism of the industrial era. Confronted with the immense socioeconomic change of the period, Philadelphians, in their collective search for order, clung to the past even as they forged a new future. These countervailing impulses shaped the character of the city and colored its economic, social, and religious development. In each of these spheres, individuals sought to preserve past prerogatives and customary privileges. Yet, as they would discover, the worlds they built and the mental visions they maintained could not keep the forces of change at bay.

Moving from the late nineteenth century to the economic heyday of the 1920s, *Church and Estate* traces the emergence of, and the struggle to sustain, a social and religious order born of industrial prosperity. Though not strictly chronological, its chapters follow a three-part trajectory of growth, consolidation, and contestation, with each chapter focusing on a discrete topic, such as philanthropic practice or religious conversion. This thematic approach serves to highlight religious differences among members of the social and financial elite and to demonstrate how different religious communities responded to similar influences.

Broadly speaking, the first three chapters explore how wealth and upper-class influence shaped institutional growth and structured authority within the religious sphere. Chapter 1 focuses on patterns of elite giving and the distinct denominational cultures that guided upper-class philanthropic practice during the age of great fortunes. It shows how wealthy individuals sought to reconcile religious imperatives with their own class sensibilities in pursuit of a morally and personally satisfying philanthropy.

Chapter 2 looks more closely at the systems of institutional finance and church governance that allowed members of the upper class to play an increasingly powerful—and officially sanctioned—role in ecclesiastical affairs. Drawing on Sam Bass Warner's classic analysis of urban development, it relates how wealthy donors applied "privatist" economic logic to their religious commitments, thus shaping the nature and direction of church growth during the late nineteenth and early twentieth centuries. The structures of church governance further allowed wealthy individuals to use their financial resources and personal influence to shape the social mission and theological message of their churches. The dominant system of congregational organization, with its emphasis on localized administration, financial autonomy, and lay authority, opened the door for those in possession of wealth, status, and professional expertise to secure positions of authority, particularly through appointment to church boards, vestries, or other administrative bodies.

In addition to holding formal positions of authority within their local churches and broader denominations, wealthy individuals had the ability to refashion religious life in more subtle, yet equally significant, ways. Their role in determining the design and decoration of their churches, in particular, gave them a means to promote their own distinctive visions of religious community. As chapter 3 reveals, artistic and architectural patronage allowed members of the upper class both to display their theological loyalties and to transform sacred spaces into the physical embodiments of their own cultural tastes and class sensibilities. In so doing, they created religious environments suitable for their spiritual needs. They also set a standard for refined worship and proper ecclesiastical style that extended their influence beyond their own local churches. However trivial they might seem individually, these aesthetic changes had a profound cumulative effect on religious communities' theological identity and spiritual praxis.

Shifting to issues of class formation, the next two chapters describe the forces that contributed to the religious consolidation of the upper class and the consequences of that consolidation for social and religious life, both locally and nationally. Chapter 4 discusses the spiritual and theological factors that motivated religious conversion among the Philadelphia elite. A substantial number were drawn to the Episcopal Church, creating a pattern of migration that contributed to a striking shift in the religious character of the city's upper class. The emergence of what E. Digby Baltzell has termed Philadelphia's "Quaker-turned-Episcopal gentry" provided a cohesive religious foundation for shared class identity.[46] Rejecting the notion that religious conversion among social and financial elite stemmed from nothing more than their search for status, the chapter examines the complex motives and high social costs that often accompanied religious conversion and the quest for the proper spiritual capital. It also explores the cumulative effect these conversions had on religious communities, both those who gained and those who lost adherents.

The consolidation of the social and financial elite along religious lines came to shape the contours of the wider religious landscape. Nowhere was this more evident than within the Episcopal Church, whose power and prestige within American life were entirely disproportionate to its numerical strength.

As chapter 5 demonstrates, members of the social and financial elite were among the prime exponents and beneficiaries of the "Episcopal Ascendancy"; their support of efforts to raise the Episcopal Church's public profile, such as the construction of the Washington Memorial Chapel at Valley Forge, served to enhance their own status as well. Through this exchange of financial and symbolic capital, members of the Episcopal Church came to see themselves as the nation's de facto religious establishment and to act accordingly. Developments within the Church further reveal how those who possessed wealth and status were able to acquire a disproportionate degree of authority within American religious life, just as they had within the nation's political and economic life.

By all appearances, the social and religious order born of industrial prosperity seemed unshakable as Philadelphia entered the modern era. The stately churches that dotted the city's landscape testified to the strength of religious conviction, while the churches' moral approbation convinced the wealthy that they were indeed entitled to their place atop the social hierarchy. Yet, as the final two chapters describe, fault lines had begun to emerge within both the social and religious spheres. In the class-charged atmosphere of the progressive era, the union of religion and wealth did not go uncontested.

Chapter 6 examines the actions of Rev. George Chalmers Richmond, Scott Nearing, and Morris E. Leeds, three figures who challenged the elite orthodoxies of early twentieth-century Philadelphia. Stirred by the progressive spirit and their own faith, each raised questions about the moral legitimacy of the patrician class and consequently elicited a powerful response from those they challenged. Individually, each man had only limited success in changing the status quo, but, taken together, their crusading efforts exposed the tenuous nature of elite authority. Philadelphia's religious communities had likewise to contend with criticism. For H. Richard Niebuhr, H. Paul Douglass, and other early twentieth-century observers of religious life in the United States, the success of these communities had come with a price. Many of the most pressing pastoral problems of the day, they argued, from the rise of "class churches" to the destabilizing effects of social and geographic mobility, were related to social class and resource allocation.

Chapter 7, the final chapter, examines how religious leaders in Philadelphia responded to the immense socioeconomic changes that had taken place within American society at large and within their own churches during the industrial era. It highlights their efforts to bridge class divisions and correct the disparity between professed theological inclusivity and experienced social exclusivity. Although efforts to mitigate class distinction met with limited success, the forces that had shaped the social and religious character of the era eventually succumbed to their own internal contradictions. The ultimate instability of wealth and status explains why, for religious life in the age of industrial prosperity, the luster did not last.

1

"Money Faithfully and Judiciously Expended"

During their visit to Rome in early 1887, Katharine Drexel and her two sisters, Elizabeth and Louise, were privileged to receive a private audience with Pope Leo XIII. On the appointed day, the pontiff graciously welcomed the three young women from Philadelphia, having been informed of their generous financial support for the work of the Catholic Church. Taking advantage of the moment, Katharine decided to speak to the pope about a religious concern close to her own heart: the anemic condition of the Church's missions in the western United States. Upon hearing her request that a priest be sent to aid the work in that field, he replied, "Why not be a missionary yourself, my child?" As Katharine would admit only years later, the pope's reply was not the response she had expected. As steward of her portion of the trust fund her father had established for her sisters and her, Katharine had always thought it her duty to fund the work of others. She had never considered it her role to take up missionary work herself. But the pope's simple question forced her to reassess her religious vocation, and it contributed to her decision a few years later to enter the convent and establish her own religious order.[1]

Katharine's decision was in many ways exceptional, but she was certainly not alone in her quest to discern the obligations her fortune demanded of her. Many who had come to share in the financial prosperity of the industrial era similarly contemplated how best to apply their financial resources for the greater good. They recognized that they owed a debt to God for the blessings bestowed upon them. Like Katharine, many turned to religious leaders for guidance and spiritual counsel. They sought the comfort that comes from knowing they had used their material resources in accordance with church teachings and divine will.

Religious belief, however, was not their sole source of inspiration. In determining how to employ their financial resources, the wealthy were also guided by societal expectations and their own class sensibilities. Over the course of the nineteenth century, the nature of giving had changed dramatically, with the more intimate charitable practices that characterized the "benevolent empire" of earlier decades yielding to the new emphasis on the efficient management of wealth that lay at the heart of the elite philanthropy of the industrial era.[2] Those who had made their fortunes in the world of business and commerce viewed charitable work as an enterprise to be governed by the same economic principles and financial logic as any other. They paid careful attention to the effects of their benefactions, mindful to administer them in a way they deemed both responsible and respectable.

Philanthropic practices reveal a great deal about the personal beliefs and social outlook that guided members of the industrial-era elite. They shed light on the motives and desires that animated those who enjoyed the privileges and bore the responsibilities of wealth. They allow us to see how individuals negotiated both class and religious imperatives in pursuit of a personally and morally satisfying philanthropy. Within the religious sphere, prominent benefactors may have felt inspired to give generously to support the work of their churches, but they were generally reluctant to cede financial control entirely to members of the clergy and other denominational officials, preferring instead to maintain a watchful eye over the initiatives they supported. Many engaged in contractual philanthropy and put in place legal safeguards to ensure their intentions were observed.[3]

Attention to philanthropy also sheds light on the tensions inherent in the financial and symbolic exchanges between the financial elite and their religious communities. Giving was a powerful act, fraught with implications for both donor and recipient. For members of the financial elite, philanthropic practice helped secure their standing within their church communities and upper-class society, but the desire for moral approbation and spiritual security also bound them to religious authority. By accepting philanthropic contributions, churches, for their part, entered into a client relationship with their wealthy benefactors and became subject to their influence. Still, church officials continued to court members of the social and financial elite, knowing that their benefactions would increase the prestige of their religious communities, sustain institutional expansion, and thereby bolster their own power and authority.

The extended reach of elite philanthropy during the industrial era sparked persistent debate over how wealth should be employed. Although few among the elite and their religious beneficiaries questioned the workings of the economic order, they did not necessarily agree on how money should be used, by whom, or under what conditions. Those who sought to shape the philanthropic agenda included not only members of the upper class concerned about the philanthropic practices of their peers but also church leaders interested in advancing their religious mission. Rarely did donors have a free hand in determining the nature of their benefactions. They followed church rules and worked within distinct denominational cultures of giving that informed their decisions. To examine elite philanthropy outside of its religious context during this period not only ignores important distinctions among the methods of giving embraced by members of the financial elite, but also creates the illusion that wealthy donors were the sole agents in determining the use of their financial gifts.

In addition to its implications for individual donors and their beneficiaries, elite philanthropy had significant consequences for the nation's social and religious life at large. The money that flowed into church coffers during the industrial era helped create and sustain the institutional networks that lay at the heart of the denominational order that defined American religious life from the middle of the nineteenth century until the latter half of the twentieth. It was during this time that "Christian" society was transformed into a constellation of competing creeds, each marked by its own assemblage of churches, schools, hospitals, and other institutions. Although support for this institutional growth came from individuals of all ranks, church leaders looked to members of the social and financial elite to provide an example of faithful stewardship. Sectarian giving, therefore, not only became an indicator of religious loyalty, but also contributed to the hardening of denominational boundaries during this period, when religious affiliation constituted an essential aspect of one's identity and public persona.

The Obligations of Wealth

Philadelphia's leading citizens had long understood the social obligations that their status and wealth demanded of them. The city's Quaker founders conceived of the Pennsylvania colony as a "holy experiment" and took it upon themselves to order society according to their unique religious testimonies. Their early dominance in political and economic affairs helped them instill their social principles among the wider community. Their social ethic, rooted in their belief in spiritual equality, could at times be radical, and throughout the eighteenth and nineteenth centuries, members of the Society of Friends stood at the vanguard of many humanitarian crusades, including abolition, prison reform, and care for the mentally ill. Philadelphians were also heirs to the legacy of enlightened civic activism advanced by Benjamin Franklin and other members of his generation. Many of the city's most venerable institutions, from the Library Company and the Philosophical Society to the Pennsylvania Hospital and the University of Pennsylvania, owe their origins to that legacy of personal and civic improvement.

Those who found their fortunes in the age of industrial opportunity built upon this tradition. In addition to sustaining established organizations and institutions, members of Philadelphia's social and financial elite used their resources to support new charitable initiatives, promote community welfare, and respond to the changing social needs of their day. The directory of charitable organizations and societies compiled by the Philadelphia Civic Club in 1895 reveals the vast array of agencies and institutions that contributed to the city's vibrant voluntary sector, from older almshouses and orphan asylums to newer immigrant aid societies and industrial training schools. Even though these organizations drew upon individuals of all backgrounds and stations in life, they actively courted the wealthy and looked to elite benefactors to sustain their work. For men and women of means, financial contributions increasingly became the measure of personal commitment to charitable initiatives, shifting emphasis from the type of direct involvement that characterized the "ladies bountiful" and "Christian gentlemen" of an earlier generation.[4]

In Philadelphia, as elsewhere, the rise of great industrial fortunes dramatically changed the nature of philanthropic practice, ushering in an era defined by large-scale giving conducted systematically according to the dominant corporate and scientific principles of the day. In contrast to the disparate charitable campaigns and social uplift movements of the early nineteenth century, "philanthropy," as the term came to be understood in the industrial era, referred to the prominent benefactions and managed giving carried out by men and women of substantial means. Across the United States, members of this new generation of philanthropists demonstrated the socially transformative power of private wealth through their support of libraries, museums, educational institutions, and other projects. By the end of the nineteenth century, every major city in the country could boast of a class of enlightened philanthropists who dedicated a portion of their wealth to the cause of social uplift and civic improvement. As one 1893 survey of the nation's millionaires noted, society had been "profoundly affected by the existence . . . of a recognized class of great capitalists who command congeries of agencies and forces which had no practical existence" in antebellum America, and whose public gifts reflected an "infectious" liberality. Among those Philadelphians the survey recognized for their philanthropic spirit were Joseph Wharton, Anthony J. Drexel, John B. Stetson, and others who supported the city's libraries, trade schools, and network of educational institutions.[5]

The benefactions of this new class of millionaire-philanthropists constituted only a portion of industrial-era philanthropy, but the unprecedented scale and often conspicuous nature of their giving made their initiatives the standard against which all others were judged. Andrew Carnegie, who did more to shape industrial-era debates over philanthropy than any of his peers, received praise for his commendable example from those who believed that the wealthy had an obligation to contribute to the betterment of society.[6] As stewards of their wealth, the industrial elite possessed the ability to shape the philanthropic agenda and establish standards for giving. Recognizing the considerable power their wealth afforded, they used their resources and influence to promote their favored causes and advance their own vision for how wealth should be expended and administered.

This shift in philanthropic practice corresponded with the ascent of a new capitalist class whose social outlook was shaped by the logic of the industrial economy. In Philadelphia, the composition of the city's social and financial elite changed significantly over the course of the nineteenth century as the industrial economy opened new doors for economic advancement. In earlier decades, wealth was concentrated in the hands of the city's merchant class and the descendants of the colonial elite, many of whom had entered the gentlemanly professions, notably medicine and law. Tax records from the Civil War confirm their established economic position, with sizable estates still held by members of these older clans. Yet those same records also reveal how the composition of the financial elite had already begun to shift. The city's two wealthiest men, Matthias Baldwin and Matthew Baird, were partners in Baldwin Locomotive, a pioneering firm in the country's nascent railroad industry. Those who joined them at the very top of the city's tax rolls came almost exclusively from the world of banking and industry. Indeed, the descendants of older Philadelphia families who had retained high economic standing were those who had moved into those fields. These economic and social transformations in Philadelphia fell in line with national trends. As Sven Beckert has demonstrated in his study of New York City, the closing decades of the nineteenth century witnessed the emergence of a new bourgeois class of industrialists, bankers, and financiers who had coalesced around a common ideology of laissez-faire liberalism and a political defense of property rights.[7]

By the close of the nineteenth century, industrial manufacturing, rail and transport, and corporate finance had become Philadelphia's main engines of wealth. Major corporations such as the Pennsylvania Railroad not only provided handsome compensation for their managers and partners, but also rewarded those who had the foresight and capacity to invest in them, thus perpetuating many family estates. "Some of the largest fortunes in the city," one 1891 newspaper report noted, "have been accumulated by buying securities at low prices and holding them for many years or by negotiating large blocks of stocks and bonds." Cash dividends for Pennsylvania Railroad stockholders, for instance, averaged 7 percent between 1855 and 1900, creating the impression that funds placed in the company would never fail to offer a stable return.[8]

The wealth produced by the city's industrial firms became a source of pride for the city, and members of the new capitalist class often found themselves the recipients of public adulation. Indeed, many prosperous business leaders actively presented themselves as models of emulation for those seeking their own fortunes. Adding to the advice manuals and self-help literature of the late nineteenth century, publisher George W. Childs offered instruction for "success in life" to young men seeking opportunity in business and industry, as did department store magnate John Wanamaker in many of his public addresses.[9] Popular guidebooks from the period similarly provided biographical sketches of business leaders and others who "have attained success and contribute to the general prosperity of the community" in order to provide the ambitious with models for "future progress."[10] Local boosters liked to point out that Philadelphia's capitalist class did not share in the reckless tendencies of their economic peers in other cities. Among those who had risen to the rank of millionaire by 1890, "there are none who have made their money by wrecking railroads, thereby ruining hundreds of small investors, or by speculating in stocks or grain, or by notorious harsh dealings with the poor and unfortunate," insisted one promotional account. Such accounts focused on the "honesty and integrity" by which members of the local business community conducted their affairs. The rise of Philadelphia's fortunes held "a moral for everybody," one booster concluded. "At their root lie toil, thrift, and caution," he argued, insisting that the city's "seasoned millions are the best rebuke to speculation and hazard."[11]

However excessive its rhetoric and however deliberate its disregard of the less-than-honorable practices of some, this insistence on the moral probity of Philadelphia's business leaders and financial elite helped protect them from the stigma of "tainted money" that had become a growing concern among beneficiaries of their philanthropy, particularly those within the religious sphere. By the late nineteenth century, church leaders had already begun to express concern about the source and nature of the donations they were receiving. The debate quickened in 1905 when Washington Gladden, a Congregational minister and chief spokesman of the Social Gospel, criticized the Congregational Church's Board of Missions for accepting a $100,000 gift from John D. Rockefeller. In a highly publicized address, Gladden urged church leaders to "neither invite nor solicit donations . . . from persons whose gains have been made by methods morally reprehensible or socially injurious."[12] In Philadelphia, the dominant discourse of upper-class integrity offered the elite a degree of protection from such judgments.

Religious leaders were also hesitant to castigate the wealthy as a class, lest they risk alienating those upon whom they relied for financial support. They likewise recognized that the moral status of most donations would be difficult to determine. Would beneficiaries be required to scrutinize every dollar they received and investigate the life and career of each donor? Even those who wished in principle to heed Gladden's warnings about "tainted money" found it difficult to do so in practice. In 1907, for instance, the *Presbyterian*, a denominational weekly published out of Philadelphia, ran an editorial that repeated Gladden's warnings, but half a year earlier, the same paper had admitted that church beneficiaries generally evinced little resistance to bequests from such wealthy individuals as Andrew Carnegie and John D. Rockefeller, whose reputations had been tarnished by the Homestead Strike and Ida Tarbell's exposé of Standard Oil, respectively.[13]

For much of the late nineteenth century, wealth, in and of itself, was not viewed as an obstacle to one's moral standing or personal salvation. Religious leaders rarely condemned the growing economic disparity of the day or the accumulation of great fortunes because they continued to see wealth as a sign of hard work and divine favor. Russell H. Conwell, Philadelphia's golden-tongued preacher of the Gospel of Success, for instance, regularly reminded his followers that God would reward hard work and upright living with material success.[14] He and other like-minded religious leaders extolled those who used their money to help the poor and advance the work of their churches. Rather than speaking out against millionaires, they castigated those who attempted "to copy the industrialists and pursue wealth at all costs" by engaging in gambling, speculation, and other economically—and morally—dangerous practices. They further defended the accumulation of wealth by declaring it the *love* of money, rather than money itself, that was the root of all evil.[15]

In an era of rapid urbanization and population growth, support from prominent benefactors helped religious communities expand their institutional reach. A survey of congregational growth within the local Presbyterian Church reveals how elite patronage provided seed money for many building projects, including those beyond donors' own congregations. Matthias Baldwin, for example, emerged as one of the most steadfast local supporters of church extension in the mid-nineteenth century. Concerned about the spiritual needs of his employees and others living near his locomotive works, Baldwin helped organize a church there in 1860 and pledged to support it for two years. In the years that followed, he donated land for other new churches in the city and helped congregations finance the purchase of their lots.[16] During the closing decades of the nineteenth century, a considerable number of other congregations likewise owed a debt to benefactors who offered sizable donations or bequests. At Berean Presbyterian Church, founded in 1880, John McGill's donation of $5,000 toward the construction of the new $33,000 church building was praised for its role in "encouraging others to give."[17]

Such examples offer a reminder that throughout the industrial era most giving remained sectarian in nature. Even as secular philanthropy grew, donations great and small flowed to local congregations and sustained the larger network of schools, hospitals, charitable agencies, and other institutions sponsored under denominational auspices. In 1901, Presbyterian leaders in Philadelphia praised businessmen for being among the "most zealous and faithful workers of Christ," and noted how the collection for "benevolences" grew from $79,377 to $274,540 between 1867 and 1900.[18] The example of John D. Rockefeller, who remained committed to Baptist causes even as he widened his philanthropic involvements, reflected the practice of countless other individuals, especially those of more modest fortunes who did not have the ability or desire to establish their own philanthropic enterprises. Religious organizations provided them with a means to exercise their stewardship collectively. In supporting churches and other religious institutions, moreover, wealthy benefactors signaled their approval of established work and expressed confidence that religious leaders would manage those resources in the best interests of society.

Indeed, as church leaders witnessed the accumulation of great fortunes, they wanted to ensure that their churches would be remembered financially. To encourage bequests, many religious institutions published model legacy clauses that individuals could copy into their wills. At the Church of the Holy Trinity, a fashionable downtown Episcopal congregation, sample bequest statements began to appear as early as the 1890s. Church officials wanted to make sure both that wills were properly executed and that they could withstand any potential court challenges. It was a legitimate concern. Following his death in 1922, the will of department store magnate John Wanamaker, a devout Presbyterian, was contested not only by the federal government, which questioned the amount reported for inheritance taxes, but also by his two daughters, who fought to ensure that their legacies would be paid out before any funds went to charitable purposes.

Expectations of giving were tied closely to denominational loyalty, a characteristic sometimes described as "churchmanship." Although the notion of churchmanship was invoked most frequently within the Episcopal Church, where it referred to one's orientation toward high, low, or broad church theology during the ritualism debates of the nineteenth century, it increasingly crept into ordinary usage as a way of describing one's religious devotion and of signaling one's firm denominational loyalty. Numerous obituaries and memorial tributes from the time employed the term to honor those active in congregational life or denominational affairs.[19] When Alexander Van Rensselaer donated a portrait of his father, Rev. Cortlandt Van Rensselaer, to the Presbyterian Historical Society in 1902, for instance, those at the ceremony spoke of how they could not recall "a better gentleman, a more loyal churchman, and a more devoted Christian" than Rev. Van Rensselaer, who had helped establish the organization.[20] This language of churchmanship signified more than mere affiliation, referring instead to those who demonstrated a sustained commitment to advancing the material interests and spiritual mission of their religious communities. When the Episcopal diocese broached the idea of closing a struggling suburban parish in 1894, prominent layman George B. Roberts wrote to the bishop to convey his strong objection to the sale of "consecrated property." To dispose of property secured through the gifts of "churchmen" for the welfare of the community violated the intention of the donors, he argued, and would do "violence to the interests of the Church."[21]

This renewed emphasis on churchmanship and denominational loyalty thus carried the expectation that members advance the material interest of their churches. The institutional growth of the late nineteenth century demanded that individuals not simply embrace the Christian message, but devote their time, talent, and treasures to building up their churches. Church guides and congregational handbooks affirmed this message, making voluntary donations central to one's Christian obligations. In a 1878 booklet, "Duties of the Church Member to the Church," Presbyterian theologian Thomas Murphy argued that in addition to advancing the spiritual work of the church through prayer, worship, and benevolences, church members must also support their local congregation by renting a pew, placing money in the collection plate, or contributing by some other means according to local custom.[22] Similar sentiments flowed not only from members of the clergy, but from prominent lay leaders as well. John Wanamaker, for example, frequently reminded his fellow laymen of their duty to aid their local congregations as well as the institutional work of the church as a whole. The 1880 membership guide for Bethany Presbyterian Church, which Wanamaker founded and supported throughout his life, explicitly stated that all members were expected to contribute something during the free-will offering.[23]

In appealing to the devotion of churchmen, religious leaders made, in effect, a claim on their wealth and sought to bring funds under congregational or denominational control. It reflected the leaders' desire to ensure not only financial support, but also the financial autonomy they needed to advance their mission. This would at times bring them into conflict with donors, who often had their own ideas about how funds should best be used or administered. However much donors agreed with the religious mission of their churches, their support was not unconditional. Though many wealthy individuals accepted the obligations of stewardship, they nevertheless guarded their own interests and used their giving to advance their own philanthropic agendas, even within the religious sphere. They may have been willing to cede a portion of their fortune to support the work of their churches, but they were often reluctant to relinquish complete control over their assets. A number of benefactors placed conditions upon their bequests in order to achieve their desired ends. Charles Macalester, a successful Philadelphia merchant best known for his foundational gift to the Minnesota college that bears his name, left money in his will in 1882 for the establishment of a Presbyterian church near his summer estates in the Torresdale district of Philadelphia. He instructed his executors to obtain an acre of ground on one of the major streets if within five years "a respectable number of persons" could be found to form a congregation and commit to erecting a church. He further promised $5,000 to be left in trust as an endowment for the church, but noted that the money would revert to the residuary estate if the five-year deadline were not met. Macalester's terms forced the local presbytery to commit missionary resources to establish the congregation before its time in a largely undeveloped district that held few prospects for growth.[24]

Macalester's bequest, though modest in comparison to later industrial-era philanthropy, nevertheless reflected a growing tension between donors and beneficiaries that would only intensify as the scale of giving increased during the late nineteenth and early twentieth centuries. Namely, it encapsulated a debate over how wealth should be expended and administered. As members of the industrial elite weighed the obligations of wealth, many looked to religious leaders for guidance and worked within existing denominational frameworks. This brought them under the authority of church officials, who courted wealth as a means of advancing their own religious mission. Even though their interests often coincided, both parties sought to control the donated assets and, in turn, the philanthropic agenda. The balance of power would shift as members of the new industrial class began to reassess traditional methods of giving and improve philanthropic practice.

Philanthropic Protocol

Few in the late nineteenth century were as keenly attuned to the potential and pitfalls of large-scale philanthropy as Andrew Carnegie, the rags-to-riches Scottish immigrant who, after making his fortune in the Pittsburgh steel industry, did more than any other person to define and promote a philanthropic philosophy for the age. He laid out his vision in a series of articles written for the *North American Review* in 1889; these were later reprinted as *The Gospel of Wealth* (1900).[25] Neither an advice manual nor an investment guide, the book served as a manifesto for new approaches to philanthropic practice that would shape the nature of upper-class giving and set the terms of philanthropic debate for much of the industrial era.

At no time did Carnegie challenge the dominant belief in an individual's natural right to wealth, viewing America's great fortunes as the inevitable fruits of democracy and capitalism. But though he saw nothing wrong with the accumulation of wealth, he believed that those who held great fortunes had a moral obligation to use their money for the good of society. "The man who dies rich," he famously declared, "dies disgraced." Carnegie further maintained that the wealthy—those who were most successful in business, management, and finance—were naturally the most qualified to administer their own philanthropic programs. Indeed, Carnegie's ethic of financial stewardship taught that many social problems were the result of the improper management of wealth. In his book, he warned that poorly conducted charity had the potential to do more harm than good. He was particularly concerned about the creation of a culture of dependency among beneficiaries and believed that philanthropy should promote self-sufficiency by helping those willing to help themselves. That same logic applied equally to churches, charitable agencies, and other institutions. Wealthy benefactors should not perpetually sustain an organization because such action risked destroying "society's own responsibility to preserve individual initiative." He therefore refused to include institutional endowments in his own philanthropy.[26]

Carnegie's writings and the managerial ethos of the era challenged many to question the nature of their giving. When it came to religious philanthropy, benefactors were often torn between religious loyalties and class sensibilities. They upheld older notions of charity even as they embraced the new philanthropic gospel. Members of the industrial elite did not want institutions in which they believed to develop an unhealthy dependence on their financial support, yet neither did they want to see those institutions fail. Despite Carnegie's advice, many benefactors continued to endow churches and other charitable organizations, particularly those they had founded or which bore their name. The economic collapse of an eponymous institution would have been particularly embarrassing, discrediting the very name the institution was intended to commemorate, or even redeem.

In Philadelphia, John Wanamaker's evolving relationship with Bethany Presbyterian provides a glimpse of how one individual struggled to balance his older sense of stewardship with the new philanthropic creed. It reveals the tension between religious obligation and the class imperatives that he and others of his generation experienced as their accustomed methods of giving were called into question. Wanamaker, Philadelphia's great "merchant prince," who rose like Carnegie from a humble background, cared for Bethany, the church that grew from the Sunday school he had founded in 1858, with a parent's love. Active in Bethany's governance throughout his life, Wanamaker faithfully attended services despite other pressing obligations: indeed, he was as committed to Bethany's success as he was to the success of the department store that bore his name. While serving as postmaster general under President Benjamin Harrison, he traveled weekly from Washington to teach his regular Sunday school class.[27] He sat on both the board of trustees and the Session—the two main governing bodies within every Presbyterian congregation—demonstrating that his concern for Bethany's spiritual as well as temporal health. By the start of twentieth century, Bethany boasted one of the largest Sunday schools in the nation and a membership of more than 4,000.[28]

Wanamaker's own faith was rooted in the evangelical Christianity of the mid-nineteenth century. He experienced a personal conversion at the age of twelve and later joined a Presbyterian congregation led by Rev. John Chambers, a crusading preacher whom Wanamaker viewed as a spiritual father. In 1858, after serving a few years as a sales clerk, he accepted a paid post as secretary of the local branch of the Young Men's Christian Association, which drew him into the temperance movement and other evangelical causes. Although he soon relinquished that post and turned to retail, he remained committed to spreading the Gospel and devoted energy to Sunday school work and revivalism. In 1871, he purchased the *Sunday School Times* and helped revive the struggling publication. During the nation's centennial year, he hosted Dwight Moody's visit to Philadelphia in his "Grand Depot," the first incarnation of his department store. He also bore witness to his faith through his business practices, leading his workers in prayer and staging grand and overtly religious displays at Christmas and Easter. By the early twentieth century, Wanamaker was recognized as one of the leading Presbyterian laymen and Christian businessmen of his generation.[29]

Though responsive to the appeals of various national causes and the needs of the international missions, Wanamaker never strayed from his religious commitments to Bethany. He worked to expand its social ministries and to grow the congregation through personal outreach. In 1890, he founded the Bethany Brotherhood, a men's fellowship whose meetings he regularly attended. Within the congregation, he led by example, both through his financial contributions and through his personal piety, and held other church members to his own high standards. When he went so far as to suggest that every Bethany member be required to make four distinct pledges of spiritual and financial commitment to the church, the pastor objected to this unusual and "drastic" measure, which clearly went beyond traditional Presbyterian teachings.[30]

As Wanamaker grew older and started to think more about his ultimate fate and personal legacy, he became concerned for Bethany's future. He wanted to wean church members from dependence on his support, yet did not want them to think that he was abandoning them. Therefore, in crafting his will, Wanamaker left $200,000 to the General Assembly of the Presbyterian Church to be held in trust for Bethany, specifying that interest income was to be distributed semiannually in a "proper business manner." The principal was not to be touched. He bequeathed several real estate holdings to Bethany as well, stipulating that profits from their sale could only be applied to "the cost of construction" of "building[s] for church work," not to daily operational expenses. Wanamaker thus protected his vision by ensuring that the trustees would manage his bequest responsibly. In addition, he placed the burden of ongoing financial support squarely on the shoulders of Bethany's members, desiring that they develop a sense of ownership in their church.[31]

Wanamaker was not alone in his efforts to dictate how bequeathed funds were to be administered. In the late nineteenth and early twentieth centuries, many benefactors would establish contracts or legally binding deeds of trust with their beneficiaries to specify how their money was to be spent. Those seeking to control church affairs from beyond the grave could, like Wanamaker, place specific instructions in their wills. They learned to circumvent laws such as one requiring dissolution of a charitable trust nine years after the death of the last trustee that were designed to prevent perpetual—mortmain ("dead hand")—control over programs and organizations. Donors could avoid the above restriction, for example, by appointing a corporate trustee that was unlikely ever to "die" or cease to exist, such as a religious body—like the Presbyterian General Assembly in Wanamaker's case—or city government. Eventually, many anti-mortmain laws were repealed as political leaders came to recognize and accept changing philanthropic protocol, such as the creation of private philanthropic foundations with their own self-perpetuating boards.[32]

Even when well intentioned, legal restrictions attached to benefactions could became a source of consternation for beneficiaries. At one Presbyterian church, the congregation's plans to erect a new parish house connected to the church ran into legal trouble when it was determined that such action would run afoul of a deed restriction that proscribed the placing of any mortgage on the property. As an attached structure, the new building would technically be a wing to the existing church, and therefore its mortgage would be conveyed to the original property as a whole and thus violate the terms of the deed.[33] Problems likewise arose when the need for which the gift was intended no longer existed, or when the donor's wishes proved too difficult to execute. The city of Philadelphia had trouble complying with the wishes of one donor when the "sufferers of yellow fever" for whom he had left funds grew scarce.[34] Several orphanage endowments, including one established by Wanamaker, similarly fell into limbo when the intended recipients refused to accept them in the first place or when the institutions they were intended to support had to close their doors.[35] Often the only way to alter the terms of a benefactor's trust was through legal action, a potentially cumbersome process. In the 1910s, the Episcopal diocese, for example, took considerable pains to amend the terms of one bequest that had provided funds to support the establishment of a diocesan cathedral when the site specified by the donor was deemed unsuitable for the project.[36]

Legal restrictions placed on trusts and inheritances could also frustrate donors, as Katharine Drexel discovered when she began her philanthropic career. The conditions of the trust fund her father had established for her two sisters and her before his untimely death in 1885 did not allow them to transfer control of its assets to any other individual or legal entity. Despite claims later made by members of her extended family, the provision was not intended to prevent Katharine from taking the veil, but to ensure that she and her sisters did not lose their financial autonomy within marriage. When Katharine decided to become a nun, she was caught in a bind. Unable to transfer the money to her religious order, and prevented from renouncing her wealth without losing it to the other charities her father had named under the terms of the trust, she was seemingly barred from using her inheritance to support her religious vocation. Ultimately, two members of the American Catholic hierarchy helped Katharine secure a special dispensation from the vow of poverty. This rare act showed that it was easier to get Rome to bend than it was to loosen the "iron bands" of her father's trust.[37]

Thus, although the rise of industrial fortunes increased the flow of resources to charitable enterprises, the increasingly legalistic and contractual nature of giving altered philanthropic practice and shifted the balance of power between donors and recipients. It allowed wealthy benefactors to protect their interests and preserve their influence by setting the conditions under which their money was to be used. In extending their control in such ways, donors challenged the dominance religious leaders had previously enjoyed in determining how money entrusted to their care would be spent.

Denominational Cultures of Giving

Debates over the proper use and administration of wealth make sense only in relation to the theological views that guided members of the upper class and conditioned their philanthropic conduct. Although influenced by class imperatives and economic logic, wealthy benefactors also followed religious teachings and looked to Scripture for guidance. In trying to explain why some members of the economic elite acquired a philanthropic impulse while others did not, historian John Hamer argues that many great philanthropists of the industrial era, including Carnegie, Rockefeller, Wanamaker, and Morgan, possessed some vision of the greater social good acquired through the example of devout parents or members of the clergy who had served as spiritual role models and moral guides.[38] Mindful of how difficult it was for the rich to enter the kingdom of heaven, many wealthy individuals wanted to know how to ensure their salvation—something adherence to the gospel of wealth alone could not do.

Within philanthropic practice, theological distinctions mattered. Whatever their professional or class imperatives, members of the industrial elite understood the obligations that came with their wealth in light of specific church teachings and their own personal religious beliefs. In Philadelphia, variations in upper-class philanthropy consequently reflected the city's religious diversity. Individuals conducted their philanthropy not just as members of a perceived class, but as members of a particular religious community. They understood their social responsibilities in light of the distinct teachings, community ethos, and social outlook they gained from their religious affiliation and faith practice. As a result, the nature of elite philanthropy cannot be understood fully without examining the religious teachings that guided members of the upper class and the denominational cultures in which they worked.

Although broadly Protestant in their orientation, members of Philadelphia's financial elite operated within distinct denominational milieus. For the purposes of this study, it is important to distinguish between the practices of Quakers, Episcopalians, and Presbyterians, the three denominations that claimed the greatest loyalty among members of the city's upper class.[39] The theological teachings, communal history, and social composition of each particular tradition affected how individuals viewed the obligations of wealth and administered their financial resources. Although finer distinctions existed within the particular denominations—such as those between Hicksite and Orthodox Quakers, the two main branches of the Society of Friends, each with its own set of disciplines on financial conduct—for the most part, the differences across denominations were more significant than those within them.

Drawing attention to denominational difference also reveals how theological teachings and organizational structures affected the degree of autonomy that donors possessed in conducting their philanthropic affairs. Protestant denominations, for instance, with their congregational polity and individualist ethic, tended to provide donors greater discretion in determining how resources were to be deployed, even when working within the denominational sphere. In contrast, Catholics and Jews tended to make stronger corporate claims on their co-religionists' wealth, seeking to ensure that resources remained within the religious community, where religious leaders had a greater voice in setting philanthropic priorities. Although Catholics and Jews stood at the margins of both proper society and the Protestant mainstream, their inclusion here not only provides a fuller view of the philanthropic landscape, but also reveals how class composition affected charitable practice during the industrial era. Broadly speaking, the communalism of Catholic and Jewish philanthropy differentiated it from the more individualized philanthropy of Quakers, Episcopalians, and Presbyterians.

Of the various strains of religious philanthropy in Philadelphia, the Quaker strain is perhaps the most distinctive and therefore merits special attention. As E. Digby Baltzell has demonstrated, long-established Quaker practices influenced other religious groups and so shaped the character of the city and its upper class.[40] Many of the city's oldest benevolent organizations and charitable associations owed their origins to the Society of Friends.[41] Quaker charity was heavily informed by the sect's unique testimonies regarding peaceable relations and personal equality, a tradition that remained strong within many industrial-era Quaker families. Generations of the Elkinton family, for instance, who had grown wealthy from the success of the family chemical firm, the Philadelphia Quartz Company, remained committed to missionary work among Native Americans.[42] Anna T. Jeanes, the daughter of a wealthy merchant and heir to the Quaker abolitionist tradition, did much to help African Americans in the post–Civil War decades.[43] Anna Wharton Morris, the daughter of steel baron Joseph Wharton, took an active interest in prison reform, also a respected part of the Quaker philanthropic tradition.[44] During the late nineteenth century, both the Orthodox and Hicksite branches of the Society affirmed that philanthropy was a manifestation of the "Inward Light." Although some conservative elements within the Society called for a further retreat from worldly affairs, Quaker leadership reaffirmed the importance of charitable work, seen in the founding of groups like the Hicksite Yearly Meeting's Committee on Philanthropic Labor in 1892.[45]

Yet, curiously, at the same time that Quakers attained prominence for their commitment to personal service and reform campaigns, they also acquired a reputation for tightfistedness. Unlike members of other denominations, Quakers were not known for large bequests. They did not build grand sanctuaries, nor did they have as vast a network of religious institutions to finance. Lavish giving was also contrary to the Quaker religious temperament. With their emphasis on simplicity, personal service, and social equality, many objected to the class inequalities inherent in much industrial-era philanthropy. Writing in her diary in 1901, an exasperated Anna Wharton Morris asked, "Why can't these patronizing, self-conscious philanthropists realize this, that it is sincerity which counts, not patronage of those they consider their inferiors, but who are often their superiors?"[46] It is also possible that some Quakers, in consciously avoiding any signs of class distinction among themselves, eschewed making large gifts for fear of revealing their true economic positions.

Wealth was something good Quakers kept to themselves, or at least kept within their families. Owing to concerns about the immorality of debts, the Quaker ethic of fiduciary responsibility tacitly included an obligation to leave one's family solvent and one's investments secure.[47] Parents were instructed to educate their children in sound economic practices. To default on financial obligations was to bring shame on oneself, one's family, and the Society of Friends. Faced with a $200 debt in 1889, one Quaker described his situation as "the mortifying and disgraceful position of being unable at present to meet my obligations, without assistance, or encroaching on the Trust income of my inheritance."[48] Wills also offer evidence of Quakers' sense of obligation to preserve the financial health of their families. When Joseph Wharton died, the bulk of his estimated $25,000,000 estate was left in trust to members of his family, with the exception of a $100,000 gift to Swarthmore College, his only sizable bequest.[49] His wife, also a devout Quaker, did likewise, leaving most of her $2,000,000 estate to her children.[50] There were always exceptions: Quaker philanthropist Anna T. Jeanes, for example, bequeathed $1,000,000 to the cause of Negro education in the South and provided several other large bequests to fund medical and charitable institutions. Jeanes never married, however, and outlived the rest of her family.[51]

Thus what appeared to be stinginess among Quakers was in part a reasoned response to moral imperatives. Quakers were neither promised spiritual blessings nor celebrated by their religious community for immense financial bequests. They did not associate simplicity with voluntary poverty as Catholics did, making it unnecessary for them to endeavor to give away their wealth. Rather, they understood simplicity as an ethical practice designed to help members ensure their financial security. Quaker sanctity was measured in part by one's ability to be a good financial steward, which required resources to manage. Wealth, therefore, was a both sign of grace and an instrument for obtaining it. In this light, it is not surprising that Quakers were active in establishing trust companies and life insurance programs.[52] These enterprises allowed them to put their principles into practice. As one history of the Provident Life and Trust Company explained, the firm's "success and reputation" resulted from its managers' commitment to fulfill the "important and sacred duties which relate to the care of the estates of deceased persons and those involved in the management of trusts." Influenced by Quaker sensibilities, several of the city's other venerable financial institutions also would come to specialize in what Nathaniel Burt refers to as "maintenance guardianships of Philadelphia fortunes."[53]

In contrast to the Quakers, Episcopalians, as heirs to the traditions of the established Church of England, conducted their charity out of a sense of noblesse oblige. As they rose within the American economic and social establishment, their sense of moral obligation to support the poor remained strong, with their benefactions reinforcing their sense of entitlement to privileged social position. Prominent Episcopal officials, like Bishop Henry Codman Potter of New York, a leading voice of the Social Gospel, rejected the extreme stance of Christian socialism and viewed wealth as a means to attain "greater happiness [for] those who expend it" in service to others.[54] Within the Episcopal Church, it was most often members of the laity who initiated charitable outreach or founded social service agencies. Many of Philadelphia's orphanages, clinics, missions, and houses of rest for the aged, though associated with the Episcopal Church, were not established by the diocese but rather by lay church members acting either independently or through their parishes. In the late nineteenth century, as urban issues claimed the attention of social reformers, numerous parishes sponsored settlement houses, industrial schools, clinics, and other community services. Because philanthropy was viewed as a social obligation rather than a strictly religious one, Episcopal outreach tended to lack the overt evangelical tone that dominated the work of other denominations.[55]

Wealthy Presbyterians shared their Episcopalian peers' sense of elite obligation to help those less fortunate, but their views on charity and philanthropy were also shaped by the denomination's Calvinist theology and evangelical orientation. As part of their reformed tradition, Presbyterians espoused a Protestant work ethic that viewed economic success as a sign of God's favor, and sought moral virtue in the marketplace. As historian Richard W. Pointer has demonstrated, Presbyterians in Philadelphia embraced the market revolution of the early nineteenth century, even though they remained conflicted about the moral legitimacy of material acquisition.[56] Alongside their acceptance of financial reward, Presbyterian leaders placed a strong emphasis on charitable giving, much of which went to support evangelization and missionary outreach. Throughout the industrial era, Presbyterian churches were required to devote a certain percentage of each week's collection to charitable causes. Their budgets and financial records distinguished between funds intended for "congregational purposes" and those raised for "benevolences."[57] At one point, Bryn Mawr Presbyterian Church, one of the wealthiest in the Philadelphia area, was sponsoring three foreign missionaries in addition to supporting the denomination's general missionary fund.[58] In 1921, the congregation directed more than 53 percent of total receipts toward benevolences.[59] In 1915, members of Overbrook Presbyterian Church, a congregation on the edge of the Main Line, celebrated the fact that they, in their first quarter century, had given more to missionary and charitable purposes than they had spent on congregational expenses.[60] Indeed, Presbyterians often took the lead in supporting tract societies, revivalist crusades, the YMCA, and other interdenominational evangelical organizations.[61] Several members of the upper class were themselves bitten by the evangelism bug, organizing Bible study classes or even laboring in the missionary fields.[62]

Catholics and Jews tended to approach philanthropy differently from Protestants, both because of their particular theological teachings and because of their minority status within American society. The hierarchical nature of the Catholic Church, for instance, placed greater authority in the hands of clerical leaders to administer funds at both the parish and the diocesan levels. Such centralized oversight helped Catholics pool limited resources more effectively than otherwise possible. As members of an immigrant church, Catholics lacked large numbers of wealthy benefactors upon whom to rely. Although some Irish and German Catholics had moved into the middle and upper classes, only a few Catholics in Philadelphia held estates of any great worth during the late nineteenth and early twentieth centuries. This financial reality fundamentally shaped how Catholics conceived of their role in supporting the work of the Church. Speaking to rich and poor alike, church leaders consistently emphasized vocations to the religious life as the ultimate form of giving. As the ranks of priests, nuns, and other vowed religious swelled, these human resources became the lifeblood of the Catholic institutional network. Consequently, Catholic organizations rarely enjoyed endowments or sizable financial reserves of any sort. Historian Mary Oates points out that the "popular sentiment" against endowments reflected not only Catholics' low socioeconomic position but also their concern "that endowments might be built at the expense of those in immediate need." Only after 1900, and then slowly, did endowments for Catholic institutions begin to grow, as it became more common for diocesan officials to "accommodate the needs of the rich for public acclaim for their benefactions" by bestowing church honors and publicizing large gifts.[63]

Members of Philadelphia's Jewish community were similarly drawn together by a blend of religious and ethnic solidarity, which motivated much of their charitable enterprises. Like Catholics, they harbored a suspicion of Protestant charity, seeing such benevolence as thinly veiled attempts at conversion, and worked to establish hospitals, schools, social service agencies, and other institutions of their own in response to perceived or experienced religious prejudice.[64] Their emphasis on communal responsibility flowed from the "tradition of Tzedakah," one's religious obligation to perform works of charity, which bound all members of the Jewish community, both rich and poor, to "care for [their] own."[65] To this end, many Jewish aid organizations were established in the city between 1880 and 1910, during the peak of eastern European Jewish immigration to the United States. In the process, the established German-Jewish elite sought to preserve their good name within wider society and alleviate public concern about immigrant poverty and the "Jewish Problem."[66] Unlike Catholic leaders, however, Jewish leaders in Philadelphia tended to be more willing to work with nonsectarian organizations and state agencies as a means of promoting cultural assimilation. This impulse was particularly strong within the educational sphere. Temple University, although founded as a Baptist institution, received considerable support from Philadelphia's Jewish community because of its inclusive enrollment policies and nonsectarian spirit.[67]

During the industrial era, therefore, patterns of giving in the city continued to reflect these and other denominational cultures even as older notions of charity gave way to the methods of modern philanthropy. For the social and financial elite, religious identity and church affiliation defined the limits of acceptable philanthropic practice. Few would have been unfamiliar with the culture of giving within their churches, and those who chose to pursue their own course had to define it against dominant religious conventions. Since the vast majority of charitable work at this time was church based or religiously affiliated, most philanthropic decisions were conditioned by denominational attitudes toward wealth and its proper use. The state had not yet become a major force in the provision of social welfare, and very few charitable initiatives were truly secular; even agencies claiming to be nonsectarian or nondenominational were generally understood to be broadly Protestant in orientation. The religious character of giving would persist among the industrial elite even as new philanthropic philosophies took hold because of the moral approbation that came from working within the religious sphere.

Divergent Philanthropic Careers

To assess more thoroughly how religious differences affected philanthropic practice, it is useful to examine the careers of two members of the Drexel family, Katharine and Anthony, one a Roman Catholic nun and the other an Episcopalian banker.[68] Both were religiously devout individuals guided by their faith, but also strong-willed members of a distinguished Philadelphia family accustomed to the privileges of their class. At times, each would challenge the boundaries established by church teachings and denominational directives. Yet, even though both exercised influence and authority in philanthropic affairs, their charitable work reflects a motivational complexity that eludes easy categorization. Their methods of giving further reveal how two members of Philadelphia's upper class negotiated religious beliefs and class sensibilities. As Katharine and Anthony sought to live moral lives, achieve personal salvation, and improve society, they did not ignore church teachings or denominational authority, but neither did they submit to either with unquestioning obedience.

The religious rift within the Drexel family had no clear origin, thus allowing divergent narratives to develop. Despite popular misconceptions—some fostered by family members themselves—the Drexels had originally been Catholic, not Protestant. The founder of the family dynasty, Francis Martin Drexel, an itinerant painter turned currency trader who arrived in the United States in 1817, was a Catholic from the Austrian Tyrol. Of his three sons, the two youngest, Anthony and Joseph, eventually joined the Episcopal Church, while the eldest, Francis, Katharine's father, remained a Catholic.[69] As members of the Protestant side of the family married into other proper upper-class Protestant families such as the Philadelphia Biddles, New York Van Rensselaers, and North Carolina Dukes, they conveniently forgot the family's Catholic roots. Indeed, to "preserve" her family's Protestant lineage, Cordelia Drexel Biddle, the wife of tobacco heir Angier Duke, tellingly makes Katharine a religious convert in her family memoir.[70]

Katharine, however, was Catholic to the core. Born in 1858, she was raised in a devout Catholic family active in the life of the Church and supportive of its social mission. Long before she and her sisters shared in the $14 million trust fund their father had established for them, they had inherited their parents' commitment to the faith. Seeking to do more than dispense charity, Katharine eventually decided that she was being called to give the ultimate gift of self by accepting a religious vocation. Although she was inclined to spiritual introspection from adolescence, the real change in Katharine's life came during her tours of the western United States, first in 1884 and again in 1887, which awakened her to the plight of Native Americans. These experiences, together with subsequent correspondence with missionary priests and her spiritual advisor, along with the gentle suggestion of Pope Leo XIII, convinced her that the best way to support the work of the Church was to become a missionary herself. In 1891, after her postulancy with the Sisters of Mercy in Pittsburgh, Katharine professed her vows as a Sister of the Blessed Sacrament, the religious order she founded for work among the "Indians and Colored People," two groups largely neglected by Catholic missionary outreach.[71]

When Katharine announced her decision to become a nun in 1889, Anthony, who had assumed responsibility for the well-being of his three nieces after their father's death in 1885, urged her to reconsider. Upon hearing of her decision, "Uncle Anthony dropped four or five tears," Katharine told her spiritual advisor. And although "he said he would not oppose anything which contributed to my happiness," she continued, "he thinks, however, that I am making the mistake of my life if I become a religious."[72] It was a curious response. Anthony knew that his late brother Francis would not have opposed the entrance of any of his three daughters into religious life. Nor was Anthony personally opposed to the Catholic faith. He openly supported the philanthropic careers of his three Catholic nieces, occasionally gave to Catholic causes himself, and included Catholics in his social world and professional affairs.[73] Rather, it is likely that his reservations about Katharine's vocation stemmed from his concern about her future within the Catholic Church, and his fear that, as a nun, Katharine would lose the ability to manage her money and conduct her philanthropy as she saw fit. He thought that she could "do so much more good by helping the [religious] Orders already established," a sentiment that Katharine herself had originally shared.[74] As a Gilded Age financier and businessman, Anthony placed a high value on his own financial autonomy, and enjoyed the privileges wealth afforded. He desired nothing less for his niece.

Anthony's concerns, however, proved unfounded since Katharine was unlike any other nun of her day. Well educated and financially astute, her dispensation from the vow of poverty allowed her to retain her financial and personal independence. Although most nuns sacrificed their identities upon entering the convent, Katharine's wealth enabled—and indeed required—her to maintain hers. In order to execute her portion of the trust fund, it was essential that Katharine retain her name and legal identity. For her religious name, she simply inverted her first and middle names to become Mother Mary Katharine Drexel. Katharine's wealth similarly allowed her to avoid the proscriptions against "singularity," or individualism, that nuns usually faced, proscriptions she had earlier doubted her ability to observe.[75] It also gave her other liberties unusual for a nun to possess, such as the ability to leave the convent and visit with family at her own discretion. In 1893, Archbishop Patrick Ryan of Philadelphia, perhaps responding to Katharine's concerns about the liberties she enjoyed, informed her that if she wanted to "remove all danger of scandal" she could "announce that I have *commanded* you to see your sister Louise as frequently as your duties will permit—certainly once a week."[76] Ryan recognized Katharine's tendency to hold herself to the same standards of poverty and sacrifice required of others in her order. He therefore used his authority on occasion to remind Katharine that she need not renounce all the benefits of her economic position. In 1907, for instance, he was "gratified" that Katharine "changed to first class" during a steamer voyage. He reminded her that she possessed "the reward of poverty & the comfort of affluence," and should not deny herself either.[77]

Katharine brought unique skills to her vocation. Born into a family of bankers, she was well versed in business methods and financial management. As biographer Dan Rottenberg notes, she was her uncle Anthony's "aptest pupil and the only entrepreneur among the family's third generation. In a letter to her spiritual advisor, Katharine mentioned how George W. Childs, one of her uncle's friends and closest business partners, had explained to her how corporate boards were arranged and operated.[78] Such skills proved invaluable when she used her trust fund income to underwrite the work of her religious order. During her long religious career, lasting until her death in 1955, she provided the funding necessary to run the churches, schools, and mission centers scattered across the country that were staffed by the Sisters of the Blessed Sacrament. Indeed, the business mentality and financial logic she inherited and cultivated so pervaded her thought that it affected even her spiritual views. In a letter to her cousin Josephine, she told of a man who left a "posterity of 203 children, grandchildren, and great-grandchildren."[79] She lamented that the Church was unable to reach that first man, a concern that makes sense in light of Katharine's financial background. Clearly, had the Church made the initial investment, the spiritual benefits would have accrued over the years, providing abundant dividends for both the man's family and the Church. To Katharine, the Church accumulated souls like compound interest.

More significantly, Katharine's wealth provided her with the ability to maneuver within Catholic authority structures and gave her a degree of independence within the Church's dominant clerical culture. Despite her vow of obedience, Katharine was able to set the terms of her philanthropy. Like other wealthy donors of her day, she engaged in contractual philanthropy, requiring financial accountability from those she supported, a demand that sometimes led to the consternation of missionary priests unaccustomed to having to account to a woman, let alone a nun.[80] Those she agreed to support could do little to interfere with her decisions since she controlled her own assets. In 1891, shortly after she had taken her vows, Archbishop Ryan made it clear that he left her "free" to spend "any sum under $10,000 so that [she] need have no scruples."[81] At a time when parish priests and other vowed religious within the archdiocese were expected to receive permission for spending even the most modest of sums, Katharine was given enviable financial discretion.

Katharine had earned this trust by conducting her religious career with as much industry, efficiency, and financial savvy as any corporate executive of her day. Although her uncle may have feared Katharine's loss of opportunity within convent walls, in reality, her position as a nun offered her opportunities unavailable to other wealthy women of her generation. Despite her financial acumen, as a woman, Katharine could not have joined the family firm. But, as the leader of a religious community, she could and did direct a national network of religious institutions and oversee a "staff" of hundreds of sisters. At the height of her order's activities, Katharine was personally supporting more than sixty schools, missions, and parishes throughout the United States.[82] Her charitable work rivaled, if not exceeded, that of other prominent female philanthropists of the era, such as Mary Elizabeth Garrett of Baltimore and Olivia Slocum Sage of New York. Had Anthony lived to see the flourishing of his niece's religious order and the aplomb with which she directed her charitable enterprises, his earlier concerns about her future would doubtless have been laid to rest.

In contrast, had Anthony remained Catholic, he would have found it difficult to work within Catholic authority structures in a manner suitable for a man of his wealth, status, and skill. Although Katharine found ways to maneuver within the Catholic Church, her position as a vowed religious made her less threatening to male clerical authority. As a layman, Anthony's role would have remained circumscribed. Thus it made sense that Anthony and his brother Joseph would gravitate toward the Episcopal Church, which was more open to lay influence, and which allowed wealthy individuals to conduct their religious affairs and philanthropy more freely. Indeed, membership in the Episcopal Church would "befit Anthony J. Drexel's prominent position," as E. Digby Baltzell observed.[83] Although speaking strictly about issues of social status, Baltzell was right to believe that the Episcopal Church would have been more accommodating to someone like Anthony, who expected to retain a great deal of personal control in his religious work and philanthropic affairs.

Admittedly, little is known about Anthony Drexel's spiritual life or personal views regarding religion. Unlike his niece, who left behind abundant correspondence and many personal spiritual writings, Anthony preserved none of his personal papers. What is known has been gleaned from a variety of sources, including his correspondence with Katharine, church records, newspaper reports, and business documents.[84] The record is silent about why or when Anthony actually decided to leave the Catholic Church. The first official marker of his conversion was his marriage in 1850 to Ellen Rozét before Rev. John Ludlow, a minister in the Dutch Reformed Church and a relative of the Rozét family. In 1856, he was listed as a founding member of the Episcopal Church of the Saviour in West Philadelphia, where he served as vestryman from 1856 to 1889 and as accounting warden from 1889 until his death in 1893. Anthony expressed his religious commitment through his many large bequests to the parish, including generous support for the construction of a new church in 1889. He associated with leading members of the Episcopal clergy and hierarchy, both locally and nationally, and at a memorial service after his death, Bishop Henry Codman Potter of New York eulogized him as "a strong and beneficent moral force."[85]

Anthony's decision to become an Episcopalian came at a time when authority in the Catholic Church was becoming more centralized within the hands of the bishops and the clergy. By the middle of the nineteenth century, the dioceses had taken control of many activities formerly under the domain of lay individuals. With this "Romanization" of the Church in Philadelphia and elsewhere, it became increasingly difficult for prominent Catholics to work outside of clerical auspices. Unlike the Episcopal Church, which welcomed the services of laymen on church boards and diocesan committees, the Catholic Church took a firm line against "trusteeism" after the issue led to numerous conflicts within local parishes, including the "Hogan Schism" of the 1820s, in which the trustees of St. Mary's Church in Philadelphia, then the cathedral parish for the diocese, locked the bishop out of the church when he attempted to remove the popular pastor Rev. William Hogan from his position. When the first Provincial Council of Baltimore convened in 1829, the bishops resolved that all church property be held in the name of the bishop of the diocese, a move that effectively eliminated any formal lay control in the temporal affairs of the Church.[86] Although Anthony would have been too young to remember these events personally, he would have had indirect knowledge of them through his family, since his father had served briefly as a trustee at St. Mary's and his parents were married there in 1821, on the eve of the trustee dispute.[87]

His shift in religious affiliation greatly affected Anthony's future philanthropy. For wealthy philanthropists of his generation, personal focus and financial independence formed the cornerstone of charitable practice. Anthony likely would have agreed with Matthew Vassar, who, in a letter to Anthony, insisted on maintaining an active role in the governance of the institutions he supported so that his money would be "faithfully and judiciously expended under [his] own eye."[88] Anthony adhered to a similar philosophy when he planned his own philanthropic legacy, most notably in the establishment of the Drexel Institute of Art, Science, and Industry in West Philadelphia, founded in 1891 as "part of a nation-wide trend towards an ever-closer and more immediately practical liaison of education with business and industrial advances."[89]

As founder, trustee, and principal benefactor of the Drexel Institute, Anthony was able to define the institute's mission and craft its identity. He consulted widely with business associates and religious leaders, yet retained ultimate authority for himself. Anthony "brooded over this large plan," Bishop Potter noted, and "selected his fellow-counselors with equal prudence and wisdom."[90] Such institutional independence would not have been possible under prevailing Catholic protocol, as seen in Catholic Thomas E. Cahill's educational philanthropy in Philadelphia. In 1890, Cahill, a wealthy coal and lumber merchant, bequeathed land and money to the archdiocese to establish a boys' high school, the first free Catholic high school in the country. The nature of his bequest reveals his deference to church leaders. They, not Cahill, appointed administrators, set the curriculum, and determined how best to manage the school. In the Catholic system, as Cahill would have recognized, there was little room for the exercise of lay influence.[91] In contrast, Anthony established the standards for his institute, often in consultation with his wife, his friend George W. Childs, and his nieces. Even though he died suddenly just two years after the institute's founding, his educational vision endured because he selected family members, friends, and business associates to serve as trustees and managers.

Such institutional independence was not simply a by-product of Anthony's wealth and status, but a reflection of the denominational culture of the Episcopal Church, which did not oppose such lay autonomy. Church leaders praised the nonsectarian Drexel Institute when it was founded, and two members of the clergy sat on the original board of managers without any apparent reservations.[92] The Episcopal Church was accustomed to having the laity establish schools and other institutions only loosely related to the Church.[93] In the Drexel case, the technical curriculum posed little need for theological scrutiny and church leaders probably assumed that a dominant culture of Protestantism would prevail, as it did at the University of Pennsylvania, the Drexel Institute's West Philadelphia neighbor.[94] Any Catholic seeking to establish and govern a nonsectarian school at this time would have had trouble maintaining favorable relations with church leaders, since bishops and clergy took a dim view of any institution not explicitly professing Catholic identity or submitting to church authority. The Episcopal Church, however, did not challenge or condemn individuals who chose to work outside of denominational confines. Rather, it offered them an avenue for religiously sanctioned philanthropy without forcing them to sacrifice personal autonomy.

Members of the industrial-era elite may have enjoyed a considerable degree of personal discretion in determining how to employ their financial resources, but as the careers of Katharine and Anthony Drexel demonstrate, church teachings and denominational culture played a considerable role in shaping their philanthropic practices, both constraining and empowering benefactors who sought to use their wealth in accordance with the dictates of conscience. Even when guided by sympathetic church leaders who sought to accommodate, and who at times shared, their class interests, they still operated within a religious framework and institutional context that shaped the nature of their giving.

The nature of industrial-era philanthropy reveals much about how members of the financial elite understood the obligations of wealth and their proper role in society. Though many were guided by sincere religious conviction and sought to follow the dictates of conscience, they were also members of a capitalist class who held their own views on the proper administration of their financial resources. Individuals worked to reconcile religious and class expectations, seeking to broker a balance between established methods of giving within their own faith tradition and the new imperatives of elite philanthropy. They listened attentively to church leaders, their social peers, and their own hearts in an effort to determine how best to employ their resources for the good of society, their churches, and their immortal souls. The ethical demands of wealth prompted considerable personal introspection, and required that individual negotiate class and religious impulses to forge a personally and morally satisfying philanthropic agenda.

The study of industrial-era philanthropy also sheds light on the relationship between members of the financial elite and their religious communities, as well as the power dynamics present between donors and their church officials. In addition to living their faith, wealthy individuals were called to support the work of their particular churches and religious communities. Church leaders had a vested interest in promoting sectarian giving, and looked to members of the industrial elite to support the network of institutions and agencies that gave visibility to the nation's denominational order. This institutional expansion also made denominational organization and church governance more complex, and opened the door for greater lay involvement in congregational and denominational affairs, particularly when it came to the management of church finances. As chapter 2 reveals, those who controlled financial assets were able to influence the social mission and theological message of the churches, not only within their local congregations but increasingly within their broader denominations, as they gained positions of authority on boards and other governing bodies.

A Controlling "Interest"

On 4 February 1889, the first service was held at the Church of St. Martin-in-the-Fields, an Episcopal parish established on the lower side of Chestnut Hill. Among those seated prominently in the new church that day was Henry Howard Houston, the person most responsible for its formation. Houston had donated land, coordinated architectural planning, and provided construction funding for the church building. He also secured the services of a rector and even helped draw members to the congregation through his investments in other community developments. According to one estimate, Houston's benefactions to the new church amounted to some $100,000, although it was not until his death in 1895 that title to the church property was officially transferred from his estate to the parish. In the decades that followed, members of the Houston family continued to support the parish in ways crucial to its success by funding church improvements, covering financial shortfalls, supporting charitable work, and participating in church governance.[1]

Described by the most recent parish history as a "venture in faith," St. Martin-in-the-Fields was likewise a financial venture for Houston, who had come to Philadelphia in 1847 as an executive of the Pennsylvania Railroad, building a fortune in rail and oil that he later invested in real estate. He believed that establishing an Episcopal parish in the sparsely populated northwest district would help draw respectable families to the area and improve the value of his holdings there. Until it did, however, St. Martin-in-the-Fields was a church in search of a congregation, sustained largely by Houston's financial support.[2]

Although unusual in the degree of influence retained by a single family, the history of St. Martin-in-the-Fields accurately reflects the internal dynamics at work within many religious communities during the industrial era. In particular, it reveals how private financial influence steered the direction of church growth and guided congregational development. In the absence of state support, the cost of building and maintaining a church fell to the voluntary contributions of its members, making religious communities particularly responsive to persons of means. Under these circumstances, many congregations, especially within the Protestant tradition, came to operate according to a "privatist" system of finance and governance, vesting power and authority in those who had a direct financial interest in their lives. This stood in contrast with the parochial system of church organization and governance found within the more centralized and hierarchical Catholic Church, which tended to restrict the financial influence of lay members within church affairs. Although a number of studies have examined the contributions of churches to community life and their role in political and social affairs, few have explored the economic realities under which churches operated, something that had considerable bearing on the success of their mission.[3]

The example of St. Martin-in-the-Fields reveals how the structures of church governance enabled members of the social and financial elite to exercise considerable power in congregational life and to extend their authority into the wider ecclesiastical sphere. During the industrial era, the systems of ecclesiastical organization determined not only how churches were formed and financed, but also how power and authority were structured within religious communities. Like other prominent donors, members of the Houston family saw their wealth and status rewarded not only with leadership positions within their local church, but also with seats on denominational boards and appointments to national church agencies. In those capacities, they used the means afforded them to advance not only the work of their church, but also their own personal, professional, and class interests.

Matters of church finance and administration had profound consequences for the shape and character of religious life in America during the late nineteenth and early twentieth centuries, when religious communities across the denominational spectrum expanded their institutional reach and grew in organizational complexity. It was during this time that religious communities, in the words of Russell E. Richey, "refined the grammar of denominational life" by strengthening church governance, clarifying structures of church authority, and creating new church agencies and organizations.[4] It was amid this institutional expansion and corporate ordering that the powers reserved for the laity became increasingly concentrated in the hands of the elite, the product of their financial influence, social prominence, and professional expertise. Although welcomed by its beneficiaries, to those who found themselves marginalized within the structures of power, the trend carried troubling implications for religious community, as the era's emergent debates over church polity indicate. There arose concern that elite influence had the potential to erode the democratic elements of religious life, just as it had in other spheres.

Church Growth

The late nineteenth and early twentieth centuries marked one of the greatest periods of institutional growth in American religious life, especially in the nation's burgeoning urban centers. In cities across the country, older churches expanded to accommodate growing congregations, new churches sprang up to serve the spiritual needs of those moving to the suburban periphery, and recent immigrants looked to re-create their accustomed religious life and its structures on American shores. Bolstered by the general prosperity of the period, these efforts not only reflected the collective determination of religious communities to announce their presence; they also gave visibility to the denominational order that would define the nation's religious life in the years following the Civil War and beyond. Many religious communities became increasingly "churchly" in their orientation and developed a heightened denominational consciousness, as seen in the increased reach of centralized governing bodies, the proliferation of denominational publications, and the growth of sectarian institutions in cities and towns across the country.[5]

Philadelphia proved no exception. Across the denominational spectrum, churches responded to rapid urbanization by increasing their institutional presence, which was made possible by the spiritual commitment, personal service, and financial contributions of countless individuals. During the administration of Bishop Ozi Whitaker, from 1887 to 1911, the Episcopal Diocese of Pennsylvania added approximately seventy new churches and missions in the five-county metropolitan region.[6] Presbyterians in the greater Philadelphia area, previously concerned that their church had "not increased as rapidly . . . as its character, position, influence, wealth, population, and responsibilities require," saw the number of their congregations swell from 112 to 171 between 1870 and 1900.[7] The network of Catholic parishes likewise expanded, with more than 100 created between 1880 and 1919, and another 45 during the 1920s.[8] If one includes all the parish houses, schools, hospitals, orphanages, old age homes, and other religious institutions founded during these years, the record of church growth becomes all the more impressive.

However measured, the churching of Philadelphia was an enormous enterprise. From a distance, it may have seemed as though the development of the dense network of religious institutions was being orchestrated by increasingly powerful, centralized, and assertive denominational bodies. In reality, however, church growth was actually a much more decentralized undertaking, with responsibility resting squarely on the shoulders of local communities. Though subject to denominational authority and discipline, most churches were organized as independent congregations. Localized and lay driven, the congregational model of organization placed personal and financial responsibility for a church's foundation in the hands of its voluntary lay members.

Even though ministers frequently helped establish new churches, clerical involvement was not required for congregational growth, especially when the local community possessed active and dedicated lay leadership. The history of the Church of the Holy Trinity typifies congregational formation within Philadelphia's elite residential districts. Though officially founded in 1857, the Episcopal congregation can trace its origins to a meeting of "gentlemen" who decided in 1855 that their rapidly developing neighborhood around Rittenhouse Square needed, and could now support, a new church. They named trustees who would be responsible for congregational finances and circulated a pledge book to record initial subscriptions in support of the building fund. They selected a name for the church and discussed possible building locations and real estate prices. Since theirs was an Episcopal assembly, they elected members to the vestry, the lay body charged with church governance, and began the search for a rector. Soon afterward, the new congregation obtained a charter from the state and petitioned the diocese for recognition, thus securing their status under both civil and canon law.[9]

Parallel examples can be found in other Protestant denominations. The Overbrook Presbyterian Church, located on the far western edge of Philadelphia, was founded under similar circumstances in response to local population growth. On 11 December 1888, Wistar Morris and his wife, a Quaker couple whose daughter had married a Presbyterian pastor, invited neighbors to their home to discuss the formation of a new congregation, whose church was to be built on a tract of land they owned across the road from their farm. After accepting the couple's gift, a small committee of prominent men secured money for the church and hired an architect and builder to construct a dignified stone edifice, which was completed in a little more than a year at a cost of $14,767.[10]

Given their celebratory nature, congregational histories often treat the success of these ecclesiastical ventures as foregone conclusions, despite the considerable personal commitment and financial wherewithal required for their success. When such support was not immediately available, congregations had to rely on other models of church extension. Some were formed as "daughter congregations" of existing churches, while others began as "chapels of ease," worship sites intended to serve members living at a distance from the main church. Congregations might also establish missions to help meet the religious needs of their poorer co-religionists in undeveloped districts, or to serve the unchurched population or minority groups within their own neighborhoods.[11] Yet however a congregation might be formed, each of these systems of church extension emphasized voluntary lay involvement. It was assumed that chapels and missions would eventually mature into independent congregations so that they would enjoy the benefits of self-governance, financial autonomy, and representation within denominational decision-making bodies.[12]

Religious communities adopted many different strategies in their effort to secure a stable base of support, but none reflected the political implications of church finance more clearly than the imposition of pew rents, a practice that had developed during the colonial era and remained in place well into the twentieth century. Although critics have charged that rents were a means of maintaining social exclusivity within a particular church, their original intent was simply to require worshippers to commit to a given congregation and to support it financially. The system rewarded those who maintained a financial interest in the church by extending them certain benefits, such as a guaranteed seat in the assembly and the right to vote in congregational elections. Pew rents thus provided one of the clearest links between private financial influence and power within congregational affairs, and established a precedent that would persist even after local churches abolished rents.[13]

At first, pews were not merely rented, but purchased outright. This formal ownership gave individuals a financial stake and real property "interest" in the church. Revenue from the initial purchase of pews allowed the church to finance construction and eliminate debts, while the accompanying annual rents provided income for salaries, maintenance, and other operational expenses. Like any real estate, pews rose and fell in value according to demand. Writing to a newspaper editor in 1826, one Philadelphia woman recalled how her husband was repeatedly outbid for the choicest pews in one of the city's fashionable new churches.[14] The public nature of pew auctions also tended to invite financial speculation. Indeed, as Mark Schantz reveals in his study of religious life in antebellum Rhode Island, it was not unheard of for individuals who had no intention of joining a church to purchase a pew as a financial investment. If the church succeeded in attracting a large congregation, the demand for seats would increase, and the pews could be resold at a profit.[15]

For churches, such competition served as a confirmation of their desirability. Such was the case for the Church of the Holy Trinity in 1906, when the press reported that Walter Lippincott paid $1,000 at auction for pew 37 in the church "at the request of his wife, who desired to be nearer the pulpit."[16]

In Philadelphia, pew rents gained acceptance, in part, because they closely resembled the city's unique system of ground rents that remained in place well into the nineteenth century. Under the system, derived from English antecedents and designed to promote real estate development without requiring large outlays of capital, individuals economized by not having to purchase property outright. Rather, they agreed to a long-term lease, in which the renter "gained all the rights of land held in 'fee simple' (the absolute ownership of land) so long as he paid the rent," which was usually "fixed at 6 percent of the value of the lot at the time the parties executed the deed."[17] In short, the system provided perpetual property rights in exchange for annual rent, which carried over to the new owner when a property was sold. For Philadelphia churchgoers, the system of pew rents made perfect sense, since the same legal principles were involved. Renter-owners could sell their pews, which were considered personal property, but purchasers had to agree to accept the continued obligation to pay annual rents. Receipts for pew rentals even employed the same legal language of ground rents, stating that a pewholder, in exchange for the purchase money, "is entitled to a fee-simple interest" in his or her pew.[18]

Although most closely associated with the Episcopal Church, pew rents were employed across the denominational spectrum. Even Catholic parishes were known to employ a version of the practice.[19] During his visit to the United States in 1853, Cardinal Gaetano Bedini, a papal envoy, lauded American Catholics for their "wonderful sense of responsibility" in dutifully "pay[ing] their pew rents" and giving to collections. At the Church of St. Edward the Confessor in North Philadelphia, church newsletters from 1896 spoke of rents being "absolutely indispensable" to the parish. In other instances, Catholic parishes collected seating fees at certain Masses, which, in addition to providing reliable revenue, regulated attendance at peak times.[20] Within many Jewish synagogues, de facto pew rents were imposed by a system of yearly congregational dues and seating fees, payment of which entitled individuals to all the privileges of the congregation, including the right to seats in the sanctuary.[21] Among the city's religious denominations, only Quakers staunchly opposed the renting of pews, viewing it as a punishable offense because it encouraged "hireling ministry."[22]

Because of their financial practicality, pew rents were not limited to fashionable or elite congregations. Bethany Presbyterian Church, for instance, with its predominantly working-class congregation, collected pew rents, although they were kept low in keeping with the congregation's evangelical orientation: "A few cents each week will pay for a seat," promised the church handbook.[23] The vestry of the Church of the Holy Apostles, a large, evangelical Episcopal congregation, similarly tried to ensure that rents were not set "beyond the means of the people." In addition, to preserve the democratic character of the congregation, they decided that there would be no gradation in rental fees. So in 1890, for example, each seat in the church was priced at 5 dollars per year (or less than 10 cents per Sunday). Such small sums, however, quickly added up, and rents provided a quarter of the church's income that year.[24]

Yet beyond their financial practicalities, pew rents and other funding models helped structure the nature of power and authority within local churches, providing a mechanism to enforce the principle that those who attended the church should contribute to its care. Effectively defining "congregation" as "contributing members," pew rents reinforced the idea that only financially supporting members should be granted congregational benefits, such as the right to vote in congregational elections or hold positions of authority within the local church. Even as the system of pew rents lost favor and was eliminated within many churches during the late nineteenth and early twentieth centuries, its legacy endured. Private financial interests continued to drive church growth and define the nature of congregational governance.

Privatist Logic

It was no secret that churches and congregations were extremely responsive to private financial influence. Writing in 1851, Stephen Colwell, one of the leading political economists of his generation, noted how "buildings are erected for the worship of God where men are found to pay for them; ministers preach where men are found to pay them; congregations assemble in costly temples which they have contributed to build [and] every manner of good work is accomplished where money can be had to pay for it." These lines appeared in Colwell's polemical book *New Themes for Protestant Clergy*, which faulted Christian churches for embracing the worldly ethic of capitalism at the expense of charity. Coming from the mouth of a devout and orthodox Presbyterian, these words carried an extra sting and elicited a fierce reaction from members of the local clergy in Philadelphia, Colwell's adopted city, who took umbrage at his insinuation that they had abandoned the precepts of Christ for the "riches of this world."[25]

Even though his frustrations stemmed as much from the moral challenges posed by the market revolution and emergent industrial economy as they did from the failures of the Christian community to bear witness to the Gospel message, Colwell correctly noted how private financial influence structured religious life. Because of this, church growth during the late nineteenth and early twentieth centuries followed an economic logic remarkably similar to the "privatism" that guided other urban development. In the absence of strong municipal governance, as historian Sam Bass Warner argued in his classic study of urban growth in Philadelphia, private financial interests determined the direction and scope of urban development. The system privileged "interested" parties who financed "improvements," placing few restraints on individual initiative. The city's first waterworks, for instance, supplied water primarily to those subscribers who paid for the service, rather than serving as a public utility. Its success or failure depended on the commitment of individual investors.[26]

Since churches were part of the urban fabric, it was only natural that they, too, were subject to privatist forces. Civic boosters, real estate developers, and congregational leaders alike viewed churches and other religious institutions as "improvements" designed to enhance communities. Like St. Martin-in-the-Fields, many churches gained financial support because of their perceived benefit to a neighborhood. St. Clement's Church, founded in 1864, received its land from a Presbyterian real estate speculator who believed that an Episcopal congregation would "enhance the attractiveness of his residential projects." Likewise, when Anthony J. Drexel and George W. Childs laid out plans for the town of Wayne in the 1880s, they set aside plots for several different religious denominations in order to attract middle-class families to the Main Line community. To these investors, church and community existed in a symbiotic relationship. Churches encouraged district development, which would in turn grow the congregation.[27]

The personal and professional conduct of George B. Roberts provides a particularly instructive case of the privatist logic that infused congregational development. A leading Episcopal layman of his generation, Roberts built his career working for the Pennsylvania Railroad, rising through the ranks from engineer to president. He was also one the largest landholders in Lower Merion Township, a portion of Montgomery County that included several fashionable Main Line communities, having inherited his family's share of the original "Welsh Tract" granted to the area's colonial settlers by William Penn.[28] When Roberts spoke of his business affairs and personal investments in his correspondence to family, friends, and business associates, he regularly employed privatist rhetoric. He supported road grading and other projects that he believed would "improve" the community of Lower Merion and increase the value of his real estate holdings there. Moreover, in keeping with privatist practice, he insisted that financial responsibility for district improvements fall on those who benefited directly from them. When approached about improvements to Montgomery Avenue, one of the township's main thoroughfares, Roberts refused to commit the resources of the Pennsylvania Railroad, but promised instead his personal support as a private landowner.[29]

Roberts applied the same logic to his ecclesiastical endeavors. Such was the case when he led efforts to establish a new Episcopal congregation, the Church of St. Asaph, at Bala. Drawing on privatist principles, he informed a neighbor in 1886 that he expected the project to "receive the aid and assistance of all those who are interested in the advancement, improvement, and care of that part of the city."[30] Similarly, when consulted by church officials a few years later about plans to erect a new building for diocesan offices, he recommended that it possess sufficient "character and beauty" so as to attract the support of all those "interested in our church."[31] Applying privatist logic even further, he believed that religious communities could not function freely unless they enjoyed financial independence. When he agreed to provide support for a downtown chapel, for instance, he nevertheless asked why it was "not under control under those who attend." As long as he financially supported the congregation, he believed its members would never truly be able to promote their own interests.[32]

Privatist logic further dictated that "interested parties" not only support projects, but also protect the value of their investments. When runoff from a pig farm threatened to pollute a stream that ran through his land, Roberts and his neighbors petitioned Philadelphia park officials for redress. Roberts acted similarly on behalf of his ecclesiastical commitments. He used his political connections to assist St. Stephen's Church, his former parish, when noisome post office stables were built nearby. Similarly, after he and his sisters donated the land for St. Asaph's from the family estate, Roberts closely regulated the development of adjoining lots. He specified that piggeries, slaughterhouses, liquor establishments, and other "nuisances" not be permitted to operate near the church, conditions his executors later codified in the land sale agreements drawn up for those properties. To pressure diocesan officials to take similar precautions, Roberts even threatened to withdraw his financial support for the new diocesan offices unless they agreed to move the project to a "more prominent spot," further from warehouses and commercial sites.[33]

Although Roberts believed that congregational autonomy was sacrosanct, the fruit of financial independence, he would also learn that privatist logic could be turned against him as other congregations endeavored to protect their own interests. When Roberts and other residents of Bala began to organize St. Asaph's, they met with opposition from members of neighboring St. John's Church. According to diocesan regulations, the three nearest congregations had to approve the erection of any new church. St. John's refused. Its leaders worried that the new church, to be located less than a mile away, would encroach upon their established work and draw away members. They were unconvinced by Roberts's assurances that new railroad connections would make the region a center of population growth and provide enough residents to support two congregations. Unable to settle the matter themselves, the two churches turned to the diocese to broker a solution. Diocesan officials, however, found themselves in a bind. They did not want to risk alienating the influential congregants at St. John's, nor did they wish to seem ungrateful for the generosity of the Roberts family and other benefactors of the proposed new church, St. Asaph's. Ultimately, since it was not in a position to challenge the privatist aspects of congregational formation, the standing committee of the diocese allowed St. Asaph's to organize. Pledged support from Roberts and other district residents essentially guaranteed the project would receive diocesan consent.[34] And although the new parish did flourish, the fears of St. John's congregants were not unfounded. Six years after St. Asaph's founding, Roberts had to make a personal appeal to the bishop to withdraw a recommendation that St. John's be closed because of membership loss and economic hardship.[35]

As this incident indicates, denominational authority was far from absolute when it came to congregational formation. Not only were denominational leaders hesitant to challenge influential congregations and wealthy donors, they generally lacked any clear enforcement mechanism to make congregations modify their plans or to participate in any comprehensive planning strategy. Other than the ability to reject or withhold approval for a project, the bishop and the standing committee of the Episcopal diocese, for instance, had no means of forcing a congregation to rescind its plans.[36] One of the few effective weapons in the diocesan arsenal was the requirement that congregations be financially self-sufficient, a rule that only reinforced privatist tendencies.[37] When, for instance, a new church was proposed for the town of Darby in 1912, Episcopalians were warned that, unless "the investment [were] made seriously . . . it will just add another small struggling parish to the number of small rural parishes already in existence."[38] Such warnings notwithstanding, as long as a proposed new congregation could demonstrate its sustainability and did not appear to harm existing congregations in any substantial way, plans to establish it generally met with approval.

Even when denominational officials challenged church plans, determined congregations could simply disregard their views or disobey them outright. Thus, in 1896, one Presbyterian congregation ordered their builder to speed up construction on their church when denominational officials expressed concern about its proposed location. By the time the officials had completed their investigation, construction was too far along to be abandoned.[39] A few years later, the local presbytery forbade Bethany Presbyterian from erecting a new church at Twenty-Eighth and Morris Streets when members of a neighboring congregation complained that it would interfere with their established ministry in the area. The ruling, however, did not stop John Wanamaker, Bethany's main financial contributor, from independently erecting a church on the site in 1902. As Kenneth Hammonds notes, "Faced with this *fait accompli* the Presbytery thanked Wanamaker for his generosity in providing this $80,000 building, and revoked its previous action forbidding development of the site."[40] Wanamaker knew that it would be impossible for the presbytery to spurn such a tremendous gift, particularly from him, one of their leading benefactors.

Even with such problems, the privatist model of congregational organization offered distinct benefits for religious communities, rewarding voluntary lay initiative and empowering individuals to join together as a congregation and establish a church wherever and whenever they felt the need. Those not served by existing churches, whether because of geographic distance or theological orientation, could act on their own behalf. Whatever the system's shortcomings, it spurred the vast expansion of religious institutions in Philadelphia and other American cities, with the strength of independent congregational initiative contributing to the vibrancy of American religious life during the industrial era and beyond.

The Parochial Model

The strengths and weaknesses of the privatist model of congregational finance and governance become clearer when contrasted with the parochial structure of the Catholic Church, which matured during the late nineteenth century. According to Catholic polity, a parish, unlike a congregation, served a particular geographic area. With few exceptions, a person belonged to the parish within whose territorial boundaries he or she resided. Since the parish and its pastor were responsible for the spiritual care of all the souls within those boundaries, membership could not be selective or restricted. Although Episcopal and other Protestant congregations also called themselves "parishes" at times, their members were free to join any parish of their choosing.[41]

Unlike their Protestant neighbors, Catholics were required to belong to the parish in whose geographic territory they resided, even if other parishes were personally preferable or more conveniently located. Unlike Protestants, who could leave a neighborhood and still continue to worship with their familiar congregations, a move of a few blocks could formally sever a Catholic from his or her parish.[42] Historical ties and emotional attachments mattered little to the bishops and priests who defended the parochial system. When two mothers appealed to the archbishop of Philadelphia in 1927 for permission to send their children to a neighboring parish school, he bluntly reminded them that "the Law of the Church is that one must attend his own parish church and send his children to the parish school of the Church to which he belongs. This law was made by our Holy Father himself." However overstated it may have been, the archbishop's reply accurately reflected local policy.[43]

This parochialism served as the bedrock upon which the Catholic system of church finance was built. Every person living within the parish counted as a potential source of financial support. Pastors wanted to maximize the number of families—and potential donors—in their parish. Parish boundaries, delineated as soon as a new parish was named, occasionally became a major point of contention because of their financial implications. The pastor of Most Precious Blood of Our Lord Roman Catholic Church, for instance, asked the archbishop to redraw his boundaries a few years after the parish's creation in 1907 because he felt the number of people was "insufficient to warrant my undertaking the work of erecting the necessary parish buildings." He insisted that he could not be expected to build a proper parish with "scarcely" 3,000 souls when neighboring parishes enjoyed the support of 8,000 or 10,000.[44] Other pastors, too, worried about the success of the parishes they were called to lead. That was the case for Rev. Patrick F. Burke, who in 1901 was named pastor of a new parish to be located in a sparsely populated area of West Philadelphia on a plot of land the bishop had already purchased. According to parish lore, when the bishop asked Burke to suggest a name for the parish, the young curate replied, "Agony in the Garden."[45]

Operationally, the Catholic parochial system was much less responsive to private financial influence and individual will of lay members. Catholics could not establish a parish simply because they had the desire and financial ability to do so. Although some parishes did spring up organically as the natural outgrowth of a local worshipping community, lay members lacked the authority to create a parish on their own. Within the parochial system, power rested with the bishop and the clergy, not with the congregation. By the middle of the nineteenth century, as the Catholic population expanded dramatically, it was generally the bishop who determined where and when new parishes would be established. Even when communities organized efforts to petition for their own parish, they usually acted through clerical intermediaries. Not only did the bishop and other diocesan officials have the authority to rein in lay initiatives; they felt no compunction about exercising that authority. In 1922, for instance, the archbishop rejected one benefactor's offer to erect an unsuitably small church building for the parish of the Holy Child, whose members had been worshipping in temporary chapels since its founding in 1909.[46]

During the first half of the twentieth century, burgeoning Catholic dioceses relied on strong episcopal leadership to guide brick-and-mortar expansion. Like other powerful bishops of his generation, Dennis Dougherty, archbishop of Philadelphia from 1918 to 1951, maintained firm financial oversight of all diocesan projects and commanded obedience from his diocesan clergy and the heads of the religious orders serving in the diocese. In 1924, for instance, he rejected an appeal from a group of Benedictine nuns from Minnesota who, after seeing "countless beautiful mansions" during a recent trip to the city, wanted to send two sisters to "visit some of the wealthy Catholics in Philadelphia" to raise money for their young community. Archbishop Dougherty informed them that he could not honor their request because "the diocese has been constantly overrun (if I may use such a word) by outside collectors." He feared such permission would drain support needed for various local needs, including his own favored projects.[47]

Despite clerical claims to the contrary, Catholic dioceses did not always possess such centralized financial authority. The earliest parishes were treated as independently incorporated congregations like their Protestant counterparts, complete with lay trustees who held parish assets and managed church finances. Catholics officials, however, moved to restrict this practice in the early nineteenth century after it gave rise to conflict between the clergy and the laity. As mentioned in chapter 1, one of the worst disputes took place in Philadelphia in the 1820s when the trustees of the cathedral parish, St. Mary's, took control of the church after clashing with the bishop over finances and clerical appointments.[48] In response to this and other temporal disputes, members of the Catholic hierarchy moved to consolidate diocesan financial authority in the office of the bishop, who acted as "corporation sole" for all diocesan funds and property. The implications of this arrangement can be seen in Archbishop Dougherty's instructions to Louise Drexel Morrell granting her permission to erect a memorial chapel on the grounds of the family estate. After reminding her of her promise to provide additional land in case the site should ever be needed for the establishment of a parish, he stipulated that the "titles to all said grounds and buildings will be vested in the Archbishop of Philadelphia."[49]

Although such centralized diocesan financial authority could certainly lend itself to abuse, it nevertheless provided distinct benefits to the Catholic community. It allowed the diocese to coordinate parish growth, pool resources, consolidate debt, and reduce financial risk. Planning for future needs, shrewd bishops in the nation's cities used diocesan funds to acquire land in advance of residential development. As historian Dennis Clark observed in his study of parish growth in nineteenth-century Philadelphia, Catholic officials possessed a "greater capacity" than their Protestant peers "to keep somewhat ahead of the homebuilding trends," following the path of gas mains and streetcar lines. Once the area began to blossom, plots could then be provided to parishes on favorable terms. If the land exceeded parish needs, parcels could be sold and proceeds returned to diocesan coffers, where they became part of the revolving fund for other projects.[50] When the Sisters of Mercy established Mater Misericordiae Hospital in West Philadelphia, they relied on a loan from the diocese to provide a down payment on the land, which allowed them to reduce their obligation to commercial lenders. Later, whenever the sisters obtained revenue, they prioritized paying off their bank loan, knowing that the diocese would be a much more lenient creditor. Writing to the bishop in 1914, Sister M. Bernard, clearly mindful of her order's more pressing debt, feigned an apology for having let their "desire to lessen our debt and our interest" to the bank overrule "our duty to your Grace."[51]

Although Protestant denominations offered similar benefits to member congregations by negotiating group insurance rates and by overseeing clerical retirement funds, they did not come close to matching Catholic dioceses in terms of financial clout. In Philadelphia, Archbishop Dougherty used the means at his disposal to support struggling parishes and diocesan institutions. Although he fully expected parishes to be self-sustaining, he also recognized that any bankruptcy or foreclosure would have reflected badly on him, the diocese, and the Catholic community in general at a time when the "Immigrant Church" was striving to secure its position and gain respectability within Protestant America.[52] The appearance of financial difficulties would also have been a devastating blow to the collective confidence of local Catholics and tarnish Dougherty's own carefully crafted self-image as "God's Bricklayer."[53] In his eyes, responsibility for maintaining the expansive system of diocesan institutions he deemed essential to religious life fell on the Catholic community as a whole, and therefore required strong centralized oversight.

Archbishop Dougherty's tactics for mobilizing parochial resources for diocesan ends can best be seen in his fundraising for the diocesan seminary, his favored cause. Rather than imposing an assessment on individual parishes, a practice used for other diocesan purposes, Dougherty instituted an annual collection for the seminary and relied on healthy parochial competition to spur giving. Every year the diocesan and other local newspapers published the results of the collection, ranking parishes by the totals collected. To reach or stay at the top of the list, many parishes (and their pastors) went to great lengths to best neighboring parishes or to improve upon their previous year's performance. Dougherty kept detailed ledger sheets for each year's collection, noting gains in black ink and losses in red and calculating the percentage change in collection totals from the previous year for each parish. This allowed him to recognize poorer parishes that had made large gains, but it also allowed him to investigate those parishes (and their pastors) whose performance did not meet his expectations.[54]

As institutional networks expanded during the industrial era, the Protestant congregational and Catholic parochial models offered two distinct approaches to church growth and finance, each with its own advantages and disadvantages. With its emphasis on lay initiative, the congregational model empowered lay members to act whenever they felt their religious needs were not being adequately met by existing institutions. Such responsiveness to the desires of interested parties, however, carried a privatist logic that privileged individual financial influence. The parochial system tempered such privatist forces, but often by imposing tight clerical control over the process of brick-and-mortar expansion. For Catholics, centralized diocesan authority helped coordinate development and ensure the viability of these sometimes immense building projects. Yet it also placed a considerable financial strain on the faithful, who were expected to support not just their own churches, but also the vast network of schools, hospitals, and other institutions that sustained the conspicuous Catholic subculture of the era and upon which many bishops had staked their ecclesiastical reputations.

In addition to shaping how churches obtained the money they needed to support their institutional networks, the two systems of finance both reflected and reinforced the dominant organizational character of their particular religious communities. Practices of giving called attention to the nature of authority within individual churches and demarcated which obligations had primacy over others. They provided the faithful with an understanding of the role they played as individuals in advancing the communal mission. They likewise spoke to the relationship between local communities and wider denominational bodies, and to the degree of autonomy each could expect. It mattered how and where money flowed.

Church Governance and Elite Authority

As religious life in the United States took its modern form, elite influence came to extend well beyond the pull of purse strings. During the industrial era, wealthy individuals were able to expand their authority within the ecclesiastical sphere precisely because congregational governance privileged those with a private financial "interest" in their churches. This was particularly the case within Protestant communities, where the tradition of lay control over temporal affairs made it possible for those with wealth and status to acquire and exercise considerable influence within their local congregations. That same trend increasingly extended into denominational affairs as well, as the network of religious institutions expanded and denominational life became more corporate during the late nineteenth and early twentieth centuries. The more highly structured nature and administrative complexity of religious life furthered the consolidation of power in the hands of the era's elite, whose financial resources, social connections, and professional expertise proved invaluable. Although the exact nature of lay authority varied within denominational communities according to their particular governance structures, the general pattern was unmistakable: those with wealth and status came to attain disproportionate power and privilege within the nation's religious life, just as they had in its economic and social life, which in turn raised concerns about the equitability of church polity and the proper distribution of power within religious community.

Among many religious communities, lay authority was deeply rooted in denominational tradition. Within the Episcopal Church, for instance, it had long been customary for clergy and laity to share authority at every level, from the local parish on up through the diocesan and national conventions. Though primarily directed toward temporal affairs, this shared power also extended to spiritual concerns, such as ruling on changes to church canons or revisions to the Book of Common Prayer. As historian Deborah Matthias Gough explains, this system was a legacy of the colonial church, when, lacking a resident bishop, lay members were able to claim a greater role in church affairs. This emphasis on lay-clerical cooperation led to a uniquely American "horizontal structure within a hierarchical church."[55] Presbyterian governance similarly provided for shared governance, although it distinguished more clearly between the temporal and spiritual spheres. At the congregational level, Presbyterians divided authority between two separate governing bodies: the board of trustees and the Session. Whereas trustees held oversight of the congregation's temporal affairs, members of the Session shared with the clergy oversight of spiritual matters, including worship, religious education, and benevolences.[56]

These arrangements were certainly not without their difficulties. Chief among them was the issue of purview. No matter how clearly responsibilities were defined, it was often difficult to distinguish between temporal and spiritual spheres. In 1883, for instance, the Presbytery of Philadelphia was forced to issue a statement concerning which body, the board of trustees or the Session, had authority over the employment of church musicians. The trustees believed it part of their jurisdiction because it pertained to salaries, but the Session—as the presbytery would ultimately agree—countered that it fell under their auspices since music was connected to public worship, and thus to spiritual affairs.[57] Even the most trivial disagreements had the potential to become major conflicts, particularly when money was involved. For several weeks in early 1909, the Session and board of trustees of Disston Memorial Presbyterian Church were locked in a bitter dispute over a $4.58 bill for printing and postage for a mailing sent to church members announcing a collection for the missions. Both sides contended that the other should cover the expense from its own budget. The pastor, concerned about the "probability of a split in the church," offered to settle the matter by paying the bill personally, but the trustees refused on principle, arguing that the special letter was a spiritual matter not connected to the ordinary business of the church.[58]

Despite such problems, churches benefited immensely from their relationship with the wealthy, prominent, and talented. Trustees and vestrymen who earned their positions on account of economic and social prestige were expected to use those gifts to the benefit of the congregation, particularly through an example of good financial stewardship. Since congregations were required to be financially self-sufficient, it made sense to place wealthy members in positions of prominence. At the Church of the Holy Apostles, banker George C. Thomas quietly covered annual parish deficits. Members of the Houston and Woodward families did the same at St. Martin-in-the-Fields. Gifts in kind, in the form of professional services, were equally welcome. At Disston Memorial Presbyterian, the treasurer of the board of trustees, a builder by trade, took a personal financial loss when he received the commission for the church's new manse. Architect Theophilus Chandler reportedly returned the fee he received for the design of St. Asaph's, preparing the plans as a favor to his wife's cousin, who sat on the vestry. In addition to work for their own parishes, Charles Biddle performed pro bono legal work and George C. Thomas served as treasurer for various initiatives within the Episcopal diocese.[59] No matter how often church leaders warned that vestry seats and other positions should not be sought for selfish reasons, it often seemed that congregations themselves chose their vestrymen and trustees on rather self-interested grounds.[60]

Given the degree to which churches relied on men of wealth and talent, lay governance often had the effect of solidifying authority in the hands of the financial, social, and professional elite. Although not always tapped to fill positions on a congregation's governing bodies, wealthy and prominent members were customarily given the right of first refusal. Indeed, it would have been impolitic if a congregation's most generous benefactor or most distinguished member failed to be nominated for a position of leadership. Congregational elections, therefore, were often foregone conclusions. At one Presbyterian assembly, each proposed nominee to a Session seat declined to be nominated, allowing the incumbent, whose term had expired, to reclaim his seat unopposed. It is possible that the incumbent used his financial, social, or spiritual clout to intimidate potential candidates and dissuade them from running. More likely, however, his potential rivals chose to decline their nominations in order to save face and prevent the congregation from displaying any sign of disunity.[61] Although elections could be extremely competitive, many were perfunctory affairs and in 1919 the executive secretary for the Diocese of Pennsylvania went so far as to describe them as "mere farce."[62]

As the power of the elite increased, so often did their sense of entitlement. Once elected, many trustees, vestrymen, and other lay officials viewed their positions as an inherited right, rather than an earned privilege.[63] Long-serving members often were reluctant to step down to allow younger members to assume control. In his first year as rector of St. Thomas's Episcopal Church in Whitemarsh, Nathanael Groton found himself in the middle of one such generational dispute. Late in 1913, several older members of the vestry mentioned that they might resign to let "younger men take their places." But, as the annual elections approached, some hesitated, including the rector's warden, William Taggert, who eventually served forty-three years on the vestry, twenty-eight of them as warden.[64] The wife of one of the other "old men" was "insulted that her husband should be 'slated' to resign."[65] In both 1925 and 1927, Bishop Thomas J. Garland used his annual address to express his concern that many parishes relied too heavily on "self-perpetuating leadership" within families.[66] In fairness, such dynasties persisted because their congregations chose to reward experience and preserve continuity in church leadership. Those who served for decades were acclaimed not only by religious officials, but even by the secular press, which regularly reported on parish elections.[67] Yet for all their power, the jobs of vestrymen and trustees were often less than glorious. Those who served in these capacities spent their nights fretting over leaky roofs, heating bills, mortgage payments, and other matters. When a congregant brought suit against Disston Memorial Presbyterian after falling down a flight of stairs, it was the trustees who had to handle the legal complexities of the case.[68] Lay officials likewise struggled to keep their congregation's various constituencies happy. Given the voluntary nature of religious life in the United States, there was always the potential that those dissatisfied with congregational administration could flock to another church. It is important, moreover, not to underestimate the awesome sense of responsibility that devout trustees and vestrymen felt. Even though positions of lay governance conferred status and added to one's store of spiritual capital, individuals did not serve for purely personal gain. Working under the watchful eye of God, they recognized their duty to ensure the temporal success of their local church and often bore the blame when problems arose. In 1916, the rector of the Church of the Messiah, Gwynedd, grew so frustrated with parish leadership that he issued a formal letter to the congregation in which he chided the vestry for failing to raise the necessary funds for the promised enlargement of the parish house and for having "put me here to work without proper tools."[69]

Indeed, the demands and duties associated with board and vestry positions sometimes made recruitment difficult. Many older downtown congregations struggled to fill vacant vestry seats with men of similar talent, wealth, and status as those who had once held them. In an effort to obtain "qualified men" to serve on the vestry in the 1910s, the rector and prominent members of Christ Church sought individuals from outside the parish who had a historical connection to the church through parents, grandparents, or even more distant ancestors.[70] The church's charter and bylaws allowed this sort of flexibility by not requiring trustees to be members in the congregation. The Presbytery of Philadelphia had similarly ruled that "there is nothing in the fundamental law of the Presbyterian Church which requires that trustees shall be members of the congregation. They are such persons as the corporation may select for that purpose."[71]

Over time, the dominant role played by lay members in church affairs broadened the definition of "church work." As religious communities absorbed the business ethos of the industrial age, there emerged a growing emphasis on financial management as ministry. Upon the death in 1873 of Thomas Potter, a ruling elder and chief benefactor of Chestnut Hill Presbyterian Church, the trustees praised him for "his energy and sound judgement in business affairs and well as his strict integrity . . . ever ready to aid by his prayers, his labors and his pecuniary contributions."[72] In 1909, the Episcopal *Churchman* similarly praised George C. Thomas for not holding back from the Church his "unwonted administrative power and business experience."[73] The language of business and professionalism that infused such memorials was revealing, equating denominational advancement and devotion with temporal expertise and economic acumen.

As churches expanded their ministries and institutional reach during this era of prosperity, proper management and oversight of ecclesiastical operations became all the more important. Congregational leaders familiar with the organization and operation of corporate boards increasingly demanded that churches be run more like businesses, and those serving on church boards helped introduce modern accounting methods, new financial strategies, and other corporate practices. In 1895, the finance committee of St. John's Church, in Wilmington, Delaware, demanded that the finances "be placed upon a more business-like basis," possibly in response to the demands of their du Pont benefactors.[74] As members of the clergy began to internalize contemporary business mentality, they too spoke about the need for greater efficiency and systemization in church work. Speaking before the Synod of Pennsylvania in 1916, one Presbyterian clergyman commented how "slack business methods . . . will do our programs more harm in the community than a half dozen of our most spiritual sermons can correct," and encouraged the church to promote better financial practices. That same year, the General Convention of the Episcopal Church adopted a new canon, "Business Methods in Church Affairs," that regularized the Church's fiscal year and spelled out requirements for the auditing of parish accounts.[75]

Amid the corporate restructuring of religious life in America, members of the professional and business classes found high demand for their services and expertise. Seminary education did little to prepare members of the clergy to administer the complex temporal affairs of their parishes. It came to be understood that such matters were best left to lay expertise, thus freeing ministers to focus their attention on spiritual matters. At the Philadelphia Divinity School, for instance, courses in "practical parochial work" placed emphasis on pastoral ministry rather than parish administration. Instruction in topics like business methods and financial management was limited to occasional lectures delivered by men prominent in the corporate and professional worlds.[76] In 1886, for example, banker George C. Thomas spoke on the subject of "The Rector in Relation to Money Matters," and C. Stuart Patterson, legal counsel for the Pennsylvania Railroad, gave an address entitled "The Legal Relations of Rectors to their Vestries and Parishioners."[77]

Even the Catholic hierarchy came to recognize the value of lay expertise in parochial affairs, especially as the financial demands of brick-and-mortar expansion exceeded the abilities of pastors and other members of the local clergy. One example can be seen in the career of Daniel B. O'Loughlin, a professional fundraiser who made a name for himself in the archdiocese by conducting capital campaigns for Catholic parishes during the 1910s and 1920s. Though pastors were at first reluctant to engage an outsider and grumbled about the fees he charged, O'Loughlin rarely failed to deliver on his promises to secure the funds they sought, no matter the amount. "All that is required of a pastor needing money for parish purposes," he insisted in his promotional brochures, "is a clear and convincing presentation of his case to the people, followed by a practical . . . procedure of collection," which he and his firm provided. Nothing proved the efficacy of O'Loughlin's methods more than his success in coordinating a two-month archdiocesan drive in late 1921 to raise money for a network of homes operated by Sisters of the Good Shepherd. Determined that the Good Shepherd Homes "shall not fail" when the state withdrew its support for sectarian institutions, Archbishop Dougherty engaged O'Loughlin, under whose direction funds raised exceeded the archdiocese's goal of $500,000 by more than half. As a self-recognized "lay pioneer" in church fundraising, O'Loughlin remained deferential to church authority and cognizant of the limits under which he worked, but his activities nevertheless reveal how professional expertise came to be recognized and welcomed even among Catholic clergy who vigilantly defended their clerical prerogatives.[78]

Concerns About the Concentration of Power

The deepening influence of the social, financial, and professional elite in ecclesiastical affairs during the late nineteenth and early twentieth centuries may have served individual congregations and religious communities well, but it also gave rise to a troubling concentration of power. As religious communities became increasingly dependent on and deferential to elite authority and professional expertise, those who felt excluded or marginalized raised questions about how power was structured, not only within their local congregations, but in their broader denominations as well. Calls for systematic reform fell mostly on deaf ears, but they nevertheless signaled growing discontent, especially among those who believed the concentration of power in the hands of the elite threatened the democratic nature of their religious communities and their structures of corporate governance.

To gauge how power at various levels of denominational life became concentrated in the hands of the elite—and the tensions it engendered—it is instructive to look at the Episcopal Church. Although perhaps not as democratic as those of other denominations, its administrative structures were nevertheless rooted in the principles of representative governance. Moreover, the fact that concerns over power and polity emerged within a hierarchical church with a traditional deference to elite authority makes the debates that emerged all the more meaningful. Even lay members who enjoyed wealth and privilege grew concerned about the allocation of power and its implications.

The organization of the Episcopal Church tended to facilitate the concentration of authority in the hands of the elite. At each level of governance, from parish vestries to the triennial General Convention of the national church, power was vested in those elected to represent the interests of their religious communities. In these decisions, as in the larger political culture of the period, "best man" ideology tended to dominate, which created a culture of deference to the social and financial elite. The pattern became even more pronounced the higher up the chain of authority one moved. The socioeconomic homogeneity of lay delegates to the General Convention, for instance, reflected the relatively high status of those elected to represent parishes at the annual diocesan conventions, from which candidates for national office were drawn. Lay members who joined the clergy in organizational and theological deliberations thus tended to be an elite among the elite. Such was the case when patrician lawyer George Wharton Pepper and real estate executive Samuel F. Houston served as the lay representatives of the Diocese of Pennsylvania at the 1928 General Convention, where they weighed in on revisions to the Book of Common Prayer and debated the possible relaxation of church canons regarding marriage and divorce.[79]

Since diocesan and national conventions were the main legislative and administrative bodies of the Episcopal Church, those elected to serve as lay deputies in the General Convention's House of Deputies possessed real and practical power within denominational affairs. They had a voice in finance and filled seats on various committees, including the executive council, the main administrative body of the national church.[80] Although theological decisions were reserved for the Church's House of Bishops and its appointed committees, lay deputies to church conventions had a role in determining how church teachings and moral principles were codified in church canons and otherwise promulgated and enforced. The issues debated by Pepper and

Houston at the 1928 convention offer clear evidence of this. Since both the General Convention's House of Deputies and the Church's House of Bishops had to approve any revisions to the Book of Common Prayer, the main liturgical guide for the Church, lay delegates could shape the spiritual practice of the entire membership of the Episcopal Church. Similarly, in voting whether to relax church canons on divorce or to revise the church's stance on birth control, lay members of diocesan and national councils helped to define morally acceptable behavior. Although it would be wrong to assume that class interests overrode all other considerations lay delegates brought with them, it would be equally incorrect to pretend that they suspended their class sensibilities when they deliberated spiritual and moral issues.

Given the importance of these administrative bodies to church life, the distribution of representation was an important—and potentially contentious—issue. Each diocese was free to set its own canons governing how it ordered its annual convention, but most, including the Diocese of Pennsylvania, allotted equal representation to each parish, traditionally seen as the basic unit of a diocese. Since wealthy parishes could sustain themselves with fewer members, and since the diocesan convention elected both lay and clerical delegates to the General Convention, these parishes gained a disproportionate voice in both diocesan and denominational affairs.[81] In 1910, for instance, the 256 registered congregants at St. Thomas's, Whitemarsh, a community dotted with elite estates, had the same voting power at the diocesan convention as the 1,900 members of Holy Apostles, an urban parish in a working-class district. Admittedly, some "fashionable" downtown congregations such as St. Mark's Church and the Church of the Holy Trinity had larger numbers of congregants (1,585 and 1,577, respectively), but these figures included those who attended parish-sponsored chapels and who, as non-pewholders, lacked an official voice in congregational affairs.[82] Large city churches also complained that it was unfair for small rural and suburban parishes that did little to support the broader work of the Church to receive the same representation as parishes that did more. Those parishes with large institutional networks believed that they should be rewarded with a greater voice in denominational affairs because they represented not only their official membership, but also a wider constituency of the city's unchurched.[83]

Reformers within the Episcopal Church periodically demanded a more equitable distribution of power; they sought a proportional representation based on membership numbers rather than equal representation by parish. In Philadelphia, motions to that effect were introduced at the diocesan convention with some regularity from the late nineteenth century onward, but none were adopted. In 1888, after one clerical delegate proposed to amend the diocese's constitution and implement a system of proportional representation that would have given parishes the right to seat as many as seven lay deputies, the matter was referred to a special committee. Two years later, noting that the proliferation of small parishes had created an imbalance of power at the convention, the committee raised questions about fairness to larger parishes. Yet it nevertheless reaffirmed the principle that lay representation be based on membership in a parish as a "sub-unit . . . on par with all other sub-units."[84] After attending what he described as the "destructive" convention of 1914, when the issue was taken up again, Rev. Nathanael Groton mused that it would remain tabled "forever & forever, I guess."[85] Bishops Philip Mercer Rhinelander and Thomas J. Garland again drew attention to the issue during the 1920s, but once more to no avail.[86]

Another concern for reformers was the secondary status of Episcopal mission churches and their members. According to church canons, only independent and financially self-sustaining parishes had a right to representation in the diocesan convention. Like those who attended parish-sponsored chapels, mission communities were effectively disenfranchised within the broader church. The numbers affected could be sizable. In 1916, for instance, there were approximately seventy missions within the Diocese of Pennsylvania, many of which served already marginalized groups, such as the "colored" population and immigrant communities.[87] Under privatist logic, these worshipping communities could not share in diocesan governance because they were not considered "interested" parties. It was expected that the parish, diocese, or other corporate body that sponsored the mission, and therefore possessed the financial "interest" in the work, would represent these groups at the convention. Without their own voice, these missions had little ability to change the system unless they became independent parishes and earned representation, at which point the matter was no longer an immediate concern for them. The extension of representation to mission churches was periodically discussed within the convention during the early twentieth century, but no substantive policy change ever resulted.[88]

Similar discussions over equitable representation surfaced at the national level, where numerically large dioceses, such as those of New York, Pennsylvania, and Massachusetts, voiced their concerns about their marginalization within denominational affairs under the system of equal apportionment. At the turn of the twentieth century, for instance, the ten most populous dioceses accounted for 46 percent of total church membership, yet together held only 17 percent of the seats in House of Deputies at the General Convention.[89] Smaller dioceses, for their part, opposed any push for proportional representation within the national church since it would have concentrated power in the hands of large urban dioceses located mostly in the eastern portion of the country. Recognizing the temptation to take unfair advantage of the system, an editorial in the *Church Standard* in 1900 warned that dioceses should not split simply to gain votes in the General Convention. Three years earlier, the Diocese of Pennsylvania had considered just such a move, though not over the narrow issue of national representation.[90] Yet to some extent, regardless of geographic divisions, elected lay representatives were drawn from the same strata of society. Even small dioceses sent their wealthiest and most distinguished lay leaders to the national convention.[91]

However much those who benefited from the status quo resisted these efforts to reform the system of lay representation, change did occasionally come, particularly at the parish level. St. Thomas's, Whitemarsh, revised its church charter and bylaws in 1922 to expand membership in the vestry from six to ten, with rotating terms of service. Other churches would adopt similar policies, often accompanied by a restriction on the number of consecutive terms an individual could serve. In keeping with congregational governance, however, such changes were not mandated, but took place church by church. The power of the diocesan convention, for instance, was limited to ruling whether term limits complied with church canons. Bishops, likewise, could only encourage congregations to revise their rules.[92]

As these developments reveal, denominational structures at both the congregational and the denominational level allowed for lay elites, whether financial or professional, to exert a considerable degree of influence within church affairs. Episcopalians may have been more accepting than others of such divisions of status and wealth within church affairs, given their traditional emphasis on hierarchical order, but even denominations that espoused a more egalitarian theology or maintained a more democratic polity were susceptible to similar pressures. As one sociological survey concluded from a 1928 national sampling of Protestant congregations, "on the whole the membership of the boards of churches is made up overwhelmingly of the favored economic classes."[93] The implications were hardly trivial.

Regardless of denominational differences, the trend was clear: the increased affluence of lay members, and the power they derived from it, profoundly affected the history and development of religious life in the United States during the late nineteenth and twentieth centuries. Even though wealth did not entirely determine the distribution of power and authority within religious communities, the nature of congregational organization and governance, with its emphasis on lay authority, opened the door for those in possession of wealth, social status, and professional expertise to gain a greater role in church life.

Through their direct involvement in ecclesiastical affairs, both at the local and the national level, financial and social elites were able to shape the theological character, ethical teachings, and social mission of their churches. Although their power was far from absolute, members of the upper class refashioned religious life in significant, albeit sometimes subtle, ways. As chapter 3 will make clear, their role in determining the design and decoration of their churches gave them a potent means to promote their own distinctive vision of religious community. Aesthetic decisions allowed members of the upper class both to display their theological loyalties and to transform sacred spaces into physical embodiments of their own cultural tastes and class sensibilities. In so doing, they created a religious environment suitable for their spiritual needs, and they set a standard for refined worship and proper ecclesiastical style that extended their influence well beyond their local churches.

A Labor "Exceedingly Magnificent"

The George W. South Memorial Church of the Advocate has long been regarded as one of Philadelphia's most architecturally stunning churches (fig. 1). With its soaring nave, ornamented spires, and rows of slender buttresses, the high French Gothic "cathedral in miniature" built between 1887 and 1897 was intended to rival its European counterparts. The church boasts a magnificent array of decorative detail, including a complete set of stained glass windows by the celebrated English firm of Clayton & Bell. Indeed, by 1889, with construction still far from complete, it had already gained recognition as one of the most notable Episcopal churches in the country.[1] Erected through the generosity of the wife and daughter of George W. South, one of the city's leading merchants of the mid-nineteenth century, it served as a memorial to South's community leadership and religious faith. It was designed with an eye to the possibility of its one day becoming the diocesan cathedral. Although guided by a desire for personal glorification, the South family was also committed to the church's spiritual mission. Whereas other churches offered in memory of wealthy benefactors were located in fashionable neighborhoods or elite enclaves, the South family decided to build its church in North Philadelphia, the city's industrial heart, to aid the diocese in its missionary outreach to the working class. They believed that the spiritually transformative power of Gothic church design should be made accessible to people from all walks of life.

The history of the Church of the Advocate reveals the power that wealthy donors wielded through their financial and artistic patronage to shape and define the spiritual character, congregational mission, and theological orientation of their religious communities. The vision for the grand church to be both mission and cathedral came not from the diocese or members of the clergy,

Fig. 1   George W. South Memorial Church of the Advocate, Philadelphia. Photo from Moses King, *Philadelphia and Notable Philadelphians* (New York: M. King, 1902), 33.

but from its donors, South's family. They were the ones who set forth the plan and funded the venture. Those responsibilities they were not equipped to handle they delegated to trusted colleagues, placing oversight and management of the project in the hands of Richard Cook, a family friend and South's executor, who was himself a wealthy merchant, financier, and leading church benefactor. As chairman of the building committee, Cook was responsible for selecting architect Charles M. Burns to design the church, a man who shared his fondness for the work of John Ruskin and other proponents of preindustrial design and craftsmanship. Cook and Burns were so committed to ecclesiastical authenticity that they skewed the orientation of the church, in defiance of the street grid, to allow the sanctuary to face true east, in keeping with the ancient practice of aligning churches with the rising sun. As a leading trustee, Cook was also instrumental in recruiting a rector sympathetic to the South family's doctrinal stance, liturgical tastes, and social commitments, one who would be supportive of high churchmanship and liturgical formalism, yet committed to missionary outreach. Through their financial generosity, the Souths and Cook fashioned a church that conformed to their own personal vision of what the Episcopal Church should be—socially, theologically, and aesthetically.[2]

This relationship between financial patronage and ecclesiastical development in the United States was perhaps never more pronounced than it was during the late nineteenth and early twentieth centuries. During this time of institutional growth, members of the upper class were able through their benefactions and commissions to build churches that reflected their own social views and theological vision. Working closely with architects and artists who could bring their aesthetic vision to life, they fashioned ecclesiastical spaces that articulated their class tastes and personal sensibilities. Collectively, they helped cultivate a shared religious outlook among members of the industrial-era elite, instilling in them a distinct religious habitus, an internalized set of shared religious subjectivities, which often transcended denominational lines.[3] The appropriation of English parish architecture, for instance, helped facilitate class formation among the elite by connecting them culturally to England's landed gentry.

The ability to shape the physical form of their churches endowed the elite with "ecclesiological" influence, through which they were able to physically define the proper relationship between faith, practice, and aesthetics.[4] Even if a donor chose a particular architectural plan or piece of ecclesiastical art merely in response to passing fashion, that choice had theological implications. As the ritualism debates of the period affirm, the appropriateness of liturgical objects and their use were matters of great controversy. The arrangement and adornment of sacred spaces not only affected the nature of worship, but also shaped how individuals attending particular churches experienced the sacred and encountered the divine. Filtering down from elite tastemakers to workaday religious communities, these aesthetic trends came to transform religious life in the United States as church buildings came to receive, reify, and transmit religious beliefs. As both historians and liturgical scholars have affirmed, their design and decoration both impart and reflect aesthetic sensibilities, regional tastes, environmental conditions, social concerns, and theological trends.[5] If Michael DeSanctis is correct that all buildings "exert a subtle but real influence" on those within, then these changes in church aesthetics during the industrial era carry greater significance than previously recognized.[6]

Crafting an Aesthetic Vision

Before exploring the impact of these aesthetic choices, we need to examine how members of the industrial-era elite were able to advance and execute their aesthetic vision. In the United States, ecclesiological influence frequently emerged as a by-product of the privatist nature of church governance.

Ecclesiastical design reflected what voluntary contributors were willing to pay for, as well as what local church leaders believed would attract "interested parties" to their congregation. Apart from a handful of denominational requirements and ecclesiastical expectations, congregations generally had a free hand in determining the design of their church buildings. Within the Protestant tradition, clerical authority and denominational oversight were generally minimal, and often limited to perfunctory plan approval.[7] Responsibility rested instead with church trustees or those appointed to church building committees, whose membership were usually derived from the congregation's core donors. Not infrequently, those who contributed the most to a project tended also to be those with the greatest voice in matters of church design.

Even though a significant number of churches in industrial-era Philadelphia bore the mark of a particular benefactor or family—as in the case of the Church of the Advocate[8]—it was more common for donors to place their stamp on the aesthetic character of their churches during the ongoing process of adornment. Indeed, most churches were not fully adorned until years, if not decades, after construction was completed. In calculating initial construction estimates, congregations rarely figured in the cost of elaborate altars, statuary, organs, or other embellishments. With ambitions almost always outstripping available resources, even the most affluent congregations were obliged to delay internal enrichments. Common practices included installing plain glass in the windows during initial construction or delaying the purchase of bells for the tower, knowing that stained glass or ranks of bells could always be added at some later date.[9] Such decisions reflected an understanding of donor mentality. Church leaders prioritized the essential, often mundane, aspects of construction over aesthetic embellishments, trusting that benefactors could later be found to fund them. As one example, when the Philadelphia Divinity School moved to its new campus in West Philadelphia in the 1920s, school officials conserved funds by leaving the school's chapel unadorned—"its windows will be filled with common glass; its floors will be uncovered concrete; its altar and its stalls will be rude and temporary"—confident that the project would attract "many memorial gifts which will make it more and more an evident center of loving interest."[10]

In seeking to improve the physical appearance of their churches, lay and clerical leaders alike saw little wrong with appealing to vanity if it led to offerings of support. In their attempt to tap the deep resources of wealthy benefactors, some made blatant class appeals. The rector of St. Mark's Episcopal Church near Rittenhouse Square "assailed the 'cheapness' in church decoration and reminded his parishioners that medieval people, unlike their modern descendants, were eager to fill churches with costly treasures."[11] In 1928, an editorial in the Episcopal diocesan newspaper called upon the prosperous men who sat "behind shining, mahogany desks in magnificently furnished offices" and the wealthy women who "enrich[ed] the interior decorators of the country" to devote the same attention to the beautification of their churches. "It is a shame," the editorial lamented, that many churches "are permitted to remain so shabby-genteel while the houses of their members are being enriched and beautified," for as King David proclaimed, the house of God should be "exceedingly magnificent."[12] Although a cynical reading of such comments would be that church leaders were obsessed with the superficial trappings of the faith, a more sympathetic one would be that they were simply encouraging wealthy parishioners to reassess their spending habits, offering a reminder that God deserved nothing less than what church members gave themselves.

If financial autonomy provided wealthy individuals with a means to exert aesthetic influence, then their direct contact and extensive collaboration with architects and artists helped enable them to realize their vision. George B. Roberts, for instance, worked closely with Theophilus P. Chandler, one of Philadelphia's most respected ecclesiastical architects, on the design and construction of the Church of St. Asaph. Roberts, the church's leading benefactor, selected Chandler because they shared aesthetic tastes, having worked together on a number of residential commissions. Roberts's deep involvement in the construction of the Pennsylvania Railroad's grand Broad Street Station, "the most elaborate and costly terminal development" of the period, further exposed him to the intricacies of architectural collaboration. Although lacking any formal architectural training, Roberts managed the design and construction of the church with the same diligence he gave to managing his corporate projects and family estate.[13] Working in conjunction with his social peers on the church vestry, he negotiated designs and styles, often without any direct clerical oversight, to fashion a church reflective of his tastes and cultural vision. He proposed, for instance, that the church, sited within the original "Welsh Tract" of the Pennsylvania colony, be modeled on a cathedral dedicated to St. Asaph in his ancestral Wales. Later, when he felt that the church's chancel was too small, Roberts asked Chandler to extend it by 15 feet, and personally covered the cost of the alterations.[14] Far from an aesthetic whim, the larger chancel reflected Roberts's high church leanings by placing emphasis on the ritualistic aspects of worship and the sacramental role of the clergy.

In addition to his regular contact with Chandler, Roberts corresponded with building material suppliers, stained glass studios, and purveyors of church furnishings. As the primary donor, Roberts had ultimate authority. Dissatisfied with the Tiffany windows Chandler intended for the church, Roberts purchased new ones from Clayton & Bell, a London firm favored by the English liturgical reformers and Gothic revival architects.[15] Although Roberts's personal involvement in parish life ended with his untimely death in 1897, members of his family remained active in church affairs for generations. Through various memorial donations and through internal improvements they both funded and directed, they exerted influence over parish life, conforming the church building to their own vision of proper liturgical function and form. The processional crosses, candles, altar linens, and liturgical objects they donated reflected their commitment to ritualism and high church theology; decorative elements from the Anglican tradition, such as a rood screen and lych-gate, highlighted the English character of the church.[16]

Such patterns of patronage greatly advanced the careers of many architects in Philadelphia, thus deepening elite influence over architectural tastes as those they favored rose in stature. Theophilus P. Chandler, Frank Furness, Addison Hutton, Milton B. Medary Jr., and Allen Evans were just a few of the many local architects who rose to professional prominence through their upper-class commissions.[17] It helped that many came from socially prominent families themselves. In the late nineteenth century, architecture was still very much a gentleman's profession. Unlike draftsmen, master architects generally held university degrees, completed studies at leading European schools such as the École des Beaux-Arts in Paris, and began their careers at prestigious firms. They were expected to be conversant with both the grand architectural traditions of Europe and contemporary upper-class tastes.[18] Frank Furness, for instance, was the son of the city's prominent Unitarian minister, William Henry Furness, and brother to the famed Shakespearian scholar Horace Howard Furness. Allen Evans, Furness's apprentice and later partner, could trace his family ancestry back to the region's original Quaker settlers. His ancestry, Main Line residence, religious affiliation (Quaker-turned-Episcopal), and club memberships provided him with the proper social credentials and offered him social contacts that helped to advance his career.[19]

In addition to class considerations, patterns of patronage fell along sectarian lines, particularly for ecclesiastical commissions. Many church architects specialized in work for one denomination, often their own. Familiarity with its distinctive religious culture and ecclesiological requirements proved advantageous, and personal religious connections helped many architects obtain commissions. It is not surprising that Addison Hutton, a faithful Quaker, completed many works for Quaker institutions, nor that he began his career under the tutelage of Walter Cope, also a member of the Society of Friends.[20] Allen Evans, similarly noted for his work for the Episcopal Church, was a devout communicant and friend to the bishop, and saw his own son enter the ministry. He gained several commissions through his religious connections, and volunteered his services to his own parish.[21] Even more than Protestant church leaders, Catholic clergy were eager to hire members of their own flock, allowing a handful of Catholic architectural firms to flourish.[22] In addition to profiting financially from their church contracts, architects who engaged in ecclesiastical work derived a certain degree of spiritual satisfaction from serving their religious communities. Theophilus P. Chandler, for example, toward the end of his career, designed and erected a new mission chapel for his Episcopal parish as a gift to the diocese. Built entirely to his personal specifications and ecclesiological vision, the project served as both a professional and spiritual exercise.[23]

Among all the architects working in Philadelphia during this period, Chandler may have been the one who best understood the ecclesiological sensibilities of the city's upper class and helped advance them. He successfully capitalized on their patronage, later using his prestige to raise the status of the local architectural community. Born into a prominent Boston family, Chandler attended Harvard for one year before going to Paris to complete his architectural training. In Europe, he developed an interest in Gothic architecture and seized an opportunity to study under English architects.[24] This decision served him well, for it anticipated the demand for English styles among the American upper class. When he arrived in Philadelphia in 1872, members of his mother's family, prominent in local circles, introduced him to the city's social and religious elite. A marriage to Sophie M. du Pont in 1873 ensured his social standing and provided him with lifelong financial security. His connection to the du Pont family would also help Chandler establish his name as an ecclesiastical architect. While still a young, unproven architect, he succeeded in obtaining a commission for renovation work at Christ Church in Christiana Hundred, Delaware, where many of his du Pont in-laws worshipped.[25]

By 1905, Chandler had become such a respected figure within ecclesiological circles, particularly within the Episcopal and Presbyterian Churches, that St. Thomas Church on Fifth Avenue in New York—arguably one of the most fashionable Episcopal churches in the country—encouraged him to enter the design competition for their new church building. They praised him for having "more thoroughly beautiful churches to your credit on purely Gothic, churchly lines, both outside and in, than any [other] architect in America."[26] Although Chandler did not receive the commission, he was never short of work, particularly in the Philadelphia area, where his ecclesiastical projects included the Swedenborgian Church of the New Jerusalem (1881), Tabernacle Presbyterian Church (1883), and Mary Elizabeth Patterson Memorial Presbyterian Church (1884), as well as numerous commissions for alterations and decorative design. The geographical distribution of Chandler's projects—mostly along the Main Line and within fashionable semisuburban neighborhoods in the city—reveals his dependence on commissions from the city's privileged and professional classes.[27]

As one of Philadelphia's most sought-after "society architects," Chandler kept in near-constant contact with members of the upper class and completed hundreds of commercial, residential, and ecclesiastical commissions for his esteemed clientele. His decisions to reside first in fashionable Chestnut Hill and later along the Main Line reflect his awareness of the social connections necessary for professional advancement. While the draftsmen at his firm labored to complete the plans for his many projects, Chandler made his rounds, calling on clients at their homes, offices, or city clubs.[28] Part of the practical training other architects acquired under Chandler, directly or indirectly, included an appreciation for the manner in which Chandler understood upper-class expectations. Two of his protégés, Walter Cope and John Stewardson, joined forces in 1885 to establish their own prestigious partnership. They likely benefited from the social contacts they made during their training under Chandler and, before him, under Addison Hutton, the leading "society architect" among Philadelphia's Quakers.[29]

Chandler, in addition to setting a standard for ecclesiastical design, did much to advance the architectural profession in Philadelphia. In 1890, he was instrumental in organizing the department of architecture at the University of Pennsylvania, which soon rivaled the established programs at Columbia and Harvard.[30] Chandler was also active in the Philadelphia branch of the American Institute of Architects (AIA), mentoring younger architects and helping to cultivate local talent.[31] According to architectural historian Sandra Tatman, "the importance of T. P. Chandler to the architectural profession in late nineteenth-century Philadelphia cannot be overestimated."[32] Chandler's leadership lent the Philadelphia architectural community a touch of sophistication that appealed to local patrons.

Just as upper-class patronage nurtured architectural talent, it also sustained those engaged in other ecclesiastical crafts. Rather than relying on church furnishing catalogs, members of the upper class commissioned artists and artisans to provide the decorative elements they desired. Among the most significant firms working in Philadelphia were the D'Ascenzo Studios (specializing in stained glass) and the Yellin Metalworks, both of which rose to prominence in the years during and immediately after World War I, when European trade was interrupted and churches turned to domestic sources for ecclesiastical decorative arts. By drawing on European traditions and capitalizing on the abundance of skilled immigrant labor, Nicola D'Ascenzo and Samuel Yellin set a national standard for ecclesiastical craftsmanship. Both acquired national followings and obtained commissions from churches across the country.[33] At its height in the 1920s, Yellin Metalworks employed more than 200 craftsmen, turning out decorative metalwork for such prestigious projects as the Washington National Cathedral, the Cathedral of St. John the Divine in New York City, and the Washington Memorial Chapel at Valley Forge, in addition to commissions for a host of residential and corporate clients.[34]

The success of D'Ascenzo and Yellin, though attributed mostly to their skill, was also due to the artistic philosophy they espoused. At a time when upper-class patrons responded to industrialization by promoting "craft idealism," both D'Ascenzo and Yellin provided decorative elements inspired by the work of the preindustrial masters. Samuel Yellin, who had trained under a Russian craftsman in his native Galicia, readily acknowledged the traditions from which his art arose. In one of his many lectures before architecture clubs and craft societies, he encouraged others to "follow the lead of the past masters and seek our inspiration from their wonderful work." The preindustrial metalworkers, he proclaimed, "saw the poetry and rhythm of iron."[35] In line with his craftsman ideals, Yellin rejected the label of "artist," and regularly referred to himself as simply a "blacksmith." Nicola D'Ascenzo espoused similar views regarding art's "humanistic function" and the "educatability" of aesthetic sensitivity.[36]

In this regard, the two men aligned themselves with the Arts and Crafts movement and the ideals of theorists like John Ruskin, William Morris, and Ralph Adams Cram, whose works were read widely by the American elite.[37] Indeed, Cram praised both D'Ascenzo and Yellin for their contributions to ecclesiastical craft and vocational training in his 1924 ecclesiological tract, *Church Building: A Study of the Principles of Architecture in Their Relation to the Church*, which served, in the words of Michael D. Clark, as "a kind of bible of church design for its era."[38] In addition to drawing attention to these two Philadelphia studios, his endorsement tacitly elevated the status of local churches that contained their pieces, and confirmed the ecclesiastical taste and artistic vision of the upper-class patrons who had donated them.

Looking at the Philadelphia scene, perhaps no project better demonstrated the ecclesiological influence of the era's elite than Bryn Athyn Cathedral, a monument to the union of industrial wealth, religious fervor, and aesthetic vision. Financed largely through the benefaction of the Pitcairn family, the cathedral was built to serve the Church of the New Jerusalem (also known as the "New Church"), a sect inspired by the writings of the eighteenth-century scientist and theologian Emanuel Swedenborg, whose mystical writings found a receptive audience among those seeking an alternative to the harsher Christian doctrines of the day. By the mid-nineteenth century, the New Church had established communities in many American cities, including Philadelphia and Pittsburgh. It was in Pittsburgh that John Pitcairn Jr., a Horatio Alger figure who emigrated from Scotland with his family in 1846, was received into the Church. A childhood friend of Andrew Carnegie and Henry Phipps, Pitcairn started as an office boy for the Pennsylvania Railroad at age fourteen and quickly rose through the managerial ranks. Although he enjoyed a stellar career with the railroad, he spied opportunity elsewhere and in 1883 used part of his savings to invest in the Pittsburgh Plate Glass Company. In 1896, he was named president of the company; under his leadership, the firm was soon producing more than 65 percent of the nation's plate glass, a key component in industrial manufacturing and urban construction. From the company's success and through his own financial acumen and prudent investments, Pitcairn earned his fortune.[39]

Remaining devoted to the New Church and its teachings throughout his life, Pitcairn became one of its leading benefactors and lay leaders. In the late 1880s, he moved from Pittsburgh to Philadelphia and selected land northwest of the city for his country estate, Cairnwood. There he also established the community of Bryn Athyn, which he envisioned as a home for the New Church where the religious community would be "free to express itself not only in worship but in all aspects of life." It was to be a place where members of the Church could reside, educate their children, and worship together.[40] At the heart of the community would be the New Church cathedral and religious academy. As head of the lay council, Pitcairn was responsible for ensuring the financial success of the religious enterprise, which often meant that he turned to his own bank account whenever the Church fell short of funds. Indeed, so closely were the Church's finances tied to Pitcairn's own that the move of the New Church to Bryn Athyn was delayed until 1897 owing to the effects of the Panic of 1896 on Pitcairn's investments. As his biographer concluded, "Had John Pitcairn not lived, the New Church, no doubt, would have survived, but it would not have experienced the growth and advance that it did at the time. The Academy of the New Church, the General Church of the New Jerusalem, and the Bryn Athyn community all owed their development, if not their very existence, to his liberal support and intelligent foresight."[41]

Although John Pitcairn provided the financial support for the cathedral through his financial bequests, it was his eldest son, Raymond, who supplied the artistic vision for the project and continued the family involvement after his father's death in 1916. Undaunted by his lack of any formal architectural training, Raymond Pitcairn gave up his legal practice in 1914 to devote his energies to the cathedral project for the next fifteen years of his life.[42] An avid collector of medieval glass and sculpture, he was deeply interested in medieval craftsmanship, and believed that the arts were an essential component of worship and spiritual life. It was Raymond who hired Ralph Adams Cram, the foremost proponent of the Gothic style in the United States, as chief architect. Even though Raymond would later dismiss Cram from the project after the two clashed over how construction should be managed, their initial affinity stemmed from their shared belief that medieval forms most authentically captured and reflected the Christian spirit.[43] In planning the Bryn Athyn Cathedral, Raymond consciously turned his attention to the "Christian symbolism and the traditions of primitive Christian faith [as] have been preserved in like manner in the great cathedrals of the Middle Ages. . . . The New Church has in them a heritage of Christian art vast and beautiful."[44]

Committed to the ideals of the Arts and Crafts movement, both Cram and Raymond Pitcairn believed that the spiritual power of art came when both patron and artist grasped the spiritual significance of their task. True art could not be manufactured or mass-produced; such productions lacked the creative spark of the human mind. As Raymond confided to his brother after the cathedral was completed, "our experience at the Church confirms fully . . . that an artist who is sincerely working along lines of a wonderful tradition can produce a work of art which has a strong emotional appeal." He wanted a cathedral that not only took medieval form, but was also constructed according to medieval methods. The project required hundreds of craftsmen with the right skill and spirit. Raymond set up workshops for wood- and metalworking, stained glass production, and stone crafting on the cathedral grounds so that all the decorative elements needed for construction could be produced under his direct supervision. He also used local stone and timber for as much of the construction as possible, both to cut costs and to affirm the principle of organic growth, showing how the cathedral could rise from its local setting. In effect, Raymond re-created the medieval guild system and built a high Gothic cathedral on the outskirts of early twentieth-century Philadelphia (fig. 2).[45]

Bryn Athyn Cathedral thus was the product of the union of religious faith and aesthetic philosophy, made possible by upper-class patronage. Spiritually, Raymond Pitcairn's intent was to produce a distinctively "New Church

Fig. 2   Bryn Athyn Cathedral. Photo courtesy of the Athenaeum of Philadelphia (Karl Lutz Collection).

Sanctuary." The building was designed to reflect the unique theology of the New Church, with its particular emphasis on the symbolism found in the Book of Revelation, and Pitcairn's own idiosyncratic architectural philosophy, which sought to embody the ideals of a romanticized medieval past. The New Church boasts that there are no straight lines or right angles to be found anywhere in the cathedral. Rather, "the walls of the building are skewed against each other, bowing out in the middle only to return at the opposite wall," with these and other "imperfections" intended to represent "the unpredictable path of human growth."[46] None of this would have been possible without the enormous financial support and personal commitment of the Pitcairn family, to whom craft excellence mattered more than financial cost, quality more than construction deadlines, and faith more than corporate success. Indeed, the final cost of the cathedral project remains unknown because Raymond kept no clear financial records, perhaps believing that no monetary value could be attached to such sacred work.

Ultimately, the history of Bryn Athyn Cathedral not only reveals the immense influence donors had in ecclesiological decisions, but also suggests the theological sincerity of their motives. It challenges the common assumption that donors supported grand ecclesiastical projects simply to achieve social prominence or to elevate their class standing. Though the Pitcairns certainly cherished the high esteem in which they were held within the New Church and the Bryn Athyn community, their devotion to the project came from their personal faith, commitment to the New Church and its teachings, and their belief in the spiritually transformative power of ecclesiastical design. In using their wealth to build a church that reflected both their religious faith and their upper-class artistic ideals, the Pitcairns set an aesthetic standard for their entire religious community. They took the theological message of the New Church and enshrined it in a space built according to their own cultural vision of proper aesthetic form. Their decisions would shape how members of the New Church conducted worship and encountered the divine for decades to come.

Class Identity and Ecclesiastical Style

As more and more churches came to bear the mark of upper-class patronage, the cumulative effects of individual aesthetic decisions would exert a subtle but steady influence on both the elite and their religious communities. By transmitting the social and cultural value embodied in them, ecclesiastical structures played a crucial role in cultivating shared religious tastes within the religious community. Fashionable churches also came to serve as cultural landmarks, helping members of the upper class identify and locate one another across the nation's often fractured social landscape. As such, they served as arenas of social interaction where individuals and families came to understand themselves as members of a cohesive class with shared cultural tastes and religious values. For religious communities, the consequences were equally pronounced as the ecclesiological influence of the elite stretched outward from local congregations to shape the broader contours of the American religious landscape. Those who financed church construction and contributed funds for ecclesiastical adornments affected the theological character and spiritual orientation of not just their own assemblies, but all who emulated them. By presenting themselves as the standard-bearers of refined worship and proper ecclesiastical form, elite congregations functioned as aesthetic arbiters for their wider religious communities. Their actions were not uncontroversial, as battles over ritualism and other ecclesiological disputes attest, but their choices had a powerful role in defining proper aesthetic form and religious practice.

In Philadelphia, the linkage between ecclesiastical patronage and the emergence of a shared upper-class identity was nowhere more visible than along the Main Line, the string of fashionable suburban communities that served as the domain of the city's industrial elite. The churches that developed alongside the region's great estates in the late nineteenth and early twentieth centuries helped define the character of the region and shaped the theological and social outlook of its residents. As new churches were built to serve the religious needs of the local population, many congregations drew inspiration from the Gothic revival in England and the example of that country's rural church architecture; indeed, the cultural tastes and theological orientation shared by Philadelphia's predominantly Anglo-Saxon Protestant elite ensured the prevalence of the English Gothic style. This "parish revival," which began in the middle of the nineteenth century but grew in strength in the period between 1880 and 1930, corresponded with the years of peak development along the Main Line. As it took hold, this ecclesiological trend had implications for both the class identity of the Philadelphia elite and the theological character of their religious communities, particularly within the Episcopal Church, which emerged as the dominant religious force in the region. These Main Line churches came to embody class distinctions and helped to unite the upper class as a religious establishment, while setting a standard for refined worship and "proper" ecclesiology.

The parish revival emerged from within the wider Gothic revival of the mid-nineteenth century, one of the most significant and far-reaching architectural movements in United States history. Over the course of a few decades, Gothic architecture went from obscurity to ubiquity, leaving its mark on ecclesiastical, institutional, and residential design in cities and towns across the country.[47] Scholars have offered many explanations for the success of this cultural phenomenon, most broadly linking it to the rise of Romanticism in art and literature during the nineteenth century. The specific appeal of the Gothic in the United States, however, generally has been viewed as a result of the "antimodernist" impulse prevalent among the industrial elite, and of the broader quest for refinement and respectability among the growing middle class. Gothic design likewise signaled a "reverence for social hierarchy" at a time when class status was in flux and underscored the growing sophistication of American architects and their willingness to challenge the dominance of colonial and classical forms.[48]

During the industrial era, many congregations gravitated to Gothic design because they believed its formal, "churchly" style conveyed a sense of permanence and prestige. Even Protestant denominations that had once been deeply suspicious of Catholic forms and elaborate decoration embraced the movement, appropriating stylistic elements that had previously aroused passionate opposition. The process unfolded gradually, as individual congregations selectively incorporated Gothic designs or decorative features into their plans.[49] It has been suggested that the rapid acceptance of Gothic in Quaker Philadelphia and Congregational New England came from those seeking an alternative to "meetinghouse plain."[50] Historian Jeanne Halgren Kilde has further proposed that the popularity of Gothic church design was related to the search for religious unity among evangelical Protestants in the mid-nineteenth century. She argues that Gothic functioned as a "generic architectural style" that transcended denominational differences because, as a new architectural idiom, no evangelical faction could lay claim to it.[51]

Amid all these cultural and social explanations, it is important to remember that at its core the Gothic revival, particularly as expressed in church architecture, contained a theological impulse, and its widespread adoption would have important religious ramifications. The roots of the ecclesiological trend lay in England, where it was part of an effort by high church advocates and architectural theorists to revive the institutional life of the Anglican Church, and to offer an alternative to the Roman tendencies of the Oxford Movement and the emergent Catholic revival.[52] In tracts and design manuals, A. Welby Pugin, F. A. Paley, and other English "ecclesiologists" expended considerable effort promoting the principles of Gothic architecture, debating proper forms and symbols, and emphasizing the theological importance of the arrangement of ecclesiastical space. They favored churches that possessed extended chancels, often elevated or separated from the nave by altar rails or rood screens, and elaborate altars frequently backed by ornate reredos or stained glass. Such designs emphasized sacramental worship, elevated the status of the clergy, and returned adornment to altars once stripped bare. They often drew inspiration from the rural parish churches of pre-Reformation England, which offered them ecclesiastical models suitable for ritualism, yet free of the taint of later Roman tendencies.[53]

The politics of ecclesiastical design were somewhat less severe in the United States, but the Gothic and parish church revivals still retained their theological edge. Since Gothic designs emphasized ritual and sacrament at the expense of preaching, the introduction of Gothic architecture challenged the dominance of the widespread evangelicalism that followed in the wake of the Second Great Awakening. Evangelicals viewed the Gothic revival with suspicion, not so much for fear of popery as for the challenge to democratic values implicit in its focus on religious hierarchies and clerical authority.[54] At the opposite end of the religious spectrum, the Gothic revival offered an antidote to the excesses of nineteenth-century religious rationalism by affirming the transcendental aspects of the faith. By building churches designed for ritual practices, congregations and their donors, some more consciously than others, made ecclesiological statements replete with deep theological implications that would shape the future character of their church. In the words of historian Ryan K. Smith, as "one Protestant congregation after another broke with tradition" to embrace Gothic architecture, "employ symbolic crosses, [and] decorate sanctuaries with flowers and candles," they would gradually "initiate a new religious landscape."[55]

Events in Philadelphia, one of the early centers of the Gothic revival in the United States, would play an important role in this national story. The city was home to the Church of St. James the Less and St. Mark's Episcopal Church, founded in 1846 and 1847, respectively, which stood at the vanguard of the movement. Their buildings were among the earliest to be constructed along the new ecclesiological lines, with an eye toward historical and theological authenticity. Both congregations were established under the auspices of the Episcopal Church, the denomination most receptive to the early Gothic revival. Support came mostly from those with high church proclivities, but, as Phoebe Stanton notes, even those Episcopalians who cared little for ritualism and sacramental theology often embraced parish church architecture and other elements of the Gothic tradition because "they suggested the English background and the distinguished lineage of their church."[56]

In the case of both of these two early Gothic revival churches, the physical manifestation of the ideals promoted by revivalists was realized through the power of local wealth and patronage. The Church of St. James the Less—the first in the United States "erected under the direct supervision of the English ecclesiologists"—had the financial backing of Robert Ralston, a wealthy merchant desirous of establishing a parish near his country estate just beyond the northwest edge of the city limits at the time. He corresponded extensively with members of the Cambridge Camden Society, a group of English scholars and architects who gave intellectual force to the movement. Through them, Ralston received detailed plans for the church and recommendations for its interior appointments and decorative elements. The result was a meticulous replica of a thirteenth-century parish church from Cambridgeshire, England. Although Ralston acceded to a few modest modifications to the plan, he refrained from making any changes that would have substantially altered the church's character, such as modifying the pitch of the roof or plastering the interior. The notable features of this diminutive, widely praised church included an extended chancel and elevated altar, and distinctively English decorative elements such its rood screen, exposed interior roof beams, and bell cote (fig. 3).[57]

Fig. 3 Church of St. James the Less, Philadelphia. Photo from Moses King, *Philadelphia and Notable Philadelphians* (New York: M. King, 1902), 54.

One year after the founding of St. James the Less, St. Mark's became the first "town church" erected in accordance with the new ecclesiology. The parish, located near Rittenhouse Square, an area destined to become one of the city's most fashionable downtown neighborhoods, was established by a handful of wealthy Episcopalians committed to high church principles. Through Ralston, they turned to an architect associated with the Cambridge Camden Society for plans and guidance, desirous of a structure suitable for ritualism and liturgical worship. Construction of the church was then placed in the hands of John Notman, a local architect of growing prominence who adapted the English design to better suit local climate conditions and the constraints of the lot. The church design features a prominent, offset tower flanking the street, a spacious, clerestoried nave with exposed hammer-dressed stone, and an extended chancel with elevated altar (fig. 4). Later embellishments, such

Fig. 4 St. Mark's Episcopal Church, Philadelphia. Photo from Moses King, *Philadelphia and Notable Philadelphians* (New York: M. King, 1902), 58.

as an ornate Lady Chapel, stained glass windows, and an intricately carved marble pulpit, complemented the original design and added to the beauty and symbolic richness of the space.[58]

Upper-class patronage thus put the English ecclesiological theories into practice in these two churches, one rural and one urban, which would serve as prototypes for Gothic design in Philadelphia and elsewhere. According to Phoebe Stanton, who remains the leading authority on the early Gothic revival, St. James the Less and St. Mark's heralded a revolution in ecclesiastical design, bringing "a new church style and a new sophistication to American architecture." The Episcopal Church may not have been as numerically dominant as other denominations, but, as Stanton points out, "it constituted a privileged and intellectually distinguished group which was able to publicize the doctrines in which it believed." The sheer prominence and visibility of these and other early Gothic revival churches contributed to their widespread influence, shaping ecclesiastical fashion even among those who did not share in the ecclesiologists' theological orientation.[59]

To some extent, this ecclesiological revolution became the victim of its own success. As early as the 1850s, Presbyterian and Congregational councils were lauding Gothic design within their denominational publications and making plans for Gothic churches available in architectural pattern books. According to Jeanne Kilde, such efforts "advanced a Gothic stylistic hegemony that would be well established by the 1860s."[60] By the late nineteenth century, Gothic monumentality had become so commonplace, particularly in the nation's burgeoning cities, that it no longer aroused ecclesiological debate, nor served as an immediate indicator of a congregation's theological orientation. Even denominations that had earlier rejected such architectural formalism because of its theological implications, particularly in regard to ritualism and hierarchy, came to embrace the style. Indeed, its very ubiquity in ecclesiastical, commercial, residential, and collegiate design had stripped the Gothic style of much of its once radical theological symbolism.

For members of the Philadelphia elite and their religious communities, however, the theological and social consequences of the Gothic revival would not only persist but increase in significance over the course of the industrial era. Within their religious communities, their embrace of Gothic form and ecclesiological formalism affected not only the outward appearance of their own churches, but also their style of worship, particularly when church plans came to include decorative elements and ecclesiastical objects that accentuated the liturgical aspects of the faith. Yet more than simply effecting a shift within their own churches, their aesthetic actions would also influence the theological character of others who took cues from their example. In Philadelphia, such patterns of innovation and emulation can be seen in the proliferation of English "parish church" design within the communities of the Main Line and other elite residential enclaves, spreading from there to become a model for suburban church architecture, most notably within the Episcopal Church, but within other denominations as well.

Though rooted in the academic ecclesiology of the 1830s and 1840s, the parish church revival emerged as a cultural force in Philadelphia during the late nineteenth and early twentieth centuries as members of the industrial elite migrated along rail lines to the suburbs, where they established their country estates and rural retreats. In seeking an ecclesiastical style appropriate for their new social environment, members of the upper class embraced the subtle grace and dignified air of English parish architecture. They turned their attention from grand urban sanctuaries to churches that were smaller, yet distinctive in physical appointment, aesthetic sophistication, and theological authenticity. Parish church designs were publicized widely in architectural guides and pattern books, and members of the upper class would have been familiar with the style from their visits to the English countryside during their grand tours of Europe.[61]

Between 1880 and 1920, the Main Line became home to at least eight of these new parish churches.[62] The style could not have been more appropriate for an upper class that believed itself heir to England's landed gentry, and that sought to re-create the atmosphere of the English countryside on the outskirts of Philadelphia.[63] These parish churches served as fitting ecclesiastical accessories to the region's great estates, whose proprietors sought to replicate the gracious living of the English aristocracy in all forms. Several operated working farms, complete with tenant farmers and roaming livestock. Both financier Robert L. Montgomery and industrialist Percival Roberts enjoyed watching their prized herds of Ayrshire cattle graze on the rolling hills of their Main Line estates.[64] The architects hired to plan these country residences took great pains to craft their patrons' desired image of preindustrial pastoralism.[65] For an upper class that emulated English modes and manners so heavily, it was only natural that many would consider the English parish to be the appropriate style upon which to model their churches.

More than the embodiment of a particular cultural ideal, parish churches and other fashionable houses of worship sanctified the region's elite suburban districts. In these elite enclaves, churches were among the first public institutions that connected members of the upper class, drawing them off of their estates and out of their private clubs. They became the sites of important social rituals and rites of passage, particularly the weddings that cemented family clans, the christenings that celebrated dynastic succession, and the funerals that honored the Christian lives of the wealthy and privileged.[66] They also provided a religious environment amenable to wealth and class distinction, their generally small size fostering a more intimate—and more exclusive—sense of community. They tended to serve a more homogenous

population than their urban counterparts, which had a harder time segregat-
ing themselves from the lower classes.[67] With suburban communities making
fewer demands on churches for social welfare ministries, their congregations,
though still generous toward numerous charitable causes, directed considerable attention toward the material condition of their own parish churches,
fashioning physical complexes that would attract others of the same rank
and class.[68]

Residents of the Main Line sought not only to attract fashionable congregations, but also to ensure that their church buildings complemented the
character of their local communities. When George W. Childs and Anthony
J. Drexel laid out plans for developing their real estate holdings in the Main
Line town of Wayne in the 1880s, for instance, they offered tracts of land to
various religious denominations in order to entice them to set down roots in
the community. They believed that churches would help draw residents to the
town and contribute to local civic life. To ensure that the churches erected
were "in keeping with the architecture and surroundings," Childs and Drexel
monitored their plans and placed stringent demands on their beneficiaries.
In return for the land they received, the town's Catholics, for instance, were
expected to erect a church valued at no less than $25,000 within three years,
or else they would have to forfeit the land and any improvements. With few
wealthy members on whom to rely, the pastor resorted to soliciting money
from other parishes to raise the funds necessary to fulfill the terms of the
agreement. Drexel and Childs may have endeared themselves to religious
communities for their liberality, but they still sought to ensure that their town
would be graced with tasteful churches of substantial worth.[69]

Through their concern about the proper style and character of their
churches, members of the upper class set and sometimes enforced a standard for church design that would influence the development of other religious communities. Such interplay can be seen in the Episcopal Church of
the Redeemer and its Catholic neighbor, the Church of Our Mother of Good
Counsel, both in the Main Line community of Bryn Mawr. Although, for the
most part, Catholics and Protestants inhabited vastly different social and religious worlds, the histories of these two suburban churches, located less than
a quarter mile apart, are inextricably linked to each other and to the development of the community. Their ecclesiastical design choices indicate how each
group responded to the other, and how each understood its social status and
theological identity.

During the second half of the nineteenth century, the sleepy village of Bryn
Mawr was transformed into one of the premier Main Line communities. The

coming of regular passenger rail service opened Bryn Mawr to increased settlement and helped spur its development, first in the 1870s and 1880s as a fashionable summer resort, and later as a residential suburb, as summer estates became year-round residences.[70] The Church of the Redeemer witnessed Bryn Mawr's evolution from rural hamlet to upper-class enclave. At the time of its founding in 1851, it was the only Episcopal church on the Main Line between the city limits and Radnor, some five miles distant, whose St. David's Episcopal Church dated to colonial days. In 1879, the parish hired architect Charles M. Burns to design a new church that would accommodate the congregation's increased membership and reflect its growing status in the community. Having recently completed improvements at the Church of St. James the Less and St. Timothy's Church, Roxborough, two of the finest examples of English parish design in the Philadelphia region, Burns brought excellent credentials to the project.[71] Dedicated in 1881, his elegant stone church stood a short distance from the rail station and the Bryn Mawr Hotel, the two nerve centers of the resort community. The structure was set back from the main road and collared by lawns and a churchyard, features that would help preserve the parish's bucolic character as the community grew and development encroached. Continued population growth in the area prompted the congregation to enlarge the church building in 1910, with the addition of two bays and a narthex that complemented Burns's original design.[72]

The first attempt to establish a Catholic parish in Bryn Mawr came in 1885, when Augustinian priests from Villanova College were asked to organize a mission in the community. Members of the local flock, then having to travel three miles or so to either Villanova or Havertown to attend religious services, were desirous of having their own church. The task would not be an easy one for the region's relatively poor Catholic community, most of whom worked as servants and groundskeepers on nearby estates.[73] The deed to the first parcel purchased by the parish, located on Montgomery Avenue, a main thoroughfare that linked many of the area's grand estates, stipulated that the purchasers must erect a "substantial stone church . . . of no less value than $5,000.00 within three years."[74] Although the stipulated minimum cost was only a fifth of that imposed by Drexel and Childs on their Catholic beneficiaries in the town of Wayne, it was a financial burden the parish was unable to meet. Having succeeded in building only a temporary chapel in the allotted time, the parish was forced to forfeit the land. Yet, undeterred, and through the financial assistance of the Augustinians at Villanova, the parish purchased a larger, unrestricted parcel of land nearby in 1888 and transported the chapel there so that services could continue to be held until a permanent church was built. In 1896, not quite a decade later, members laid the cornerstone to the new Church of Our Mother of Good Counsel, designed by prominent Philadelphia architect Edwin Durang and erected at a cost of $41,000.[75]

Perhaps the most intriguing thing about Our Mother of Good Counsel is its architectural similarity to the Church of the Redeemer (fig. 5). Even though Catholics at that time were consistently cautioned against falling prey to Protestant influences, Good Counsel's design reveals that its parishioners—or, at the very least, its clergy—were not only cognizant of their Protestant neighbors, but also desirous of emulating them. As the two churches stood in 1890, Good Counsel may have lacked the landscaped churchyard that provided the Church of the Redeemer with a more picturesque setting, but its "old English Gothic style" echoed many of Redeemer's features.[76] Both churches consisted of a clerestoried nave flanked by two side aisles, although Durang's design gabled the aisle windows of Good Counsel and added a rear transept to create a cruciform floor plan. Both also featured an offset square tower, though, here again, Durang made some modifications by placing Good Counsel's more prominently at the front of the church and adding bell-shaped finials, perhaps to draw the attention of passing railway passengers (fig. 6). Casual observers would likewise be drawn to the similarity between the tapered rose windows of the two churches, both of

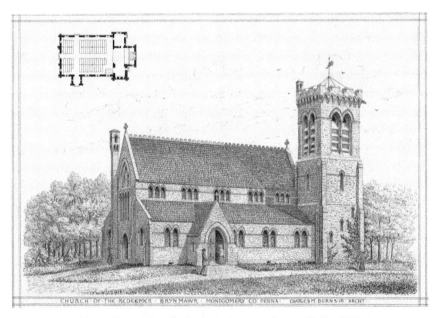

Fig. 5 Episcopal Church of the Redeemer, Bryn Mawr. Architect: Charles M. Burns, 1881. Photo courtesy of the Athenaeum of Philadelphia.

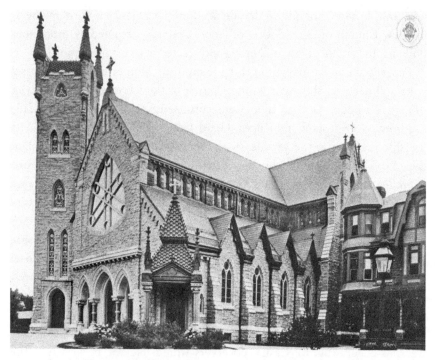

Fig. 6 Church of Our Mother of Good Counsel, Bryn Mawr. Photo from *E. F. Durang's Architectural Album* (Philadelphia, [ca. 1900]). Courtesy of the Philadelphia Archdiocesan Historical Research Center.

which were situated at the peak of a Gothic arch. On a lesser, but still significant note, the addition of a porte cochere at Good Counsel, one of the more distinctive and unusual features of Durang's design, further implied a conscious attempt to mimic upper-class tastes. Though convenient for those who arrived by carriage, the architectural flourish was neither essential nor standard for a Catholic church.

Even if Durang did not directly imitate the Church of the Redeemer in designing Our Mother of Good Counsel, he had to have seen the close resemblance of the two. No records exist that describe how Durang chose his design or what features he was instructed to include. Many matters were likely settled in face-to-face discussions between Durang and representatives of the parish. Nevertheless, visual evidence suggests that in his foray into suburban church architecture, Durang did not draw upon the common Catholic design vocabulary. Of his dozens of other archdiocesan commissions, mostly for urban churches, none resembles Our Mother of Good Counsel, the inspiration for which seems to have come from Main Line suburban ecclesiastical architecture, particularly that of its neighbor, the Church of the Redeemer.[77] As a point of comparison, Durang's design for the nearby church on the campus of Villanova College, completed in 1887, hews more closely to Catholic convention. Even though the church is not particularly large, and the central portion of its façade, with its notable bell cote, echoes the design of St. James the Less, its twin spires, purportedly modeled on one at Chartres Cathedral, and prominent position atop a hill overlooking Lancaster Pike make for a more imposing structure premised on a desire for Catholic distinctiveness.[78]

Good Counsel's peculiar design thus reveals something curious about the Catholic community's sense of self. The standard narrative of American Catholic history identifies the early twentieth century as a period marked by overwhelming Catholic "confidence" as the "immigrant Church" came of age. The monumental churches built during the time announced Catholic presence and distinction. Paula Kane has describes this trend as "architecture as apologetic" for a Catholic American identity that blended traditionalism and triumphalism.[79] Although the Church of Our Mother of Good Counsel predates that era slightly, it nonetheless conveys Catholics' sense of confidence, albeit a confidence in their ability to gain social respectability by conforming to the dominant religious character of the Main Line community in which they lived. In the eyes of its Protestant neighbors, the new church may have been on the "wrong side of the tracks," but it was an appropriately fashionable Main Line church, which from all outward appearances might have been mistaken as Protestant.

There were, of course, limits, to Catholic emulation. Despite external similarities, the interiors of the two churches bore little resemblance to each other. At Good Counsel, Catholics surrounded themselves with saintly iconography and devotional objects. Early photographs of the interior of the church reveal such prominent features as the reliquary and the statue of the Sacred Heart that occupy niches just before the transept crossing. In contrast, the Church of the Redeemer was embellished with items consistent with English church design, such as a rood screen, eagle lectern, and sanctuary choir stalls (fig. 7). Redeemer's congregants attempted to maintain the intimate feel of medieval church design by employing dark woods and leaving exposed the stone and brick walls and the roof's hammer-beam construction. Good Counsel's interior is larger and brighter, with supporting columns eliminated and the walls covered in a light shade of plaster (fig. 8). This openness allowed worshippers to witness the Eucharistic sacrifice during Mass and better view the tabernacle that held the reserved Sacrament. These interior differences reflect the contrasting cultural tastes and devotional needs of each congregation, and show that, because of its inherent

Fig. 7 Episcopal Church of the Redeemer, interior. Architect: Charles M. Burns, 1881. Photo courtesy of the Athenaeum of Philadelphia.

theological implications, ecclesiological design was not always denominationally interchangeable.

As "proper" ecclesiological expression grew ever more essential to members of the upper class and their religious communities, so did the need for a clearer

Fig. 8 Church of Our Mother of Good Counsel, interior, 1897. Photo from *E. F. Durang's Architectural Album* (Philadelphia, [ca. 1900]). Courtesy of the Philadelphia Archdiocesan Historical Research Center.

definition of what constituted appropriate form and acceptable style. Nowhere was the tension between subjective aesthetic tastes and theological orthodoxy more apparent than within the Episcopal Church, whose reputation for elaborate architecture and sumptuous display had increased through its close ties with the industrial elite. As Peter Williams has noted, the denomination offered a receptive spiritual home for collectors and other cultural philanthropists engaged in promoting the "Gospel of Art." It helped to legitimize artistic display among and provided wealthy individuals with an institutional context where their impulse toward "material accumulation could be channeled into activities that were religiously and culturally edifying."[80] Yet there remained a segment within the Episcopal Church who stood opposed to aesthetic innovations and ecclesiological changes because they recognized their theological implications. Through their gifts of church furnishings and devotional objects in particular, elite patrons could alter the character of denominational life in significant ways, encouraging a renewed emphasis on liturgical practice, sacramental worship, and symbolic expression. Even if donors supported aesthetic enrichments for less than pious reasons, their actions nevertheless carried a theological message that had broad implications for the Church as a whole. Their aesthetic choices had the potential to effect fundamental shifts in theology, worship, and denominational culture. This raised a foundational issue of who ultimately was entitled to determine what constituted proper ecclesiastical style and church form, with church officials and donors defending their respective theological and aesthetic authority.

The acrimony that surrounded ecclesiological changes confirms their consequential nature. When the ritualist movement first gained force within the Episcopal Church in the mid-nineteenth century, members of the denomination's low church, evangelical wing sought to curtail liturgical innovations and decorative embellishments.[81] They charged that ritualists were violating the unity of worship by introducing practices not recognized by the Book of Common Prayer or church canons. In 1868, evangelical representatives at the General Convention sought to enact canons expressly prohibiting the use of incense, the elevation of the Communion elements "in such a manner as to expose them to view of the people as objects towards which adoration is to be made," and "bowings, crossings, genuflections, reverences, bowing down upon or kissing the holy table, etc." They also sought to ban crucifixes, processional crosses, altar candles, and other ecclesiastical objects.[82] The dispute was left unsettled until the convention of 1874, when delegates decided that the interpretation of the liturgical rubrics, or instructions, contained in the Book of Common Prayer would be left to local bishops.[83]

As low church advocates recognized, even ostensibly benign acts, such as the placement of candlesticks and crosses upon the altar, had theological consequences whether or not that was the donor's intention. For this reason, the politics of church patronage emerged as a major flashpoint in these early ecclesiastical debates. By presenting their churches with ritual objects, donors placed their religious leaders in a bind. If they were to reject a gift of candlesticks or altar cloths, they risked alienating their benefactors. Yet in accepting them, pastors and vestries tacitly approved donors' theological agenda and risked upsetting the theological sensibilities of other congregants or violating denominational custom. Well before the ritualist controversies of the General Convention between 1868 and 1874, the vestry of St. Mark's Church, Philadelphia, voted to return a "richly embroidered" altar cloth donated by a member of the congregation when the vestry and the rector could not agree on its appropriate use. At a time when ritualism was still a matter of great controversy, despite its theological support for high church practices, the parish was forced to act cautiously to avoid a potential clash with the bishop.[84]

In the years to come, with the ritualism debates far from settled, similar scenes would repeat themselves at other parishes. In many instances, it was the vestry that served as the final arbiter in these matters.[85] Recognizing the potential for congregational divisiveness that such gifts could bring, rectors were understandably reluctant to issue a decision themselves, and therefore turned matters over to the church's elected lay representatives. By placing the decision in their hands, this action provided a degree of protection for both rector and parish by declaring such matters to be a temporal, rather than spiritual, concern. It also frustrated opponents' efforts to curtail liturgical innovation because, once declared a "temporal" matter, the issue stood beyond the traditional purview of the bishop or other diocesan officials. As a matter of course, such strategies further strengthened the authority of the vestry, giving those prominent individuals who sat on the body the power to determine the theological character of their church.

By shifting responsibility to the laity, this course of action also allowed clergy to avoid censure when they had a role in introducing or advancing liturgical changes. Such was the defense employed in 1880 by Rev. Oliver S. Prescott, the rector of St. Clement's Church, Philadelphia, when he found himself at the center of an ecclesiological firestorm. The trouble had started ten years earlier, when ceremonies and practices not explicitly proscribed by the Book of Common Prayer, including the use of ritual objects, were instituted at the parish by the previous rector.[86] Prescott found himself defending his predecessor's decision against criticism in the wake of recent ritualism debates at the General Convention and the schism effected by the formation of the evangelical Reformed Episcopal Church in 1874.[87] Although the case could have been settled quietly within the congregation, the militantly low church bishop of the diocese, William Bacon Stevens, chose to exercise his episcopal authority and use the dispute at St. Clement's to make a theological and political statement. Stevens charged Prescott with introducing ceremonies and practices "setting forth or symbolizing erroneous or doubtful doctrines during the celebration of the Holy Communion" in violation of church canons. Prescott denied the charges of "ritualistic rascality," insisting that he had not breached canonical rules because he had not *introduced* the practices. Rather, he had merely conformed to what he found at the parish when he was appointed rector. The ritual items and practices, he argued, had been first employed by the previous rector and, although challenged by some members of the vestry at the time, they had not been rejected.[88]

In this and other ritualism debates within the Episcopal Church, the Book of Common Prayer became one of the main flashpoints of conflict. Both sides looked to its text, as the main liturgical guide for the Church, to defend and uphold their position. Ritualists were eager to have their liturgical practices receive official sanction in the Prayer Book, and pressed repeatedly for the liberalization of its rubrics. Opponents scoured proposed changes for any sign of Roman tendencies, fearing that the introduction of liturgical innovations would compromise the integrity of the faith. As one commentator observed, the lack of firm episcopal control over worship within the Church "throw[s] the Prayer Book as it stands into a most unusual prominence" as a source of liturgical authority.[89] For this reason, any proposed changes to prayer texts, rubrics, or devotional guidelines held the potential for acrimonious debate. Despite the bitter controversy, the tide of opinion gradually turned in favor of those seeking license to adopt ritual practices and high church theology. When the Book of Common Prayer was revised in 1892 and more thoroughly in 1928, the national church authorized the use of ritual objects and sanctioned greater formalism in worship, essentially ruling that they would not attempt to restrict the liturgical changes that congregations had already adopted.[90]

Many of the ecclesiological debates of the industrial era, however, could not be settled by the rubrics contained in the Prayer Book, for they involved matters not of permissibility, but of quality and style. As ritualism gained more widespread acceptance in the 1910s and 1920s, many Episcopalians turned their attention to defining what constituted authentic church design and the proper character of liturgical objects. In Philadelphia, editorials in the *Church News of the Diocese of Pennsylvania*, known simply as the *Church News*, addressed such pressing ecclesiological issues as "Shrubbery" and "The Latest Trends in Tombstones" in an attempt to prevent aesthetic offenses. Another editorial cautioned against the use of concrete for paving, reminding readers that "cinders and burnt clay" were suggestive not of heaven, but "of a much less desirable place."[91] Although church officials certainly possessed the authority to rule on the suitability of ritual objects, ecclesiastical design, and the arrangement of sacred space, defining what constituted an essential element or appropriate form was fluid and often arbitrary. Consequently, wealthy donors and elite tastemakers were able to influence denominational life through their cultural dictates, imposing their class sensibilities on the wider worshipping community.

Nothing captures the debate over appropriate church style within the Episcopal Church better than two disputes over church chimes that erupted in Philadelphia at either end of this period of ritualistic foment. The first and more famous incident occurred in 1877, when a group of neighborhood residents petitioned the court for an injunction against St. Mark's Church, the parish founded thirty years earlier by proponents of the new ecclesiology, to silence the church bells it had installed the year before in commemoration of the nation's centennial. Although changing liturgical practice and differing theological opinions clearly precipitated the lawsuit, the petitioners focused predominantly on the matter of noise. Led by George L. Harrison, himself a devout Episcopalian and leading church benefactor, they stated that the ringing disturbed the tranquility of the neighborhood, lowered their property values, and created a public nuisance. The daughter of one of the lawyers for the petitioners recalled how the parish, "proud of their possession," rang the bells "so inordinately often" that neighbors were left with no option but to seek a court injunction "to have the ecclesiastical zeal kept within bounds."[92] The wealthy residents of the district, who were deeply divided on the issue, recruited a steady stream of real estate agents, architects, theologians, scientists, doctors, members of the clergy, and other experts to offer opinions on both sides of the debate. S. Weir Mitchell, the prominent local physician famous for developing the "rest cure" to treat neurasthenia, testified that the "frequent" and "prolonged" ringing could have deleterious health effects, particularly for women. The rector and vestry countered that the church's chimes were "sweet and harmonious," and that their daily pealing conformed "with the custom of all denominations . . . throughout the civilized world." Hearing these arguments, the city Court of Common Pleas sided with the petitioners and enjoined St. Mark's from ringing the bells until "a mode of chiming can be devised that will not be attended with injurious consequences." Only on appeal did the parish receive permission to resume ringing the bells on a limited schedule.[93]

Some fifty years later, views had changed dramatically. With bells largely accepted as a part of church design and their routine ringing a part of church life, the debate shifted to matters of style and substance. By the 1920s, advances in phonographic technology made it possible for churches to employ recorded chimes in place of actual bells. Indeed, advertisements for home phonographs from the decade were known to describe their tone to be "as clear as the Sabbath church chimes."[94] For some, however, these innovations were an affront to religious sensibilities. In 1930, an editorial in the *Church News* came out against "amplified phonographic chimes." "How will churches retain their distinctiveness," it asked, when any church "can put a record of the Bok Carillon on its little victrola and amplify it out of a broken second-story window," thinking it will sound "just as sweet and rich" as "real Belgian chimes?"[95] The editorial even suggested that it might be necessary for churches to seek legislation restricting the use of amplified chimes. Although these protestations did not carry very far, the piece reveals how concern had shifted from the use of bells to the authenticity of the sound. Since affordable phonographic equipment made it possible for any church to mimic real bells, wealthy congregations needed to find a way to safeguard their investment. They therefore railed against the cheapening of sacred sound and sought to preserve their aesthetic ideal by claiming it to be the only one suitable for divine praise.

Among mainline Protestant denominations, the effects of architectural and aesthetic change were perhaps most pronounced within the Episcopal Church, a product of the general affluence of its members and their tradition of liturgical formalism. In gradually accepting high church influences over the course of the late nineteenth and early twentieth centuries, Episcopalians increasingly espoused what might be described as a "materialistic faith." Despite the superficiality described by the term, the refinement of ecclesiastical space and the introduction of ritual objects into communal worship and church life was nothing less than theologically transformative. It provided the Episcopal Church with a means of rediscovering its ecclesiastical roots, and distinguishing itself from other denominations. And, as contentious as changes in ecclesiology could be, over time they came to serve as points of denominational distinctiveness and unity. Indeed, every dispute over rubrics and ecclesiological practice simply reinforced how central liturgical objects, forms, and architecture had become in defining religious identity for Episcopalians. By embracing English parish architecture, Episcopalians found an architectural form to express their denomination's unique identity as fully Catholic yet thoroughly Protestant. Moreover, the style reaffirmed ties to the mother Church in England and, by extension, the spiritual authority of the episcopate and centuries of tradition.

Even though some of these aesthetic and ecclesiological debates may now seem trivial, they had a powerful cumulative effect on religious life in the United States. Amid the institutional growth of the late nineteenth and early twentieth centuries, the introduction of new architectural styles, artistic adornments, and liturgical furnishings amounted to a refashioning of ecclesiastical space, significantly affecting how religious communities worshipped.

When assessing ecclesiastical change in the industrial era, one could argue that form followed function. The Gothic revival and parish church architecture, as noted, crafted spaces that accommodated ritualism and high church adornments. They respected the growing distinction between clergy and laity, separating the chancel from the nave and making the altar, rather than the pulpit, the focal point. But one could also argue that form—and ecclesiology—followed finance.[96] Through their patronage, members of the upper class and financial elite were able to direct ecclesiastical aesthetics and, by extension, influence theology and denominational identity. Because they were given discretion in architectural design and the material character of their churches, they built spaces reflective of their cultural tastes and class sensibilities. Though their authority and ambitions did not go uncontested, members of the financial and cultural elite exercised considerable theological influence through their artistic patronage, setting a standard for proper aesthetic character and form that would influence the development of religious life in their own congregations, their broader denominations, and beyond.

The "Quaker-Turned-Episcopal Gentry"

William Ellis Scull married Florence Prall at her family's parish, St. Paul's Episcopal Church, in Paterson, New Jersey, in 1887. Scull's father, despite having traveled from Philadelphia for the occasion, was not in attendance. He stood at the door and watched his son approach the altar, "but when the wedding ceremony began he left as a silent testimony to the Friends' conscientious objection to 'hireling ministry.'" Scull was understandably saddened by his father's action, but as one raised in a tight-knit Quaker community, he understood the consequences of his decision to marry "out of meeting"— outside the faith—including the moral challenge it presented for his father and other members of his family who maintained strict adherence to Quaker principles.[1]

Shortly after his marriage, to avoid "disownment"—expulsion from the Quaker fold—Scull approached the Twelfth Street Meeting (Monthly Meeting of Friends of Philadelphia for the Western District; Orthodox) and admitted his transgression. Upon consideration of his appeal, the meeting recognized Scull's "earnest desire to be retained as a member of the Society of Friends" and expressed its hope that his "marriage with one not a Friend would not interfere with it."[2] The meeting was delighted that Scull sought reconciliation: his removal from the community would have been a significant loss. He was a member of a distinguished Quaker clan with deep roots in the Philadelphia community. Both his father and grandfather were "weighty" members of the Twelfth Street Meeting, and he had kinship ties to many other prominent Quaker families.

Ultimately, though, Scull's renewed commitment to his Quaker faith lasted only a few years, and in March 1891, he was baptized into the Episcopal Church.

In his autobiography, Scull expressed his appreciation for "the high spiritual development" of the Quaker community and the benefits "bestowed by the influence of meetings, discipline and family life." He noted how the members sent to convince him to reconsider his decision expressed their regret that they could not and "graciously bid me 'farewell' and happiness in my new faith." Yet he also expressed his dissatisfaction with the strictness of Quaker teachings and with the Society's willingness to disown members "who from weakness may fall from . . . adherence to these high standards." Scull was energized by the spiritual vitality he felt within the Episcopal Church, and he described his decision to leave the Quaker fold as driven by a desire to join "a church militant."[3]

Scull's remarks reveal mindful deliberation, but may not reveal the full complexity of his motives or his true reasons for breaking with the Quakers and joining the Episcopal fold. Writing for posterity, and mindful of his Quaker relations, Scull needed to justify his decision without bringing offense. Although he chose to emphasize the firmness of his new convictions, his conversion may also have been prompted by his inability to adhere to the Quaker faith's "high standards," including its strictures against worldliness that would have weighed particularly upon a man of his wealth and status. The rift between him and the Society may also have been greater than he felt comfortable admitting. Despite these lingering questions, one thing is certain: Scull's decision was not one he made lightly.

Whatever his true motives, Scull followed a well-trod religious path in joining the ranks of those E. Digby Baltzell termed Philadelphia's "Quaker-turned-Episcopal Gentry." The pattern was as old as the city itself, starting with William Penn's own sons, and grew more pronounced during the industrial era, when membership in the Episcopal Church came to be regarded as a marker of status. Given the "good taste of its architecture, the dignity and breeding of its clergy, and the richness of its ritual," as Baltzell has noted, the Episcopal Church attracted many who sought to advance their own social standing by coming into contact with other respectable families.[4] Even though Quakers like Scull already enjoyed high status in Philadelphia society, membership in the Episcopal Church allowed him to position himself within a wider social and religious network than did membership in the Society of Friends. Through their individual actions, he and other members of the Quaker-turned-Episcopal gentry served as the most notable local manifestation of a national trend that contributed to the religious consolidation of the social and financial elite.

Yet, as pronounced as that pattern was, to suggest that Quakers migrated to the Episcopal Church merely for the social status it conferred[5] grossly oversimplifies the personal and religious complexity of such decisions. It treats religious affiliation as nothing more than passing fashion, presenting Quakers and other upper-class converts as little more than slaves to social expectation. It ignores the personal dimensions of the conversion experience and fails to take into account the wider religious context surrounding such decisions. During the latter half of the nineteenth century, there was a sense among Quakers that the spiritual vitality of the Society had waned, a sentiment that could only have contributed to the growing number of industrial-era conversions. If individuals felt their current faith lacking, it should come as no surprise that they sought spiritual fulfillment elsewhere. As Scull's autobiography reveals, the decision to convert involved a complex web of motives. It took place within the contexts of family, society, and religious community and could have profound cumulative consequences, for the chosen faith of one generation inevitably shaped the next. Conversions had the potential to alienate an individual from family, friends, and social peers, making the acquisition of social and spiritual capital never as straightforward as it seemed.

Exploring the rise of Philadelphia's Quaker-turned-Episcopal gentry thus sheds light on the social and religious consequences of upper-class conversion, both for individuals and their broader religious communities. In particular, it reveals the internal struggles such conversions engendered within religious communities. The loss of prominent members prompted theological and social introspection among faithful adherents, who sought to identify and address the grounds for the conversions. In the case of the Quakers, much discussion focused on whether the Society should modify its positions on wealth and marriage since those matters seemed to weigh most heavily in conversion decisions, particularly among the elite. Beyond the theological particulars, this discussion reveals a deeper debate over the extent to which the Society should adjust its teachings and practices, if at all, to accommodate the needs and interests of its most prominent members. The stakes were indeed high since the growing number of conversions had the potential to drain the Society of its spiritual vitality and weaken its social position.

In tracing these developments, my goal is neither to question the sincerity of individual conversions nor to fit the Quaker-turned-Episcopal gentry within a particular model of conversion experience.[6] Rather, it is to situate the pattern of conversion within its social and religious context and to gain a fuller sense of the tensions inherent in the religious consolidation of the upper class. Here it is particularly instructive to examine how the elite interpreted and explained the religious paths they or their ancestors had taken. The conversion narratives contained within family histories and personal memoirs offer a window onto the social considerations that accompanied the refashioning of religious identity. Although some went to great lengths to justify their conversion, many came to embrace their hybrid identity as a unique marker of status in its own right, thus turning a potential liability into a distinct asset.

Spiritual Troubles

Individual conversions could at times be sudden, but the rise of the Quaker-turned-Episcopal gentry had been conditioned by broader spiritual trends within the Society of Friends and fell in line with a long-standing pattern of disaffiliation. Indeed, few religious communities in Philadelphia have been as conscious of the realities of membership loss as the Quakers, whose accounts generally acknowledge the prevalence of members' migration to other faiths, a trend not confined to any particular era.[7] Quaker leaders knew that such migration was to be expected. The founders of the Society, as converts them-selves, understood that not everyone had the fortitude to adhere to Quaker testimonies. They therefore established policies to allow for the removal of those individuals who violated the sect's norms. The reports of disownment proceedings, entered into the record of local meetings, placed membership losses squarely before the eyes of the Quaker community and drew attention to the causes for those losses. During the Revolutionary War, for instance, many Quakers were disowned for their support of the military struggle. Another sizable segment of the early Quaker population was seduced by the allure of worldliness and wealth; because these Quakers no longer adhered to a strict interpretation of testimonies regarding simplicity and plainness, though not officially disowned, they stood at the margins of the Society.

The 1827 doctrinal schism between Orthodox and Hicksite Friends com-pounded the challenges of maintaining community cohesion in the years that followed. The two groups cut off relations with each other, both claiming to be the faithful remnant of the Society, even though they espoused nearly identical teachings.[8] The bitterness of the dispute persisted into the early twen-tieth century. In response to a 1907 article in *American Friend* that referred to "both branches of Friends," one reader chastised the editor for daring to speak of Hicksites and Orthodox as belonging to the same Society: he fer-vently adhered to the belief taught him in his youth that the Hicksite branch "has neither moral nor legal right to the name of Friends."[9] In Philadelphia, those who did not succumb to infighting and recrimination tended to shy away from public attention. Direct Quaker influence in civic affairs declined steadily and had essentially ceased by the late nineteenth century. The few influential Friends who attempted to preserve Quakers' public presence were more likely to come from academic circles than business or politics.

These developments worked to sap the Quaker faith of much of the strength and unity it needed to remain a vital force in society at large. With the exception of a Quaker concentration in Germantown, and a sizable number of Friends in the Old City and Rittenhouse Square districts, Quaker communities in the city of Philadelphia had largely faded from public view by the start of the twentieth century. As early as 1880, fewer than 1 percent of the city's residents were Quakers. Membership in the Yearly Meeting of Orthodox Friends of Philadelphia, which included the surrounding counties in both Pennsylvania and New Jersey, was approximately 5,600 that year; the more numerous Hicksites counted only 13,500 members.[10] Moreover, even these modest figures exaggerate the number of true Quakers in the Philadelphia area. As Howell John Harris notes, about half of those in either camp "were Quakers through family tradition rather than real conviction; these nominal 'birthright Friends' scarcely participated in its religious or benevolent activities."[11]

By the mid-nineteenth century, numerical decline and factionalism had taken its toll on the Society in the Philadelphia region and contributed to the spiritual hardships experienced by individual Friends.[12] Among those who documented their spiritual struggles was Isabella Pennock Huston, a member of a wealthy Chester County family belonging to the Hicksite branch. During the 1850s and 1860s, Huston experienced a profound spiritual crisis, and sought advice from friends and relatives to improve her "low estate." She described her spiritual condition to her aunt in early 1856: "There has been a long period of poverty and it is but seldom I catch my ray of that heavenly influence for which my soul pains yet of which I know, it is all unworthy. . . . Never since last summer has there been a return of the feelings I then confided to thee." Although today Huston might be said to suffer from severe depression, likely brought on by the death of her mother and sister, she interpreted her turmoil in the idiom available to her, as a crisis of faith.[13]

Throughout her spiritual trials, Huston admired the faith of her fellow Quakers and wished for the type of religious experience and spiritual security they seemed to possess. "It is comforting to see the effects of vital religion in others, even when we cannot find it in ourselves," she remarked in another letter to her aunt. She prayed earnestly to hear the "still small voice" and wondered whether she had not fallen under the "delusion of the enemy."[14]

Family and friends recommended devotional readings, shared their own struggles in faith, and pointed out the blessings in her life, but their efforts did not bring the spiritual comfort she desperately desired. Despite her own economic security and other "temporal blessings" showered upon her and her family by the "favors of Providence," Huston considered herself "truly poor and needy." On a few occasions, she even looked beyond the Quaker community for succor, attending evangelical revivals and experimenting with faith cures.[15]

As Huston's spiritual crisis worsened, she expressed doubts about her ability to raise her children properly and worried that she was not doing enough to keep them in the Quaker fold. She confided to her aunt that she had "much to do to prepare the fallow ground—for the reception of the heavenly seed [so] that they may grow up good men and women, living in the fear of the Lord, which is wisdom!" For a woman unsure of her own religious state and doubtful of her own spiritual talents, preparing fallow ground proved to be a daunting task. To assuage her anxiety, Huston turned to the Quaker community to help provide for her children's spiritual care. She sent her son to Quaker-run Haverford College, where, as a fellow Friend assured her, he would "be kept in a tender, susceptible state of mind so that the good seed of the kingdom may grow and flourish."[16]

Huston's letters often described the troubled state of the Quaker faith in her rural community, with frequent references to the paucity of Friends who attended the local meeting. Its membership was "reduced" and "scattered," she remarked, with "our two families mak[ing] up the larger part" of its small number.[17] Friends with whom she corresponded similarly noted the "decay" and "anxiety" affecting the Society in their communities.[18] However subjective these assessments may be, they point to genuine challenges facing the Society of Friends in the latter part of the nineteenth century.

The task of breathing new life into the Quaker community during this time fell upon the shoulders of a handful of "ministering Friends" who helped others develop their spiritual gifts. Committed to the renewal and re-evangelization of the Society, they preached at meetings, visited rural districts, and wrote letters of support to those struggling with spiritual doubts. Huston's circle of correspondents included several of these ministering Friends, among them Elizabeth Evans, Evan Evans, and John S. Stokes. Their accounts share the sentiment that the Society lacked its earlier vitality. In his diary, John Stokes spoke of the "poverty of spirit" he encountered while visiting farming communities in Pennsylvania and New Jersey, including Huston's.[19] Conditions were not necessarily better among urban Quakers. As Elizabeth Evans reminded

Huston, rural isolation presented a distinct challenge, but "there is no situation free from trials [even] if [you are] living in Germantown or Philadelphia."[20] Although historian Thomas D. Hamm has described the 1860s and 1870s as a period of "renewal" and "revival" in American Quakerism, especially among Midwestern Friends who came under the sway of the emergent holiness tradition of the period, efforts to rekindle religious energy were evidently intermittent.[21]

In addition to its effects on individuals, the perceived spiritual malaise afflicting the Society of Friends during the latter half of the nineteenth century had the potential to contribute to membership decline even further by weakening the transmission of faith from one generation to the next. As parents came to doubt their own spiritual state, they found it harder to inspire religious conviction in their children. According to the *Christian Advices*, a spiritual guide issued by the Yearly Meeting of Orthodox Friends, parents possessed a "duty to watch over their youth for good, and early guarding them against those deviations from simplicity in speech, behaviour and apparel, by which many have been betrayed into injurious company and unsuitable connections, and some in an entire renunciation of the religious principles and profession of their fathers."[22] Coupled with the erosion of a once-vibrant religious community that had steeped young Quakers in the faith's distinctive customs, rituals, and codes of conduct, the decline of spiritual fervor among the older generation had the potential to adversely affect the spiritual development of the rising generation.

At the same time, many parents had begun to loosen religious reins in order to expand their children's professional and social opportunities. The parents of George B. Roberts, for instance, who had entrusted him to the care of a Quaker school for his elementary education, later allowed him to receive his professional training at the non-Quaker Rensselaer Polytechnic Institute in Troy, New York, one of the leading engineering schools in the country. Separated from the protective Quaker environment of his youth, George began to drift spiritually shortly after his arrival in New York in 1848. He continued to attend Quaker meetings occasionally, but he attended other church services with his non-Quaker acquaintances. After graduation, when his work as an engineer for the Pennsylvania Railroad took him to remote regions of the state, he became even more removed from Quaker influence.[23]

Like other Quaker families, George's weighed religious concerns against social aspirations and professional ambitions. During his education and early career, George's parents seemed to worry less about his decline in Quaker practice than about his need for professional and social advancement. They did not reproach him for attending the services of another faith, although Quaker testimonies specifically forbade the practice.[24] Likely speaking for the family, George's sister, Gainor, reminded him that he "must not forget to go to meeting or church," speaking as though the two were interchangeable.[25] The family apparently came to a consensus that it did not matter where George worshipped as long as the religious message was suitable for an individual of his social class. They were more concerned that he might not be meeting the "proper society." In 1852, his sister admitted that she felt "very anxious for your advancement not in a pecuniary point of view but as regards the station you will occupy in Society. I therefore cannot help feeling a desire your home should not be in Cambria Co[unty] as I think the Society you mingle with will certainly leave its stamp and in my opinion it is much better to be without any than in that Society from which there is no benefit to be derived."[26]

The response of George's parents to his drifting from the Quaker faith matched their response to the religious paths taken by their other children, most of whom migrated to the Episcopal Church.[27] Although they may have had their own private reservations, there is no evidence in their correspondence that they fought to keep their children in the Society or even that they were disappointed with their children's drift from the fold. When their eldest child, Mary, married Owen Jones out of meeting, her relations with her parents did not seem to be affected. It was, after all, an auspicious marriage that united two distinguished families, both wealthy landowners descended from the Pennsylvania colony's original Quaker families.[28] The family even supported the benefit fair for the new Episcopal church to which Mary and Owen belonged.[29]

Though not unique in their permissiveness, George and Rosalinda Roberts clearly understood how crucial religious associations were to their son's professional advancement. As part of the Society's testimonies, Quakers emphasized the communal nature of business and enterprise, and took it as their obligation to mentor the rising generation. This tradition continued to serve young Friends well, particularly those seeking positions within fields such as banking and commerce, where Quaker firms had an established presence. For those seeking opportunity in the new industrial order, however, ambition could all too easily draw them away from the local Quaker community. In his professional pursuits, George B. Roberts was typical of many Quakers of his generation. Although George's father and uncle continued to farm and oversee tenants on land that had been in the family since the 1600s, George, his brother Algernon, and cousin Percival each turned to industry. George steadily moved up the ranks of railroad management, while his brother and cousin founded the Pencoyd Iron Works, a firm that eventually became part of the U. S. Steel empire.[30] Their contemporary, Joseph Wharton, although sent by his parents to apprentice on a farm, similarly turned his attention to the business of metal production, first zinc, then nickel, and ultimately steel.[31] Among this generation, economic prospects more often lay beyond the guarded world and localism of their youth.

The spiritual anxieties of the latter half of the nineteenth century within the Society of Friends, therefore, not only contributed to a decline in membership, but also shaped the professional and social trajectories of the rising generation. As the religious bonds that had once undergirded commercial networks and familial association came under strain, individuals increasingly cultivated connections beyond the local Quaker community. With industrial expansion and the increasingly national scope of economic activity, professional ambitions brought Quakers into contact with a wider social world and upset established religious and class configurations. As more Quakers slipped from the fold, matters of personal conscience became a communal concern.

Debating Disciplinary Demands

The collective weight of individual conversions kindled debate among Friends over the essence of Quaker teachings and disciplinary demands. For a religious community that had thrived in relative isolation, the national opportunities of the industrial era presented a distinct challenge to the faith, as educational needs, corporate responsibilities, and industrial ambitions drew young Quakers away from the "guarded" environment that had nurtured the faith of past generations. For some, religious conviction proved too weak to survive separation from the larger Quaker community or to resist the temptations of worldliness. Joseph Wharton, himself faithful to Hicksite teachings, blamed the apostasy of his nephew, a convert to the Episcopal Church, on the lack of a strong Quaker community in Bethlehem, Pennsylvania, where Wharton's steel works were located.[32] As Frederick Tolles explains, Quakers, although engaged in the world, had built "hedges" around themselves to provide "the necessary conditions for a culturally insulated and autonomous existence" that would enable them to preserve the faith.[33] When these hedges were cut down by conversion and the decline of a cohesive Quaker subculture, it became more difficult for Quakers to withstand exposure to new influences and preserve the integrity of their religious community.

For those concerned about decline within the Society, the issue often came down to boundaries. Friends were conflicted over whether membership loss was the product of religious disciplines too strictly or too loosely enforced. In 1873, Thomas H. Speakman criticized Quakers' "too frequent" disownment of members "for merely disciplinary offenses" rather than moral wrongs, and called for more liberal policies, noting that the Society could not be "kept up" by "disciplinary coercion."[34] In contrast, ministering Friend John S. Stokes had warned just two years earlier that "innovations" within the Society were causing testimonies to be "laid waste." He was troubled by members' weakening commitment to plainness of speech, behavior, and apparel, and he was appalled by the Yearly Meeting's failure to correct those Friends found to have attended services held by other denominations.[35] Stokes and Speakman would have agreed that essential Quaker principles—such as belief in the presence of the Inner Light within every individual—could not be compromised. But they differed significantly in their response to those who failed to adhere to particular testimonies—such as plain dress or the rejection of paid ministry—that had long served to distinguish the Society of Friends from other faiths. In contrast to Stokes's defense of traditional modes, Speakman criticized the Society for its "morbid conservatism" and tendency to elevate customary practices to the level of unassailable dogma.[36]

To advance the cause of reform, Speakman, a Hicksite Friend living on the outskirts of Philadelphia, authored a series of articles in 1872 and 1873 that addressed the sources of religious decline within the Quaker community. His broad-ranging diagnosis found fault with the Society's rigid adherence to established custom, its failure to keep pace with "the advancing intelligence of the age," and the tendency toward ritualism and an "approximation of the doctrines of the Established church."[37] Although Speakman's concerns did not lay specifically with the loss of members among the social and financial elite, he noted that others had attributed it to the strictness of Quaker proscriptions concerning wealth and marriage, two matters of particular import to them.

Even though Speakman's personal embrace of evangelical theology colored his vision of Quakerism, his writings signaled a shift in the nature of the debate from individual faithfulness to communal governance. Unlike Isabella Huston, who agonized over her low spiritual state and worried about what effect it would have on her children, Speakman attributed spiritual aridity and religious decline to "errors in the conduct of Society affairs." He contended that the older generation's demand for adherence to "formal observances" has reached the point that "few of the strict class of members are able to bring up their children in the ways they deem so essential."[38] This concern for the rising generation, a theme that runs through his articles, led him to question the effectiveness of "disciplinary coercion" and argue for a more "liberal policy" that would bring "younger members into more general participation in Society affairs."[39] Although Speakman's specific proposals, such as changing the times of meetings to make them more convenient, may not have reflected what younger Friends themselves desired, his articles did underscore a growing generational divergence within the Society.

Despite the growing sentiment that the rigidity of some strictures had become both impediments to personal sanctity and barriers to evangelization, the Quaker community as a whole remained wary of formally modifying the Society's teachings. It was not until 1910 that Philadelphia's Orthodox Quakers, the wealthier of the Society's two branches, prepared a "substantial" revision of the *Discipline*.[40] Only minor changes were made, however, such as the modernization of language and clarification of phrasing. The official Quaker stance toward simplicity and marriage remained essentially unchanged. Members of the Society still risked disownment for marriage out of meeting and were regularly urged "seriously to consider the plainness and simplicity which the gospel enjoins, and to manifest an adherence to this testimony, in their speech, apparel, furniture, business, salutations and conversation."[41] Yet even these limited changes were nevertheless a dramatic step for the generally cautious Quaker community, where traditionalist members feared that the repudiation of the Society's distinctive testimonies would weaken communal identity and undermine the integrity of the faith. By admitting, albeit with intentionally vague language, that some testimonies had lost their social applicability, the Quaker community sanctioned ongoing conversation about the nature and necessity of their disciplinary requirements.

One place to gauge the significance of these developments—particularly in relation to the elite—is within the Germantown Monthly Meeting of Orthodox Friends, which comprised many of the city's oldest, wealthiest, and "weightiest" Quaker families. During the early twentieth century, for instance, their annual responses to the query on simplicity showed signs of accommodation to worldly desires, with practice seemingly secondary to principle. In 1916, the meeting admitted that most members found it difficult to live according to Gospel simplicity, but insisted that "many are sincerely desirous to keep that standard before us." In later years, the meeting again declared that the ideal should remain an essential part of religious teaching, even though very few actually met the "high standards of simplicity."[42] But, even though it was unwilling to moderate its stated principles, in recognizing the communal weakness of its members, the meeting essentially let it be known that it would not challenge those who failed to conform to the requirements of Quaker simplicity.

Such responses to the query on simplicity were nothing new. For generations, worldly Quakers had fashioned ways to reconcile faith and social practice. During the colonial period, wealthy Quakers filled their homes with furniture and other objects that were of a "plain style, but finest." They justified their possessions by selecting expensive goods that sacrificed stylistic flourishes for quality materials and skilled craftsmanship.[43] Industrial-era Quakers similarly developed their own creative interpretations. Tyson Stokes, a member of a distinguished Quaker clan, recalled his relatives in Germantown possessing "substantial yet unpretentious" stone houses, "appropriate for nineteenth century Orthodox Friends who scrupulously avoided any evidence of display."[44] Some went to unusual lengths to avoid appearing in violation of Quaker proscriptions. In his memoirs, William Ellis Scull recounted the story of an uncle, "a very strict Quaker," who "had on his parlor floor a Brussels carpet. He felt that its large, bright, flowing pattern was too gay, however, so he had it turned upside down on the floor until his death."[45] When it came to selecting a summer resort, a number of wealthy Quaker families from Philadelphia built cottages at Jamestown, Rhode Island, to isolate themselves from the excesses of Newport, while still remaining within its social orbit. It was within that "colony" that Joseph Wharton built his large—but architecturally simple—mansion in an effort to meet social expectations without violating his religious principles.[46] In revising the discipline, therefore, the Quaker community simply sanctioned an interpretive openness that individual Quakers had long been practicing.

Although this flexibility meant that Quakers were rarely disowned for breaches of simplicity, it did not lessen the burden of the teaching. The Quaker faith required constant introspection on wealth, a perennial topic in periodicals and a common theme in prescriptive literature.[47] Quakers regularly read the *Advices* on plainness and simplicity, and those who attended meetings were required to listen and respond to a series of "queries" on the subject, which made some apprehensive about their moral standing in light of their economic status. In 1865, lumber merchant Francis Stokes confessed to his wife that his "mind seems often & most engaged in devising means of making money, which often gives me uneasiness."[48] Anna Wharton Morris, the daughter of steel magnate Joseph Wharton, once commented how she disliked "the feeling of being among the millionaires, being on the side of the oppressor."[49] Morris E. Leeds, a leading member of his generation of young Friends, similarly noted in 1913 that he considered wealth "a very great hindrance to righteousness," with "efforts to accumulate it . . . dangerous and perhaps wrong.[50] Such forthright admissions about the spiritual burden caused by wealth or by the desire for it were hardly common, but the sentiments they captured were probably not unusual. Although Stokes, Morris, and Leeds each remained a member of the Society, other wealthy Quakers may have found constant introspection on wealth too onerous. Few, if any, other faiths placed the issue of wealth and its display before their members as explicitly and as regularly as the Quaker faith did.

Despite the challenges of simplicity, it was the testimony against inter-marriage that most often threatened the status of wealthy Quakers within the Society. With it, there was little room for creative interpretation: a person either married within meeting or without. Since marriage was a public affair, violations could not be kept private. The Quaker proscription against marriage outside the faith was originally intended to protect the integrity of the young sect, but, by the early twentieth century, many felt it unnecessary to maintain this self-imposed isolation.[51] As far back as the 1860s, the London Yearly Meeting had ceased disowning members for marrying out of meeting. For faithful Friends in industrial-era Philadelphia, however, whose social activities brought them into ever-increasing contact with non-Quakers, the proscription remained a burden.[52] Those already on the margins of the community may not have felt troubled by it, but the proscription weighed heavily on those who strived for faithful adherence to Quaker teachings and social expectations. As Quaker membership declined, those desirous of marrying within the Society were forced to select partners from a dwindling number of families. Faced with the lack of suitable marriage partners, but granted the freedom to pursue economic opportunities outside the home, many Quaker women chose not to marry. Indeed, one sampling of the women belonging to the Philadelphia meetings between 1880 and 1920 indicates that 40 percent had never married, a development that did not help the Society's prospects for growth.[53]

To understand how a more prominent segment of the Quaker population responded to changing sentiments on marriage, the experience of the Germantown community is again telling. The late nineteenth-century records of the Frankford Monthly Meeting (which represented Germantown until 1906) showed that it actively investigated violations of the marriage testimony. As was customary, the meeting would send a committee of two or three Friends to visit those reported to have married out of meeting in an effort to convince the offending parties to acknowledge their transgression, holding out the possibility of disownment should they refuse. By the early twentieth century, however, the meeting minute books no longer show active pursuit of such violations. The reasons for this shift are not entirely clear. Some within the community may have felt that this corrective outreach had little effect on those who already felt alienated from the community, while others may simply have deemed intrusive interventions to be impolitic. Letters of acknowledgment for marriage out of meeting continued to appear, but they were no longer prompted by investigations. As communal disciplinary efforts waned, recorded disownments also decreased significantly. Whereas the minute book of the Frankford Monthly Meeting for 1852–1889 lists approximately eighty cases of disownment for all reasons, the book for 1890–1906 lists only eight. In the minute book of the Germantown Monthly Meeting for 1906–1916, "disownment" is listed in the index but is not accompanied by any cases; in the book for 1916–1924, the heading disappears entirely, evidently from lack of use. The minute books continued to maintain lists of those who married non-Quakers, but the meeting no longer prosecuted these individuals, nor did it seem willing to disown them for this violation alone.[54]

As attitudes changed, the leadership of the Germantown Monthly Meeting began to take a more pastoral approach toward Friends who married out of meeting. They recognized that Quaker religious principles would have little weight if the Society continued to remove members who failed live up to those ideals. In 1908, the overseers of the Germantown Men's Meeting issued a statement on marriage that revealed a new spirit of toleration within the community. Recognizing that "an increasing number of our young Friends have joined in marriage with those not in membership with us," the overseers agreed that there was an "earnest" interest "for the solemnization of marriages between members and nonmembers in our meetings for Divine Worship" and promised to submit the matter to the Monthly Meeting for its consideration. Though still inherently cautious, the statement nevertheless reveals that the leaders of the Germantown community recognized the need for a more generous response to the increasing number of Friends who married out of meeting.[55]

Even though the Germantown records indicate that those who sought reconciliation after violating the marriage testimony were routinely received straightforwardly, the community concluded that the absolute nature of the existing prohibition risked alienating members unnecessarily, particularly those "young Friends" most in need of religious guidance and on whom the future vitality of the Society depended. In the absence of widespread evangelization efforts to increase the number of "convinced" Friends, as converts to the Quaker faith were known, the community relied on birthright members to maintain its ranks. The overseers' statement reveals an effort on the part of Germantown Friends to address changing social conditions by urging an official reform and, most important, by reaching out to Friends who desired both to marry out of meeting and to remain members of the Society in good standing. Among the Orthodox, the more conservative branch with regard to the marriage testimony, the victory for reformers came in 1916, when the Yearly Meeting permitted mixed marriages to occur under Quaker supervision. Yet, for some, this accommodation came too late.[56]

Finding New Spiritual Homes

The degree of personal introspection and communal discussion that Quakers exhibited over matters such as marriage and worldliness challenges the facile assumption that religious conversion among the Quaker elite was prompted purely by social aspiration. Debates within the Germantown Monthly Meeting demonstrate that social concerns could not be separated from their spiritual underpinnings. Concerns over wealth and marriage were not simply about social status, but also about the theological teachings that governed the relations of Quakers with the outside world, and the social boundaries set and maintained by the religious community. Whereas some sought to reform Quaker teachings in light of changing social realities, others concluded that the Society's ethical demands and moral strictures no longer provided a practical guide for their lives and left the fold in search of a more personally satisfying religious faith.

To argue that Quakers converted to other faiths simply to avoid the Society's proscription against intermarriage and the display of wealth ignores the sincere spiritual yearnings of most converts. Those distressed by the low spiritual state of the Quaker faith had reason to search for greener spiritual pastures elsewhere. The strength of evangelical Quakerism in the closing decades of the nineteenth century, though muted in conservative Philadelphia, reflects a spiritual yearning across a broad swath of the Quaker community, not just the elite.[57] As William Ellis Scull's autobiography suggests, he and others of his class had a genuine desire for sound teachings, meaningful worship, and spiritual fulfillment. In order to understand Philadelphia's Quaker-turned-Episcopal gentry, therefore, it is important to consider not just what individuals rejected, but what they came to embrace.

It has been argued that the Episcopal Church, with its openness to intellectual inquiry, provided an attractive alternative for those who tired of doctrinal disputes within their own denominations during the late nineteenth century.[58] The Quaker experience, however, runs somewhat counter to this argument since the Society of Friends, with its emphasis on individual conscience, accommodated a considerable degree of theological disagreement. Indeed, some Quakers would insist that one of the defining features of their faith was its lack of absolute doctrines. When the Hicksite Yearly Meeting considered adding a "fragment of creed" to the discipline in 1894, Joseph Wharton "urgently protest[ed] against the assumption that any person or body of persons has the right to set up dogmatic tests for which I can be held responsible either by the Society of Friends or by the community in which I live."[59] Thus, in proclaiming their acceptance of the Episcopal Church's formal creeds and doctrines, Quaker converts made a profound theological profession. Among the reasons William Ellis Scull gave for his decision to join the Episcopal Church was his conviction that the Society of Friends lacked "historical and biblical authority."[60] Scull's views may not have reflected the belief of all Quaker converts, many of whom would probably not have been as dismissive of the Society's claims to biblical authority, but they reflect his own high church orientation and his desire to frame his conversion in terms of theological assent rather than dissent.

The presence of an ordained clergy may have also contributed to the Episcopal Church's appeal, providing converts with a type of spiritual leadership not found within the Quaker community. Quakers rejected the "hireling ministry" because it violated the spiritual egalitarianism they professed, with all Christians sharing in the gift of the Inward Light.[61] But for those seeking spiritual direction, ministerial guidance possessed a distinct appeal. By the early twentieth century, younger Friends had begun to push for the appointment of stated ministers within the Society, a practice that had taken hold in some Quaker communities by 1900, albeit not in the conservative stronghold of Philadelphia.[62] Ministering Friends offered an acceptable equivalent, but in an age marked by increased professionalism, some seeking religious guidance may have felt that their words did not carry the same weight as the advice of clergy educated for their vocation. Others found themselves drawn to churches whose well-trained clergy could present theological views in a language and style that met their intellectual standards. When George B. Roberts was separated from "good society" on one of his early engineering projects, church sermons were one of the few sources of intellectual stimulation he could find. In one letter, he informed his family, "I went to Church this morning (Episcopal of course) and heard a sermon from one of their most talented ministers."[63]

For those who found Quaker worship stark, the ritualism and aesthetics of the Episcopal Church could be spiritually transformative. The Quaker faith, explained William Wistar Comfort, a leading voice within the Society in the first half of the twentieth century, was a contemplative faith whose "method of worship is the most exacting of all methods in the demands it makes upon the mind and spirit."[64] Indeed, constant personal introspection in an atmosphere of silence could be mentally and spiritually taxing. Isabella Pennock Huston repeatedly confided to family and friends that she gained nothing from Quaker meetings for worship, speaking of her lack of spiritual progress and her inability to sense the guidance of the Inward Light. For others who shared these frustrations, Episcopal services might have provided an alternative means to achieve spiritual communion. Whether high, low, or broad in character, Episcopal churches offered a degree of ritual that connected worshippers with the divine in ways not found in "unprogrammed" Quaker meetings.[65] Participation in a communal ritual could provide a sense of spiritual fulfillment absent during silent worship.

With their often ornate architecture and rich imagery, Episcopal churches conveyed a spiritual power in ways that unadorned Quaker meetinghouses could not.[66] Whereas, in Quaker meetings, the spiritual intensity emanated from the silent gathering and stark simplicity of the worship space, Episcopal services drew from the Church's liturgical and symbolic traditions to provide a different path toward spiritual uplift. For those unable to sense God's immanence through the workings of the Inward Light in their own persons, Episcopal ecclesiastical spaces held forth the potential of making the divine present in both visible and tangible ways. Personal devotional objects served a similar function within the home. Mary Williams Brinton, the niece of George B. Roberts, cherished her mother's prie-dieu not only for its aesthetic beauty, but also for its sentimental and spiritual value: "It was Mother's prayer stool, and Clarence [Mary's husband] and I solved many problems kneeling on its sloping cushion."[67] Items like these—and the spiritual power reflected in them—helped cement Brinton's transformation from the residual Quakerism of her father to her own Episcopalianism. Music likewise drew some Quakers to the Episcopal Church. "Quaker singer" David Bispham recalled that the "desire to enter upon a musical career came to me, I am sure, through the influence of the music I heard in the Episcopal Church at Moorestown, [New Jersey,] where now and then I went with my father, who sang occasionally in the little choir."[68] The spiritual aesthetic of the Episcopal Church found a receptive audience among those who found Quaker meetings wanting.

For members of the Quaker-turned-Episcopal gentry, conversion stemmed not only from frustrations over the strictness of Quaker social discipline, but also from the quest for meaningful spiritual instruction. "Worldly" Friends found a home in the Episcopal Church where they could hear teachings about prosperity that were spiritually comforting. Their new faith, moreover, was not a social club gathered under Gothic spires; it was a religious community that offered a distinct theological message and form of spirituality. For Quakers suffering from spiritual malaise, Episcopal intellectualism and aestheticism beckoned, offering religious instruction and spiritual experiences not found within the Society.

Admittedly, not all wealthy Quakers who were dissatisfied with the theological demands or social isolation of their faith chose to join the Episcopal Church. Charles Lukens Huston was drawn to the Presbyterian Church, as was Mary Morris, wife of Wistar Morris, a wealthy landowner. Nor, of course, was every convert to the Episcopal Church originally a Quaker. Rodman and Thomas Wanamaker left behind their father's evangelical Presbyterian faith, while Anthony and Joseph Drexel migrated from the Catholic fold.[69] Joseph Drexel's wife, Lucy Wharton Drexel, came from a Quaker-turned-Episcopal family, but defied social expectations later in life by converting to the Catholic Church.[70] Within the Waln family, three spinster sisters spent their Sundays with three very different congregations: Ellen remained a Quaker, Sally became an Episcopalian, and Anne joined the Presbyterians.[71] Although such anecdotes reveal the difficulty of generalizing about the motivations that lay behind conversion decisions, the Quaker-turned-Episcopal gentry nevertheless remained the most visible manifestation of a spiritual restlessness among the Philadelphia elite, one that would have considerable consequences for both them and their religious communities.

From Stigma to Status

As the steady migration of Quakers to the Episcopal Church changed the religious composition of many prominent Philadelphia families, it made the conversion experience a defining feature of their history. But conversion offered social benefit only if others accepted its legitimacy. Given the centrality of religious affiliation to upper-class identity, in recounting their religious histories, it was important for families to present their conversions in a socially acceptable way. Family annals, personal memoirs, autobiographies, reminiscences, and other accounts provide a glimpse of how members of the upper class interpreted their own religious histories and that of their ancestors. These sources shed light on the aspects of family history that families deemed suitable for private commemoration or public consumption, and show how explanations for conversion changed over time and across generations. They reveal not only how members of the upper class came to terms with their new religious identities, but also how they made them socially respectable and culturally valuable.

In keeping with Quaker custom, Friends were encouraged to keep journals and compose autobiographical accounts as spiritual exercises to testify to the working of the Inward Light in their lives. In the absence of formal doctrinal statements, the Society relied on members to "tell their story" across generations.[72] The lives of early Friends, such as George Fox, Margaret Fox, William Penn, and John Woolman, were almost required reading for members of the Society. These and other accounts were widely available to nineteenth-century Quakers as part of the *Friends' Library* series, which provided a wholesome alternative to "pernicious reading."[73] When Isabella Pennock Huston was struggling with her faith, she turned to such accounts for comfort and inspiration. Helen Thomas Flexner, the sister of Bryn Mawr College president M. Carey Thomas, recalled how her mother read Quaker biographies and Christian histories for comfort and guidance when she was suffering from cancer. Quaker children likewise had their own library of didactic literature, intended to inspire an appreciation of the Society's customs and principles.[74]

Among the notable Philadelphia Quakers who wrote in this tradition was Hannah Whitall Smith, whose widely reprinted autobiography, *A Christian's Secret to a Happy Life*, promoted spiritual renewal within the Society by drawing upon the emergent holiness tradition in Anglo-American religion. First published in 1875, Smith's book became a classic among evangelical Friends, particularly outside of Philadelphia.[75] She also wrote a biography of her father, John Whitall, in the Quaker inspirational tradition. In praising his religious devotion, she attributed the success of the family business to the fact that he "made the Lord literally his partner, and did nothing without consulting Him, and seeking to discover His will." As in other Quaker writings of its kind, Smith offered evidence of her father's spiritual gifts and religious status: she included a family tree to confirm his birthright membership in the Society, and she listed his religious tracts to show the working of the Inward Light in his life.[76]

By the next generation, the style of family biography had changed. As their writings indicate, Smith's children had developed distaste for the conservative ways of Philadelphia Quakers, but it did not inspire them to work toward the spiritual renewal of the Society as she had. Instead, Smith's children turned away from the faith and distanced themselves, both socially and geographically, from the world of their childhood. Mary, the eldest daughter, deserted her Irish husband to join the famed art scholar and agent, Bernard Berenson, in his world of patronage and wealth. Rather than looking to her mother's life for spiritual guidance, she used Hannah's rebellious embrace of evangelicalism and universalist theology as an excuse for her own rejection of the Quakers' social and religious norms. "Thee, who is such a rebel against orthodoxy in religion," she informed her mother, "cannot be surprised or shocked if I am a rebel against orthodoxy in conduct."[77] Mary's brother, Logan Pearsall Smith, took refuge in the world of letters at Oxford, and had even harsher opinions about his religious upbringing. His autobiography, *Unforgotten Years*, presented the narrative of his escape from it. Writing in 1937, he recalled his parents with fondness, but rejected the "fiery background" of their evangelism and scorned the provincial attitudes of Philadelphia Quakers, whom he described as a "secluded community, carefully entrenched and guarded from all contact with what we call the 'world,'" and rife with hypocrisy and clannish disputes.[78] Writing *Unforgotten Years* allowed him to cleanse his soul and justify his rejection of Quaker principles.[79]

As other members of the upper class explained why they or their relatives left the Quaker fold, they sought to put events in the best possible light. One solution was to turn conversion into a heroic act, especially if motivated by love. Charles W. Thayer, for instance, admired the resolve of his Quaker grandmother, who insisted on marrying an Episcopalian despite her parents' refusal to attend the ceremony. Perhaps projecting some of his own views of Quakers on her, Thayer claimed that his grandmother saw a "release from the restricted existence of a pious Quaker household" in her marriage to a prosperous banker.[80] When conversion was precipitated by marriage out of meeting, there also was a tendency to blame the inflexibility of Quaker strictures. George Wharton Pepper acknowledged that his maternal grandfather and paternal grandmother had each faced a "barrier" of separation from the Quaker community when their marriages led them to join the Episcopal Church.[81] By placing responsibility for soured relations squarely on Quaker strictures, he did not have to entertain the possibility that his grandparents might deliberately have chosen to distance themselves from the Quaker community.

Another common explanation for conversions among one's forebears was disownment for military service during the Revolutionary War, with patriotic valor serving as a more socially acceptable defense than spiritual restlessness or worldly aspiration.[82] When T. Williams Roberts received an inquiry about his family's religious genealogy, he replied that the family had not been Quaker since Revolutionary times.[83] Although members of the Roberts family had indeed been disowned during the war, some later made their peace with the Society, a fact he failed to acknowledge. The family's final rejection of the Quaker faith did not occur until the latter half of the nineteenth century, when his father and aunts joined the Episcopal Church.[84] Whether Roberts's response reflects ignorance, deliberate distortion, or a simple desire to answer concisely, he clearly felt more comfortable citing revolutionary patriotism than social aspiration or religious fashion as the reason for his family's conversion. Like other members of the Episcopal upper class, he created a more usable past through the retelling of his family's religious wanderings.

So common were disownment for military service and marriage out of meeting as reasons for Quakers' conversion to other faiths that they were popularized in local literature. In S. Weir Mitchell's *Hugh Wynne, Free Quaker*, first published in 1896, the protagonist rejects the strict faith of his father, fights in the Revolution, and later marries in an Episcopal ceremony.[85] Although Mitchell, the famous promoter of the rest cure, was not a member of the Quaker-turned-Episcopal gentry, he moved within elite circles and knew many who could identify with such themes.[86] Despite objections from the local Quaker community for its glorification of the "the man who fights," the novel was well received in Philadelphia, where most of Mitchell's readers would have found patriotism and love to be socially acceptable reasons for conversion, as well as the basis for an exciting narrative.[87]

As time passed and conversion became still more common, Philadelphia's Quaker-turned-Episcopal gentry felt less need to defend the past decisions of their families. Those further removed from the restrictive Quaker community and its demanding testimonies were less inclined to speak with acrimony or alienation. Separated by historical distance, they began to fashion a romantic vision of Quakers, finding beauty and charm in the customs of Philadelphia's "peculiar people." Mary Williams Brinton delighted in remembering how her Episcopalian father would sometimes forgo the usual prayer before meals and call for a "silent Quaker Grace."[88] In his own memoirs, her father recalled childhood visits with his "lovely Quaker aunts," and described how he had longed to join them when he saw them heading off to meeting in plain dress.[89] By the third generation, the memory of Hannah Whitall Smith's religious temperament softened considerably, with Ray Strachey, Mary Berenson's daughter, writing affectionately about the wisdom and kindliness of her "Quaker Grandmother."[90] For her and others, Quaker cultural habits came to acquire quaint appeal. Some former Quakers, for instance, continued to use the distinctive Quaker forms of address or dating throughout their lives, particularly when corresponding with other Quakers. Charles Lukens Huston, who discarded Quaker theology for evangelical hymns and premillennial theology in the late nineteenth century, never ceased using Quaker idioms. Indeed, his Presbyterian wife "so loved" his Quaker "Bible language, thee, thou and thy" that she eventually adopted it herself in family correspondence.[91]

Remarkably, through such acts, members of the upper class came to re-embrace their Quaker ancestry and to turn it into a distinctive marker of status. Quaker ancestry, regardless of religious practice, helped confirm a family's inherited place within the social establishment. Those who could trace their lineage back to colonial settlement were eligible to join the Welcome Society. Named after the ship that carried William Penn to his colony and founded in 1906, the Welcome Society served as the Philadelphia equivalent of the Mayflower Society to honor those with the proper genealogical credentials.[92] Quaker heritage also was credited both as the source of distinctive upper-class personality traits and as a defining feature of their worldview.[93] Horace Mather Lippincott, a member of the prominent publishing family, attributed the "simplicity, dignity, and reserve" of old Philadelphians to a residual Quaker ethos.[94] Reflecting on his own Quaker heritage, Henry Seidel Canby likewise suggested that "there may be found a certain tenderness of mind, an openness of heart toward all the simple things . . . among men and women of Quaker descent."[95] By the early twentieth century, families that had rejected the Society's strictures nevertheless embraced the Quaker virtues, such as thriftiness and trustworthiness, which became seen as innate personality traits passed down from one generation to the next. In effect, converts and their descendants recast their Quaker heritage in ethnic, rather than religious, terms. They claimed Quaker social and cultural attributes as their own, without being bound to its theological demands.

Indeed, Philadelphians as a whole became more interested in celebrating and preserving their Quaker heritage during the industrial era. As the Quaker population declined, there was a collective nostalgic desire to reaffirm Philadelphia's identity as the Quaker City. One of the more visible signs of this desire was the placement of the statue of William Penn atop City Hall in 1894.[96] It was also around this time that the "Quaker" moniker came to be associated with the University of Pennsylvania.[97] To some extent, this nostalgia can be seen as a reaction to the rapid changes of the time. For those who invoked the term, "Quaker" served as shorthand for the city's past virtue and the moral probity of its residents. In response to the influx of southern and eastern European immigrants into the city's once-fashionable Old City neighborhoods, Elizabeth Robins Pennell longed for the days when "quiet, dignified men in broad-brimmed hats, [and] sweet-faced women in delicate grays and browns," filled the streets.[98] As the embodiment of the city's finest qualities, the "historic" Quaker community provided an image of stability for those uncertain about the effects of industrialization, urban growth, and demographic change.[99]

Among the city's social and financial elite, those of Quaker ancestry, regardless of their current religious affiliation, enhanced their own status by reclaiming a heritage credited for the city's growth and prosperity. Doing so provided them with a historical identity that linked them to the city's earliest days as well as a moral foundation for their class authority.

In the end, members of Philadelphia's Quaker-turned-Episcopal gentry had not entirely turned their backs on the Quaker faith but had come to possess the best of both religious worlds. They gained the social benefits of membership in the Episcopal Church, yet retained the distinction of Quaker ancestry and its associated virtues. In some ways, "Quaker-turned-Episcopal" became a distinct religious identity in its own right, a relatively rare and valuable pedigree. Conversion, once seen as a social liability, had been transformed into a symbol of status.

Religious life in the United States has long been characterized by its fluidity, a product of the nation's vibrant religious marketplace. Yet, no matter how commonplace conversion was among the population as a whole, the religious wandering of the elite was nevertheless distinctive because of its symbolic weight. In industrial era Philadelphia, the loss of prosperous and influential Friends served as a bellwether of sorts for the spiritual health of the Quaker community and could not therefore be easily dismissed. Ongoing decline left the community searching for explanations and prompted debates over the degree to which Quakers should modify the Society's teachings or ease its discipline in order to accommodate elite expectations. They did not wish to eviscerate the testimonies of their faith, but neither, quite literally, could they afford the steady loss of their most wealthy and prominent members.

The rise of the Quaker-turned-Episcopal gentry, in addition to the concern it elicited among Friends, would also have broader implications for others in industrial-era Philadelphia, altering the contours of the city's social and religious landscape. This pattern of elite conversion helped raise the social profile of the Episcopal Church and promote class consolidation along religious lines. Though unique to Philadelphia, this religious realignment paralleled national trends and helped give rise to a more visible and cohesive ruling class centered around the Episcopal Church, whose members employed their collective might and resources to elevate the Church to a position of prominence within the American religious landscape. They came to view themselves, more than ever before, as the nation's religious establishment.

The Episcopal Ascendancy

In 1919, the Episcopal Churchwomen of the Diocese of Pennsylvania traveled to Valley Forge for their annual social outing. During their visit, they were met by Rev. W. Herbert Burk, who guided them on a tour of the chapel being built within the Valley Forge State Park. The chapel, Burk's labor of love for nearly two decades, commemorated George Washington and all the patriots who had fought for independence, marking the site as hallowed ground. In extolling his grand vision for the famous Revolutionary encampment, Burk praised the chapel as a sign of "Church unity." He urged the prominent women who stood before him to support his initiative for the sake of the "thousands of people of all creeds [who] come here to worship and visit this great national shrine. Here, at Valley Forge, where the temptation is to make it a picnic ground, the Church bears witness to Christ and his Holy Religion."[1]

Neither Burk nor his audience doubted that responsibility for this momentous enterprise must fall upon Episcopalian shoulders. No other denomination, they believed, was as well suited to provide moral leadership for the nation and serve as steward of its spiritual heritage. This sentiment was particularly pronounced among the Episcopal elite, who were committed to a patrician creed of social responsibility informed by a sense of noblesse oblige. By the time of the churchwomen's outing, the Episcopal Church professed to be the church of the nation, the fullest embodiment of the national spirit.

But how did members of the Episcopal Church come to regard themselves as the religious establishment? This conceit, which seemed so natural to them, would have been inconceivable even a few decades earlier since it relied upon a sense of denominational unity and common religious mission that members had not always shared.[2] The belief that the Episcopal Church could serve as a unifying force in the nation's religious life had emerged in the late nineteenth century, most notably in the writings of William Reed Huntington, who influenced the formulation of the 1888 Chicago-Lambeth Quadrilateral, an articulation of the four essential aspects of the Episcopal faith that would serve as a foundation for discussions of Christian unity and provide a defense of the "national church" ideal.[3] Such efforts served as a theological foundation for the nationalist vision that took hold within the Episcopal Church in the early twentieth century, when it gained more widespread cultural currency among the clergy and laity.

The rise of the Episcopal establishment in the early twentieth century served as the religious counterpart to the class consolidation that had been taking place among the financial elite since the end of the nineteenth. During this period, members of the financial elite came to wield progressively greater influence within the nation's religious life, just as they had within its economic and political affairs. With many in its ranks drawn from this privileged class, the Episcopal Church enjoyed power and prestige entirely disproportionate to its numerical size. By the 1920s, when Episcopalians' national influence was at its peak, they represented only about 1 percent of the total population of the United States.[4] They served as the standard-bearers of the white Anglo-Saxon Protestant (WASP) culture that, in the words of Peter Schrag, provided the "integrating ethic of American life."[5]

Developments in the Diocese of Pennsylvania, one of the largest, wealthiest, and most prominent within the national church, provide an opportunity to trace the contours of the Episcopal ascendancy.[6] They reveal how its members overcame their prevailing parochialism, strengthened their denominational identity, and propelled their Church to a position of prominence over the course of the early twentieth century. By the 1920s, they had acquired an air of religious authority that enabled them to present a unified religious vision for the nation, offering spiritual and cultural leadership at a time when many native-born Americans worried about the consequences of massive immigration, divided national and religious loyalties, and general social instability.[7]

Among the prime exponents and beneficiaries of the Episcopal Church's ascendancy were members of the social and financial elite, who enhanced their own status by supporting efforts that raised their Church to a position of prominence. They helped articulate what Frank Sugeno has described as the Church's "establishmentarian" mission through their support of ecclesiastical projects that reflected and reinforced their sense of privilege within the nation's religious life.[8] Three particular sites in the Diocese of Pennsylvania offer a revealing glimpse of how such abstract ideals found form in physical space: the proposed diocesan cathedral, historic Christ Church, and the Washington Memorial Chapel. These manifestations of the establishment mentality helped fashion the public image of the Episcopal Church as the nation's religious authority. They demonstrated its members' sense of confidence and collective unity and served as a catalyst for Episcopalians' emergence as a dominant force in the religious and cultural life of the nation.

Promoting Unity

The Episcopal Church had long possessed a strong presence in Philadelphia, a city crucial to its early history. During the colonial era, the Quaker commitment to religious toleration allowed the Anglican Church (precursor to the Episcopal Church) to prosper in Pennsylvania, disproving those who believed that the Church could not survive without official state recognition, as it possessed in Virginia and elsewhere. Ironically, having developed within an environment of religious pluralism and having adjusted to the conditions of financial and political autonomy, Anglicans in Pennsylvania were well positioned to adjust to the new realities of religious life that emerged after Independence. Their experience became a model for church leaders when they met in Philadelphia in 1784 for their first national convention. Five years later, Philadelphia became the birthplace of the Episcopal Church when delegates ratified its governing constitution and canons, affirming their common membership in one national religious body. A further testament to the importance of the Diocese of Pennsylvania to the formation of the Episcopal Church was the leadership of William White, the first bishop of the diocese. In addition to placing his own diocese on firm footing, White, a conciliatory figure, helped devise the denomination's bicameral governing structure (modeled after the U.S. Congress) that accommodated both the clericalism championed by the New England delegates and the lay privilege championed by the Southern churchmen, thus ensuring that the Episcopal Church was able to overcome its first great challenge to unity.[9]

Despite their common faith and shared organizational structure, members of the Diocese of Pennsylvania, like their co-religionists in other dioceses, did not always function as a cohesive religious body. Many were ardent supporters of their local parishes, where pew ownership and vestry positions were frequently passed down within families, but their parochial loyalties did not always translate into support for the diocese or the Church as a whole, particularly among those who wanted to preserve the denomination's decentralized authority structures.[10] Starting in the late nineteenth century, population growth and residential expansion into the suburban periphery created the need for new churches, which tended to further the diocese's fragmentation. By 1910, members of the diocese were funding 190 parishes and missions, some 70 of which had been established in just the preceding three decades.[11]

For diocesan leaders, staunch parochialism stood as a potential obstacle to diocesan cohesiveness. Statements from Ozi Whitaker, who served as the diocesan bishop from 1887 until his death in 1911, were filled with references to the reluctance of members to look beyond their own parishes and support the greater work of the Church. He faulted individuals for their insularity and reproved his own clergy for their unwillingness to encourage a more expansive vision of religious responsibility.[12] His successor, Philip Mercer Rhinelander, similarly criticized the narrowness of "Episcopal loyalty." He regularly reminded delegates to the diocesan convention (the main governing body for the diocese) that their loyalties were to the wider Church and must extend beyond their own vestries and parochial self-interest.[13]

Another factor that contributed to the parochial character of Philadelphia Episcopalians was the history of party factionalism within the diocese, which stemmed from the influence of the Oxford Movement within the Anglican Communion during the mid-nineteenth century. What had begun as an academic exercise among English "tractarians" soon became a major fault line within the Episcopal Church when the Catholic revival spread across the Atlantic, raising questions about apostolic heritage, doctrinal authority, and the proper mode of worship. The theological foment forced Episcopalians to confront the conflicted identity of their denomination, with roots in both Catholicism and Protestantism. As like-minded Episcopalians in the Diocese of Pennsylvania gravitated toward each other, local congregations became a notoriously cantankerous lot, divided among high, low, and broad church orientations. The delegations at the annual diocesan conventions were similarly splintered, making governance difficult. In Philadelphia, no one orientation ever became strong enough to silence the other two.[14]

The persistence of parochialism in the diocese may also have been exacerbated by the residual influence of Quaker sympathies among converts, particularly among the social and financial elite who often held positions on church vestries and other decision-making bodies. Whereas some converts embraced ritualism and high church influences, others insisted on low church style and practices more in keeping with Quaker custom. Thus, in an argument over the use of floor candles at All Saints' Church in suburban Wynnewood, one vestryman disclosed his Quaker roots by objecting that "the use of candles would destroy the 'simplicity' of the service."[15] Such disputes, whatever their origin, reflected the intensity of theological conviction within local congregations.

Entrenched parochialism and strong party loyalties thus raised concern among diocesan leaders who desired unity within the local church. To assess their response, it is useful to contrast the careers of Bishops Ozi Whitaker and Philip Mercer Rhinelander, who represented a generational shift in diocesan leadership. Whitaker was named the diocesan bishop in 1887, succeeding William Bacon Stevens, a militant defender of the broad and evangelical wings of the Church who had fought to suppress high church practices within the diocese.[16] Stevens's confrontational manner, however, did little to quiet the disputes between high and low church parties, placing the burden of reconciliation on Whitaker, a convert from the Congregational Church who came to Philadelphia after serving as a missionary bishop in the western United States. In an effort to divert attention from parochial disputes, Whitaker encouraged members of the diocese to commit support to the national church and its missionary efforts, a cause close to his own heart. His cautious approach was an understandable attempt to avoid worsening denominational rifts at a time when the Episcopal Church was still nursing the wounds of the schism effected by members of the Church's evangelical wing in the 1870s.[17]

Rhinelander was cut from different cloth. Though a moderate high churchman of judicious temperament, he was an ambitious cleric from a distinguished family rooted deeply in the Episcopal Church. He was elected diocesan bishop in 1911 at the age of only forty-two, when the two low church candidates on the ballot split the vote at the diocesan convention.[18] Despite the narrowness of his election, Rhinelander wasted no time in outlining his vision for the diocese, announcing to the convention the themes that would dominate his episcopate: diocesan unity and personal service, the two "halves of one great whole."[19]

Rhinelander's emphasis on "diocesan unity" was significant. When Whitaker had raised the issue of unity, he generally spoke of the need for "church unity," an effort to elicit pan-Protestant loyalties among Episcopalians, encouraging them to be more broadly Christian rather than narrowly sectarian.[20] Rhinelander's emphasis on the diocese made his vision more distinctly Episcopalian. He recognized the power of the Church's administrative structures and historical ecclesiastical organization. At the 1917 diocesan convention, he encouraged delegates to strive "for a larger and more generous recognition of the Diocese as such[, for] the Diocese, rather than the Parish, is both the working unit of the Church's organization and the cell of its organic life and growth."[21]

Rhinelander recognized that diocesan unity required strengthening both episcopal authority and diocesan administration. He sought ways to exercise diocesan prerogatives without impinging upon the rights and privileges traditionally reserved for parishes and their vestries. He worked steadily to increase the authority of diocesan commissions and slowly brought more funds under diocesan control. In 1913, for instance, he established the Church Building Commission to oversee architectural designs for institutions under diocesan sponsorship, a matter previously left to local boards. He also instituted centralized fundraising campaigns to support diocesan extension and to offset reliance on parish-led initiatives.[22]

Credit for diocesan restructuring also rested with Thomas J. Garland, who was elected in 1911 to serve as the diocese's suffragan bishop, and who was then elected to succeed Rhinelander as head of the diocese in 1924. Having worked as an executive in the steel industry before entering the ministry, Garland understood organizational imperatives and grasped the intricacies of financial management. Under his leadership, the diocese consolidated offices and centralized administration, incorporating prevailing attitudes toward order and efficiency into church governance. These changes, which mirrored the organizational restructuring implemented by the national church in 1919, generally earned the approval of the prominent laymen who served alongside members of the clergy on the standing committee and other important diocesan bodies. Many of these laymen were drawn from corporate ranks themselves and recognized the benefits of placing the diocese on more businesslike lines.[23]

In addition to his strengthening diocesan authority through administrative restructuring, Rhinelander also emphasized the bishop's pastoral authority within the diocese. He saw himself as a defender of the Church's theological teachings and traditions. Although he resisted the temptation to push for greater theological unity among the parishes of the diocese, he made it clear that certain religious doctrines could not be compromised. He was especially adamant in his defense of the creed, which he saw as the essential point of theological unity for all Episcopalians. Rhinelander's firm stance was, in part, a response to "higher criticism," Darwinism, and other early twentieth-century challenges to religious faith, but it also reflected his changing attitudes toward diocesan politics. Though he allowed parishes to maintain their high or low church orientations in their style of worship, he would not allow divergent views on those doctrinal matters he deemed essential to the faith.[24]

Rhinelander was particularly adept at finding ways to promote his vision for the diocese and bring others into agreement with his policies. In addressing lay and clerical delegates at the annual diocesan conventions, he communicated clear goals for the work of the Church in ways that his predecessors had not. Rhinelander was also instrumental in launching the *Church News of the Diocese of Pennsylvania* in 1912. Known simply as the *Church News*, the monthly newspaper served as the official voice of the diocese (and loyal defender of Rhinelander's policies). To win the support of the clergy, particularly the younger generation, Rhinelander took an active role in the affairs of the Philadelphia Divinity School.[25] A former seminary professor himself, he encouraged the junior clergy of the diocese to meet regularly for theological discussions and greater sociability, occasionally inviting them to his own residence.[26]

Those opposed to Rhinelander's program of diocesan renewal and accustomed to weaker episcopal leadership accused him of being a "Romanizer" and did so with such frequency that he was forced to defend himself publicly. At the 1919 diocesan convention, he refuted the charge by reaffirming his commitment to lay leadership in the diocese.[27] This may have reassured some of the delegates, but even those sympathetic to the goal of "building up" the diocese regretted the division that "unity" seemed to be creating. Indeed, after hearing Bishop Rhinelander speak at the diocesan convention a few years before, one rector commented in his diary that "the Bp. preached once more on his favorite theme, Unity within the Diocese. The more he preaches, the further we seem to become separated."[28]

Rhinelander recognized that diocesan unity would not be accomplished through administrative reform alone. It also required that individuals look beyond their parochial loyalties and identify more closely with the diocese and the Episcopal Church as a whole. He was particularly interested in promoting a creed of personal service, the other half of his "one great whole," by cultivating a class of leaders among the laity who would serve as the Church's ambassadors to wider society. Living one's faith, he believed, entailed fulfilling public obligations to church, community, and nation. This message resonated powerfully among the social and economic elite since it conformed to their own patrician attitudes, including their commitment to demonstrate moral leadership as the "best element" in society. It also corresponded with the waning of low church evangelicalism and the rise of the Social Gospel within the Episcopal Church during the late nineteenth century, which brought with them a shift in the central emphasis of active faith among Episcopalians, from cultivating personal morality to promoting civic responsibility and social influence.[29]

Among those who exemplified this creed of personal service was Charles Custis Harrison, a devout Episcopalian and one of the leading voices of the city's patrician class. After a successful career as the head of his family's sugar-refining firm, he retired from business in 1892 to devote himself to his alma mater, the University of Pennsylvania, the training ground for the sons of the city's privileged class.[30] During his tenure at the university, both as trustee from 1876 to his death in 1929 and as provost from 1894 to 1910, Harrison stressed the importance of educated service to one's church, and the church's responsibility to cultivate leadership. In an 1898 report to the university, he suggested that influence, religious or otherwise, "trickles downward." If, as "representatives of all that is best in the intellectual life of the nation," he told his audience, "they shall be recognized as peers and companions and sympathetic coworkers with the best representatives of all that is noble in the national life and thought, then the influence of culture will be favorable to their ministry and will commend and dignify their service even to the uncultivated classes." His elitist message epitomized the type of "personal service" Rhinelander would later stress.[31]

Another leading proponent of the patrician creed was George Wharton Pepper, one of Philadelphia's leading legal talents, a respected U.S. senator, and a firm advocate of upper-class responsibility for good citizenship. He was also active in the life of the Episcopal Church, sitting on his parish vestry and representing the diocese as a lay delegate to the primary governing body for the national church, the General Convention, on numerous occasions. Pepper, whose uncle had preceded Harrison as provost of the University of Pennsylvania, believed that a true Christian "develops all the qualities of the good citizen and becomes the sort of fellow one covets as a companion. If he rejects the teaching, he shrivels spiritually and emerges as a social liability."[32] Like Harrison, Pepper championed civic leadership, moral duty, and other qualities already associated with the patrician upper class. For these two men and their peers, the Episcopal creed reinforced their class sensibilities, providing moral sanction for their dominant social position.

Although it is difficult to determine the degree to which the influence of the Episcopalian elite actually did trickle down to the lower classes in society, it is clear that upper-class Episcopalians successfully blended religious and class imperatives. They believed that they had a moral obligation to exercise public leadership and serve as models for emulation. The Church likewise affirmed upper-class identity as the "best sort" in society and commissioned them to go and make disciples of the same.[33] In this subtle form of evangelism, the goal was often subjective. Not even Bishop Rhinelander himself was able to meet the high standards that some members of the laity professed. Rev. Nathanael Groton recalled how two women in his parish "denounced the Bishop as well as the clergy, who, they said, were dragging the Church down to the level of the man on the street rather than lifting him up to its own high level!"[34] Despite the blatant Anglo-Saxon pretension and class bias of such sentiments, many upper-class Episcopalians truly believed they were setting an example of self-improvement for the other classes.

Rhinelander's call for diocesan unity and commitment to personal service pleased a great many of his flock, who were convinced of its merit. Nothing reflects this better than the support Rhinelander received upon proposing one of the largest undertakings in the history of the Episcopal Church in Philadelphia. With Episcopal cathedrals already under construction in New York and Washington, D.C., Rhinelander saw construction of a cathedral in Philadelphia as an opportunity not only to raise the profile of the mother diocese of the Episcopal Church, but also to bring its members together in support of one grand enterprise. The cathedral would provide a place for members of the diocese to worship together and establish a central campus for various diocesan offices and ministries.[35]

This proposal was more controversial than it might at first seem. Like other dioceses, the Diocese of Pennsylvania had originally refrained from naming a "bishop's church" because of the political implications of exalting ecclesiastical authority in the period following the Revolution. Having grown accustomed to a weak episcopate, local congregations throughout the nineteenth century generally opposed any action that would increase the bishop's real or symbolic power. Past proposals for a cathedral had met with widespread resistance among clergy and laity alike. Even diocesan leaders were ambivalent about the need for a cathedral. Bishop Whitaker, for instance, who had overseen the construction of "Church House" in 1894 as headquarters for diocesan offices, refused to consent to naming or erecting a cathedral, contending that "the Rectors and Laymen of the diocese preferred the existing distribution of work among the Parishes rather than centralization of it in and around a cathedral."[36]

By the time Rhinelander took office, however, popular sentiment had changed sufficiently to allow him to advance the case for a cathedral, which he knew would elevate the office of bishop by providing him and his successors with a majestic episcopal seat. He received some of his strongest backing from members of the social and financial elite, whose support was crucial to the cathedral's success. Many of the women active in the Cathedral League, for example, came from wealthy and distinguished families. They brought to the project the financial strength of many of the city's leading firms, including Curtis Publishing, the Drexel Bank, and the Pennsylvania Railroad.[37] Their male counterparts in the Cathedral Chapter were an equally distinguished lot. They wined and dined prospective donors and coordinated promotional campaigns. George Wharton Pepper, although better known for his support for the National Cathedral in Washington, D.C., championed the hometown project by composing a pamphlet entitled "The Evolution of a Cathedral" for distribution within the diocese.[38]

Knowing that many of the cathedral's most ardent advocates came from the upper class, diocesan leaders spoke with that audience in mind. When Bishop Garland, Rhinelander's successor, addressed cathedral supporters in 1924, he did not hide the fact that the cathedral was a prestige project for the city. He reminded his listeners that Philadelphia should have a cathedral as grand as those planned for Washington, D.C., and New York City. At the diocesan convention the following year, Garland again appealed to local loyalties. He reminded delegates that, as Pennsylvanians, their "vital interest" should be the Philadelphia cathedral. "The future of the Cathedral of the Diocese of Pennsylvania," he declared, "awaits the generosity of the Churchmen and Churchwomen who have vision and faith and financial means to make possible the construction of this enterprise for the greater glory of God and the salvation and refreshment and inspiration of the souls of men."[39]

It is likely that some Episcopalians in Philadelphia cared less about the cathedral's importance to the office of the bishop than they did about its social significance to their city and diocese. Many supported the project out of a sense of local religious pride. They believed that their diocese deserved a triumphant cathedral befitting its position as one of the oldest and most influential dioceses within the national church. According to the initial plans unveiled in 1927, the Gothic edifice would stretch a total length of 460 feet, with the larger of its two towers rising 279 feet above the transept crossing (fig. 9). It would be built on a 100-acre tract acquired in upper Roxborough, then a largely undeveloped area in the northwest section of the city, but near the geographic center of the diocese, with convenient access for both urban and suburban churchgoers. As "a permanent center of diocesan life," the cathedral complex would eventually include a bishop's house, deanery, administrative offices, schools, and other diocesan institutions, making it the symbol and source of diocesan unity and manifestation of service.[40]

Despite their efforts and enthusiasm, members of the diocese never succeeded in building their cathedral. The diocese may have been wealthier and more unified than ever before, but planning delays and other insurmountable problems took their toll. Ground for the cathedral was not broken until 1932, when the Great Depression was drying up diocesan resources. Even though the project was scaled back, the diocese still attempted, with little success, to erect a building characteristic of its 1920s prosperity. By the time it decided in

Fig. 9 Model showing proposed Cathedral Church of Christ of the Diocese of Pennsylvania. Only the circled portion of the cathedral was completed before the project was abandoned. Photo courtesy of St. Mary's Church, Cathedral Road, Philadelphia.

the 1960s to abandon the project and convert the land to other uses, only the Lady Chapel and deanery had been built.[41]

The failure to complete the cathedral, however, did not detract from the project's significance to the diocese and the Church at large. The plans embodied the collective mentality of church leaders and their most ardent supporters. During the early twentieth century, the Episcopal Church possessed the wealth, influential membership, and confidence that allowed it to embrace such a triumphal vision. Like their counterparts throughout the country, those in the Diocese of Pennsylvania believed that the Episcopal Church needed houses of worship befitting its status within the nation's religious life. Cathedral building was not simply an architectural exercise; it reflected and reinforced Episcopalians' conviction that they were the nation's religious establishment, charged with the responsibility for bringing the nation together in prayer, worship, and shared religious destiny. The cathedral was to be not just a diocesan institution, but a "house of prayer for all God's people," a unifying force in American religious life.[42] It reflected a theological and social vision that situated the Episcopal Church at the height of the nation's religious hierarchy.

Establishment Ambitions

The success of the Episcopal ascendancy required not only denominational unity and adherence to a creed of personal service among the elite. It also demanded that Americans of all creeds recognize Episcopalians' moral leadership and status as the nation's religious establishment. The Episcopal vision needed to filter into popular perception, allowing the Episcopal Church to function as a dominant force in the nation's religious and cultural life. The successful evangelizing of others to the Episcopal ethos ultimately rested on the Church's ability to bind itself more closely to the nation and assume a custodial role over its spiritual heritage, with projects that tangibly demonstrated the Church's mission to serve as the nation's moral guardian and guide.

By the early twentieth century, Episcopalians in the Diocese of Pennsylvania had come to believe that they belonged not just to a national church, but to an *American* church, destined to unite the country in a common faith and safeguard its spiritual welfare. As Bishop Rhinelander declared in 1918 to members of the diocesan women's auxiliary, "We are the most national church of the country, the hands that drew up the Constitution, being the hands of Churchmen, and we have a national responsibility to unify the church of America."[43] To him and his audience, the Episcopal Church and its members were the religious foundation upon which the nation was built, and the wellspring of American virtue.

Philadelphia's importance to the revolutionary struggle and the founding of the nation made it easy for local Episcopalians to insert themselves into the national saga and claim responsibility for planting the seeds of the national spirit. Within the Diocese of Pennsylvania, this emergent historical sensibility was most clearly articulated at two churches—historic Christ Church in Philadelphia and the Washington Memorial Chapel at Valley Forge—where the nation's past came to be celebrated and sanctified under Episcopal aegis. At these two sites, members of the diocese crafted a vision of the Episcopal Church's role in the nation's religious life, a vision they would present to the American public and one that would inspire Episcopalians not only to demonstrate their spiritual leadership, but also to transcend their parochial divisions and theological disputes.

Central to the success of this nationalistic enterprise was the appropriation of patriotic symbols and imagery within ecclesiastical space. The design and decoration of the Washington Memorial Chapel and Christ Church made the connection between the Episcopal Church and the nation visible in profound ways. As scholars of church architecture have demonstrated, church buildings embody and broadcast ideals, constituting texts that can be read by those who visit or worship.[44] With national heroes enshrined in stained glass and statuary, the message of these two sanctuaries was unmistakable. Ceremony and pageantry further reinforced the link between church and state integral to the establishmentarian ethos. The liturgical revival that had taken hold within the Episcopal Church during the late nineteenth and early twentieth centuries enabled Christ Church and the Washington Memorial Chapel to function as important ritual spaces for the celebration of the nation and its history.[45]

Christ Church, located just north of Independence Hall, has a long and revered history. It was founded in 1695 as the first Anglican congregation in Philadelphia and soon became the spiritual home for many important families in the city. Construction of the stately Georgian redbrick building was started in 1727 and completed in 1744, with the addition of the tower and steeple a decade later. When revolutionary fervor struck the city, the congregation was split between those supporting Independence and those loyal to the Crown. Although it survived the war, Christ Church found itself in a tenuous position, with reduced membership, severed ties to its spiritual leadership in England, and little to distinguish itself from other parishes in Philadelphia. Fortunes began to turn, however, when William White, the first bishop of Pennsylvania and leading force behind the establishment of the Episcopal Church, chose Christ Church as his episcopal seat in 1787. For much of the nineteenth century, the parish enjoyed a place of esteem in the diocese.[46]

By the late nineteenth century, faced with neighborhood transition, declining membership, and rising debt, Christ Church had again fallen on hard times. Needing to find new life and renewed purpose, the parish looked to its past to secure its future. In 1894, the rector and vestry of the church solicited donations for a series of six memorial windows that would "represent events in the history of the church from the life of Christ through the founding of the Anglican and then Protestant Episcopal Church."[47] Installed over the span of four decades as financing was secured, the windows included several scenes from the Revolutionary era, a clear sign that Christ Church was affirming its role in the history of American Independence. Of particular note were the lower panels of the "American Window" (1908; fig. 10) and "Liberty Window" (1925). The first depicted patriots seated for worship in Christ Church, while the second, based on an 1848 painting by Tompkins H. Matteson, an artist known for his historic canvasses, showed a minister from Christ Church, Rev. Jacob Duché, leading delegates to the first Continental Congress in fervent prayer.[48]

Throughout the early twentieth century, parish officials regularly invoked Christ Church's historic importance. During World War I, the vestry invited the city to prayer at the "Patriots' sanctuary" and vowed to support the war effort "in the spirit of the Revolutionary Fathers who knelt in this sanctuary." In conjunction with the nation's sesquicentennial in 1926, the parish

Fig. 10 The American Window, Christ Church, Philadelphia. The upper panel depicts prayer at Jamestown, Virginia; the lower shows patriots at worship at Christ Church. Photo by Will Brown. Courtesy Christ Church, Philadelphia.

unveiled a tablet commemorating the seven signers of the Declaration of Independence buried at Christ Church. The ceremony, which was attended by many of the city's leading citizens, allowed the parish to showcase how it helped to nourish the founding fathers' moral convictions. That same year, the diocese prominently featured Christ Church in a brochure entitled "Spiritual Sources from which Signers Drew Their Inspiration" that was distributed at the Sesquicentennial Exposition held in the city. The diocese also displayed a model of Christ Church at their exposition booth, allowing visitors to "look in through the roof to observe the pew where Washington and other patriots worshipped."[49]

Although such expressions of patriotic sentiment ignore the loyalist convictions of many colonial Anglicans and the once-pervasive fears among non-Anglican colonists about the appointment of a resident bishop, they attest to the fact that the Episcopal Church's historic ties to England had ceased to be a liability by the early twentieth century.[50] Indeed, the triumphant Anglo-Saxonism of the early twentieth century enabled Christ Church and other Episcopal congregations to celebrate both their English roots and their American birthright. Other Protestant denominations may have had a less ambiguous relationship with the Revolution, but the Episcopal Church's ties to initial colonial settlement, as seen in the American Window's depiction of prayer at Jamestown, strengthened its claims to be the true embodiment of the national spirit.

As Christ Church rediscovered its colonial heritage in the early twentieth century, an Episcopal minister by the name of W. Herbert Burk sought to erect a "wayside chapel" to honor the memory of George Washington at Valley Forge. He first articulated his plans to his congregation in February 1903.[51] His sermon "Washington the Churchman" presented an image of the commanding general as a pious Episcopalian and loyal churchman. In keeping with dominant religious influences of the time, Burk's Washington was both manly and devout, a model for laymen in the Church. Burk also transformed Washington into a proponent of private piety and public devotion, although it was known, even in Burk's day, that Washington had deist sympathies and was ambivalent about public expressions of religious devotion.[52]

Undaunted, and like his co-religionists at Christ Church, Burk mined history to discover a usable past. He found several minor episodes in Washington's life to make the case for his churchly loyalties, including Washington's Anglican ancestry and his education by members of the clergy. To prove that Washington practiced his faith, Burk described a time when Washington used the funeral rite from the Book of Common Prayer to preside over the burial of a fallen British soldier. He also pointed to Washington's involvement at a local parish in Virginia, although he could not confirm that Washington was a formal communicant. Throughout his sermon, Burk encouraged his congregation to reflect on Washington's "character" and "influence," and to look with gratitude upon the man who did not fear to infuse his public life—and by extension the nation's—with a spirit of religious devotion. Burk's efforts reflect the emergence of a patriotic "civil religion" in the late nineteenth and early twentieth centuries, when, according to historian Michael Kammen, "an increased number of people turned toward history as a source of inspirational value."[53]

A consummate promoter, Burk skillfully marketed his vision. To recast Washington as a loyal churchman and to convince the public of his devout faith, Burk used the diocesan newspaper to advertise his memorial chapel project, and popularized a fictitious story of Washington kneeling in prayer amid the snow at Valley Forge that appeared frequently in devotional periodical literature of the day.[54] He also wrote feature pieces about his work at Valley Forge for local and national publications. After his death, Burk's wife published a history of Valley Forge and the chapel that preserved Burk's vision of the life of Washington and praised his dedication to preserving Washington's religious legacy.[55]

The best promotional piece, however, was the chapel itself (fig. 11). Although Milton B. Medary Jr., one of Philadelphia's leading architects, designed the building, Burk was solely responsible for setting out how Washington would be commemorated in the chapel's plan. In the end, he created a striking, yet peculiar, space. Everything in the Gothic sanctuary, from the graceful arches to the intense reds and blues of the stained glass windows, evokes spiritual power, but, all along the nave, where one might expect to find statues of saints, biblical scenes, or images of the divine, there are instead depictions of Washington, or images evoking the revolutionary struggle. The great window above the chapel's main entrance depicts thirty-six scenes from the life of Washington from his baptism to his final days at Mount Vernon, while the windows flanking the nave display various patriotic figures whose lives demonstrated the virtues of the young nation. The flags that hang in the sanctuary, the carved soldiers who stand guard over the choir stalls, and the numerous dedicatory plaques found throughout the chapel likewise all pay tribute to the Revolution. Only in the small chancel does one find traditional Christian imagery.

In his plan for the chapel, Burk intentionally blurred the line between the sacred and the secular by elevating the figure of Washington to saintly

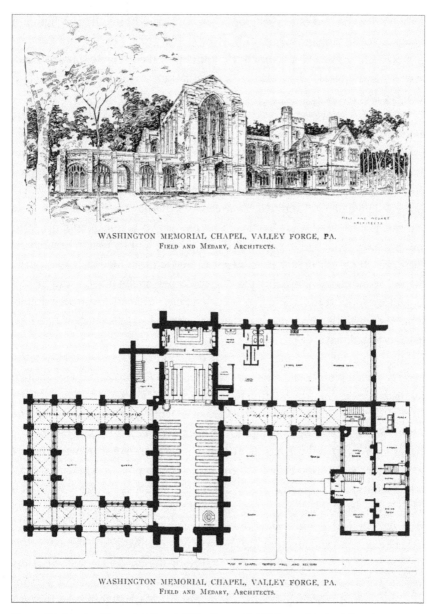

WASHINGTON MEMORIAL CHAPEL, VALLEY FORGE, PA.
FIELD AND MEDARY, ARCHITECTS.

WASHINGTON MEMORIAL CHAPEL, VALLEY FORGE, PA.
FIELD AND MEDARY, ARCHITECTS.

Fig. 11 Washington Memorial Chapel, Valley Forge. *AIA/T-Square Yearbook* (1907), 99–100. Photo courtesy of the Athenaeum of Philadelphia.

extremes. He created a didactic space in which the story of "Washington the Churchman" could be preserved, displayed, and revered. As historian Lorett Treese has argued, "at a time when the park commission was offering no active interpretation of the Valley Forge experience," the chapel allowed revolutionary history to be "distilled and promulgated in conformity with the tenets of the Protestant religion, then considered the official religion of America by its largely Protestant leaders."[56] The project might more appropriately be described as a distinctively Episcopalian enterprise since its effectiveness and appeal relied on the denomination's theological emphasis on imagery and ritual.

The chapel, however, proved easier to envision than to erect. From the time ground was broken in June 1903, the project was chronically in deficit despite Burk's constant efforts at fundraising. He placed appeals in the diocesan newspaper, sought money from Sunday school children, and issued "founders' certificates" for those who contributed to the project.[57] But when, ten years after he first outlined his dream, the money to make it come true had not materialized, Burk realized that he needed to solicit support from the two sources he had left untapped: the diocese and its wealthy members. His pride stung twice, he had to admit to himself that his modest "wayside chapel" required more funding than he could personally muster, and he had to petition support from church leaders who had originally expressed doubts about the feasibility of his plan to establish a parish in what was then a remote, sparsely populated area.[58]

In 1913, a group of laymen under the direction of Thomas J. Garland, the suffragan bishop of the diocese, took an interest in the project. Their first step entailed transferring the title of the property to diocesan trustees "so that no matter what might be the character or intention of some vestry in the future, the chapel property could not be alienated or mismanaged." From the diocesan point of view, it was likely that mismanagement fears were more a present than a future concern, given Burk's still-unproven financial skills.[59] When Charles Custis Harrison first surveyed the chapel site, he wrote that it was a "scene of desolation," and commented that "nothing of importance had been accomplished there except the endowment of the pews."[60]

Harrison, who had just retired as provost of the University of Pennsylvania, quickly became the most important figure of the chapel's new leadership. A skilled and socially connected fundraiser, Harrison soon raised or personally contributed more than $200,000 for the project, or more than thirteen times the $15,000 that Burk had collected in the previous decade. Lorett Treese has suggested that Harrison's interest in the Valley Forge chapel was a reflection of his fascination with history and his wife's involvement in the Colonial Dames, one of the patriotic societies supportive of Burk's efforts.[61] Supporting the chapel was also a matter of family pride since Harrison could trace his lineage to the Custis family of Virginia, which counted Martha Washington among its ranks through her first marriage to Daniel Parke Custis.[62]

More significant, perhaps, Harrison and Burk both believed in the positive influence of religion in public life. As his leadership at the University of Pennsylvania attests, Harrison sought to inculcate a patrician creed of personal service among the rising generation. With his "trickle-down" theory of religious influence, Harrison may well have found a convincing religious role model in Burk's Washington, who, like Harrison himself, believed that it was the patriotic duty of the elite to set a religious example for the nation.[63] For Harrison and other members of his patrician class, religion was not a private matter. From their education at elite academies affiliated with the Episcopal Church or other respectable denominations to their participation in proper society, they were socialized to witness publicly to their faith, support the work of their church, and demonstrate moral rectitude.[64]

Even though their strong wills were known to clash over financial and administrative matters, Harrison and Burk were of one mind on the place of the Episcopal Church in the nation's life. Neither doubted that the Episcopal Church embodied American virtues and was therefore best suited to establish the national shrine at Valley Forge. Through their financial support, Harrison and other donors endorsed Burk's plan to erect an "American Westminster," a "House of Prayer large enough for all who gather there, beautiful enough to inspire all who enter it, great enough to be the Nation's symbol of thankfulness to God for his manifold gifts, and comprehensive enough to embrace all the children of God in its service of prayer and praise."[65] Such sentiments not only reflect a sense of collective purpose among the leading class of Episcopalians, but also attest to their establishment mentality. In equating Valley Forge to Westminster Abbey—the resting place of English monarchs and shrine to the English people—they claimed guardianship over the nation's spiritual heritage like their counterparts in the Church of England.

True to Burk's vision, the Washington Memorial Chapel has become an important public theater for the celebration of the connection between God and country. It hosts special patriotic services throughout the year and remembers one of the fifty states or the District of Columbia in prayer every Sunday. Indeed, the chapel has become so successful in cultivating its image as a shrine to military heroism and the founding of the nation that many visitors fail to realize that it remains an independent Episcopal congregation. It sits on privately held land within what has since become Valley Forge National Historical Park, and has never been affiliated with, nor supported by, the national government in any official capacity.[66]

Christ Church has trod a similar path. During World War II and immediately after, Christ Church promoted itself as the "nation's church," proclaiming a truly expansive view of its vocation. As an ongoing part of its mission, the parish opens its doors to various patriotic societies, hosts special services on days of national importance, and works to raise awareness of the nation's foundational religious principles. Congress designated Christ Church a national shrine in 1947, and, two years later, the church entered into a formal relationship with the National Park Service. The parish continues to operate as an independent Episcopal congregation, but with an extended mission to preserve and interpret the nation's history.[67]

Across the country, other Episcopal churches have blended ecclesiastical and national history with equal aplomb. St. John's Church in Washington, D.C., has come to call itself the "Church of the Presidents" in celebration of the fact that every president since James Madison has attended services there. Boston's Old North Church professes its role in the struggle to secure liberty and freedom. The National Cathedral, however, probably serves as the clearest symbol of the religious authority of the Episcopal Church. Episcopalians are generally recognized as being the first to establish a national church in the capital, obtaining a charter from Congress in 1893 for the project. Its proponents viewed the National Cathedral as the fulfillment of the "national house of prayer" envisioned by George Washington and Pierre L'Enfant when they laid out the district.[68] At the time, only the Episcopal Church had the theological capacity, organizational structure, financial strength, and social vision to plan and execute such a monumental enterprise. Roman Catholics, Presbyterians, and members of several other denominations would later establish their own national churches in the capital, but none would match the status of the National Cathedral.[69]

In its ability to glorify American history and enshrine national heroes in its ecclesiastical space, the Episcopal Church became a leading force in the cultivation of a national "civil religion," the force that binds people in loyalty to the state.[70] Sites like Christ Church and the Washington Memorial Chapel show how the Episcopal Church successfully glorified both God and country. Ironically, the dual theological heritage of being both Protestant and Catholic that had previously caused tension within the Episcopal Church now provided a source of strength. Episcopalians conformed to the tenets of the Protestant tradition, yet possessed a Catholic lexicon that enabled them to articulate the universality of their mission. They understood themselves as not simply one denomination among many, but as America's national church, responsible for the spiritual care of all its citizens.

The United States has never had an established religion, but by the early decades of the twentieth century, many Episcopalians had come to think of themselves as the religious establishment. Even without the benefit of official state recognition, they assumed the duties and privileges that establishment status entailed, convinced that the Episcopal Church best embodied the virtues and principles upon which the nation had been founded. They believed it was their mission to unite all people in faith and to ensure that the United States forever remained a Christian nation. Proudly bearing the mantle of religious leadership, they made themselves moral arbiters for the nation and custodians of its spiritual heritage.

The history of the Episcopal Church in Philadelphia reveals how a religious minority came to possess a commanding influence in the nation's religious life. In the early twentieth century, Episcopalians were arguably the leading voice within mainline Protestantism, even though they were far from the most numerous denomination. As a national religious body with a clear hierarchical organization, the Episcopal Church had a unique ability to speak on behalf of the nation. Through its close association with the financial and social elite, the Episcopal Church was also able to cultivate a powerful leadership class that could represent its interests. Under Episcopal auspices, the elite advanced a patrician creed that conformed to both their religious and their class sensibilities. They supported the Church's mission, recognizing that their own status benefited from the prominence their Church accrued.

Ultimately, however, power and status proved not as secure as they had once seemed. In the class-charged atmosphere of the progressive era, members of Philadelphia's social and religious establishment would find that the union of economic and moral authority did not go unchallenged, not even within their own ranks. Both Quakers and Episcopalians of the upper class would struggle to preserve their spiritual capital during the 1910s and 1920s as religious reformers advanced new social creeds and held the elite accountable to their own professed ethical standards. And though the elite would not be deposed, their sterling reputations would lose some of their luster.

6

Confronting the "Money Interests"

On Sunday, 20 June 1915, Rev. George Chalmers Richmond preached a sermon in defense of Professor Scott Nearing, who had been dismissed from
the Wharton School faculty the preceding Monday, when the trustees of the
University of Pennsylvania had simply informed him, without explanation,
that they would not renew his teaching contract for the forthcoming academic year. At first glance, it may seem odd that Richmond, the rector of
St. John's Church, a humble parish in one of the city's poorer neighborhoods,
and an outspoken critic of the "money interests" that dominated the Episcopal
Church, should advocate on behalf of an academic dismissed from the faculty
of a prestigious university. Yet Richmond saw a deep kinship between himself
and Nearing: both had been mistreated by the city's social and economic elite,
whose moral standing both had questioned. Although the "Nearing case" has
been widely studied as one of the earliest tests of academic freedom in the
country, most accounts overlook the religious tensions that gave rise to it:
Nearing's progressive message challenged not only the university trustees'
dominant social and economic beliefs, but their religious self-image as well.
"I have known for years," Richmond declared, "that the same forces which
have desired my deposition from the ministry in the Episcopal Church have
also been seeking Nearing's downfall." And, indeed, a few short months later,
Richmond was brought before an ecclesiastical court for the first of a series of
trials that would lead to his suspension and eventual defrocking.[1]

The Nearing case and the Richmond trial might easily have remained internal institutional affairs. But in the class-charged atmosphere of the progressive
era, they captured public interest and drew attention to the union of economic
and religious interests that had come to dominate affairs in Philadelphia—and

indeed the nation. Authority rested locally in the hands of an elite class that, by virtue of pedigree and prowess, controlled the city's principal social, financial, educational, and religious institutions. Many of the same university officials who pushed for Nearing's dismissal were leading laymen of the Episcopal diocese, whose considerable influence in denominational affairs Richmond assailed. They viewed themselves as a patrician class with the moral sanction to exercise their authority.

As the two intertwined controversies engaged the members of Philadelphia's Episcopal establishment, currents of social reform were also stirring up tensions within the city's Quaker community. In 1917, the Yearly Meeting of Orthodox Friends established a "Committee on Social and Industrial Problems," whose task it was to study the social and economic conditions of the day. Although the committee's initial charge was limited to the "consideration of social questions," its members soon felt compelled to go further. Sensing "the seeds of war in our own social order," they committed themselves to investigating the ways in which traditional Quaker principles could be reinterpreted and applied to the needs of contemporary society. Led by Morris E. Leeds, the "Social Order Committee," as the committee came to be known, pushed for inclusion of a new paragraph to the *Advices* and for adding a line to a "social query" in the Quaker *Discipline*. The proposal was modest but nonetheless unsettling to those Friends who came under its moral scrutiny. The history of the committee's actions demonstrates the dangers inherent in challenging established orthodoxies.[2]

Taken together, these three developments not only call attention to the moral fervor that energized progressive activists; they also reveal the ways in which religion structured class authority and how members of the social and financial elite responded to the currents of social reform moving through society during the early twentieth century. Richmond, Nearing, and Leeds may not have been the most prominent voices of reform in the city, but they struck at powerful nerves. In their individual crusades, they met with concerted resistance from the city's elite not simply because they challenged labor laws, advocated for the redistribution of wealth, or investigated social conditions, but because they called into question the elite's sense of moral certitude and patrician self-image. By grounding their arguments in accepted church teachings and approved religious tradition, they sought to hold members of the social and religious establishment accountable to their own professed beliefs. As Ken Fones-Wolf and other scholars of the era have noted, religion was a contested sphere, able both to support and to challenge the class order. Spiritual capital was at stake.[3]

Yet, going further, the actions of Richmond, Nearing, and Leeds were all the more threatening because of their ability to confront the elite within their own religious assemblies and hallowed halls of learning. Their efforts signaled not only an effort to influence moral discourse, but also to control the very soul of two institutions—church and university—that shaped the establishment's moral vision, sustained their conception of the social order, and served as sites for the "cultural reproduction" of their upper-class values. Given the stakes, the threat was too great to be ignored. Members of the city's ruling class therefore mobilized to shore up their authority. Yet, even though Nearing and Richmond were ultimately silenced and Leeds had limited success in amending Quaker discipline, their actions breached the establishment's religious bulwark and chipped away at the moral foundations upon which elite authority rested.

The Richmond Trial

George Chalmers Richmond came to Philadelphia with impressive credentials. A graduate of Yale University, in 1903 he was ordained as an Episcopal minister in the Diocese of Central New York by Bishop Frederic Dan Huntington, a proponent of the Social Gospel and leading force behind the formation of the Church Association for the Advancement of the Interests of Labor. Prior to his ordination, Richmond had served as Huntington's private secretary, a post he retained until Huntington's death in 1904. His career took him to Syracuse, New York City, and Rochester, before he accepted a call in 1909 to serve as rector of St. John's Church in the Northern Liberties district of Philadelphia.[4] One of the oldest parishes in the diocese, St. John's had seen its fortunes fall as an influx of poor Catholic and Jewish immigrants changed the religious and economic character of its neighborhood. Not many ministers would have been eager to serve a declining congregation in the heart of a poor industrial district, but Richmond, inspired by the example of Huntington and other proponents of Social Christianity, had come to Philadelphia with grand ideas of how the Episcopal Church could improve the condition of the working class. He supported the cause of organized labor, advocated for municipal reform and for investigations into economic conditions, and even spoke out against lynching when an incident occurred in a neighboring county.[5]

By enlisting the Church's influence to serve the poor and marginalized in Philadelphia, Richmond imagined that he could do for St. John's what his fellow clergyman, William Rainsford, had done at St. George's Episcopal Church in New York City, reviving a struggling parish and making it a center for neighborhood spiritual and social life.[6] Unlike Rainsford, however, Richmond did not have prominent financier J. P. Morgan as a generous benefactor. Nor was it likely that he ever would, given his penchant for antagonizing members of the upper class. Richmond first gained notoriety in 1911 when he publicly denounced John Jacob Astor IV for divorcing his wife and marrying his eighteen-year-old mistress.[7] The next year, he again commanded headlines when he described the sinking of the *Titanic* as a sign of divine retribution against Astor and "his crowd of New York and Newport associates[, who] for years paid not the slightest attention to the laws of church or state which have seemed to contravene their personal pleasures or sensual delights."[8] In the years that followed, he kept his name in the press by speaking openly about the "money power" that dominated both society and the churches.[9]

Whereas most clergymen labored with quiet resolve, Richmond seemed to court controversy. Invited in 1906 to preach in Stamford, Connecticut, and to address members of the city's Board of Trade, he infuriated many when he chastised employers for ignoring the needs of the "laboring classes" and criticized members of the clergy for being too far removed from the ordinary conditions "in which most of us must do our work." Later that year, in Rochester, he attacked the local political boss and a prominent brewer, two members of that city's Episcopal elite, for their greed and corruption. Warnings from his superiors seemed only to encourage him all the more, confirming in his mind the degree to which church leaders had become beholden to men of wealth and privilege and were conspiring against him.[10]

Nor did Richmond temper his tone upon his arrival in Philadelphia. In 1911, he openly opposed Philip Mercer Rhinelander's candidacy for diocesan bishop, finding him too conservative theologically and socially. Two years later, as quoted in the press, he criticized Rhinelander's handling of diocesan affairs and accused the bishop of being "under the influence of corporations." Charging that several leading laymen of the diocese had gone to Rhinelander to have action taken against him for his recent sermons, Richmond threatened to defy the bishop's rulings "till you break away from the corrupting and slothful combine which controls our ecclesiastical life."[11]

Richmond's public actions and confrontations with his episcopal superiors forced a diocesan investigation that led to a series of trials before an ecclesiastical court. In the most prominent trial, which ran from December 1916 to July 1917, Richmond was accused of conduct unbecoming a clergyman, and charged with violating his ordination vows.[12] Unable to afford a lawyer during the latter portions of the trial, Richmond served as his own advocate, examining and cross-examining witnesses, including himself. His behavior at trial was often erratic. On several occasions, he had to be warned against attacking witnesses testifying in his defense. At one point, he even claimed that its bishops had turned Philadelphia into the "diocese of [the] Anti-Christ."[13] During another exchange, he referred to Bishop Rhinelander as "Rehoboam," an allusion to the Old Testament king known, in Richmond's words, as "the most degraded man in the world, a liar, a villain, a thief, and whoremonger, and everything else."[14]

The lengthy trial transcripts give an impression of Richmond as an utter eccentric, a man with no regard for his future in the ministry. In reality, however, Richmond was far more shrewd. He knew the diocese had a difficult case to make against him. As Henry Budd, the chancellor of the diocese, stated in the "charge of the court," the canons that Richmond allegedly violated were unfortunately vague. They spoke only of "conduct" unbecoming a clergyman, not "actions," thus implying sustained behavior, rather than occasional misdeeds.[15] In addition, there was little clear evidence that Richmond had, in fact, violated his ordination vows since many of the accusations against him could be neither substantiated nor corroborated. Budd reminded the clerical "triers" how difficult it had been to find the "facts" of the case, and informed them that they could consider extenuating circumstances, including whether "the respondent believed that he was being hounded, spied upon, refused the ordinary right of access to his spiritual superior, [or] that members of his vestry were encouraged in tale-bearing while he was not even informed of what was brought against him."[16]

Richmond also had the support of some local clergy who were concerned about the diocese's treatment of one of their colleagues. One of the clerical triers, Rev. Fordyce H. Argo, considered it shameful that the diocese failed to provide Richmond with counsel, given the abundance of legal talent among its members. He saw Richmond as a representative of the many "humbler clergy" who found themselves "impotent in the presence of power and influence" within their own congregations and the diocese as a whole. He further viewed Richmond as a martyr at the hand of the new bishop, Philip Mercer Rhinelander, whose efforts to centralize diocesan authority had angered those who favored the established system of decentralized governance and greater clerical autonomy.[17] Yet, ecclesiastical politics notwithstanding, Rhinelander's testimony at trial raised doubts about his own personal integrity, especially when it emerged that he had allowed his advisors to dissuade him from meeting with Richmond as the duties of his office required. At the conclusion of the trial, Argo stated in his dissenting opinion that "there is guilt in this case—grave, moral and Canonical guilt, possibly criminal guilt, but it rests elsewhere than upon Mr. Richmond."[18] His words signaled that the trial had become as much a referendum on episcopal leadership and diocesan governance as on Richmond's own offenses.

For the diocese, the ecclesiastical trial came as a last resort. Those who opposed Richmond most likely did not wish to see him defrocked or deposed, simply silenced or sent elsewhere. Diocesan officials initially cautioned Richmond about issuing political attacks from the pulpit and tried to keep him isolated, as evidenced by Richmond's complaint at trial that Rhinelander and his predecessor had interfered with his personal relationships, attempting to restrict his contact with several younger members of the diocesan clergy. Although Richmond was a nuisance, church canons dictated that neither the bishop nor the diocesan convention had the authority to sever the relationship between a congregation and its rector unless some violation of church discipline were involved.[19] Accordingly, the ecclesiastical trial was the diocese's only available recourse to rein in a troublesome priest who held the loyalty of the majority of his parishioners. As Chancellor Budd reported, "Not a single member of Mr. Richmond's parish signed the presentment, and not a single member of any adjoining parish had anything to do with bringing on the trial."[20]

Sensing that he held the upper hand, Richmond took the opportunity to use the court proceedings for a bit of grandstanding. He felt no compunction in invoking inflammatory issues, such as the Episcopal Church's perceived support for the wealthy and disregard for the poor. He said that the only ones within his parish who opposed him were the "curbstone vestry," some of the wealthier men of the congregation who saw their position of authority within the parish as an inherited right rather than an earned privilege. Richmond claimed that these men had "never been among our workers" and had provided only meager financial contributions to the work of the church. He even accused one of "never allow[ing] the church or her religious interests to interfere with his business or social duties."[21] Though not the first rector to clash with his vestry, nor the last, Richmond could have been more tactful. Among the actions that brought him to trial was his use of the pulpit to attack some vestrymen for "financial irregularities" within the parish, a matter that could have been handled with greater discretion.[22]

Those who initiated proceedings against Richmond, however, saw more at stake than his relationship with his vestry. Had the problem been simply poor pastoral leadership, Richmond's troubles would likely have remained confined to his own congregation. In the end, his activities came to the attention of diocesan officials and prominent churchmen because he threatened to tarnish the Church's public image at a time when its members looked to claim the mantle of moral leadership for the nation. His critique of the "money powers" that dominated the Episcopal Church and his intemperate remarks about his ecclesiastical superiors challenged the Church's establishmentarian ethos and cast doubt on its worthiness to assume religious and cultural leadership. Among those named during the trial as having expressed concern to the bishop about Richmond's suitability for the ministry were many prominent laymen well known within diocesan circles for their involvement in church governance and support of Rhinelander's policies, including banker Francis A. Lewis, industrialist J. Vaughan Merrick Jr., and lawyer George Wharton Pepper. To Richmond, these men and other members of what he had called "the corrupting and slothful combine which controls our ecclesiastical life" were invested not in truth and justice, but in the protection of their own status and reputations. He claimed that the bishop had turned against him, choosing to bow to the wishes and self-interested advice offered by those men of influence who had his ear. But, as Richmond had earlier declared in a letter to Rhinelander, "no combination of corporate lawyers, financiers and social aristocrats can do my thinking for me, or tell me what I can preach and what I can't."[23]

To members of the Episcopal establishment, Richmond's denunciations were more than the sputterings of an overzealous cleric. They were a stinging attack on their own self-image, and a failure to appreciate their valuable contributions to the work of the Church and its social mission. The Merricks, for instance, were the principal benefactors of St. Timothy's Church and Hospital in the Roxborough district of the city. They also supported St. Timothy's Workingmen's Club and Institute, which provided a library and other recreations for those employed in the local mills.[24] J. Vaughan Merrick Sr., a successful industrialist whose father had been the first president of the Pennsylvania Railroad, was particularly proud of his role as founding member of the national Free Church Association, which advocated for the elimination of pew rents in the Episcopal Church.[25] His son, J. Vaughan Merrick Jr., inherited his father's religious commitments. He was active in diocesan affairs and served as a trusted counselor to several bishops.[26] The Peppers were an equally distinguished clan. George Wharton Pepper was a leading churchman who served as a delegate to the General Convention and regularly bore public witness to his faith throughout his legal and political career. His cousin William Pepper served as provost of the University of Pennsylvania for many years, helping to strengthen the school's Episcopalian spirit.[27]

Having witnessed firsthand the struggles of the working-class poor, Richmond insisted that patrician pleasantries did little to remedy the ills of industrial society. Speaking before the Convocation of North Philadelphia in 1912, he insisted that more needed to be done. In "A Vision of What the Episcopal Church Might Do," he called on his listeners "to get into line with other churches around us and grapple with the social and industrial problems which concern ordinary men." Among the reasons he cited for the Episcopal Church's failure to support the "war for better wages" and other vital struggles of the age was that its leadership had come to stand "with wealth and luxury." Their prophetic voice had been silenced by their desire to preserve class privilege and maintain social respectability. In his address, he singled out the bishop of New Jersey, John Scarborough, as an example of one deaf to the pleas of labor. At the trial, Richmond recounted a conversation with Scarborough over dinner in 1910, shortly after the Philadelphia streetcarmen's strike had erupted in violence. Richmond claimed that the bishop had commented to him privately that, "the working man should know his place, and keep it, and if he doesn't like what's given to him, let him get out and hustle for himself."[28] To Richmond, such comments captured the Church's defense of privilege and callous disregard for the plight of the working class.

When questioned at trial about the charges he leveled against the bishop and the propriety of publicly criticizing members of the episcopacy, Richmond asserted that, though he did not "attack individuals as a rule," he and other religious leaders had a duty to speak on public issues and to question those in power.[29] Such assertions made Richmond a danger to those members of the city's elite who relied on the Episcopal Church and its representatives for moral approbation. For that reason, diocesan officials needed to ensure that Richmond would not become a representative figure. Indeed, when Richmond became involved with the Central Labor Union—the group responsible for the 1910 streetcarmen's strike—he was asked by the bishop to state publicly that he represented only himself, and not the diocese or the Church in any official capacity. Richmond, however, brazenly announced in response that he represented something bigger than the Episcopal Church—"humanity."[30]

Although the ecclesiastical trial ostensibly arose in response to allegations of clerical misconduct and addressed canonical procedures for the removal of a minister from office, those were not the issues that ultimately mattered. The case garnered attention because it brought to light the pervasive elite influences and unspoken class interests that dominated the Diocese of Pennsylvania and, by extension, the Episcopal Church itself. Richmond issued a stinging condemnation of what he perceived as the rule of wealth not only within the local diocese, but within the nation's religious life as a whole. At trial, he repeated claims he had made in a published sermon on the influence of "money power" on the Protestant churches, declaring that "the moral vision of the clergy [has] been restricted by the glare and glitter of present day advantage. Their mouths have been stopped continually by the power of special interests, vested rights and rich laymen who profess to have a great interest in the salvation of men's souls."[31] To Richmond, nothing less than the Episcopal Church's moral credibility was at stake. If bishops and other ministers were beholden to the social and financial elite, they could no longer consider themselves servants of the Gospel. In a sense, Richmond turned the tables on his superiors, leveling against them the very same charge of conduct unbecoming a clergyman that they had brought against him: they, not he, were the ones who had abrogated their Christian duty and violated their ordination vows.

In the end, the various attacks, recriminations, and countless unsubstantiated claims that surfaced during the trial were more than mere bluster. Richmond's testimony resonated powerfully among those who believed the Church was indeed plagued by the overweening influence of its elite members and the complacency of its clergy. His treatment at the hands of his ecclesiastical superiors and leading laymen of the diocese simply confirmed existing suspicions. And even if church officials succeeded in discrediting Richmond, they could not do so without airing their dirty laundry in public. They found themselves in an untenable situation. Allowing Richmond to continue unchecked was to risk further scandal, yet attempting to censure or silence him would only fuel further speculation and appear to confirm his conspiratorial tales. Thus, whether they responded with action or inaction, they found themselves on the defensive, struggling to keep their house in order. The same trial that led to Richmond's suspension and contributed to his eventual defrocking dealt a considerable blow to the Episcopal Church's public image and moral authority. It turned the Church's close association with the industrial elite, something once viewed as an unmitigated asset, into a moral liability.

The Scott Nearing Case

For members of the Philadelphia social and religious establishment, the travails of the Richmond trial came on the heels of a much more public controversy at the University of Pennsylvania. In April 1915, the board of trustees declined to renew Scott Nearing's teaching contract for the forthcoming academic year.

Although the board's staffing decisions were normally of little concern to those outside the university community, this particular decision came under scrutiny because of the figure it affected. An assistant professor of economics in the Wharton School, Nearing had acquired a reputation for stirring up controversy. In his crusades against social injustices, he frequently lashed out against powerful men of affairs on whom the university relied for support, including members of the board themselves. In short, Nearing had become a liability to the university; his dismissal came to be seen as a reprisal for his indiscretions. Placing these classroom politics within their broader social context reveals that the case was not simply about the nature and limits of academic freedom. It was also an effort on the part of the university establishment to protect the class interests and moral authority of its members.

The case raised a number of troubling issues for the university. The board's decision angered the faculty, violating as it did the accepted practice of deferring to faculty recommendations on hiring and contracts. "It has always been tacitly understood," one faculty member asserted, "that when the professors of a department and the faculty recommended a man to the board of trustees, the board would not totally disregard such recommendations and fail to reappoint." The faculty acknowledged that the trustees had both the right and the obligation to dismiss individuals for good reason, but, in Nearing's case, they had given no such reason. The trustees' failure to explain their decision further angered the faculty and fueled speculation about the board's intentions. From the faculty's perspective, Nearing's dismissal was the "first move" on the part of the board "to assert its right to censor the opinions of men whom it has called or may call to membership in one of its faculties." An official from the Association of American Professors described it as "one of the heaviest blows that has been struck against academic freedom for some time." To him and others within the academy, the case carried national significance because it emerged at a time when many prominent institutions of higher education, the University of Pennsylvania among them, were in the process of reforming their curricula and institutional governance to meet the standards of the modern research university. Consequently, the Nearing case became a test of those new structures and relationships.[32]

Viewing events solely through the lens of faculty concerns about academic freedom, however, overlooks what else the trustees and their supporters understood to be at stake. Why the need to silence Nearing? On one level, they sought to protect the reputation of the institution entrusted to their care by removing a problematic professor. On a deeper level, however, they sought to protect their own class interests and moral authority from internal dissent.

Although Nearing was not a member of the city's social or economic establishment, his position at the University of Pennsylvania placed him within their walls of power. During the opening decades of the twentieth century, the university played a prominent role in upper-class life. It functioned as a crucial training ground for members of the Philadelphia elite and served as a site of their socialization into the city's leadership class. Through his classroom instruction and social advocacy, Nearing did more than challenge economic orthodoxy; he also threatened to disrupt a critical pathway for the cultural reproduction of upper-class values. More than simply denouncing the elite, he was undermining an institution responsible for much of their intellectual, social, and moral formation.

Little in Nearing's early years would have predicted his later radicalism. He was born into comfort in 1883 in north central Pennsylvania's Tioga County, where his grandfather ran a successful coal company, employing many of the hard-nosed managerial tactics typical of the era. Life in coal country was marked by extremes of wealth and poverty, but Nearing's family endeavored to insulate his siblings and him from exposure to its harsh realities. As part of the local ruling class, he and his family enjoyed "all the economic necessities, most of the comforts, and for the day many of the luxuries" of life, even though they were far removed from the nation's centers of power and influence. When Nearing was fifteen, his parents set up a residence in Philadelphia so that their children could have access to an "advanced education." Those years in Philadelphia marked a "crucial period of transition" in his young life, Nearing would write in his autobiography; they opened his eyes to the social conditions of the day.[33]

After attending one of the city's public high schools, Nearing entered the University of Pennsylvania in 1901. Upon graduation, he studied law for one year before transferring to the Wharton School, where he earned his doctoral degree in 1909. Nearing's autobiography speaks of his early frustrations with the social climate at the university, which was heavily influenced by the city's upper class and religious establishment. He was "repelled by the big business domination of the law and lawyers" there, as well as by the complacency toward corruption that marked Philadelphia politics of this era, most famously captured by Lincoln Steffens in *The Shame of the Cities*.[34] He found his university training "severely limited by the economic and social interests of those who founded and financed the institution [and who] supported the Establishment quite frankly and openly."[35] He had also grown disenchanted with the religious message he heard in the city, particularly Russell Conwell's "Gospel of Success," which seemed to him to turn religion into the bridegroom of "monopolistic capitalism."[36]

But the real change in Nearing's life came when he encountered Simon N. Patten, the chair of the economics department at the Wharton School and the school's director from 1896 to 1912. A brilliant scholar and charismatic teacher, Patten transformed the Wharton School's mission, recasting the classical discipline of economics into a "social" science. As part of a larger circle of reformers that included Richard T. Ely and Jane Addams, Patten advanced a progressive agenda guided by moral vision and pragmatic philosophy.[37] Under his leadership, the Wharton School developed a "practical reform-oriented curriculum" that included both courses on sociological theory and fieldwork that examined specific social and industrial problems of the day. During Patten's tenure, the Wharton School sponsored important sociological studies, such as W. E. B. Du Bois's *The Philadelphia Negro*, and pathbreaking economic investigations, such as those exposing the exploitative practices of Philadelphia's municipal utility companies.[38] As biographer John A. Saltmarsh argues, Patten "offered Nearing a way of reconciling progressive social science with the ideals retained from the moral universe of his youth." Or, in Nearing's own words, Patten turned him "from preaching to teaching."[39]

Nearing's first foray into social reform came in 1905, when he was named assistant secretary of the Pennsylvania Child Labor Committee. He threw himself into his new job, personally investigating child labor abuses across the state and speaking out against the union of political and industrial interests that allowed such abuses to persist. In 1910, the U.S. Census Bureau reported that child laborers accounted for 20 percent of all children between the ages of 10 and 15; the following year, Nearing authored a study on the topic, in which he argued that the solution to the child labor problem lay in ensuring that working men earned enough to raise their families "without some outside aid" and that children had access to proper education as an alternative to employment.[40] That same year, he issued a report presenting statistical evidence that "a large portion of American workmen are unable to maintain an efficiency standard of living."[41] In 1913, he directed his message toward the churches with the publication of *Social Religion*, which grew out of a series of talks he gave before the Friends' General Conference a few years earlier. Though his work may have lacked the theological sophistication of other proponents of Social Christianity, reducing religion to a creed of personal service, it succeeded in presenting economic concerns as matters of conscience. And though he had largely cut his ties with organized religion and the Baptist faith of his youth, Nearing retained an evangelical zeal, redirecting it toward the work of social reform.[42]

As Patten and Nearing brought new life to the Wharton School, they came into conflict with the university administration and the city's business elite. Their attacks on lax labor laws, industrial monopolies, corporate consolidation, and financial corruption appealed to progressive audiences, but not to Philadelphia's men of affairs. One local industrialist whom Nearing denounced for his opposition to state child labor legislation reportedly used his political connections to hold up a $1 million state appropriation to the university.[43] In their private discussions, university officials expressed grave concern that this shift in focus at the Wharton School would frustrate their efforts to attract the class of donors needed to help shore up the university's precarious finances, the result of ambitious expansion in preceding decades.[44] On one occasion, to illustrate a lesson on the "economics of distribution," Nearing contrasted a lavish dinner hosted by Edward T. Stotesbury (as reported in the press) with the conditions of the city's unemployed and working poor. One of the city's leading bankers and a member of the university's board of trustees, Stotesbury was incensed to be cast in such a "Dives and Lazarus" scenario. Given that Stotesbury's stepson had been in Nearing's class at the time, this "illustration" proved "academically suicidal." As historian Steven Sass has written, for Nearing, "the issue was no longer introductory economics, but sin and social salvation." It was shortly after this event that the trustees, in response to internal and external pressure, moved to dismiss Nearing.[45]

In the absence of any statement from the trustees, many potential explanations emerged for Nearing's dismissal. One popular story suggested that Nearing was dismissed for insulting the Episcopal Academy, one of the oldest and most prestigious schools in the city, and a major source of students for the university.[46] More reliable accounts reported that Nearing's dismissal had resulted from his advocacy of child labor reform and his "unorthodox" economic views. Although initially silent on the matter of his dismissal, Nearing would later admit in his autobiography that he had been warned that his teachings would land him in trouble.[47] That likelihood grew following the appointment of several new trustees to the board in 1910 and 1911, tilting its composition in favor of business and corporate interests. According to the *Alumni Register*, the restructuring placed those "who stand as an active force along education lines . . . in the minority."[48] The year before his dismissal, five out of fourteen members of the committee charged with reviewing his candidacy for an assistant professorship voted against him. In the end, however, the most convincing explanation is probably the simplest one: Nearing was, in the words of one observer, a "victim of the interests."[49]

The "interests" of the university trustees, administration, alumni, and others aligned against Nearing were sufficiently alike to bode poorly for him. As members of the city's social and professional establishment, the trustees and their supporters were committed to training their sons for positions in business, banking, medicine, and law. Faculty notwithstanding, there was little dissent to the board's decision: the only two trustees to oppose the decision were Wharton Barker and Harrison S. Morris, the nephew and son-in-law of Joseph Wharton, the school's founder. And even though Morris publicly defended Nearing's right to free speech, Morris's actions may in fact have been partly motivated by a desire to defy and embarrass members of the city's upper class for an earlier social snub.[50] The trustees also received the overwhelming support of the alumni, who maintained that the trustees had the right to determine the fitness of individual faculty members and to protect the public reputation of the institution. Indeed, apart from faculty members, few protested the board's decision. Among the notable few was Henry Budd, the diocesan chancellor who would preside over the Richmond ecclesiastical trial the following year, and who demanded that the trustees issue a public explanation.[51]

News reports focused heavily on Nearing's subversive economic and political views, largely overlooking the religious undercurrents of the dispute. His clash with the trustees came at a time when the university was in the midst of a religious revival. Concerned that they were failing in their duty to provide students with proper moral guidance, school officials sought to ensure that religion remained a vital part of the university's institutional character. Under provosts William Pepper (1881–1894), Charles Custis Harrison (1894–1910), and Edgar Fahs Smith (1910–1920), the "Quaker" university took a decisive turn toward the Episcopal Church. Though it had long maintained an informal association with the diocese, with bishops and prominent churchmen serving on the board of trustees, as Philadelphia's upper class consolidated around the Episcopal Church, university leaders began to infuse university life with the Episcopal creed.[52] As early as 1895, Provost Harrison envisioned a Gothic chapel as the centerpiece of the new campus dormitory quadrangle. Although it was never built, he believed that a strong religious presence would contribute to the mission of the university whereby "the moral life [would be] clarified and illumined, not only by didactic teaching, but by a very atmosphere of noble living; and the religious life made natural by having its scope and opportunities in students' services and students' worship."[53] In 1914, just one year before the Nearing case, Provost Smith sought to reinstitute mandatory chapel attendance for all students, although he later relented in response to protests from Jewish and Catholic leaders who objected to the Protestant orientation of the ostensibly nonsectarian services.[54] George Wharton Pepper, one of the few trustees to speak publicly about the decision to dismiss Nearing, had several times addressed the dangers of secularized education. In the wake of the Nearing case, Pepper contended that free speech did not give an individual license to advocate "a disregard of moral principles regarded by the rest of us as fundamental."[55]

Indeed, it was the fundamentals that were in dispute. The tensions between Nearing and the trustees stemmed in no small part from their divergent views on the proper role of religion in public life and their efforts to advance two competing moral discourses. As representatives of the Episcopal establishment, the trustees espoused a patrician creed, whereas Nearing championed the Social Gospel. Indeed, through his classroom instruction and social advocacy, Nearing challenged the moral authority of the city's ruling class and threatened its hold on the moral imaginations of the students entrusted to the university's care. The fact that Nearing received the support of many of his students became a troubling sign of intellectual upheaval. The trustees worried that the proliferation of radical doctrines would alienate influential alumni and dissuade parents from sending their sons to the school, a fear borne out by enrollment statistics that indicated that only about one-quarter of young men from the city's "ruling social group" had been electing in recent years to attend the University of Pennsylvania.[56]

The clash of religious views exhibited itself perhaps most clearly in February 1915, just months before Nearing's dismissal, in his protestations against the decision of university officials to invite Billy Sunday to address the student body as part of Sunday's evangelical crusade in the city. In a letter to Sunday that was reprinted in one of the local newspapers, Nearing chastised the great revivalist for his moralizing and hypocrisy; he urged him to abandon his "theological pleasantries" and to address the "truths" of "exploitation and social injustice" among the working-class poor. Like Richmond, Nearing saw the prophetic voice of religious leaders silenced by their connection to special interests. Nearing challenged the revivalist to recognize that "the well-fed people, whose ease and luxury are built upon this poverty, child labor and exploitation, sit in your congregation, contribute to your campaign funds, entertain you socially, and invite you to hold prayer meetings in their homes. These are they that bind grievous burdens on men's shoulders."[57] University officials and other members of the Philadelphia establishment saw things differently, however. They supported Sunday, as historian Ken Fones-Wolf has suggested, because his message encouraged the cultivation of personal piety and Christian service without calling into question the prevailing social order. Sunday had come to Philadelphia at the request of the city's leading industrialists in order to quiet labor agitation and promote, in the words of Alba Johnson, the president of Baldwin Locomotive, "purity, modesty, contentment, and thrift."[58] To Nearing, the university's refusal to allow Samuel Gompers, the nation's foremost trade unionist, to speak on campus the following month offered final confirmation of their social agenda and disregard for academic debate.

In the end, Nearing was terminated, not only "because he dared to advocate industrial and municipal reforms inimical to the private interests of millionaire members of the board of trustees," as George Wharton Pepper explained, but because he struck at the moral underpinnings of upper-class authority by reinterpreting religious obligation. Even worse, he had the audacity to do so within the elite's own hallowed university grounds, where he had the potential to subvert the entire local establishment by clouding the minds of their sons with new economic and social doctrines. Like Richmond, who rightly regarded him as a kindred spirit, Nearing sought to strip the patrician class of its mantle of moral authority. However unrelated the Richmond trial and the Nearing case might seem at first glance, both forced the city's elite to defend their spiritual capital.

The Social Order Committee

Despite their small numbers in the early twentieth century, Quakers commanded an unrivaled degree of moral authority in Philadelphia, especially in economic and business affairs, where they maintained a reputation for personal probity and commitment to fairness. No other religious community had made financial responsibility so central to its faith or monitored the economic conduct of its members so closely.[59] Quakers viewed the marketplace as an arena where moral decisions were made, and they sought, through their example, to promote virtue within the economic sphere. Among the manifestations of this Quaker commitment was the Wharton School itself. Established in 1881 through the benefactions of the prominent Quaker industrialist Joseph Wharton, the school's mission was defined by policy guidelines Wharton himself incorporated within its deed of trust. In addition to providing students with a course of study in classical economics and political philosophy, he required that the school espouse and advance a body of principles derived from Quaker teachings on wealth and business. In keeping with the

Society of Friends' established proscriptions against gambling and speculation, for instance, Wharton instructed that the school teach the "immorality . . . of seeking to acquire wealth by winning" and "the necessity of rigorously punishing by legal penalties and by social exclusion those persons who commit frauds, betray trusts, or steal public funds, directly or indirectly." He believed that a sound business education would prepare "young men of inherited intellect, means, and refinement" to "manage their property . . . while husbanding it to benefit the community." For Wharton, commerce was to serve as a sphere of religious witness, and his decision to establish his school at the University of Pennsylvania rather than Swarthmore College—the local Quaker institution on whose board he had served—reflected his desire to bring the Society's values to bear on the broader community.[60]

Yet as the nation's industrial economy reached new heights in the early twentieth century, some within the Quaker community began to express concern that Friends had grown complacent—or at least less vigilant—in maintaining their ethical standards. Reflecting on Philadelphia during those "unforgotten years," essayist Logan Pearsall Smith claimed that members of the Quaker business community seemed only faintly interested in applying their religious principles "to the treatment of their employees." For them, "business was business; it was a world apart, without the slightest relation to the Heavenly Kingdom."[61] Others within the Quaker community were less concerned about the abandonment of principles than about how Quaker teachings might be applied to the new economic realities. Did the rise of corporate capitalism and the new imperatives of the mature industrial order demand a fundamental rethinking of Quaker practices? How might peaceable relations be maintained in large firms, as once they had within family enterprises? How might the Quaker community monitor the financial practices of its members as partnerships grew into large industrial concerns with increasingly complex financial arrangements?

These and other such questions weighed heavily on the mind of Morris E. Leeds when he gathered with twelve other Orthodox Friends on 9 April 1917 as part of the Philadelphia Yearly Meeting's newly established "Committee on Social and Industrial Problems." Leeds and his colleagues took their inspiration from the example of the London Yearly Meeting, whose members had been propelled by the shockwaves of war to renew their moral witness on social and economic matters.[62] Their goal, as outlined in their statement of principles, was to determine "the part which the religious Society of Friends should take in the present day application of efforts to promote the kingdom of God on earth particularly as it relates to social, political and industrial conditions."[63] Although this effort hardly seemed radical, the committee's history reveals just how controversial the call for renewal could be. The established order had its defenders.

The initial goals of the Social Order Committee were rather modest. Members limited their agenda to the "consideration of social questions," without committing themselves to any specific course of action.[64] Initial meetings focused on establishing procedures and setting priorities. Over the course of the year, the committee formed subcommittees and working groups to address particular areas of concern. While Leeds and fellow industrialists Bernard Waring and Henry T. Brown focused on business problems, other members of the committee investigated agricultural issues, women's concerns, and educational reform. As part of their investigations, they commissioned social surveys and sent out questionnaires to fellow Friends. They also met regularly to discuss their findings, exchanged information with other Quaker communities, and disseminated reports to local meetings to increase awareness of their work. In true Quaker fashion, the committee took measured steps. They had no intention of diving into a program of social reform without having first assessed the situation, gathered facts, and studied their findings.[65]

The Social Order Committee served as part of a much larger Quaker response to the tremendous social and economic change brought about, on an immediate level, by the First World War, which roused Philadelphia's Quakers from their quietism and complacency, spurring them to reaffirm their commitment to the "peace testimony" and other Quaker teachings,[66] and, on a broader level, by the currents of reform that had been flowing through the United States and Europe during the progressive era. Morris E. Leeds, in particular, had become a student of transatlantic reform. After completing his education at the Westtown School and Haverford College, two venerable local Quaker institutions, Leeds had traveled to Germany in 1892 to pursue graduate studies in engineering. During his time there, he was inspired by the work of Ernst Abbe of the Carl Zeiss Optical Works in Jena, where he witnessed for the first time the possibilities of industrial welfare programs. Upon his return to Philadelphia, Leeds applied these ideas to his own professional affairs, and, as early as 1908, he began to encourage other Quaker employers to do the same.[67]

Leeds's own reformist vision combined religious and technocratic strains of progressive thought, the product of his Quaker upbringing and his professional training. A birthright Friend, Leeds was born in 1869 in the Germantown district of Philadelphia, a Quaker stronghold. Though nurtured within the Orthodox branch, he was part of a rising generation of Friends less interested in perpetuating those old divisions. Like many other men coming of age in the late nineteenth century, he sought opportunity in the industrial professions. After his studies in Europe, he returned to Philadelphia, where he found employment at the manufacturing firm of James W. Queen & Company. Through the financial support of members of the local Quaker community, Leeds established his own firm, Morris E. Leeds & Company, in 1889, later joining with a partner in 1903 to establish Leeds & Northrup, which specialized in the manufacture of precision instruments. Inspired by the example of Zeiss and progressive employers, including the Quaker Cadburys and Rowntrees in England, Leeds embraced the notion of welfare capitalism and made his company a pioneer in profit sharing and cooperative employee governance. Sustained in his commitment to improving workplace relations by his strong Quaker convictions, and wary of those elements in society calling for revolutionary change, Leeds had begun early in his career to formulate a religious response to the problems of the industrial order. Thus, in a speech before a gathering of Friends in 1909, he drew on traditional Quaker teachings on the management of wealth to argue for its more "equitable distribution."[68] Leeds's cautious remarks reflected his attempt to develop an authentically Quaker response to the social and industrial problems of the day.

Leeds insisted that reform required more "self-controlled, self-governing, high-souled people, prepared to enter intelligently and unselfishly into the world life."[69] He and other members of the Social Order Committee therefore attempted to reconnect Quakers of the present generation with the radicalism of past generations, inviting them to consider anew how they were to live out their espousal of spiritual equality, dedication to peaceable relations, and commitment to simplicity. The committee was concerned that Quakers had become too complacent in their social responsibilities and had grown lax in their commitment to maintaining the Society's distinctive—and demanding—practices. Writing to recent college graduates in 1919, the committee remarked how the Society "on the whole … has accepted the prevailing social and industrial standards" of the day, allowing the desire for material acquisition to supplant the spirit of service. It challenged these young Friends to use their "spiritual, moral and intellectual advantages" to support the committee in its reform efforts and to place themselves in the company of those Friends who labored "to recognize and abolish certain great outstanding evils."[70] By invoking the history of past Quaker witness, the committee sent a clear message to its fellow Friends: their abandonment of social activism was nothing less than an affront to their spiritual heritage.

The committee's efforts to awaken a renewed commitment to Quaker testimonies quickly revealed its radical potential. As committee members studied social conditions and searched their souls, they came to the conclusion that the causes of war and social discord were rooted in the inequalities of the industrial order and the capitalist system. Christian duty, therefore, required more than the mitigation of ills in times of crisis, but a fundamental reordering of economic relations to prevent future conflict. If Friends were sincere in their desire "to promote the Kingdom of God on Earth," the committee forthrightly asked in its report to the Yearly Meeting in 1919, then "are we not also ready to pronounce un-Christian a social order which withholds from the masses of mankind those means to a self-respecting life which we so highly prize?"[71] The following year, in the wake of the bitter strikes and widespread industrial turmoil that seized the nation, the committee spoke more directly to the need for the "right ordering of wealth" and urged Friends to support opportunities for "workers to participate or to be heard in the management of industry." Doubts lingered as to whether industrial capitalism could "be stripped of its abuses and made to serve a beneficent purpose," but the committee remained confident in the value of their work and Friends' willingness to reexamine their personal and corporate practices.[72]

Even though the committee had yet to endorse any specific reforms, the introspection it invited could be unsettling in and of itself. In 1918, it had commended to the Yearly Meeting five points for Friends' consideration, asking them to ponder "a sympathetic study of the condition of labor and the causes of poverty"; schemes for the democratization of industry; the nature of their financial investments; their commitment to simplicity; and "the daily practices towards all of that sympathy and good-will which is more than indiscriminate kindliness."[73] Two years later, the committee circulated a questionnaire among its members, asking them to give their views on specific economic issues, ranging from tax policy and wage rates to unemployment insurance and collective bargaining. The responses were not preserved in the committee's records, but one can imagine how members wrestled over these issues, especially the ones that seemed to call for greater government intervention in economic affairs and labor relations.[74]

Given the privileges that many Quakers enjoyed, not all were anxious to reassess the Society's teachings on social responsibility and economic morality. Many saw no reason to alter the methods and principles that had served them and the Quaker community so well in the past. Members of the older generation, in particular, were reluctant to disrupt the status quo and question those ethical formulations which had enabled them to see themselves as faithful to their Christian duty in business and finance. One member of the Business Problems Group admitted his own difficulty dispelling the "feudalistic notions" ingrained in him by his father and seeing "industrial matters with the eyes of the worker."[75] Even those sympathetic to the work of the committee called for caution. Writing to their fellow committee members in 1919, Harold and Sylvia Evans expressed concern that "experiments along the lines of democratic control and minimum standards" carry great risk and "if not successful, may seriously injure or totally wreck his business." Given the moral implications of bankruptcy, the couple had reason to be wary of the consequences of even the most well-intentioned industrial reforms.[76]

Quakers' conservative outlook on social and economic matters can also be attributed to the occupational composition of the religious community. As the twentieth century wore on, fewer and fewer Quakers had direct, firsthand experience with the industrial economy and the plight of labor. According to a 1920 census conducted by the Philadelphia Yearly Meeting (Orthodox), only 2.5 percent of respondents identified themselves as wage earners (laborers). More than one in four were involved in business either as owners or managers (10.4 percent) or as salaried workers (17 percent). Others worked in education (4.6 percent), the professions (6.5 percent), or agriculture (6.8 percent). The remainder were either non-wage-earning housekeepers (27.9 percent) or persons living on income (26.8 percent), such as students, the elderly, and an undisclosed number of "gentlemen."[77] Although many of these individuals may have been generous in their charity and sympathetic to social reform, those who enjoyed the fruits of prosperity were presumably also heavily invested in the economic status quo.

Convinced that the "tremendous problems before us" required nothing less than the "sympathy and co-operation of every member of our Yearly Meeting," Leeds and other members of the Social Order Committee were determined to formalize their work and make ethical reflection part of the official "queries" and "advices" found within the Quaker *Discipline.*[78] After an extended period of study and deliberation, the committee began to prepare its proposal. In an initial version, members of the drafting subcommittee amended three of the existing eight official queries and added a ninth. This version was rejected by the committee as a whole, however. The reason was not recorded, but it likely stemmed from the extensiveness of the subcommittee's changes and the pointed language of the proposed new social order query. Calling on Friends to "understand the social and industrial conditions of the day" and to embrace service, the new query challenged them both to consider the extent to which "your own standards of living, and opportunities [are] within the reach of your employees" and to assess the willingness "to surrender your own advantages in order that others may have greater opportunities to develop themselves for service."[79] Some committee members might have viewed the language as too condemnatory or as demanding more sacrifice than many Friends would be comfortable with.

The committee's revised proposal, forwarded to the appropriate representative bodies within the Society, was significantly softened in tone; it left existing queries largely unchanged, but added a line to one that asked Friends to consider whether they "were endeavoring to carry out the principles" indicated in the new, and more cautious, paragraph the committee proposed for inclusion in the *Advices*:

> Let us remember that as followers of Christ we are called to help in bringing the Kingdom of God upon earth. May our sense of brotherhood with all men be strong, leading us—as workers, as employers, and in all our relations—to make the chief aim of our lives service rather than gain. May it inspire in us a deeper sympathy with those whose development is stunted by meager income, insufficient education, and too little freedom in directing their own lives. May it lead us not only to minister to those in need but to seek to understand the causes of social and industrial ills and to do our part, as individuals, and as a Society, for their removal.[80]

The revised proposal still called on Friends to work for the elimination of social ills, but it shifted emphasis from sacrifice to service. In addressing both workers and employers, it also eliminated the assumption of Quakers' privileged status within the industrial order that could be sensed within the initial proposal, which spoke only of Quakers in their role as employers.

The Yearly Meeting in 1922 accepted the committee's new paragraph for inclusion in the *Advices* with only minor changes in language, but it rejected the line the committee proposed to add to the queries. Still, the inclusion of a social order statement within the *Advices* carried great moral force, placing it before Friends for their consideration alongside their other testimonies.[81] Moreover, the committee also succeeded in having a lengthy social order statement incorporated in the more discursive sections of the *Discipline*. Speaking extensively and more freely about the problems of industrial society and the need for both moral and structural reform, the statement called on Friends "to surrender some of our rights of property" and chastised employers who pursued self-interest without proper regard for the common welfare. It even encouraged cooperative workplace governance and accepted as legitimate a state role in the regulation of wages as paths to industrial peace.[82]

Even with these gains, however, it remained up to individual Friends to reassess their economic conduct or alter their managerial practices. Members of the committee could, at best, lead by example, as Morris Leeds did through his efforts to promote industrial democracy and implement a profit-sharing plan within his own firm. As the 1920s wore on, the committee continued to study industrial conditions, commission reports, host discussions, circulate literature, and raise awareness about the problems of the social order, though it did little to speak to those outside the Quaker community. But for all the committee's efforts at changing the perspective of the Society's own members, it sometimes seemed that Quakers were more interested in the conversation than in its conclusions.

Although the Social Order Committee may have played a relatively minor part in the history of social reform in the United States, its significance for members of Philadelphia's Quaker community was considerable. The committee's actions reveal the determined efforts of one segment of Orthodox Friends, the smaller but wealthier of the two branches, to reconsider the ethical demands of Quaker teachings and hold members of the religious community accountable to their professed beliefs. Inspired by the rich reform tradition of British Friends, the committee sought to stir members of the local Quaker community from their complacency and help the Society reclaim its moral voice, particularly in the economic sphere. By conducting investigations, fostering discussion, and securing the addition of a new social order statement to the *Advices*, it sought to have Friends wrestle with the moral obligations of their own wealth and status and consider anew how they could contribute to the betterment of society. By steering discussion in new directions and unsettling old orthodoxies, it placed new demands on the Quaker conscience and made it more difficult for those in positions of economic authority to rest comfortably within the industrial order. Those who wished to claim moral legitimacy within economic life and business affairs were called to do more than simply uphold their fiduciary responsibilities or maintain a commitment to fair dealings. They had now to weigh the imperatives of structural reform and contend with economic disparity. The integrity of the economic order that sustained their status stood in greater doubt.

When all was said and done, it would seem that the reform campaigns led by Morris E. Leeds, George Chalmers Richmond, and Scott Nearing ultimately did little to change prevailing social structures or alter the overall course of affairs. For all the energy these three figures released, they offer a lesson in the limitations of progressive-era reform, in the inherent difficulty of supplanting existing orthodoxies and displacing an entrenched elite determined to preserve its social and religious authority. In the years following the First World War, members of the Protestant ruling class stood at the pinnacle of their social, political, and economic power. The Episcopalian elite, in particular, enjoyed the fruits of religious and class unity, employing their collective might to extend their influence in local and national affairs. They preserved their place atop the social order and credited themselves for the nation's return to normalcy and economic prosperity.

Yet whatever their limitations, the three campaigns should not be construed as insignificant. Had they been, they would not have garnered the response they did from members of the city's ruling elite. Indeed, the fact that those in power felt the need to stifle proposed reforms and silence the criticism directed against them clearly indicates that they felt the stakes too great to ignore. By dismissing patrician bromides for the nation's ills and preaching a new social creed, Richmond and Nearing clearly posed a threat to members of the Episcopal establishment accustomed to hearing only affirming voices in church pulpits and university classrooms. Morris E. Leeds and members of the Social Order Committee conducted their affairs more quietly, but their actions were no less unsettling for those Friends who felt justified in their professional conduct and financial dealings. Those who adhered to established testimonies did not welcome efforts to amend Quaker teachings, especially when they called for substantial structural reforms within the capitalist system, the wellspring of their wealth and status. Adding to establishment anxieties was the distinctive nature of these three campaigns. In contrast to many other crusades of the era, whether led by labor organizers, socialist agitators, or populist preachers, all three campaigns attacked the moral foundations of class authority from within the very institutional structures which the elite themselves had customarily expected to command. And the leaders of all three campaigns held positions that carried authority and demanded a degree of respect, which explains their opponents' urgent need to remove them from their posts or, in the case of Leeds, to substantially temper his influence.

Taken together, these campaigns helped awaken the Philadelphia establishment to the fact that, even though religion could be used to preserve social values, it could also be used to challenge the established order. As progressivism and Social Christianity reached full tide in the 1910s and 1920s, members of the ruling class, long accustomed to conforming their lives and actions to the moral standards they themselves defined, suddenly found themselves held accountable to new ethical norms and having to defend religious conceptions that seemed so certain and absolute not too long before. They discovered just how tenuous and problematic the union of religion and wealth could be. And, as we shall see in chapter 7, their religious communities would come to this same realization at much the same time. The churches and congregations that had come to rely on industrial wealth for their own prosperity discovered that their good fortunes came at a price.

Changing Fortunes

Writing to his congregation in early 1927, Rev. George H. Toop, the rector of Philadelphia's Episcopal Church of the Holy Apostles, made a rather unusual appeal. He encouraged parishioners living at a distance from the church to purchase automobiles so that they might more easily travel to services. He even promised to employ a man to patrol the street on Sunday mornings and keep an eye on the cars while their owners were in church. As automobile ownership increased during the 1920s, some church leaders had argued that the allure of country rides, weekend getaways, and other excursions would, quite literally, drive people from their religious observances. Toop, however, viewed the convenience and comfort of travel by motor car as a welcome advance, one that promised to help individuals remain active in the life of the church since physical distance would no longer be an impediment.[1]

Yet for all its hopefulness, Toop's message conveyed an air of desperation. Ever since he assumed the rectorship of the church in 1914, Toop had watched his parish rolls decline steadily, as more and more families left for newer residential districts on the city's suburban periphery. This out-migration, a trend that predated Toop's arrival, had slowly hollowed out the congregation, which once boasted one of the largest Sunday schools in the city. Nevertheless, Toop was confident that, once freed from travel constraints, many who had left the parish neighborhood would "insist on keeping their membership" in the congregation out of "affection for the old church." Aware that the problems of residential mobility extended well beyond his own congregation, he believed that increased automobile ownership promised "help in solving the attendance problem of centrally located churches." Though also aware that automobiles would be no panacea for

Holy Apostles's ills, he saw no harm in attempting to lure back the scattered members of his flock.[2]

However trivial it might seem, Toop's effort to turn automobile ownership into a moral obligation speaks to the institutional challenges confronting religious communities during the early twentieth century. The theological battles and moral crusades of the era may have garnered greater media attention, but they were in many ways less critical to the lives of ordinary churchgoers and their pastoral leaders than routine concerns over maintaining healthy membership rolls and sound balance sheets.[3] Toop spoke for many congregations in voicing concern about declining church attendance and demographic shifts. Thinking beyond the plight of his own congregation, he recognized that the consequences of the dramatic social and economic transformations of the period extended across the ecclesiastical landscape, threatening not simply the vitality of individual churches, but the integrity of the entire denominational order that had taken shape during the industrial era. As upwardly mobile families withdrew from older neighborhoods, taking their financial resources with them, they weakened the social and financial foundations of the religious institutions that earlier generations had built as monuments for the ages. Congregations that could not attract new members often had little choice but to close or relocate, even if it meant abandoning those communities most in need of their presence and ministry, an act considered by some to be an unconscionable abrogation of religious mission.

Toop was far from alone in his broader concerns. During the 1910s and 1920s, a growing number of theologians, social scientists, and church officials challenged the prevailing optimism of the industrial era. Drawing on personal experiences, community studies, and the lessons of history, they offered a less sanguine assessment of the nation's spiritual health. Among the most influential were H. Richard Niebuhr and H. Paul Douglass, who, respectively, marshaled theological and sociological evidence to alert church leaders to the troubling disparities present within American religious life. Despite their disciplinary differences, each called attention to the unforeseen perils of prosperity that affected the nation's churches.

These critics confirmed what had already become painfully apparent to many local church leaders who saw the effects that internal class divisions and growing economic inequalities had come to have on their religious communities. While Toop contended with the consequences of his parishioners' geographic mobility and sought strategies to reverse the decline of downtown congregations, others struggled to bridge social divides. Persistent apprehension about the existence of "class churches" reflected a prevailing concern about the character and composition of religious communities. For churches that professed theological inclusivity, the pervasive social exclusivity of the time was cause for scandal, spurring efforts to eliminate pew rents and other obstacles to cross-class unity. The pastoral problems of wealth and the particular religious anxieties that emerged during the era of industrial prosperity would force churches to reckon with the unintended consequences of their own success.

Class Composition

In the early decades of the twentieth century, class divisions within the nation's religious life were unmistakable. Distinct social hierarchies existed within and among denominations, particularly in urban areas where churches and congregations reflected the diverse religious, ethnic, and social composition of the population. Like membership in other organizations, religious affiliation contributed to an awareness of class status and social position by situating individuals among their peers and separating them from those they deemed superior or inferior. Although churches had the potential to unify individuals across class lines, they more often than not patterned and reinforced social divisions, accelerating a trend evident in older urban communities since at least the antebellum period.[4] In Philadelphia, as elsewhere, patterns of social and financial patronage allowed "fashionable" churches and denominations to distinguish themselves within the local religious marketplace. Among the industrial elite, Sunday morning services were social showcases, as the well-dressed streamed in and out of their equally well-appointed churches. The society pages further publicized the spectacle, ensuring that everyone knew where the wealthy and prominent worshipped and wed. The class boundaries that delineated religious communities were often starkly drawn.

These trends elicited no shortage of commentary within local religious circles, where many spoke of the superficiality of religious devotion among the well-to-do. In June 1928, a minister writing for the *Presbyterian* introduced his readers to the little-known sin of "club-icity," declaring it "common knowledge that there are many who consider membership in the Christian church on the same plane as that of belonging to a recognized club. In it one finds a few congenial friends, a warm room, comfortable seats, and a little entertainment." Speaking before the annual convention for the Diocese of Pennsylvania in 1921, Bishop Philip Mercer Rhinelander announced that the problem of church extension and missionary outreach would never be solved until "the rank and file of our people have forever ceased to regard their Parish Church as a 'reluctant Sunday Morning Club.'" In his diary, Quaker Joseph S. Elkinton preserved a newspaper clipping from 1890 that spoke of Protestant churches as "pleasant and fashionable Sunday clubs, where wearied business men have their intellectual palates tickled once a week with good music, good society, and soothing reflections on life, and death and judgment." Even more sharply, the famed Baptist preacher Russell H. Conwell denounced wealthy congregations who built grand churches for use a few hours each Sunday, only to leave them "shut up all the rest of the week." His neighbor on North Broad Street, Rabbi Joseph Krauskopf, criticized those Jews who shopped around for membership in the most fashionable synagogues. Whether directing their remarks toward members of their own flock or others, each saw a lack of sincere spiritual commitment or true theological conviction on the part of many.[5]

Although such criticism may not have been entirely new, the widening gap between rich and poor pervading all aspects of American society in the early twentieth century had caused more and more religious leaders to take notice of how their own communities had been affected. Mainline Protestant denominations that had focused on evangelization and outreach to immigrant groups and the laboring classes now cast a more critical gaze on the internal conditions that stood as obstacles to missionary outreach, church unity, and the flourishing of Christian society. Commentators from across the denominational spectrum began to speak with concern about the emergence of "class churches" and how their religious communities had become, in the words of one Presbyterian minister, "largely committed to the point of view of the possessing element."[6] Even if they did not always offer clear solutions to the problem of class divisions within their midst, those who spoke on the issue helped to transform the nature of debate. What was to others a social and economic concern had sparked in them a theological crisis. For those who believed that theological assent, not economic position, defined religious community, both the existence and the very notion of "class churches" were deeply troubling.

Among those who brought attention to this issue was H. Richard Niebuhr, a young theologian and educator, who saw Christianity and its message compromised by accommodation to the "caste system of human society." In his groundbreaking study *The Social Sources of Denominationalism*, Niebuhr challenged the accepted wisdom that attributed sectarian division to theological divergence. Rather, he argued that denominational rifts had always been conditioned by underlying social conditions, including divisions in wealth and status. Completed shortly before the onset of the Great

Depression, Niebuhr's work seemed to take a cue from the social realities of the industrial era. Drawing attention to the ways in which class interests and other social forces had influenced denominational development, it revealed the deep-seated obstacles to Christian unity. To those who shared Niebuhr's concern about the "ethical problems of denominationalism," class presented a particularly intractable problem.[7] For churches to deny the existence of class divisions made them seem blind to reality, yet for them to identify too closely with a particular class or social group left them beholden to those interests and limited their wider appeal. There seemed no easy way to respond.

In Philadelphia, perhaps nowhere were these tensions more evident than in the career and ministry of Russell H. Conwell, the driving force behind Grace Baptist Temple and founder of Temple College. Born in 1843 and ordained at age thirty-seven, Conwell, a native of Massachusetts, blazed onto the Philadelphia religious scene in the early 1880s, preaching a "gospel of success" to those struggling to find their place in the new industrial economy. Developing and honing his message over the course of more than four decades, he taught that the virtuous would be rewarded financially and lectured audiences on their "duty to succeed."[8] In his best-known sermon, "Acres of Diamonds," which he reportedly delivered more than 6,000 times over the course of his career in venues across the country, Conwell proclaimed that the poor had only themselves to fault for their poverty since opportunities for material success abounded.[9] Reflecting on his own congregation, he once claimed that in twenty-five years "there was not known to be a single member of that church out of work [for even] a month who desired a position."[10] Like other prophets of prosperity, Conwell defended the accumulation of wealth, insisting that "the sin is not in the having of money," but in not using it "for the good of mankind."[11] The popularity of his sermons and publications—with titles such as *Praying for Money* and *The Key to Success*—helped make his Baptist Temple the largest Protestant church in the country, at least according to his own estimates.[12]

By preaching to the aspiring classes about financial success as a sign of divine favor, Conwell tailored a message that effectively gave his blessing to the city's economic elite. His many sermons and public pronouncements declared his faith in the power of the capitalist class to better society. Among those he honored were John Wanamaker, the city's great "merchant prince," who promoted a similar version of the gospel of success, and Matthias Baldwin, founder of Baldwin Locomotive Works, one of the city's major employers, whose main manufacturing facilities were not far from Conwell's church.[13] As ones devoted to their faith who each rose from rags to riches, their biographies conformed nicely to Conwell's own theological narrative. Those who filled the pews of his church or attended his lecture tours may not have always shared Conwell's high opinion of the capitalist class, but he never failed to lavish generous praise upon those whose lives confirmed the existence of opportunity and proved the veracity of his religious message.

Yet, for all his rhetoric about success and his untiring faith in the potential for material prosperity, Conwell was conflicted about the place of the elite within society. He vacillated between adulation and excoriation. He heaped praise on the city's financial elite but lashed out against money interests; he extolled the virtue of the common man while wanting each to rise above the common condition. Convinced that the consolidation of wealth in the hands of the few had created an "American Aristocracy" inimical to democracy, he supported the promotion of an "aristocracy of genius" in which "every poor boy and girl [would] have an opportunity equal with the rich to obtain the highest education of the land."[14] To that end, he started offering night classes to a group of young men in 1884, the seed from which Temple University would grow. Neither an elite academy nor a charity school, it served those of modest means striving for self-betterment. In keeping with his own teachings about financial stewardship and social responsibility, Conwell reinvested a large share of his lecture earnings in the school. As he worked to build up the institution, he became his own most reliable benefactor.[15]

Conwell was equally uncertain about the place of the elite within church life. He was extremely critical of the vast wealth possessed by some churches, and he passed judgment in a 1922 sermon on the "many great churches costing hundreds of thousands of dollars to which only a few people go." Echoing those who promoted the income tax as a means of economic justice, Conwell went so far as to suggest a tax on churches. "It is not right," he contended, "that so much money should be locked up just for worship by a few people."[16] Yet, at the same time, he needed and actively sought upper-class financial support for his own religious and educational enterprises. Even though he loved his inspirational "History of the Fifty-Seven Cents," which credited the mite offering of a dying girl for establishing a foundation for the church's future prosperity, the history of his Baptist Temple tells a story of financial uncertainty.[17] Had it not been for a handful of generous benefactors, Conwell's grand plans might never have been realized. In 1886, when the congregation was preparing to erect its stately new Romanesque sanctuary on North Broad Street, they acquired a lot on generous financial terms from a supportive landowner. They likewise benefited from a $10,000 contribution from William Bucknell, a devout Baptist and wealthy real estate developer who had also contributed to the congregation before Conwell's arrival.[18] Though he denied his own dependence on the financial elite, Conwell never stopped courting them. He paid several visits to Anthony J. Drexel in search of financial assistance, claiming at one point that he was the one who had given Drexel the idea of establishing the Drexel Institute of Art, Science, and Industry.[19] Conwell even wrote to John D. Rockefeller, hoping that the oil baron's Baptist loyalties would inspire a large contribution. Though he once declared that "rich men . . . have never let themselves be interested" in his work, he consistently exhibited a keen interest in them.[20]

Conwell may have had his fair share of critics, including those who mocked his plans for the grand Grace Baptist Temple as "Conwell's Folly," but his ministry flourished in no small part because of his ability to read the city's social landscape, a skill he used to his advantage in building up his flock. Indeed, his accomplishments were nothing short of remarkable. He took over a struggling Baptist congregation in 1882 and catapulted it to prominence through his tireless labors. When the new church opened in 1891, standing-room crowds regularly packed the sanctuary designed with a seating capacity in excess of 3,100.[21] By the time of his death in 1925, he had secured his place among the city's leading citizens. An engaging speaker, Conwell responded to the spiritual yearnings of those who dreamed of financial security and upward social mobility. He tailored his message to individuals uncertain of their economic prospects and offered them the assurance that God would reward their faithfulness and hard work.

Yet Conwell also recognized that the very financial success he promised his followers could gradually undermine his ministry. Having attained their acres of diamonds, would they still flock to hear his message? As his own experiences revealed, the financial elite had little personal need for his theological teachings. Admittedly, the chances of achieving universal prosperity were exceedingly slim, but still he had to be careful in his praise of wealth not to unduly extol the wealthy. In his sermons and writings, he regularly denounced the aristocratic spirit that pervaded the nation and pointed to the shallowness of upper-class religiosity in order to affirm the moral standing of the common folk upon whom he relied for financial support. He sought the promise of wealth without its accompanying perils.

Some of these same struggles were shared by Conwell's neighbor, Rabbi Joseph Krauskopf of Keneseth Israel, Philadelphia's most prominent reform congregation. Founded in 1847 by a group of German-speaking Jews, the congregation grew steadily, drawing those attracted by its learned leadership and progressive theology. In 1890, it made plans to erect a new synagogue on North Broad Street, on a parcel of land adjacent to the Mercantile Club, a bastion of the city's German-Jewish merchants and manufacturers. The commanding Italian Renaissance structure, clad in Indiana limestone and flanked by a 150-foot tower modeled on the campanile at St. Mark's Basilica in Venice, stood just one block south of the new Grace Baptist Temple, adding to the ecclesiastical splendor of the neighborhood.[22] Despite their theological differences, Krauskopf and Conwell developed a long and lasting friendship, sharing both personal ambition and a commitment to civic engagement. Perhaps finding a common bond in their shared status as newcomers to the city, they actively supported each other's work in a spirit of interreligious cooperation.[23] Among the areas where they found common ground, their shared belief in opportunity and advancement stands out most clearly. One can detect more than a hint of Conwell's "Acres of Diamonds" mentality in Krauskopf's own thought, as seen in one letter in which he credited his accomplishments to his habit of never sitting "idle waiting for an opportunity to turn up."[24]

Although he shared Conwell's faith in material prosperity, Krauskopf understood even more acutely than his friend the social and pastoral challenges it posed. As members of the Jewish community struggled to situate themselves within the social order of industrial America, they found themselves vilified by non-Jews for being at once too rich and too poor. Among Philadelphians, this conflicted view of Jews can be seen in the writings of Elizabeth Robins Pennell, a respected author known for her biographies and travel accounts. In her 1914 work, *Our Philadelphia*, whose title evoked that of the nativist tract *Our Country* by Josiah Strong, Pennell lamented, in one breath, how the Old City neighborhood of her childhood had become "a slum, captured by the Russian Jew" and, in another, how Jews had forced their way into the schools and professions that had "been looked upon as the sacred right of certain Philadelphia families for almost a couple of centuries."[25] For her and many others, Jewish poverty was a problem and Jewish affluence a threat.

In the face of such prejudice, Krauskopf became an ardent apologist for the Jewish community and relied on his congregation to demonstrate the potential for social advancement and cultural assimilation. He knew from personal experience both the obstacles and opportunities of the era, having emigrated from Prussia in 1872 at age fourteen and having worked as a store clerk before entering Hebrew Union College, an emergent center of the reform movement within American Judaism. Though a staunch defender of Jewish identity, he rejected a "slavish adherence to dead form [that] clashed with the spirit of modern thought" and sought to free Judaism from its association with the ghetto, whether in Europe or urban America.²⁶ When he assumed leadership of Keneseth Israel in 1887, he recognized both the enormous responsibility and the benefit of his new position. With the financial commitment of many of Philadelphia's most prosperous Jewish families, his new congregation offered resources, visibility, and reach his previous congregation in Kansas City, Missouri, lacked.²⁷ Connections with those families would prove crucial to Keneseth Israel's success, as well as his own, and so he worked tirelessly to cultivate them. Over the years, Krauskopf and other congregational leaders actively courted those whose membership would enhance the congregation's prestige. In 1920, for instance, upon hearing that Lessing J. Rosenwald, the son of Sears, Roebuck president Julius Rosenwald, would soon be moving to Philadelphia, Krauskopf wrote to encourage him to join the congregation. "It would mean a great deal for us to have a man of his prominence associated with our congregation," Krauskopf confided to Ellis Gimbel, the head of one of Philadelphia's leading department stores, in an effort to enlist his help in the recruiting effort. He knew who counted, and he welcomed any whose connection might prove beneficial, including non-Philadelphians and members of the nouveaux riches.²⁸

Yet despite the affluence of many of the congregation's members, Krauskopf's efforts to raise its social profile, and the emergence of a more cohesive and visible Jewish upper class centered in the area, Keneseth Israel did not define itself as an elite congregation. Rather, its members viewed themselves as the embodiment of middle-class virtue and distinguished themselves from those who sought only to enrich themselves. In 1922, at the banquet celebrating the congregation's diamond jubilee, members expressed their sense of class identity in a series of verses written for the occasion. One, set to the tune of "London Bridge Is Falling Down," ran:

> God bless the middle class, middle class, middle class
> God bless the middle class
> That's the Doctor's cry.
> God help the upper crust, upper crust, upper crust
> God help the upper crust . . .
> Or they'll surely die.

Another, in praise of Krauskopf, included the following lines:

> He tells us all our many faults
> Which lots don't like to hear

That's why he gets the upper crust
Just two days in the year.[29]

Although intended as lighthearted amusement, the songs provide a clear sense of the congregation's self-image. With Jewish wealth and Jewish poverty both social handicaps, middle-class identity had become the only safe alternative. It further allowed them to avoid the stigma of class distinction that could damage the cohesiveness of the community.

The congregation's sentiments corresponded with Krauskopf's own vision of Jewish advancement and his views on the path to social respectability. He defended wealth and honest moneymaking, but he denounced unscrupulous gains and the shallowness of many members of America's elite, including those members of the Jewish community who failed in their obligations to support charitable works or engage in philanthropic enterprises. Writing in his diary in 1891, he criticized those for whom "from the first money not culture, success not character, present prosperity not past fraud, was looked to, & was given value."[30] He also understood that Jewish poverty, particularly when linked to socialism, radicalism, and vice, hurt Jewish chances for social acceptance, going so far as to implicate Jews for contributing to anti-Semitism when their behavior conformed to stereotypes. In one impassioned speech in 1907, he urged his Jewish listeners to "resolve to strip away from our religious and social life all that tends to lessen the esteem of the Jew and Judaism in the eyes of the world."[31] Another time, he claimed that the "rich and vulgar and pretentious Jews of the big American cities are the source of most of our troubles." It was these "moneytheists," he argued, who sullied the reputation of the Jewish community.[32] He believed that if Jews were refined and cultured— that is, if they mimicked the customs and behavior of the Protestant elite— they would be less likely to face exclusion from fashionable hotels, exclusive clubs, and prestigious schools, a trend that had worsened during the renewed anti-Semitism in the 1920s, when the use of restrictive covenants and quotas increased.[33]

Across his career, Krauskopf seemed often to be of two minds when it came to material gain. On the one hand, he defended wealth and social advancement, which he sought to direct for the good of the wider Jewish community. Keneseth Israel used its resources to sponsor a range of social outreach ministries, from housing reform to wartime relief, echoing the work of the "institutional church" movement of the time. Krauskopf knew full well that the success of his advocacy work and other reform initiatives, most especially the National Farm School, an agricultural college near Philadelphia that he founded in 1896, depended on his ability to attract and retain donors.³⁴ Throughout his career, he masterfully cultivated relationships with social and financial elites, both Jewish and non-Jewish, in Philadelphia and across the nation. While visiting San Francisco during an 1891 cross-country tour, he met with banker Philip Lilienthal, whom he described as "one of those $5,000 men I wanted to find" to support his publication society.³⁵ Indeed, Krauskopf never passed up an opportunity to appeal to anyone he thought would be able to offer a financial contribution or public endorsement.

On the other hand, Krauskopf recognized the temptations that material and social success could bring. From his own experience as rabbi, he knew that wealth and upward mobility frequently led to a decline in religious commitment. Troubled by the reluctance of wealthy Jews to support synagogues and other religious institutions, he criticized those secular Jews who had forgotten "the God that made their prosperity possible."³⁶ In a 1913 address on the state of Judaism entitled "Hear, O Israel," an invocation of the Shema, the chief Jewish prayer, he called Jews to faithfulness, particularly those of "high culture and commanding wealth" who had converted to Christianity or lapsed into atheism.³⁷ Years earlier, during his 1891 tour, Krauskopf complained that "the Jews are up to the time in building for themselves palatial residences, but they have, as yet, as a rule, no money to erect Houses of Worship for a monument to Judaism."³⁸ Although some Jews may have shunned public expressions of religious devotion for fear of social backlash, Krauskopf believed that a strong institutional presence would help Jews attain social respectability and cultural acceptance. It was a strategy he saw working for Catholics: "You will everywhere find the Catholics owning the most valuable sites & imposing structures upon them. . . . But the Jew as a rule buys a little lot on a side street, erects an unsightly & cheap building upon it & thinks he has made sacrifices for his religion. His Club House he erects on the most fashionable str[eet], makes it attractive by reason of its costliness & then he thinks that by so doing he shows to the world that he is not ashamed of his race."³⁹

In effect, Krauskopf desired success and socioeconomic advancement for members of the Jewish community without accompanying secularization, which he saw as a greater and more immediate threat than the rise of class divisions. Indeed, he worked actively to accommodate the elite because, in both the figurative and literal sense, he knew that the Jewish community could not afford to lose them. In his 1913 sermon on the state of Judaism, he noted how conversion to Christianity and intermarriage among prominent Jews in Germany had left Judaism there "robbed of the support of thousands of people of high culture and commanding wealth whose labors among Jews could not but place our faith in a most favorable light before the world and command that respect for which is its due."[40] Though he supported the goal of assimilation, he understood that the strength of the Jewish community lay in its bonds of ethnic and religious solidarity, tinged with the shared experience of prejudice and persecution. Thus he willingly accommodated class interests as a means of advancing more fundamental *religious* interests. He sought to inspire Jews to remain committed to their faith, regardless of their social or economic standing. This underscored a key difference between how Krauskopf and Conwell understood "success." Even though both promoted economic advancement and upward social mobility, Krauskopf sought the collective advancement of the Jewish community, rather than the starkly individualistic advancement that Conwell did in his gospel of success, with personal success serving the economic and social success of the entire community.

Freeing the Churches

As much as some religious communities accommodated themselves to the class structure of American society and benefited from the social and economic advancement of their members, others felt considerably less comfortable with the pronounced disparities they witnessed. Many believed that class divisions had no place within church life and that conscience demanded that individuals strive to eliminate social obstacles to unity. "The more the distinctions between different classes are broken down," one Episcopal minister noted in 1887, "the larger will be the number of persons brought into the church."[41] As time passed, such sentiments only grew, particularly within the Episcopal Church and other mainline Protestant denominations that had a national presence and establishmentarian ambitions. Perhaps counterintuitively, the communities that had benefited disproportionately from the prosperity of the industrial era often seemed most ill at ease with the resulting divisions.

Privilege proved an impediment to cross-class unity, especially among the assemblies that acquired a reputation for being "class churches." As elite assemblies sought to understand why the poor felt alienated from their churches, many turned their attention to the social and financial barriers that made the masses feel unwelcome. Among the explanations offered, the system of pew rents often drew the most attention. At times deaf to labor activists and other outsiders who spoke about how the churches were beholden to monied interests, many elite assemblies came to see pew rents as the primary impediment to inclusivity and the clearest symbol of the social divisions that plagued their religious communities. Even though the rental system had developed out of financial expedience and was employed by churches both rich and poor, to its critics it was nothing more than the institutional legitimization of power and authority based on economic privilege. As such, pew rents became a primary target for those seeking to free themselves of the "class church" stigma.

In Philadelphia, the sustained campaign against pew rents emerged gradually during the late nineteenth century. Early critics tended to present theological arguments against the system, viewing rents as inimical to the spirit of Christianity. Writing in 1892, Presbyterian elder Robert C. Ogden, a member of a local Philadelphia congregation and active member in several denominational agencies, argued that pew rents could not be justified in light of the teachings of the Gospel. For one thing, a pew rent could not be considered a version of the tithe since a tithe "did not secure a proprietary legal right to any particular, exclusive private portion of the temple for the use of the tithe-payer." For another, through the system of pew rents, those "seeking social precedence" were "willing to buy at any price . . . a conspicuous place in a conspicuous church simply and only for the social distinction it confers." Claiming that the system was "necessarily discriminating, partial, incomplete and not universal," he urged his audience to recognize that true giving must be voluntary, a free offering based on the worshipper's own abilities.[42] Five years earlier, Henry Budd, a prominent Episcopalian who would later serve as chancellor of the diocese, had likewise expressed his belief that "there should be no private property in the house of God."[43] A generation later, George Wharton Pepper, a leading voice of social privilege, shared his own concern that pew rents had created un-Christian divisions within religious communities. In a series of lectures given at Yale University in 1914, Pepper confessed that for years he had "chafed under a system of pews privately owned. Under such a system I do not see how Christian fellowship can ever be more than a name."[44]

Critics further argued that pew rents hindered evangelization, particularly among the working classes and urban poor. In making a case for a "free pew" system, one minister noted that the largest urban congregations, including Philadelphia's Grace Baptist, had seen membership gains exactly because they had no pew rents.[45] Another, fearing Catholic gains, warned that if Protestantism were to remain a viable force, protecting American democracy from the forces of tyranny, pew rents would have to be eliminated since the Protestant churches could not afford to replace an "aristocracy of priests" with an equally powerful aristocracy of wealth.[46] Some even argued that the system of pew rents created walls of separation between the classes that would drive poorer congregants into the arms of socialist agitators. As historian Ken Fones-Wolf has shown, many members of Philadelphia's working class harbored a deep suspicion of organized religion, perceiving that it served the interests of the capitalist class. Speaking at a meeting of Philadelphia's Central Labor Union in December 1901, Ben Tillett, a British labor leader and socialist, pointed to the hypocrisy of clergymen who "preach to us and dine with the rich." To men like Tillett, pew rents were simply one more symptom of the churches' general disregard for the needs of ordinary workers.[47]

Perhaps more important, the system of pew rents began to unravel financially. It was all too common for individuals to fall in arrears in their payments, and many congregations found that revenues received rarely kept pace with expenses. At Chestnut Hill Presbyterian Church, the treasurer reported in 1876 that of the $777 in unpaid pew rents due the congregation, he expected to be able to collect no more than $100. He further warned that projections showed rental income unable to meet "ordinary expenditures," let alone provide a surplus for repairs or other future needs. During the 1880s and 1890s, rents tended to account for only two-thirds of the congregation's income.[48] Proposals that rents be raised met with concern that some members would be priced out of the congregation or that the rate of delinquency would increase. Conversely, church officials also worried that a lack of available pews would cause the congregation to "lose its influence and relative importance" since "nothing will retard its increase more than a feeling among new comers that there is no room for them or if they attend its services, they must sit in pews rented by others & are not welcome."[49] Similar concerns over seating fees plagued Joseph Krauskopf during the 1910s and 1920s. With his congregation's budget strained by construction debts and extensive social service ministries, he wrote to several leading ministers in Philadelphia to inquire about their funding practices. In particular, he wanted to know what others did when income from pew rents no longer met budgetary expectations. He did not want to raise seating fees for his synagogue since the congregation already lacked a sufficient number of "cheap seats," nor did he wish to upset those members who questioned the "rightfulness of making collections" from those who had already contributed their annual dues and fees. It is unclear how many responses Krauskopf received, but the nature of his appeal suggests that many shared his difficulties.[50]

Those opposed to pew rents capitalized on these various strains of discontent, and the practice declined steadily over the course of the late nineteenth and early twentieth centuries as plate collections and the envelope system became more prevalent.[51] Nevertheless, quite a few churches were reluctant to abandon the practice, for both financial and practical reasons. Church officials had doubts that freewill offerings would sufficiently replace the revenue lost once pew rents were abolished. As a result, some churches maintained a hybrid system that combined rents and weekly envelopes in order to gradually train members in "the habits of systematic giving." At times, however, those accustomed to the older practice stubbornly refused to participate in new methods of giving, as Rev. Nathanael Groton discovered when his congregation switched to an envelope system.[52] Moreover, within a number of older congregations, where pews had originally been sold and not merely rented, the system could not be eliminated without infringing on the property rights of individual pew owners. Legally, a congregation could not reclaim its pews as long as the owners continued to fulfill their contractual obligations and pay the annual rents, even if they never attended services. For this reason, the rector of the Church of the Holy Trinity encouraged families holding pews to consider bequeathing or otherwise returning them to the parish as a memorial and thus making them "free forever."[53]

To gain a better sense of how the campaign against pew rents unfolded, it is particularly instructive to look at the history of the Free Church Association, an organization within the Episcopal Church whose American branch was established in Philadelphia in 1875. It was an offshoot of the Free and Open Church Association, which had been founded in 1866 by members of the Church of England who felt "that nothing has done so much to alienate and drive away the masses from the Church as [the] appropriation [of pews] and closed churches."[54] In the United States, the association embraced a threefold mission. First, they adhered to, "as a principle, the freedom of all seats in Churches." Second, they committed themselves to promoting "the abandonment of the sale and rental of pews and sittings, and in place thereof, the adoption of the principle of systematic freewill offerings by all the worshippers in our churches, according to their ability." Finally, they supported the offertory as "an act of Christian worship" and "a Scriptural means of raising money for pious and charitable uses."[55] Many who joined the association, whether in England or the United States, had been influenced by the Catholic revival within the Anglican Communion, and found it increasingly difficult to reconcile the practice of private pew ownership or exclusive-use rental with their inclusive theology.[56] Indeed, the Cambridge Camden Society, whose architectural and liturgical studies had contributed to the "parish church" revival in both England and the United States, had condemned pew rents as early as 1841, describing them as a symbol of "the intrusion of human pride, and selfishness, and indolence, into the worship of God."[57] Despite (or perhaps because of) the prevalence of pew rents in Philadelphia, members of the diocese were soon among the strongest free church advocates within the Episcopal Church. Their efforts soon spread to other dioceses and their reports drew national attention.[58]

The force of theological conviction that gave rise to free church principles can be seen locally in the thought of individuals such as Rev. G. Woolsey Hodge, a founding member of the association and one of its leading clerical voices. Hodge was a staunch Anglo-Catholic who supported "the awakening of the Church to a sense of its historical position and its Catholic privileges and character."[59] In 1880, after a stint as assistant minister at Calvary Chapel, a free chapel associated with Christ Church, Philadelphia, he became rector of the Episcopal Church of the Ascension, where he was instrumental in convincing the vestry to abandon pew rents when the congregation occupied their new sanctuary in 1885.[60] At the consecration service, Hodge reminded his audience that the Episcopal Church could never be a genuinely "catholic Church" as long as pew rents continued to exist. He argued that rents put the Church "in a false light; conveying the impression that it is a private preserve; something intended only for those who have the pecuniary ability to contribute a considerable sum for its maintenance." Returning to his theme of catholicity, he then added, "The Church is the one place on earth where no distinction of classes or wealth or culture should be allowed to enter."[61]

For other members of the association, however, the decision to abandon pew rents grew out of more practical concerns born of congregational experience. This was very much the case of J. Vaughan Merrick Sr., another leading member of the association and a self-professed convert to the movement. In his memoirs, Merrick, a prominent layman and wealthy engineer, admitted to having been at first a "strenuous opponent" of the free church movement because of the financial struggles many free churches faced.[62] His views were undoubtedly conditioned by his own experience at St. Timothy's Church, Roxborough, which his family had been instrumental in founding in 1859. Although established as a free church in an effort to attract workers from nearby mill districts, financial difficulties forced the parish to adopt pew rents in the early 1860s. The parish history claims that free church principles were preserved in spirit since 68 of the church's 178 seats remained free, but the parish's poor financial state suggests that some of those pews were free only by virtue of low demand.[63] After first supporting pew rents, Merrick changed his mind when they failed to solve the congregation's financial problems. He therefore supported the parish's 1873 decision to abolish pew rents, an act he associated with its later success.[64] Within a few years of the "change at St. Timothy's," the church's annual offerings nearly tripled, as did its annual baptisms.[65] This dramatic growth prompted the parish to expand its sanctuary and parish house in 1885. Even though Merrick, who served as chairman of the building committee, subsidized these projects, he downplayed his own contribution, insisting that the more than $18,000 raised "could not have been so secured had not the growth of free church principles been so sound." To him, "material growth had really resulted from spiritual growth."[66]

To the practical-minded Merrick, demonstrable gains in church income offered the best argument for abolishing pew rents. Even though he accepted the theological arguments against the rental system, he knew that parish vestries would only abandon the practice if they could know that lost revenue would be offset by greater freewill gains. Because congregations were expected to be financially self-sustaining, the bottom line was crucial. For this reason, it was essential to him that the free church program flourish at St. Timothy's, so that the parish could serve as an example to others. Over time, as more and more congregations abolished rents, the evidence became more convincing, and the Free Church Association made steady and significant progress toward its goals. When the association met in Philadelphia in 1925 for their forty-ninth annual meeting, they reported that 92 percent of all pews in the Episcopal Church were free, and that 42 percent of all dioceses (30 out of 72) had no rented seats whatsoever.[67] Pew rents remained in place at a number of older churches in Philadelphia, where law and custom made them difficult to eliminate, but, on the whole, the practice was quickly becoming a vestige of the past.[68]

Ultimately, however, success was not quite what it seemed. Although abolishing pew rents eliminated a financial obstacle to religious unity across class lines, it did not eliminate the problem of "class churches." At St. Timothy's, the parish discovered that free pews, in and of themselves, did not guarantee that they would succeed in attracting those once excluded. Even with its support for outreach initiatives like the St. Timothy Workingmen's Club and Institute, the parish did not differ much from other suburban or semirural Episcopal congregations in its social composition. Members were by no means drawn exclusively from the elite, but most came from native-born families who enjoyed a degree of economic security and could afford to live in the wealthier district of the city where the church was located.[69] This points to an irony: in many instances, pew rents declined not because religious communities had grown more committed to bridging class divides, but because many churches recognized that imposing them was no longer necessary to shape the composition of their congregations or to maintain social exclusivity. Residential segmentation within growing metropolitan regions served the same purpose; market forces and residential zoning, among other factors, helped ensure the socioeconomic homogeneity of their communities.[70] Simply put, pew rents had become superfluous, and therefore expendable. But, as religious communities would soon discover, the pastoral problems of wealth extended far beyond pew rents. Demographic changes and socioeconomic mobility born of economic prosperity created challenges they would be much less able to control.

Social Mobility and Institutional Instability

As the twentieth century wore on, it became increasingly apparent to many church leaders and denominational officials that the religious order they viewed as inviolable was neither as stable nor as secure as it seemed. In older downtown districts, in particular, shifting demographics and fleeting finances placed an acute strain on many congregations, eroding their once-solid foundations and threatening their viability. Giving credence to these concerns was a growing body of evidence gathered by planning officials and social investigators. Interested in discovering how churches could be more responsive to contemporary social needs, especially in the nation's urban centers, they studied neighborhood conditions and sought models of successful "adaptation" to changing circumstances. Intended to help religious communities improve the effectiveness and efficiency of their efforts, their conclusions often presented a sobering portrait of the nation's religious life. They pointed to the tenuous state of many congregations and to the lack of cooperative or coordinated responses to systematic problems. More strikingly, they revealed how the same financial forces and privatist logic that had sustained church growth and given rise to the denominational order had also contained the seeds of their undoing.[71]

The figure most responsible for informing these discussions was H. Paul Douglass, the head of the Institute for Social and Religious Research, a New York–based agency founded in 1921 though the support of the Rockefeller family. Born in Iowa in 1871, Douglass came to his career in sociology later in life, after studying for the ministry at the Chicago Theological Seminary and spending several years as a Congregationalist pastor. In 1906, he was named the superintendent of education for the American Missionary Association and later served as the association's corresponding secretary. His work there not only convinced him of the benefits of interdenominational cooperation and improved organizational management, but also introduced him to field research and statistical investigation.[72] Upon joining the institute staff, he assumed responsibility for completing a religious canvass of St. Louis that had been initiated by the Interchurch World Movement. Modeled on earlier progressive-era neighborhood studies such as the 1908 *Pittsburgh Survey*, his resulting 1924 book, *The St. Louis Church Survey*, offered a comprehensive portrait of the city's religious life and institutional trends.

Working with another team of researchers, Douglass gathered similar data from cities across the country, which became the basis for his 1926 work, *1,000 City Churches*, in which he more fully developed his ideas about organizational adaptation. By tracing membership statistics and tabulating the number of church-sponsored ministries, he assessed how well churches had adapted to the needs and conditions of their urban environments, labeling those which supported the greatest number of services "well adapted" to urban conditions. The churches that fared best in these surveys were large urban congregations that supported a broad network of community outreach programs along the lines of the "institutional church" movement. Despite criticism from some of his contemporaries for its methodology, which assigned equal statistical weight to all church ministries, Douglass's work helped set the terms of the debate for the study of religious institutions and drew attention to the structural challenges they faced.[73]

Like Niebuhr, Douglass exhibited a keen awareness of the social and economic conditions that affected religious communities. In *The St. Louis Church Survey*, Douglass carefully delineated the city's shifting "social and religious fortunes" and described how economic and demographic changes had shaped the city's religious geography.[74] Also like Niebuhr, he believed that internal divisions within Protestantism hindered its Christian mission. A recognized figure within the ecumenical movement of the early twentieth century, Douglass was committed to the cause of Christian unity and worked closely with the Federal Council of Churches and other interdenominational agencies, often conducting his research with their support and sponsorship.[75] In contrast to Niebuhr, however, Douglass provided practical policy advice and recommended concrete courses of action, most of which called for better planning and coordination among churches and denominational bodies. His advocacy for greater "comity" among religious communities "stood in direct opposition to the fierce pace of competition" that had characterized religious developments of the preceding decades.[76]

Less directly, Douglass's work also called attention to the unintended consequences of privatist finance and congregational polity, which allowed free market principles and economic self-interest to dictate the direction of denominational growth. These forces gave rise to the vast expansion of religious infrastructure in the industrial city, but they also drove congregations to seek "institutional advantage" by following "the more desirable population from place to place." Too often, "adaptation" to new social and economic conditions resulted in congregational relocation or merger, and the subsequent abandonment of urban ministry.[77] In St. Louis, Douglass's research identified no fewer than seventy instances of congregational movement from the downtown core toward outlying residential districts between 1871 and 1921. Although he accepted the inevitability of some congregational movement, he was shocked at the regularity and unquestioning acceptance of church relocation: that congregations "should so largely have moved . . . in the direction of prestige and advantage to themselves showed total lack of constructive policy and the effective will to serve all of the city equally."[78] Though never an easy decision, relocation was often the only way congregations thought they could ensure their survival. Governed by denominational rules that required financial independence, congregations kept a careful eye on their membership rolls and their balance sheets. Even small declines in membership could have considerable financial repercussions since those who could afford to move to better neighborhoods were often those whose monetary support was most vital to a congregation. As temporal institutions dependent on voluntary financial support to sustain their mission, churches often had little choice but to follow their ever-mobile membership. Congregational autonomy, moreover, limited the ability of denominational authorities to intervene.

Developments were no different in Philadelphia, where the centrifugal forces of urban development and high rates of residential mobility posed a constant threat to institutional stability.[79] The history of the Church of the Mediator offers one illustrative example of how religious communities struggled under the weight of demographic considerations and economic pressures. Founded in 1848, the Episcopal congregation, which was neither rich nor poor, had begun to experience steady membership decline during the closing decades of the nineteenth century. With families moving to newer residential districts, the future of the downtown congregation stood in jeopardy, and, in early 1905, the issue of "removal" (relocation) was put before the pewholders. Although they voted 32 to 29 to remain at their present location, the vestry, which held ultimate authority in the matter, declared the vote a practical tie and approved the sale of the property to St. Mark's Church, a neighboring Episcopal congregation, which wanted to open a mission chapel for the "colored" population on the site. The vestry sensed that interest in the congregation would only further wane in the coming years, and therefore looked for an opportunity to relocate in a growing community with more promising financial prospects. They had made an agreement with the diocese to take over a mission church in West Philadelphia, with the understanding that they could build their parish church within a four-block radius. But after selecting a site, a neighboring congregation objected and brought their concerns about parochial competition before the bishop. When negotiations with the diocese and the other congregation failed, members of the Mediator's congregation had little choice but to shelve their plans. Financially weakened, the congregation agreed to become a chapel of the Church of the Holy Apostles in 1906, and later joined two other congregations in establishing a church at Fifty-First and Spruce Streets, near the new campus of the Philadelphia Divinity School.[80]

Members of the Church of the Mediator may have thought of their experiences as an isolated occurrence, and the relocation of a particular congregation may not have attracted much attention outside of its immediate neighborhood, but statistical data pointed to a more systematic pattern of institutional transience that would prove increasingly difficult to accept as part of the natural progression of religious development. Indeed, the weight of the evidence became difficult to dismiss. Taking note of this pattern in his 1912 doctoral dissertation, Clarence A. Young traced institutional trends among Philadelphia's downtown congregations and demonstrated how widely institutional decline—or "decadence" as he termed it—cut across denominational lines. Even though Young focused on churches in the urban core rather than in the city as a whole, he nevertheless anticipated many of the conclusions of Douglass's broader community surveys. As a minister in the Reformed Presbyterian Church, Young shared Douglass's pastoral sensitivities and hoped that a scientific investigation of social, economic, and religious conditions would aid religious communities in developing more "efficient" organizational strategies and more comprehensive responses to social needs. Although it is unclear how widely Young's findings circulated, news of his work did appear in the Philadelphia press and denominational publications, and likely came to the attention of at least some local church officials.[81]

Comparing denominational trends between 1880 and 1910, Young attempted to identify the factors that enabled congregations to "adjust" to changing conditions and to maintain their vibrant presence in the city. He looked not only at Protestant but also at Catholic and Jewish congregations, drawing upon membership statistics to measure the "success" and "efficiency" of each religious community as defined by "its ability to attract, hold, and thus influence more or less continuously the people for whom it ought to be responsible."[82] Because Young was more interested in assessing social outreach than theological teachings, the congregations that fared best in his study were those with strong clerical leadership that directed resources and energy toward meeting the needs of the local population. He praised the Methodists and Baptists for training church workers and for directing their efforts toward the immigrant communities, even though these efforts had yet to translate into membership growth. Conversely, he faulted the Presbyterians for not making "adequate use of their large resources." Despite laudable efforts on the part of some congregations during the three decades he studied, the number of downtown Presbyterian churches declined sharply, from 21 to 6, as congregations disbanded or "moved to better neighborhoods." Among Protestants, he found the Episcopal Church exhibited the most "progressive spirit and social vision," with extensive programs conducted along "institutional church" lines.[83]

To Young, the organizational weaknesses of Protestant denominations loomed largest when contrasted with the strengths of the Catholic Church. As Douglass would likewise note in his studies, Catholic parishes seemed immune to the trends afflicting Protestant congregations, exhibiting remarkable institutional stability in an era of social and economic flux. Though he attributed some of the Catholic Church's success to the ethnic loyalties of its members and the "dogmatism of its claims," Young gave considerable credit to the Church's "wonderful organization." Not only did the ranks of priests and sisters keep parishes well staffed and make them a "real force in the community," the nature of the parochial system allowed Catholics to avoid the destructive competition and "overlapping" work that was "the bane of Protestantism." As Young observed, not a single Catholic parish closed or relocated at a time when the number of downtown Protestant congregations diminished by more than half on account of relocation, dissolution, or merger.[84]

Such figures, however, are somewhat misleading. Catholic parishes were fortunate that whatever membership losses they suffered as upwardly mobile families moved to better neighborhoods were offset by immigration or masked by the large family size of those who remained. Even Catholic officials who regularly extolled the immutability of their institutions were all too aware of the dramatic demographic shifts taking place. Speaking at the cornerstone dedication of a new parish in West Philadelphia in 1922, Cardinal Dougherty, for instance, remarked how in the joy of the occasion his thoughts turned to "those fine old parishes" in other districts of the city "whose life blood is being given" to support these new ventures.[85] A few years later, the archdiocese made plans to relocate the Roman Catholic High School from its downtown location to a new site in North Philadelphia to accommodate a larger enrollment closer to the new center of the Catholic population, a move that echoed the "removal" of the Episcopal Academy from the city to suburban Overbrook in 1921.[86]

As much as religious communities derived benefit from the upward social and economic mobility of their members, the steady flow of families and resources from older residential districts and downtown areas awakened them to the unintended consequences of their own prosperity. Cutting across denominational lines, the effects of this "drift," as one report politely termed the trend, posed considerable pastoral challenges for individual church leaders and tempered the religious optimism of the age.[87] At a time when religious identity and denominational mission had grown so inextricably bound to institutional structures, there was a growing awareness that more than the fate of individual congregations was at stake. To those who had invested so much in these denominational enterprises, the demographic trends signaled a crisis of the institutional order. They elicited considerable anxiety among church leaders and spurred discussion, at both the congregational and denominational levels, over how churches could revive their flagging fortunes or insulate themselves against the consequences of these trends. Sensing that their problems could not be solved simply by increased evangelization, churches came to recognize that their plight stemmed from the very financial forces that had once given them vitality.

No one questioned the basic fact that churches needed money to support their operations, but the challenge stood in overcoming the transitory nature of wealth. Congregations needed to find a way to maintain their financial stability in the face of demographic change and the destabilizing effects of their members' social and geographic mobility. In looking at the remarkable staying power of Philadelphia's Episcopal congregations, Young observed how nearly all of them possessed substantial endowments, averaging $150,000, but with some far in excess of that amount. He further noted that of the six churches that disbanded or moved, only one had an endowment of any substantial size. Though he cautioned that "the mere existence of an endowment" was "not enough to ensure an efficient church," he nevertheless admitted that one reason for Episcopalians' relative success lay "in their financial power" and their ability to draw on endowments to equip "their plants for effective service."[88] Additionally, Episcopal churches often benefited from their connections to the city's social and economic elite, many of whom maintained seasonal downtown residences and continued to support their historic parishes out of a sense of family loyalty and civic obligation long after they had moved to the Main Line or other suburban districts. By dedicating funds to support a church in perpetuity, endowments essentially provided a bulwark against the inevitable effects of social and economic mobility.

Although most congregations did not have the financial luxury to set aside resources for the future, even those that did were often slow to recognize the need, especially when their prospects continued to look promising. With such foresight rare, the exceptions become all the more notable. The Church of the Holy Trinity offers a case in point. As early as 1884, at the height of the Rittenhouse Square district's Victorian splendor, the rector recognized the need to guard the church from the "vicissitudes which are incident to a city's history." Writing to members of the parish in his annual address, he remarked how "the experience of many churches in this and other cities ought to teach us this lesson—churches which were once as prosperous as ours is today . . . are now crippled in this work, and in some cases have been compelled to relinquish it entirely, because other people who now surround them are not able to support them."[89] He may have perhaps been mindful of St. James's Church, the third oldest Episcopal congregation in the city, which had in 1870 erected its new sanctuary two blocks to the west of Holy Trinity after judging its prospects too diminished to allow it to remain at its previous location in the older part of the city.[90] Regardless of his inspiration, he and his successors worked aggressively to build the church's endowment through dedicated collections and regular appeals, in part calculating that it would help offset the income lost from declining pew rents. By the 1920s, the endowment had grown to more than $500,000, an impressive figure for the time.[91] At nearby St. Mark's Church, the parish likewise steadily sequestered funds, raising more than $250,000 for its endowment by 1928 and moving to acquire land to the east of the church to "protect for all time the precincts" from the ravages of urban development.[92] Although such efforts certainly demonstrated considerable wisdom and prudence, they also reflected deep anxieties about the effects of economic advancement, residential mobility, and changing religious loyalties. Not even the most wealthy and fashionable congregations could take their continued prosperity for granted.

As much as endowments furnished a degree of financial security for those congregations with the foresight to establish them, they did little to deal systematically with the crisis of institutional decline. By stemming the flight of resources, moreover, they also prevented them from flowing to where the need was greatest, sustaining "class churches" at the expense of the poor. For those interested in the well-being of the institutional order as a whole, the concern was not merely social and economic mobility, but the deleterious effects of religious competition and the unequal distribution of resources. Writing in 1922, Rev. William H. Leach placed fault for the weakness of Protestant denominations in American cities on the parochial mentality that insisted that "each church" be "sufficient unto itself."[93] An early authority in church management, Leach advocated for improved cooperation both within and across denominational lines, a view he shared with a steadily widening circle of planning experts and social investigators, including Douglass and his associates at the Institute for Social and Religious Research.

Efforts to promote denominational cooperation and to encourage church planning developed in response to sobering realities. Such was the case when the Presbytery of Philadelphia commissioned William P. Shriver, the director of the Board of National Missions for the Presbyterian Church and a member of Douglass's research team in St. Louis, to survey local conditions and recommend a plan of action. To illustrate that the problems facing the Presbyterian Church did not all stem from a lack of resources, Shriver began his 1930 report with an account of the 1928 merger of First Presbyterian Church with one of its daughter congregations, Calvary Presbyterian, a move that consolidated the financial resources of two wealthy congregations and reduced Presbyterian presence in one of the city's poorest neighborhoods. Even though First Presbyterian was faced with a dwindling congregation and an aging sanctuary in need of costly repairs, Shriver considered the merger an unconscionable act. To him, it was merely the most recent manifestation of the Presbyterian Church's deeper ills: an increasing disparity of wealth among Presbyterian congregations, the denomination's retreat from its religious mission, and the lack of effective denominational oversight of member congregations. He noted, in particular, the lack of any formal response on the part of church officials to the fate of "down-town and city churches" that had seen "a large number of their most influential and supporting families leave for the suburbs."[94]

In advocating greater planning, Shriver recognized that the nature of church polity precluded denominational officials from dictating congregational action, but he also saw the weaknesses in the Presbyterian Church's own administrative structures. As part of his report, he recommended that the two local presbyteries with oversight of the city, Philadelphia and Philadelphia North, unite and formulate a regional plan to better monitor and advise congregations. He pointed out that much of the membership growth in the Presbytery of Philadelphia North was simply the result of individuals transferring from the Presbytery of Philadelphia. Shriver further believed that improved data and awareness of denominational trends would help individual congregations recognize the need for cooperation. In areas where the decline of the city's Presbyterian population was most acute, he recommended that denominational officials pressure congregations to consolidate rather than relocate, which would not only help ensure the denomination's continued religious presence in the city, but would also help prevent congregational congestion in other districts. This course of action, he insisted, represented both a sound "denominational strategy" and "a wise conservation of Protestant resources."[95]

Similar calls for greater planning emerged within the Episcopal Church during the 1920s. In March 1926, one minister urged the Diocese of Pennsylvania to "make a general survey, geographical, economic, social, as well as spiritual," as part of its missionary strategy. Later that year, a standardized "survey of needs" was conducted in conjunction with the launch of the diocese's $3.5 million Campaign for Missions and Ministries, a drive promoted by Bishop Thomas J. Garland as part of his effort to "build up" and unify the diocese. Although mission churches were to benefit from the funds collected, even here priority was given to the "outlying districts" where "the great development of the Church of the future must take place," a move that angered advocates for urban ministry.[96] In a December 1928 editorial, the *Church News* chastised Episcopalians for their indifference to the ecclesiastical transformation taking place in the city: "If tomorrow it were announced that Holy Trinity was going to sell out and move to Bryn Mawr [or] St. James's to Bala, there would be a general feeling that the moves were wise and that the 'Church was following the people.' What such moves would really mean is that the Church was deserting the people. They would be open confessions that the Church has no place and no message in a great city." The editorial stressed that physical presence was essential for the Church's successful ministry in Philadelphia. Without it, the Episcopal Church would have literally and figuratively no grounding in the city. For that reason, "someone needs to cry out . . . 'Wake up, Philadelphia Episcopalians!'"[97]

Just as Shriver pointed out the weaknesses of the city's Presbyterian administrative structures, its Episcopalians likewise argued that their diocese was doing too little to preserve the Church's institutional presence in poorer districts. Rev. David M. Steele expressed his exasperation that the diocese had no legal power or canonical authority to preserve city churches when congregations chose to relocate.[98] Since most urban missions and outreach ministries were sponsored by individual congregations, rather than by the diocese itself, he recognized how the cumulative effects of "removal" bore most heavily on those in greatest need, a constituency with no financial stake, and therefore no recognized voice, in those decisions. A former social worker, Steele had served as rector of the Church of St. Luke and the Epiphany since 1904. During his tenure, he attempted to revive the parish by expanding its social outreach ministries, a task that became increasingly difficult when the congregation continued to lose membership and financial support. Disheartened by the general complacency of the diocese toward the plight of urban parishes, he resigned his rectorship in protest in 1933. "We central city rectors, none of us, are leaving Philadelphia," he announced, "Philadelphia has simply left us."[99]

Even with such outcries, the diocese as a whole was slow to develop any concrete policies to shore up its urban ministry. In 1934, a "Report of the Committee on Problems of City Churches" at the diocesan convention urged delegates to revise diocesan financial policies, particularly assessments, to help sustain city churches. The dissenting minority to the report argued that the problem required spiritual commitment in the form of stewardship and outreach—that church members needed to be reminded of their obligation "to sacrificially serve."[100] Reluctant to throw money at failing urban parishes, some of which had become redundant and unsustainable, the minority believed it wiser to fund construction of churches in the city's suburbs, where the prospects for new parishes were far more promising. As H. Paul Douglass had stressed in *The St. Louis Church Survey*, most of the nation's religious communities simply had "no method of effective planning for, nor of adequately financing churches through periods of strain and transition by reason of shifts in population, nor of supporting them for permanent service in regions of permanent disadvantage."[101]

Even if their recommendations were not fully implemented, these planning reports called attention to the unforeseen consequences of financial success. As religious leaders now clearly recognized, economic advancement, residential mobility, and social stratification had not only created barriers to theological unity; they now also posed a threat to the long-term stability of religious institutions. Indeed, strategies to sustain downtown congregations reveal how the fate of the nation's religious life was tied to its changing social and economic fortunes. Religious competition, voluntary membership, congregational autonomy, and financial independence, once seen as the lifeblood of religious community, also contributed to the instability of religious communities and their institutions.

Although early twentieth-century debates over the social composition of religious communities and concerns about the fate of downtown congregations may have been primarily of internal institutional interest, taken together, they reflected the deeper anxieties and contradictions of the age. The established order was passing away, both for those who relied on religious association for the conferral of status and for those who considered the strength of institutional networks integral to the success of churches' religious mission. What once seemed certain and inviolable now proved fleeting, the victim of the dramatic social and economic transformations of the industrial era. Churches that had once drawn the most respectable families to their congregations and whose edifices had been built for the ages now saw their prospects fade as a result of the upward social and economic mobility made possible by the very prosperity that had once lifted their fortunes.

In the end, developments in industrial-era Philadelphia attest both to the symbiotic relationship between religion and wealth, which helped structure class relations and sustain the denominational order, and to its inherent fragility. Just as members of the social and financial elite struggled to preserve their spiritual authority and class status in the wake of moral challenges, so religious communities came to recognize the theological consequences and pastoral implications of their dependence on wealth. During the late nineteenth and early twentieth centuries, religious life in the United States came to reflect both the splendor and the inequalities of the age.

Conclusion

LEGACIES

Philadelphia owes much to the legacy of industrial wealth. The economic prosperity of the late nineteenth and early twentieth centuries reshaped the local landscape, serving as a catalyst for the city's emergence as a modern metropolis. It also refashioned social relations, widening the gulf between rich and poor and contributing to the rise of a powerful and cohesive ruling class whose members viewed themselves not only as proper Philadelphians, but also as the finest representatives of civic and moral virtue. Though prone to the excesses of the age, they nevertheless dedicated themselves to enhancing the stature of the city they claimed as their own; they supported a wide range of civic causes, cultural institutions, and educational initiatives that promoted their vision for society. Their commitments also extended deeply into the religious sphere, where their benefactions helped faith communities flourish and sustained the vast institutional network of churches, schools, hospitals, social service agencies, and affiliated organizations that defined the denominational order as it took its modern form. In patterning these changes, Philadelphia mirrored other cities and served as a microcosm for the nation.

Yet, as *Church and Estate* demonstrates, neither industrial wealth nor the social and religious order it created proved as secure as their beneficiaries imagined. Even before the economic convulsions of the 1930s took their toll, the social and religious worlds of the industrial era had become unsustainable, victims of their own success. The moral standing of the city's ruling class came under scrutiny by religious reformers within their own communities. The institutions they established suffered when financial support proved fleeting, the consequence of the social and geographic mobility that prosperity had made possible. Indeed, history reveals just how contrived and ephemeral notions of class status and moral authority were. Country estates, social registers, and majestic sanctuaries reflected the ambitions of the industrial age, offering only notional permanence in an era of immense flux.

Those hopeful that the economic prosperity of the post–World War II years would restore the old order met with disappointment. Though vestiges of industrial-era privilege and exclusivity remained, there was no returning to the way things had been. By midcentury, members of the self-appointed upper class no longer commanded the same social, cultural, or religious authority they once had. They no longer had the financial resources or individual will to sustain the world they had created. In one notable episode, Percival Roberts Jr., a steel baron and member of the distinguished local clan, decided to abandon his Lower Merion estate and raze his seventy-five-room mansion in 1939 when he lost his fight to stop the township from erecting an incinerator nearby. He could not bear having the sight of a smokestack ruin his view and destroy the pastoral vision he had meticulously cultivated over the years. No longer able to maintain the illusion, he had it all wiped away. The saga of his estate was a fitting allegory for the age.[1]

With every passing year, more of the old order slipped away. Across the Philadelphia region, estates were sold off to developers as the tax burden and cost of maintenance became too much to bear. Some were donated to their municipalities for public use, but many others were converted into schools, retirement homes, conference centers, and other enterprises. A good number were acquired by Catholic, Jewish, and other religious communities whose members had long been excluded from proper society. One can only imagine the conversations that transpired when Woodmont, the grand Gladwyne estate of steel magnate Alan Wood Jr., whose mansion had been modeled on the Biltmore House in North Carolina, was purchased by Father Divine to serve as the headquarters for his International Peace Mission.[2] Although the churches built during the era of industrial prosperity tended to fare better than the region's opulent estates and fashionable townhomes, even they struggled to retain their past splendor. And although those located in the city's suburbs frequently gained new vigor in the postwar years, all too many downtown churches continued to see their membership and finances erode. Had it not been for endowment income and other financial bequests, the pattern of congregational decline would have been even more acute. But such dependence only accentuated the fact that many of the region's grand churches stood as monuments to a bygone era.

These developments embodied the dual disestablishment that took place within American social and religious life during the middle decades of the twentieth century. The decline of the status markers and material trappings of the industrial-era elite reflected their waning command on the nation's consciousness. Those with wealth still wielded immense influence, but their collective claim to social and religious authority became increasingly tenuous. Though not as pronounced as the one following the American Revolution, when notions of privilege within the social and religious sphere succumbed to the leveling spirit of the age, the disestablishment after World War II was nevertheless quite real. Fascination with high society certainly lived on, but the WASP establishment would never recapture the civic or religious dominance it enjoyed during the early decades of the twentieth century.

Just as the postwar years witnessed the decline of the Main Line and other elite enclaves as the embodiments of proper society, so the middle decades of the twentieth century also saw the waning of mainline Protestantism's privileged position within the nation's religious life. The emergence of "tri-faith pluralism," as Kevin Schultz has recently demonstrated, brought Catholics and Jews more fully into the mainstream, prompting the nation "to alter the way power was meted out" and to reconceive "who was deserving of social, political, and cultural recognition."[3] The religious hegemony of mainline Protestantism was further challenged by the resurgence of evangelicalism as both a cultural and political force from the late 1960s onward. When combined with suburban growth and regional population shifts from the Northeast and upper Midwest to the South and Sunbelt, and with the gradual decline of formal religious affiliation among Americans, the established order came under considerable strain. This religious realignment and cultural fragmentation made it more difficult for any one denomination or religious tradition to claim to speak on behalf of the nation. In short, the postwar years gave rise to a vastly different social and religious landscape—one in which old certainties no longer held.

Setting aside those who lamented the loss of their own privileges and those who advanced a facile nostalgia for simpler times, there was nevertheless a distinctly negative side to the decentering of social and religious authority and the decline of the ruling class. A wide array of cultural critics, social observers, and scholars have noted how much more difficult it has become to speak of normative values or a collective national ethos. In Daniel T. Rodgers's recent summation, the notions of consensus and mutual obligation that dominated American culture during the years immediately after World War II gave way to an "age of fracture" in which "strong metaphors of society were supplanted by weaker ones," "imagined collectivities shrank" and "notions of structure and power thinned out."[4] Not coincidentally, those forgotten attributes were the very ones that the industrial-era elite ascribed to their leadership and example. The passing of a self-proclaimed social and religious establishment has left a void that, for good or ill, remains unfilled.

The loss of a ruling class has also created a notable absence at the local level. After surveying conditions in Philadelphia during the economic boom of the 1990s, Nicholas Lemann declared Philadelphia to be "no man's town." He noted how the city no longer possessed a "defined coterie" of individuals drawn from the economic sphere who felt it incumbent upon themselves to sustain the city and its institutions. The globalized economy and social fluidity had worked to erode institutional rootedness and eviscerate a collective commitment to place.[5] During the industrial era, in contrast, members of the financial elite constituted a patrician class that took an active, continuing interest in civic, cultural, and religious affairs. They understood that with great privilege came great responsibilities. They also understood that their own status depended on the city's well-being, for it served as a reflection of their own leadership and liberality. Certainly some of that old spirit remains, as exhibited by the successful community campaign in 2006 to acquire *The Gross Clinic*, the famous painting by celebrated Philadelphia artist Thomas Eakins, when it was put up for sale. Viewing the work as part of the city's artistic patrimony, a group of civic leaders and local philanthropies banded together to prevent its acquisition by the Crystal Bridges Museum of American Art in Bentonville, Arkansas. Although the episode gave renewed visibility to local power brokers, mobilized in no small part by resentment toward financial parvenus for trying to steal a Philadelphia treasure, any sense that they represented the city's establishment had largely faded within Philadelphians' collective consciousness.[6]

In recent decades, the link between class status and religious association has also weakened significantly. Social convention, by and large, no longer requires that individuals maintain a particular religious affiliation or give public proof of their religious devotion in order to enter the upper echelons of society. In addition, not only is there less public awareness of the religious affiliations of today's men and women of wealth, donors also have more freedom to pursue philanthropic agendas outside of denominational auspices. Even though members of today's financial elite are often just as generous in their support of their local churches and other denominational organizations as their predecessors had been, religious bodies no longer have as secure a claim on their wealth. By midcentury, elite philanthropy had come to operate within a dramatically altered system of financial, social, and religious relationships. As individuals sought to shelter their assets from taxation, charitable giving came increasingly to be mediated through family foundations, which served as the conservators of private wealth. Funds to churches and other religious institutions increasingly came in the form of grants for defined purposes or immediate needs rather than as endowments or bequests for ongoing support or unrestricted use, as had once been the case. Under such arrangements, the ultimate control over a donor's legacy remained beyond the hands of church authorities.[7]

The passing of the industrial order, however, has brought an end neither to the connection between religion and wealth nor to the power of wealthy individuals within religious life or the civic arena. Rather, the history of industrial-era Philadelphia urges us to recognize both the enduring resonance of religious belief and the pervasiveness of elite influence, whether operating in overt or subtle ways. To understand the role of the social and financial elite in church life, one must give credence to the religious beliefs and moral cosmologies that have shaped their social outlook, conditioned their class sensibilities, and informed their personal and professional lives. Likewise, to understand the nature of religious community and the character of religious life in the United States, one must recognize the financial forces and class influence at work. Those who contribute most generously to their religious communities expect to receive a degree of deference, if not actual control. The nature of church finance and the structures of church governance enable the elite to exercise considerable authority within the religious sphere and make their churches, both physically and communally, reflective of their own class tastes and sensibilities.

Now that another period of economic prosperity has come and gone, it is perhaps timely to look back at the industrial era. Recent experiences and developments are strikingly, if not eerily, similar to those of a century ago. Much as Andrew Carnegie and others of his generation wrestled with the moral obligations of wealth and sought more enlightened ways to dispense their money, the past few years have seen a new class of capitalists embrace Carnegie's notion that "the man who dies rich, dies disgraced" and pledge to give away their fortunes. Led by the example of Warren Buffett, who made a personal promise in 2006 to donate 99 percent of his fortune to charity, Bill Gates, Ted Turner, Michael Bloomberg, Philadelphian Gerry Lenfest, and others have taken his "giving pledge," promising to donate at least half of their fortune to charity.[8] Proposed in 2010, in the wake of simmering class antagonism and public criticism directed toward the excesses of the "1 percent," the initiative reflects an effort on the part of today's financial elite to burnish their public image and demonstrate the transformative power of private philanthropy. More broadly, however, economic prosperity has again become a driving force for social and cultural change, as it was then.

The most recent era of prosperity has likewise shaped the character and development of the nation's religious life. Across the denominational spectrum, religious communities have actively courted wealth in their efforts to enhance ministries, improve facilities, and expand their reach. As in the industrial era, wealth has acquired spiritual significance. Over the course of the past three decades, a new generation of preachers has attracted large followings by echoing the promise of abundance that Russell Conwell so masterfully promoted a century ago. Aspirations soaring, megachurches have become the new cathedrals of the age, though, if the recent sale of the Crystal Cathedral offers any indication, their dreams of permanence may well prove as elusive as in the past.[9]

Yet, in what is perhaps a more significant parallel of the industrial era, financial imperatives and corporate mentality have subtly worked their way into the religious sphere, gradually shaping how churches administer their affairs, make their decisions, and evaluate their operations. One notable example can be seen in the August 2012 decision by the Archdiocese of Philadelphia to transfer management of its secondary school system to an independent private foundation responsible for overseeing fundraising, marketing, and financial operations. According to officials involved with the project, which affects seventeen high schools and four special education schools, the foundation will provide a "metrics-driven management structure" and promote "entrepreneurial partnerships"; through its promotion of corporate best practices, it hopes to revitalize and stabilize the school system after years of enrollment decline and financial insecurity.[10] This effort reflects the ongoing struggle on the part of religious communities to maintain institutional viability amid economic and demographic change. Today, as then, the success of the religious mission remains inextricably bound to the changing fortunes of society.

NOTES

Abbreviations

ASBS   Archives, Sisters of the Blessed Sacrament
AthP   Athenaeum of Philadelphia
CCHP   Charles Custis Harrison Papers
Church News   *Church News of the Diocese of Pennsylvania*
FHLSC   Friends Historical Library, Swarthmore College
GBRLB   George B. Roberts Letterpress Books
GCRP   George Chalmers Richmond Papers
HFP   Huston Family Papers
HML   Hagley Museum and Library
HSP   Historical Society of Pennsylvania
JKP   Joseph Krauskopf Papers
*Journal of the
  Diocesan
  Convention*   *Journal of the Annual Convention of the Diocese of Pennsylvania*
LMHS   Lower Merion Historical Society
MELP   Morris E. Leeds Papers
PAHRC   Philadelphia Archdiocesan Historical Research Center
PHS   Presbyterian Historical Society
PYM   Philadelphia Yearly Meeting
QCHC   Quaker Collections, Haverford College
RFP   Roberts Family Papers
Richmond Trial George Chalmers Richmond Ecclesiastical Trial
SOC   Social Order Committee
TPCC   Theophilus P. Chandler Collection
TUUA   Temple University Urban Archives
UPA   University of Pennsylvania Archives

Introduction

1. "Increasing Your Income: The Service of Provident Mutual Annuities" (ca. 1920s), Box 12, Provident Mutual Life Insurance Company Records, Acc. 1930, HML.

2. On the history of the firm, see Provident Life Insurance and Trust Company of Philadelphia, "Charter and By-laws" (1865); Ashbrook, *Fifty Years*; and Provident Mutual Life Insurance Company, "75 Years of Provident Protection." For its advertising records, see Boxes 12–15, Provident Mutual Life Insurance Company Records, Acc. 1930, HML.

3. Wing, as quoted in Ashbrook, *Fifty Years*, 68, and in "Insurance Company Marks Half Century," *Philadelphia Inquirer*, 23 March 1915, 7.

4. From its incorporation in 1865 to 1952, Provident knew only three presidents, Samuel R. Shipley, Asa S. Wing, and M. Albert Linton, all of whom were respected Friends. Since members of the board held life terms, serving until their death or resignation, the Quaker

influence at the upper levels of Provident's management remained steady. For a list of the directors between 1865 and 1915, see Ashbrook, *Fifty Years*, appendix I.

5. See Box 12, Provident Mutual Life Insurance Company Records, Acc. 1930, HML.

6. On the use of William Penn in local advertising, see Kashatus, "Images of William Penn," 11–12.

7. Efforts by the Society of Friends to protect their corporate identity can be seen most clearly in their campaign against Quaker Oats, a company with no connection to the Society or its members, for its use of the "Quaker" moniker. See *To Prohibit the Use of the Name of Any Religious Denomination, Society, or Association for the Purposes of Trade and Commerce*, H. R. 435 (1916).

8. Zuckerman, *Friends and Neighbors: Group Life in America's First Plural Society*.

9. For an overview of Philadelphia's religious history, see Moss, *Historic Sacred Places of Philadelphia*, 3–27. On particular religious communities, see Moore, *Friends in the Delaware Valley*; Twelves, *A History of the Diocese of Pennsylvania*; Smylie, *A Brief History of the Presbyterians*, 102; Friedman, *When Philadelphia Was the Capital of Jewish America*; and Connelly, *The History of the Archdiocese of Philadelphia*.

10. The Diocese of Pennsylvania was surpassed in membership only by the Diocese of New York during this period. See, for instance, "General Table of Statistics," *Living Church Annual* (1911): 350–53; and, "General Table of Statistics," *Living Church Annual* (1931): 504–9.

11. It was not until 1928 that the Chicago Presbytery surpassed Philadelphia for second place in membership. The Pennsylvania synod, however, remained the largest in the Presbyterian Church (USA). See "Statistics of the Presbyterian Church for Year as Given in Minutes of 1928," *Presbyterian*, 30 August 1928.

12. Older accounts on America's upper class include Myers, *History of the Great American Fortunes*; Josephson, *The Robber Barons*; Wecter, *The Saga of American Society*; and Lundberg, *America's 60 Families*. The waning of the social establishment in the post–World War II years inspired new works such as Birmingham, *The Right People*; Amory, *Who Killed Society?*; and Aldrich, *Old Money*. But by midcentury, interest had also shifted from the upper class to political elites, as seen in works such as Mills, *The Power Elite*; Domhoff, *The Higher Circles*; and Silk and Silk, *The American Establishment*. For examinations of urban elites, see Jaher, *The Urban Establishment*; Ingham, *The Iron Barons*; and Beckert, *The Monied Metropolis*. For more recent accounts that have focused on the shift from social establishment to meritocracy, see Lemann, *The Big Test*; and Brooks, *Bobos in Paradise*.

13. See Lears, *No Place of Grace*; and Veblen, *The Theory of the Leisure Class*.

14. E. Digby Baltzell has been credited with popularizing the term "WASP," which came into usage in the 1950s, when, as a group, WASPs had already begun their irreversible decline. See Baltzell, *The Protestant Establishment*; Schrag, *The Decline of the WASP*; Christopher, *Crashing the Gates*; and Kaufmann, *The Rise and Fall of Anglo-America*.

15. For recent biographies of Gilded Age greats that take their subjects' religious beliefs seriously, see Chernow, *Titan*; Strouse, *Morgan*; Rottenberg, *The Man Who Made Wall Street*; and Krass, *Carnegie*.

16. On theological responses to market capitalism, see Noll, *God and Mammon*; Davenport, *Friends of the Unrighteous Mammon*; Hudnut-Beumler, *In Pursuit of the Almighty's Dollar*; and Woods, *The Church Confronts Modernity*. For a discussion of the state of research in this area, see Hackett et al., "Forum: American Religion and Class."

17. Representative works using rational choice economic models to describe religious life in America include Finke and Stark, *The Churching of America, 1776–1990*; Moore, *Selling God*; and Schmidt, *Consumer Rites*.

18. On the democratic nature of religion in the United States, see Hatch, *The Democratization of American Christianity*; and Noll, *America's God*. Also exploring the theme, although with greater attention to gender and race, is Heyrman, *Southern Cross*.

19. For more on elite influence within the nation's social and political life, a prevalent theme in political science, see Phillips, *Wealth and Democracy*; and Fraser and Gerstle, *Ruling America*.

20. Baltzell's canon includes *Philadelphia Gentlemen*; *The Protestant Establishment*; and *Puritan Boston and Quaker Philadelphia*.

21. Beckert, *The Monied Metropolis*.

22. On religion's role among the American middle class, see Johnson, *A Shopkeeper's Millennium*; Ryan, *Cradle of the Middle Class*; and, in an English context, Davidoff and Hall, *Family Fortunes*. The treatment of religion in these three works contrasts with the absence of religious analysis in other prominent studies of the middle class, including Blumin, *The Emergence of the Middle Class*; Hepp, *The Middle Class City*; and Johnston, *The Radical Middle Class*. On the working class and the shift from religious identity to new associations, see Cohen, *Making a New Deal*; and Gerstle, *Working-Class Americanism*; but see also, as a recent corrective, Sterne, *Ballots and Bibles*. For two examples of the persistence of religious identity among immigrants, the poor, and marginalized, see Handlin, *The Uprooted*; and Grossman, *Land of Hope*.

23. Beckert, "Comments on 'Studying the Middle Class in the Modern City,'" 396. See also Aronowitz, *How Class Works*.

24. See Putnam, *Bowling Alone*; Schmidt, *Religion as Social Capital*; and Dilworth, *Social Capital in the City*. See also the studies generated by the John Templeton Foundation's Spiritual Capital Research Program, available on the program's website, http://www.metanexus.net/archive/spiritualcapitalresearchprogram/index.asp.html. Particularly useful studies include Finke, "Spiritual Capital: Definitions, Applications, and New Frontiers"; and Iannaccone and Klick, "Spiritual Capital: An Introduction and Literature Review."

25. See Bourdieu, *Distinction*, and *The Field of Cultural Production*; Varter, "Spiritual Capital"; and Dianteill, "Pierre Bourdieu and the Sociology of Religion."

26. Bourdieu, *Distinction*, 7. Bourdieu's analysis does not specifically address the role of religion in class formation, but it does provide a framework for examining the nature of the relationship between the two. Sean McCloud, for instance, has recently applied Bourdieu's insights to demonstrate the saliency of class within American religious life. Finding class a "neglected variable" in the academic study of religion, he makes a case for its inclusion among those "socially habituated subjectivities" that shape religious practice and inform moral sensibilities. On this point, see McCloud, *Divine Hierarchies*, 7, 9.

27. On wealth as a means to promote the social good, see Lapham, *Money and Class in America*.

28. Katznelson, "Levels of Class Formation," 145–48.

29. Burt, *The Perennial Philadelphians*, 11.

30. The essential guides to the Philadelphia upper class are Baltzell, *Philadelphia Gentlemen*; Burt, *The Perennial Philadelphians*; and Lukacs, *Philadelphia Patricians and Philistines*.

31. Pennell, *Our Philadelphia*, 1.

32. Baltzell, *Philadelphia Gentlemen*, 174.

33. Lewis, *The Worlds of Chippy Patterson*, 31.

34. On the history of the Main Line, see Lower Merion Historical Society, *The First 300*; and Morrison, *The Main Line*.

35. Morley, *Kitty Foyle*; and Barry, *The Philadelphia Story*. Although Morley's work is less known today, both it and *The Philadelphia Story* were turned into major motion pictures in 1940.

36. Dudden, "The City Embraces 'Normalcy,' 1919–1929," 596.

37. For a general survey of Philadelphia's economic history, see Weigley, *Philadelphia: A 300-Year History*, particularly, 474–87 and 532–33; and Scranton, *Endless Novelty*. For a list of the city's major employers at the start of the twentieth century, see the data compiled in Scranton, "Large Firms and Industrial Restructuring." For pictorial views of Philadelphia's

economic landscape at the turn of the last century, see King, *Philadelphia and Notable Philadelphians.*

38. Hearn, as quoted in Lukacs, *Philadelphia Patricians and Philistines*, 17. See also Rhodes, "Who Is a Philadelphian?" (1916).

39. Repplier, *Philadelphia: The Place and the People*, 389.

40. See Baltzell, *Puritan Boston and Quaker Philadelphia*; and Fischer, *Albion's Seed.*

41. Writings that capture the glorification of Philadelphia's Quaker past include Faris, *The Romance of Old Philadelphia* (1918); Lippincott, *Early Philadelphia* (1917); and Henry Seidel Canby, "The People Called Quakers," *Century Magazine*, June 1912, 266–79.

42. King, *Philadelphia and Notable Philadelphians*, 29.

43. See Scranton, *Proprietary Capitalism*; and Harris, *Bloodless Victories.*

44. "The City of William Penn," *Philadelphia Inquirer*, 22 May 1896, 13; and Burt and Davies, "The Iron Age, 1876–1905," 495.

45. See Richey, "Denominations and Denominationalism"; Bratt, "The Reorientation of American Protestantism, 1835–1845"; and Chaves and Sutton, "Organizational Consolidation in American Protestant Denominations, 1890–1900."

46. Baltzell, *Philadelphia Gentlemen*, 236.

Chapter 1

1. Baldwin, *Saint Katharine Drexel*, 1–2; Letterhouse, *The Frances A. Drexel Family*, 304; and Duffy, *Katharine Drexel*, 100.

2. For general surveys of the history of American philanthropy, see Bremner, *American Philanthropy*; Friedman and McGarvie, *Charity, Philanthropy, and Civility in American History*; and Zunz, *Philanthropy in America.*

3. On the role of philanthropy in shaping upper-class identity, both presently and in the past, see McCarthy, *Noblesse Oblige*; and Ostrower, *Why the Wealthy Give.*

4. See *Civic Club Digest of the Educational and Charitable Institutions and Societies in Philadelphia* (1895); and McCarthy, *American Creed.*

5. "American Millionaires and Their Public Gifts," *Review of Reviews* (1893), 48–60, quotation on 48.

6. Ibid., 50.

7. Baltzell, *Philadelphia Gentlemen*, 108–9; and Beckert, *The Monied Metropolis.*

8. "The Millionaires of Our City," *Philadelphia Inquirer*, 14 June 1891, 6; and "The Pennsylvania as a Financial Power," *Railway Age*, 7 December 1900, 445.

9. The essay "Success in Life" is included in the appendix to Childs, *Recollections* (1892). On Wanamaker, see Speeches: Perkiomen Seminary (1902), Box 20, John Wanamaker Papers, Coll 2188, HSP.

10. *Philadelphia and Popular Philadelphians*, 5. See also King, *Philadelphia and Notable Philadelphians*; and Oberholtzer, *Philadelphia: A History of the City and Its People.*

11. "The Millionaires of Our City," 6; *Philadelphia and Popular Philadelphians*, 129; and Marcosson, "The Millionaire Yield of Philadelphia," 505.

12. "The Rev. Washington Gladden Shuns Tainted Money" (1905), in Resek, *The Progressives*, 154.

13. On the *Presbyterian*, see Scharf, *History of Philadelphia*, 3:1997.

14. Conwell, *Acres of Diamonds* (1915); and Smith, *The Search for Social Salvation*, 107.

15. 1 Timothy 6:10. "Mammon Worship," *Presbyterian*, 5 June 1901; Conwell, *Acres of Diamonds* (1915), 24; and Worcester, *The Power and Weakness of Money* (1889).

16. See, for instance, the histories of the North Broad Street, Oxford, and Hermon Presbyterian Churches in White and Scott, *The Presbyterian Church in Philadelphia.*

17. Ibid., 169; and "Memorial Service to John McGill, Esq." (1910), PHS.

18. Rev. Dr. W. M. Rice, "Philadelphia Presbyterianism," *Presbyterian*, 9 January 1901, 7, 28.

19. For a tribute to a prominent Episcopalian active in church affairs, see the tribute to George B. Roberts in Wilson, *History of the Pennsylvania Railroad Company*, 2:247; and Jordan, *A History of Delaware County, Pennsylvania*, 3:911.

20. Ledwith, "The Record of Fifty Years, 1852–1902" (1902), 429.

21. George B. Roberts to Bishop Ozi Whitaker, 20 April 1894, GBRLB, LMHS.

22. See Murphy, "Duties of the Church Member to the Church."

23. "Bethany's Illustrated Year Book and Church Membership Guide for 1880," Pamphlets, Philadelphia Churches, vol. 5, HSP.

24. Charles Macalester, "Extracts from the Will of October 15, 1875," and Macalester Legal File, no. 33712, PHS. See also Hammonds, *Historical Directory of Presbyterian Churches and Presbyteries of Greater Philadelphia*, 129.

25. Carnegie, *The Gospel of Wealth*.

26. One of the best overviews of Carnegie's life and career remains Wall, *Andrew Carnegie*, quotation on 813. See also Nasaw, *Andrew Carnegie*.

27. On John Wanamaker's life and career, see Gibbons, *John Wanamaker*; Appel, *The Business Biography of John Wanamaker*; and Ershkowitz, *John Wanamaker, Philadelphia Merchant*.

28. See Smith, *The Search for Social Salvation*, 247; Rev. John Marlin Rittler, *One Man and His God: An Historical Memento of John Wanamaker and Bethany Presbyterian Church of Philadelphia, Pa.* (1969), PHS; and List of Elders and their committee assignments, 13 March 1918, Loose Papers, Bethany Presbyterian Church Records, PHS.

29. Evensen, *God's Man for the Gilded Age*, 79–91; and Schmidt, *Consumer Rites*, 161–96.

30. See point 10, John Wanamaker, "My Holiday Thoughts as to The Bethany Future," n.d.; and attached reply of Rev. George F. Pentecost to John Wanamaker, 13 March 1916, Package 1, Bethany Presbyterian Church Papers, PHS.

31. Paragraphs 17 and 18, Will of John Wanamaker, Book 457/page 84/no. 1929 (1923), in Loose Papers, Bethany Presbyterian Church Records, PHS.

32. See Ostrower, "Donor Control and Perpetual Trusts: Does Anything Last Forever?"

33. Trustee Minutes, 7 December 1923, Disston Memorial Presbyterian Church, PHS.

34. Matthew P. Blanchard, "Altruistic Trusts Bestow Gifts from Beyond the Grave," *Philadelphia Inquirer*, 18 July 2004.

35. See "Wanamaker's $56,000 for Boys Waiting for Best Claimant," *Philadelphia Record*, 25 April 1949, in John Wanamaker Clipping File, Free Library of Philadelphia. The Presbyterian Church renounced its right to funds Wanamaker left for the care of delinquent orphan boys. The orphanage founded by J. Edgar Thomson, the president of the Pennsylvania Railroad, to care for the orphaned children of railway workers closed in 1935 and money from the endowment went to fund scholarships. See Ward, *J. Edgar Thomson*, 218–19.

36. Bishop's Address, *Journal of the Diocesan Convention* (1916): 108–10. See also "Death of Henry W. Watson," *Church News*, October 1933, 26.

37. Biddle, *My Philadelphia Father*, 99; and Lynch, *Sharing the Bread in Service*, 1:47. For the conditions of the trust, see Baldwin, *Saint Katharine Drexel*, 50–54.

38. See Hamer, *America, Philanthropy, and the Moral Order*.

39. Baltzell, *Philadelphia Gentlemen*, 236.

40. See Baltzell, *Puritan Boston and Quaker Philadelphia*.

41. See Bonner, "Quaker Voluntary Organizations in Three Centuries," 196–98. For a broader and celebratory account of Quaker influence in the work of social betterment, see Newman, *A Procession of Friends*.

42. On work among the Native Americans and other missionary activities of Elkinton family members, see Elkinton, *Selections from the Diary and Correspondence of Joseph S. Elkinton, 1830–1905*; and Elkinton and Elkinton, *Joseph Elkinton, 1859–1920*.

43. Anderson, *The Education of Blacks in the South*, chap. 5.

44. References to prison reform work appear regularly in Morris's journal from 1914 onward, including many references to her work with prison reform advocate Thomas Mott Osborne. Representative entries include 1 January 1914 and 28 April 1915, Anna Wharton Morris, Journal, Box 53, Anna Wharton Morris Papers, RG 5/106, FHLSC.

45. See Benjamin, *Philadelphia Quakers in the Industrial Age, 1865–1920*, chap. 5; Moore, *Friends in the Delaware Valley*; and Eckert, *Guide to the Records of Philadelphia Yearly Meeting*, 246–64.

46. Anna Wharton Morris, Journal, 31 August 1901, Box 53, Anna Wharton Morris Papers, RG 5/106, FHLSC.

47. Warnings about debts were included in the *Christian Advices*, such as those included under the topic of "Trade" in the 1879 edition issued by the Philadelphia Yearly Meeting (Orthodox). For a discussion of Quaker business practices and economic beliefs in Philadelphia, see Tolles, *Meeting House and Counting House*.

48. J[ames] P. P. H[uston] to Charlie [Charles Lukens Huston], 23 May 1889, Box 6, HFP, Acc. 1174, HML.

49. See "Petition for Distribution" (1910), in Wharton Estate Papers, Box 3, Anna Wharton Morris Papers, RG 5/106, FHLSC. Joseph Wharton's only sizable bequest was $100,000 to Swarthmore College. He had intended a $500,000 gift to the Wharton School, but he withdrew the offer after a feud erupted between him and members of the university's board of trustees. See "Wharton Ignored Own Foundation in Late Codicil," *Philadelphia Inquirer*, 16 January 1909, clipping in Box 11, Joseph Wharton Family Papers, RG 5/162, FHLSC.

50. Anna Lovering Wharton, Wills, Box 3, Anna Wharton Morris Papers, RG 5/106, FHLSC. Anna's attitude toward charitable giving is reflected in the fact that in revising her 1898 will in 1909, she doubled the amount each of her daughters was to receive outright, from $25,000 to $50,000, but she did not increase the value of the handful of $1,000 and $500 charitable bequests.

51. "Anna Thomas Jeanes," *American National Biography*, 11:896–97; and "Aged Quaker Woman's Gift," *Presbyterian*, 1 May 1907.

52. Ashbrook, *Fifty Years*; and Lippincott, *Chronicles of the Penn Mutual Life Insurance Company of Philadelphia*, 39. On the history of the life insurance industry, see Zelizer, *Morals and Markets*; and Murphy, *Investing in Life*.

53. *Philadelphia and Popular Philadelphians*, 96; and Burt, *The Perennial Philadelphians*, 141.

54. Potter, "The Gospel for Wealth," in *The Scholar and the State*, 238; and "The Bull Lectures: Bishop Potter on 'the Modern Man and His Fellow Man,'" *Church Standard*, 1 February 1902, 520–21.

55. For a history of Episcopalian charitable work in Philadelphia, see Richards, "The Episcopalians," 141–53; and parish histories in Twelves, *A History of the Diocese of Pennsylvania*.

56. See Pointer, "Philadelphia Presbyterians, Capitalism, and the Morality of Economic Success."

57. For a representative example of split budgeting by churches in Philadelphia, see Trustee Minutes, 1906–1911, Church of the Covenant Records (Bala Cynwyd), PHS.

58. Bryn Mawr Presbyterian Church, *Messenger*, January 1922, 1, Bryn Mawr Presbyterian Church Archives.

59. Out of $50,310.37 collected by Bryn Mawr Presbyterian in 1921, $27,115.80 went for benevolences. See Bryn Mawr Presbyterian Church, *Messenger*, 15 May 1921, 2, Bryn Mawr Presbyterian Church Archives.

60. Overbrook Presbyterian Church, *The Place Where Thy Glory Dwells*, 30.

61. Davis, "Presbyterian Organizations in Philadelphia," 189–95.

62. In addition to John Wanamaker, whose work with Bethany Presbyterian Church has already been mentioned, the Huston family was also involved in evangelism. Charles Lukens Huston of Lukens Steel was active in Coatesville Presbyterian and supported prayer meetings,

crusades, and other local evangelical work. Ruth Huston, his daughter, was engaged in Presbyterian missionary work in Kentucky starting in the mid-1920s. See Charles L. Huston General Correspondence, Box 6; and correspondence between Ruth Huston and her mother, Annie S. Huston, Box 106, HFP, Acc. 1174, HML. For other references to the Hustons' local church activities, see the Presbyterian Church of Coatesville, *Handbook* (1947), PHS.

63. Oates, *The Catholic Philanthropic Tradition*, quotations on 129–30 and 133.

64. See, for instance, "Deny Jews Need to be Americanized: Indignation Meeting Held to Resent Charges of Bishop Garland and Rev. Dr. Zacker," *New York Times*, 25 November 1919, 15; and "Deny Proselyting: Pennsylvania Episcopalians Reply to Jewish Statement," *New York Times*, 26 September 1919, 12.

65. Rosen, "German Jews vs. Russian Jews in Philadelphia Philanthropy," 199.

66. See Wolf, "The German-Jewish Influence in Philadelphia's Jewish Charities."

67. Russell Conwell's close friendship with and great respect for Rabbi Joseph Krauskopf helped earn Jewish support for the Grace Baptist Temple. See "Jewish Contributors to Russell H. Conwell Foundation Fund" (1927), and correspondence between Albert M. Greenfield and potential donors to the fund, Box 32, Folder 49, Albert M. Greenfield Papers, Coll. 1959, HSP.

68. For an excellent comparison of the careers of Katharine and Anthony Drexel, see Rottenberg, *The Shared Vision of Saint Katharine Drexel and Anthony J. Drexel*.

69. See Letterhouse, *The Francis A. Drexel Family*; and Baltzell, *Philadelphia Gentlemen*, 256n.

70. Biddle, *My Philadelphia Father*, 99–100.

71. For a detailed analysis of Katharine's spiritual life, see the *positio* compiled for her canonization in Martino, *Catharinae Mariae Drexel*, ASBS.

72. The historical record does not tell us how Anthony responded to Katharine's decision to become a nun in his own words. For Katharine's account, see Katharine Drexel to Bishop James O'Connor, 6 April 1889, ASBS. See also Baldwin, *Saint Katharine Drexel*, 73; and Francis A. Drexel to Anthony J. Drexel, 5 September 1884, Francis A. Drexel Family Letters, ASBS.

73. Francis A. Drexel to Anthony J. Drexel, 5 September 1884, Francis A. Drexel Family Letters, ASBS; and Rottenberg, *The Man Who Made Wall Street*, 151–52.

74. Katharine Drexel to Bishop James O'Connor, 6 April 1889, ASBS.

75. While discerning her vocation, Katharine recorded her feelings for and against entering religious life in her journal. Under "My Objections to Entering Religion," Katharine wrote, "Superiors are frequently selected on account of their holiness, not for ability. I should hate to owe submission to a woman whom I felt to be stupid and whose orders showed her thorough want of judgment." Katharine Drexel, May 21, 1883, Writing no. 3207, ASBS. On the issue of "singularity" among female religious, see Coburn and Smith, *Spirited Lives*, 80–81.

76. Archbishop Ryan to Katharine Drexel, undated [1893], Box 8, Archbishop Ryan Papers, PAHRC.

77. Archbishop Ryan to Katharine Drexel, 7 May 1907, Box 8, Archbishop Ryan Papers, PAHRC.

78. Rottenberg, *The Man Who Made Wall Street*, quotation in caption within photo insert after p. 126; and Katharine Drexel to Fr. James O'Connor, 13 February 1889, Writing no. 58, ASBS.

79. Katharine Drexel to Josephine Seton Henry, 3 November 1937, Administration, Box 2, Folder 4, ASBS.

80. One example of Katharine's contractual approach to philanthropy can be seen in a letter to a priest at St. Stephen's Mission in Wyoming. In promising to pay for the expenses of nineteen Indian students, she requested that he "kindly at expiration of each [quarter] send us a [record] of total attendance at the school. . . . Those pupils we pay for are to receive the same board and tuition as is called for by the Government. If you agree to these conditions will you kindly copy them and subscribe your name before a witness." See Katharine Drexel to Rev. Feusi, S.J., 18 October 1894, Writing no. 3203, ASBS. Many of Katharine's philanthropic

promises included the proviso "if I live," since she recognized the legal nature of her trust fund. Since she had no children, Katharine's share of the trust fund would revert, upon her death, to her sisters, their children, or if none existed, as was ultimately the case, to the charities selected by her father in the original terms of trust.

81. Archbishop Ryan to Katharine Drexel, 19 April 1891, Box 8, Archbishop Ryan Papers, PAHRC. Although given the latitude by the archbishop to spend any sum smaller than $10,000, Katharine was required to receive the approval of the governing council of her order for larger expenditures.

82. Sisters of the Blessed Sacrament, *Century Book*, 8.

83. Baltzell, *Puritan Boston and Quaker Philadelphia*, 420–21.

84. Much of the research into Anthony's spiritual life and religious beliefs has been skillfully performed by Dan Rottenberg, whose *The Man Who Made Wall Street* is the only book-length biography of Anthony J. Drexel.

85. Ibid., 35, 52. On Drexel's relationship with the Episcopal Church of the Saviour, see Rev. Dr. Robert Johnston, "Church of the Saviour," *Church News*, January 1917, 128–33. Codman's remark is taken from the "Memorial Service Held in the Auditorium of the Drexel Institute on the Twentieth of January, 1894," 4, Anthony J. Drexel Vertical File, Drexel Family Collection, Drexel University Archives.

86. For an interesting discussion of the influence of lay elites within the Catholic Church in Philadelphia before the elimination of lay control in 1829, see Warren, "Displaced 'Pan-Americans' and the Transformation of the Catholic Church in Philadelphia." On the Hogan Schism and trustee issues in Philadelphia in the 1820s, see Light, *Rome and the New Republic*; Carey, *People, Priests, and Prelates*; and Ennis, "The New Diocese of Philadelphia."

87. Rottenberg, *The Man Who Made Wall Street*, 43.

88. Matthew Vassar to Anthony J. Drexel, 25 March 1862; Vassar, as quoted in McDonald and Hinton, *Drexel Institute of Technology*, 17.

89. McDonald and Hinton, *Drexel Institute of Technology*, 16–36, quotation on 30. Anthony had originally intended to establish a religiously affiliated charity school for women in one of Philadelphia's fashionable Main Line suburbs, but later, perhaps influenced by his relationship with Katharine, decided in favor of a nonsectarian industrial school. When Anthony mentioned in passing that his school would be nonsectarian, Katharine told her spiritual advisor she considered that to be "the *cream* of the entire quotation." See Katharine Drexel to Rev. James O'Connor, Feast of St. Louis [August 25, 1889], Writing no. 71, ASBS.

90. Potter, "Nobility in Business" in *The Scholar and the State*, 211.

91. On the bequest, see "Will of Thomas E. Cahill" (1878), PAHRC. On Cahill, see *The Harvest of Years* (1940), PAHRC; and Consuelo, "The Church of Philadelphia, 1884–1918," 302.

92. McDonald and Hinton, *Drexel Institute of Technology*, 34.

93. On nominally Episcopal schools and other institutions established by lay church members, see Yanagihara, "Some Educational Attitudes of the Protestant Episcopal Church in America." An instance of such can be seen in the 1865 founding of Lehigh University in Bethlehem, Pennsylvania, as discussed in Yates, *Lehigh University*, 22–35.

94. On the religious character of the University of Pennsylvania during the industrial era, see Baltzell, *Philadelphia Gentlemen*, 322.

Chapter 2

1. On Houston's financing of the Church of St. Martin-in-the-Fields, see Contosta, *A Philadelphia Family*, 29; on the church more generally, see Contosta, *A Venture in Faith*.

2. Contosta, *A Philadelphia Family*, 24–29.

3. For representative works on churches and community life, see Orsi, *The Madonna of 115th Street*; McGreevy, *Parish Boundaries*; Shepherd, *Avenues of Faith*; and Sterne, *Ballots and Bibles*. For an exception that addresses church finance, see Hudnut-Beumler, *In Pursuit of the Almighty's Dollar*.

4. Richey, "Denominations and Denominationalism," 84.

5. On urban church growth during the industrial era, see Butler, "Protestant Success in the New American City." On the development of the American denominational order, see Richey, "Denominations and Denominationalism"; Bratt, "The Reorientation of American Protestantism, 1835–1845"; and Chaves and Sutton, "Organizational Consolidation in American Protestant Denominations, 1890–1900."

6. Twelves, *A History of the Diocese of Pennsylvania*, 31.

7. "Committee of Church Extension" in *Acts and Debates of the General Assembly of the Presbyterian Church* (1856), 370–71; and Hammonds, *Historical Directory of Presbyterian Churches and Presbyteries of Greater Philadelphia*, 4.

8. "Chronology of Parish Foundations," in Catholic Standard and Times, *The Catholic Directory* (1997), 154–56, where the number of congregations refers only to those parishes currently located within the five counties—Philadelphia, Bucks, Chester, Delaware, and Montgomery—that now constitute the Archdiocese of Philadelphia. The number would be even greater if it were to include those parishes in counties that were split off from the archdiocese in 1961 to establish the Diocese of Allentown.

9. Aspinwall, *A Hundred Years*, 9–10.

10. See Overbrook Presbyterian Church, *The Place Where They Glory Dwells*; and Hammonds, *Historical Directory of Presbyterian Churches and Presbyteries of Greater Philadelphia*, 102.

11. The various forms of church growth were well established within denominational governance and are reflected in local church histories. For Philadelphia, see the brief church histories found in Twelves, *A History of the Diocese of Pennsylvania*; and Hammonds, *Historical Directory of Presbyterian Churches and Presbyteries of Greater Philadelphia*.

12. See Canons 10, 11, and 12 in *Constitutions and Canons for the Government of the Protestant Episcopal Church in the Diocese of Pennsylvania* (1923), 46–61; and "Process of Organizing a Particular Church" in Hopkins, *Manual of Church Polity* (1878), 96–97.

13. As important as pew rents were to the history of congregational formation and church development in America, they have gone largely unnoticed in scholarly literature. For an older overview, see Heales, *The History and Law of Church Seats or Pews*. On their connection to the loss of state support in New England, see Olds, "Privatizing the Church." For an English comparison, see Brown, "The Costs of Pew-Renting."

14. "A Pew Holder's Letter," in Anonymous, *Philadelphia: Or, Glances at Lawyers, Physicians, First-Circle, Wistar-Parties, &c. &c* (1826), 34–35.

15. Schantz, *Piety in Providence*, 16–25.

16. "Pennsylvania," *Church Standard*, 17 February 1906, 516.

17. Rilling, *Making Houses, Crafting Capitalism*, 45. See also Allinson and Penrose, *Ground Rents in Philadelphia*.

18. Pew Rent Receipt Booklet, Box 1, St. Andrew's Church Records, Coll. 1517, HSP.

19. For evidence of the practice of pew rents in Philadelphia, see the list of pewholders included in *The Souvenir Sketch of St. Patrick's Church, Philadelphia, 1842–1892*, 82–89, Parish History Collection, PAHRC.

20. Connelly, "The Visit of Archbishop Gaetano Bedini," 213; "Pews and Pew Rents," *St. Edward the Confessor Parish Calendar* (August 1896), PAHRC; and Dolan, *The Immigrant Church*, 51–52.

21. At Reform Congregation Keneseth Israel, seating fees effectively functioned like pew rents. See, for instance, the financial report that appears in the congregation's *Yearbook* (1891), 13, Reform Congregation Keneseth Israel Archives (Elkins Park).

22. *Christian Advices Issued by the Yearly Meeting of Friends, Held in Philadelphia* (Orthodox; 1879), 57–58. For an instance of disownment for pew rental, see the memoirs of John W. Townsend, dated 28 July 1910, in appendix A of Townsend, *My Life and Heritage*, 3–4.

23. "Bethany's Illustrated Year Book and Church Membership Guide for 1880," 34, in Pamphlets, Philadelphia Churches, vol. 10, HSP.

24. "Sixteenth Annual Report of the Parish Association of the Church of the Holy Apostles" (1890), 10, in Pamphlets, Philadelphia Churches, vol. 14, HSP.

25. Colwell, *New Themes for Protestant Clergy*, quotation on 129–30. On Colwell's influence, see Carey, *A Memoir of Stephen Colwell*; and Davenport, *Friends of Unrighteous Mammon*, 115–20.

26. On the role of privatism in urban development, see Warner, *The Private City*; as well as Teaford, *The Unheralded Triumph*; Einhorn, *Property Rules*; and Keating, *Building Chicago*.

27. Lilly, *The Story of St. Clement's Church*, 3; *St. Katharine of Siena, 1893–1993*, 10, Parish History Collection, PAHRC; and Ashmead, *History of Delaware County, Pennsylvania*, 682–84.

28. Loth, *Pencoyd and the Roberts Family*. On the development of Lower Merion Township, see also Lower Merion Historical Society, *The First 300*.

29. George B. Roberts to S. B. Brown, 5 February 1886, GBRLB, LMHS.

30. George B. Roberts to Robert Lewis, 30 September 1887, GBRLB, LMHS.

31. George B. Roberts to Dr. McConnell, 10 February 1892, GBRLB, LMHS. For a description of fundraising efforts for the new "Diocesan House," see also *Memorial Sermon and Addresses Delivered on the Occasion of the Twenty-Fifth Anniversary of the Consecration to the Episcopate of the Right Reverend O. W. Whitaker, DD*, 20–21.

32. George B. Roberts to Rev. R. Francis Wood, 8 November 1886, GBRLB, LMHS.

33. On runoff from the pig farm, see George B. Roberts to Russell Thayer, 20 July 1885 and 31 August 1885; on post office stables near St. Stephen's, see George B. Roberts to Senator Matthew Quay, 19 February 1894; and on the new diocesan offices, see George B. Roberts to J. Vaughan Merrick, 1 March 1894, all in GBRLB, LMHS. See also "Restrictions on all St. Asaph Road Lots" (1899), R114, Roberts Family Collection, LMHS.

34. Spencer Ervin, *History of the Church of St. Asaph, 1888–1938*, Archives, Church of St. Asaph (Bala Cynwyd). This history provided much of the information that appeared in Roberts, *Our First One Hundred Years*, 1–13. See also William Allen, "One Hundred Years of Parish Life," n.d., St. John's Church File, LMHS.

35. George B. Roberts to Bishop Ozi Whitaker, 20 April 1894, GBRLB, LMHS.

36. On the procedures for establishing a new parish, see Canons 11 and 12, *Constitutions and Canons for the Government of the Protestant Episcopal Church in the Diocese of Pennsylvania* (1923). For a narrative description of the establishment of a new Episcopal church, see Conger, *An Historical Sermon Delivered in the Memorial Church of the Good Shepherd*, 3–10.

37. Under Episcopal (and Roman Catholic) canons, for instance, churches could not be consecrated until the building and land were free of all "encumbrances." See Canon 50, "Of the Consecration of Churches," in *Constitution and Canons for the Government of the Protestant Episcopal Church in the United States of America* (1924), 783–86; and "Consecration," in *Catholic Encyclopedia* (1913), 4:276–82. For a narrative account of an Episcopal church consecration, see Knowles, *Reminiscences of a Parish Priest*, chap. 4.

38. "Darby—The Opportunity and the Problem," *Church News*, December 1912, 15.

39. Hammonds, *Historical Directory of Presbyterian Churches and Presbyteries of Greater Philadelphia*, 61.

40. Ibid., 63.

41. "Parish," in *Catholic Encyclopedia* (1911), 11:499–503, and for one instance of proposed Episcopal parish boundaries, see the map of churches in the diocese's Northeast Convocation in "Philadelphia," *Church Standard*, 6 November 1897, 13.

42. See McGreevy, *Parish Boundaries*; and Gamm, *Urban Exodus*, 18.

43. Cardinal Dougherty to Anna Cascio and Anna Sana, 14 February 1927, 80.3060, Cardinal Dougherty Papers, PAHRC.

44. Joseph Kerlin to Archbishop Prendergast, n.d., 71.140ach, Archbishop Prendergast Papers, PAHRC.

45. "History of the Church of the Most Blessed Sacrament, Philadelphia: Grand Souvenir $50,000 Parish Campaign, 1927," Parish History Collection, PAHRC.

46. *Holy Child Parish, 1909–1984: 75th Jubilee Celebration* (1984), Parish History Collection, PAHRC.

47. Mother M. Eustacia, OSB, to Cardinal Dougherty, 25 March 1924, and Cardinal Dougherty to Mother M. Eustacia, OSB, 29 March 1924, 80.8539, Cardinal Dougherty Papers, PAHRC.

48. On the trustee controversy at St. Mary's Church, see Ennis, "The New Diocese of Philadelphia," 70–79; Carey, *People, Priests, and Prelates*, 164–66; and Light, *Rome and the New Republic*, 97–131.

49. See Dignan, *A History of the Legal Incorporation of Catholic Church Property in the United States*; and Cardinal Dougherty to Louise Drexel Morrell, 7 April 1919, 80.7350, Cardinal Dougherty Papers, PAHRC.

50. Clark, "A Pattern of Urban Growth," 166.

51. Sister M. Bernard to Archbishop Edmund Prendergast, 6 August 1914, 71.378Ai, Archbishop Prendergast Papers, PAHRC.

52. See, for instance, John Patrick Walsh to Cardinal Dougherty, 11 May 1930, 80.8404, Cardinal Dougherty Papers, PAHRC. Walsh warns that the collapse of building and loan associations that bore parish names might reflect badly on the Catholic Church.

53. Morris, *American Catholic*, 170.

54. See "St. Charles' Fund Exceeds $365,779," *Public Ledger*, 11 April 1927, 4; and "$365,779.32 is Contribution of Diocese to the Seminary," *Catholic Standard and Times*, 16 April 1927, 1; and Seminary Collection Ledger Sheets, 1928–1929 and 1929–1930, 80.3874, Cardinal Dougherty Papers, PAHRC.

55. Gough, "The Roots of Episcopalian Authority Structures: The Church of England in Colonial Philadelphia," 91, quotation on 110. See also Addison, "The Growth of the Layman's Power in the Episcopal Church," 65–77.

56. See "Of the Church Session," in *Constitution of the Presbyterian Church in the United States of America* (1892), 291–93.

57. See *Rights and Duties of Sessions and Trustees in Presbyterian Churches* (1883), 6–7. The decision on which body had the authority to hire church musicians, dated 7 May 1883, was authored by the committee of Samuel C. Perkins, Robert Adair, and S. W. Dana. A similar debate is recorded in Session Minutes, 13 May 1905, Disston Memorial Presbyterian Church Records, PHS.

58. Trustee Minutes, 7 January 1909, Disston Memorial Presbyterian Church Records, PHS.

59. For Thomas's role as diocesan treasurer, see MacAfee, *The First Ninety Years of the Parish of the Holy Apostles*, 66; and *Journal of the Diocesan Convention* (1930): 244; for the Houstons' and Woodwards' involvement in St. Martin-in-the-Fields, see Contosta, *A Venture in Faith*, 42; for Disston's service as treasurer of the board of trustees, see Trustee Minutes, 8 February 1909, Disston Memorial Presbyterian Church Records, PHS; for Chandler and St. Asaph's, see Ervin, *History of the Church of St. Asaph*, 13, Archives, Church of St. Asaph (Bala Cynwyd); and for Biddle and the Church of the Holy Apostles, see "Charles Biddle," *Church News*, March 1924, 217–18.

60. See, for instance, "Wardens and Vestrymen," *Church Standard*, 23 March 1901, 730; and "The Ideal of a Vestry," *Church Standard*, 22 July 1905, 379–80; 29 July 1905, 410–11.

61. Session Minutes, 6 October 1901, Church of the Covenant Records, PHS.

62. Reynolds D. Brown, "A Letter Sent by the Executive Secretary to the Rectors and Wardens of the Churches in the Diocese," *Church News*, January 1920, 80.

63. On concern about elected church members' sense of inherited entitlement, see "The Call of Vestrymen," *Church News*, May 1913, 6; Reynolds D. Brown, "A Letter Sent by the Executive Secretary to the Rectors and Wardens of the Churches in the Diocese," *Church News*, January 1920, 80–81; and Bishop's Address, *Journal of the Diocesan Convention* (1927): 86.

64. A memorial tribute to Taggart appeared in the parish newsletter, *St. Thomas Messenger*, December 1921, St. Thomas's Episcopal Church Archives (Whitemarsh).

65. Nathanael Groton, Diary, 20 March, 29 March, and 13 April 1914. (The diary is held privately by Nathanael Groton Jr.)

66. Bishop's Address, *Journal of the Diocesan Convention* (1925 and 1927).

67. "Vestries Chosen in Many Churches. William Waterall Elected by Grace Episcopal Congregation for 50th Consecutive Year," *Public Ledger*, 19 April 1927, 10. There is no shortage of examples of long-serving vestrymen: Lewis H. Redner held a seat on the vestry of the Church of the Holy Trinity for thirty-four years; Anthony J. Drexel was on the vestry of the Episcopal Church of the Saviour for thirty-seven years, from its founding in 1856 until his death in 1893; Edward H. Bonsall served forty-nine years as vestryman at St. Matthew's Episcopal Church, Francisville; and Samuel F. Houston served the Church of St. Martin-in-the-Fields, Chestnut Hill, for a remarkable sixty-three years.

68. Trustee Minutes, 12 June 1911, Disston Memorial Presbyterian Church Records, PHS.

69. Wainwright, *History of the Church of the Messiah, Gwynedd*, 29.

70. Gough, *Christ Church*, 305. Similar difficulties in recruiting new trustees and vestrymen were encountered at the Church of St. Luke and the Epiphany; see Newton, *River of Years*, 260.

71. "The Rights and Duties of Sessions and Trustees in Presbyterian Churches," 12.

72. Trustee Minutes, 14 October 1878, Chestnut Hill Presbyterian Church Records, PHS.

73. Cited in MacAfee, *The First Ninety Years of the Parish of the Holy Apostles*, 66.

74. Edward G. Bradford, William Fisher, and George A. Elliott, Treasurer, to the Vestry of St. John's Episcopal, Wilmington, Del., 6 May 1895; and, on Francis Gurney du Pont's views on parish management, Rev. Leighton Coleman to Francis Gurney du Pont, 31 January 1888, in Box 30, Francis Gurney du Pont Papers, Acc. 504, HML.

75. Rev. William Charles Hogg, "The Every Member Report," *Minutes of the Thirty-Fifth Annual Session of the Synod of Pennsylvania of the Presbyterian Church in the United States of America* (1916), 35–36; and *Constitutions and Canons for the Government of the Protestant Episcopal Church in the United States of America* (1924), 824–29. See also Rev. E. Van Dyke Wright, "Business in the Church," *Presbyterian*, 25 May 1922; and "Business Methods in the Church," *Church News*, January 1918, 112–13.

76. Efforts of the school trustees to institute a program of "practical parochial work" in 1893 are mentioned in West, *Centennial History of the Philadelphia Divinity School*, 81. A description of the overall curriculum with a reference to "practical training" can be found in the *Philadelphia Divinity School Catalog* (1895), 27, Philadelphia Divinity School Records, Episcopal Divinity School Archives (Cambridge, Massachusetts).

77. On the lectures, see Faculty Minutes, 13 January 1887, RG 4, Philadelphia Divinity School Records, Episcopal Divinity School Archives (Cambridge, Massachusetts).

78. On O'Loughlin's fundraising generally, see D. B. O'Loughlin, "Working a Parish to Death," in *O'Loughlin Serve-us* (September 1924), PAHRC; on the Good Shepherd fundraising campaign, see "$750,964.15 received as $500,000 Drive Ends," *Catholic Standard and Times*, 9 December 1921; and for a fuller account of O'Loughlin's career, see Rzeznik, "The Parochial Enterprise."

79. The list of deputies from the Diocese of Pennsylvania appeared in *Church News*, October 1928, 6. For a short biography of Pepper, see Lukacs, *Philadelphia Patricians and Philistines*, 219–39. On Houston, see Contosta, *A Philadelphia Family*. On the proceedings of the 1928 convention, including specific references to George Wharton Pepper, see E. Clowes Chorley,

"Day by Day at General Convention," *Churchman*, 27 October 1928, 13–16, 24–25. For more on the 1928 revisions to the Book of Common Prayer, see Sydnor, *The Real Prayer Book*, 69–83.

80. For a listing of the administrative bodies of the Episcopal Church and the organization of the general convention, see "The Church in the United States," and "The National Organization of the Church in the United States," in *Living Church Annual* (1931), 153–72. For a present-day organizational chart for the administrative bodies of the national church, see "The Canonical Structure of the Church," *Episcopal Church Annual* (2003), 24.

81. For a good explanation of the representation procedures and the significance of the diocesan convention, see Rev. Francis C. Hartshorne, "The Coming Diocesan Convention. So What?" *Church News*, April 1937, 239–40.

82. Congregational records were taken from those reported in *Lloyd's Clerical Directory* (1910).

83. In 1930, for instance, the chancellor of the diocese raised the question of whether "small and diminishing congregations" that do "a minimum of work should have equal voting power with the largest and most active." The matter was referred for further study. See "Report of the Chancellor and the Committee on Canons in re S. John, Northern Liberties," *Journal of the Diocesan Convention* (1930): 42.

84. "Last Day's Session," *Philadelphia Inquirer*, 19 May 1888, 2; and Rev. Dr. McConnell, "Report of the Special Commission of Proportionate Lay Representation of the Parishes," *Journal of the Diocesan Convention* (1890): 125–26.

85. Nathanael Groton, Diary, 6 May 1914; and Rector's Letter, *St. Thomas Messenger*, May 1922, St. Thomas's Episcopal Church Archives (Whitemarsh).

86. Bishop's Address, *Church News*, June 1920, 253–54; and Rev. George Copeland, "The 143rd Annual Convention of the Diocese," *Church News*, May–June 1927, 266.

87. The number of missions within the Diocese of Pennsylvania in 1916 is taken from "Five Years," *Church News*, October 1916, 6. For a complete listing of parishes and missions, including the designated racial or ethnic communities they served, see *Journal of the Diocesan Convention* (1917). Figures for the Church of the Holy Trinity provide one example of the degree of disenfranchisement. The parish statistics for 1916 reported that, of the parish's 3,166 members, only 1,764 belonged to Holy Trinity. The remaining 1,402, or 44 percent of the total population, belonged to one of the parish's three chapels. See Church of the Holy Trinity, *Yearbook* (1917), Church of the Holy Trinity Archives (Philadelphia).

88. For mention of such efforts, see Copeland, "The 143rd Annual Convention of the Diocese," 270; and Hartshorne, "The Coming Diocesan Convention. So What?" 239–40.

89. As reported in the 1901 *Journal of the General Convention* of the Episcopal Church, the ten largest dioceses accounted for 343,070 of the 743,622 total members within the Church, yet were apportioned the same representation as even the smallest of the Church's fifty-nine dioceses. This figure includes members of missionary districts in the membership totals, but does not count their nonvoting delegates in the representation calculation. Missionary districts, like missionary chapels at the diocesan level, did not enjoy the privileges of governance until they became self-sufficient dioceses. Not until the 1928 General Convention was an amendment passed to provide each missionary district with a one-fourth vote. See "Report of the Committee on Communication from the General Convention of 1928," *Journal of the Diocesan Convention* (1930): 330–32.

90. See the editorial response to "The Fond du Lac Function," *Church Standard* (1900), 195. A mention of efforts to divide the Diocese of Pennsylvania appears in Bishop's Address, *Journal of the Diocesan Convention* (1897): 74–80.

91. Although there has been no systematic analysis of the membership of the General Convention or diocesan conventions of the Episcopal Church, the general class character of lay delegates can be gleaned from the delegate rosters contained in the convention reports. For an explanation of the nature of Episcopal Church polity, see Dator, *Many Parts, One Body*.

92. "Rotation in Office of Vestrymen," *Church News*, April 1931, 305; and Silliman, *The Episcopal Church in Delaware*, 476.

93. Davis, "A Study of Protestant Church Boards of Control," 429.

Chapter 3

1. Shinn, *King's Handbook of Notable Episcopal Churches in the United States*, 233–34.

2. This account of the Church of the Advocate is derived from the National Historic Landmark nomination form prepared by Susan Glassman, dated 23 June 1995, available at http://www.cr.nps.gov/nhl/designations/samples/pa/advocate.pdf. On the decision not to make the Church of the Advocate the diocesan cathedral, see "The Bishop Announces Selection of Site for Cathedral," *Church News*, January 1927, 114.

3. See Bourdieu, *Distinction*, 56; and Nelson, "At Ease with Our Own Kind: Worship Practices and Class Segregation in American Religion," 57–59.

4. "Ecclesiology" as used here refers to the study or practice of constructing and decorating churches. For a history of the field, which first developed in England in the 1830s and 1840s, see Stanton, *The Gothic Revival*, introduction and chap. 1. It differs from the theological discipline of ecclesiology—the study of the origins, nature, and purpose of churches (faiths).

5. On the history of ecclesiastical architecture in America, see Williams, *Houses of God*; Kilde, *When Church Became Theatre*; and Howe, *Houses of Worship*. On liturgical practice, see DeSanctis, *Building from Belief*; Giles, *Re-Pitching the Tent*; Seasoltz, *A Sense of the Sacred*; and Wuthnow, *All in Sync*. On ecclesiastical architecture in Philadelphia, see Moss, *Historic Sacred Spaces of Philadelphia*; and Farnsworth, Croce, and Chorpenning, *Stained Glass in Catholic Philadelphia*.

6. Alison Lurie, "God's Houses," part I, *New York Review of Books*, 3 July 2003, 30–32, DeSanctis quotation on 30.

7. Within the Episcopal Church, regulations were set by individual dioceses. See Canon 57, "Of Parishes and Congregations," in *Constitutions and Canons for the Government of the Protestant Episcopal Church in the United States of America* (1924); and Canons 11 and 12, in *Constitutions and Canons for the Government of the Protestant Episcopal Church in the Diocese of Pennsylvania* (1923).

8. Within the Episcopal diocese, examples include the Church of St. Asaph, Bala Cynwyd (1888), connected with the Roberts family; the Church of St. Martin-in-the-Fields, Chestnut Hill (1889), financed by Henry Howard Houston and his family; Trinity Episcopal Church, Ambler (1891), built by R. V. Mattison in memory of his daughter; St. Paul's Memorial Church, Philadelphia (1904), donated by George C. Thomas in honor of his parents; the Chapel of the Mediator, Philadelphia (1906), a tribute to George C. Thomas by his wife; the Memorial Church of the Good Shepherd, Germantown (1919), funded by the sons of Henry W. and Alice P. Brown; and the Nevil Memorial Church of St. George, Ardmore (1932), given by George Washington Nevil.

Similar examples can be found among Presbyterians in Philadelphia, including: Ann Carmichael Memorial Presbyterian Church (1877) given by Thomas Potter in memory of his sister; Mary Elizabeth Patterson Memorial Presbyterian Church (1880) given through a bequest from Morris Patterson in honor of his daughter; and Disston Memorial Presbyterian Church (1886) supported by Mrs. Henry Disston and other members of the family. For parish and congregation histories, see entries for these churches in Twelves, *A History of the Diocese of Pennsylvania*; and Hammonds, *Historical Directory of Presbyterian Churches and Presbyteries of Greater Philadelphia*.

9. For an example of a decision to economize with plain glass windows, see Trustee Minutes, 28 April 1913, Church of the Covenant (Bala Cynwyd), PHS. On bells, see Manton, *A Splendid Legacy*, 67.

10. "The Divinity School: Its Character and Purpose," in the Philadelphia Divinity School, *Catalog* (1924–1925), Philadelphia Divinity School Records, Episcopal Divinity School Archives (Cambridge, Massachusetts).

11. Lears, *No Place of Grace*, 199.

12. "Renovation," *Church News*, October 1928, 230–31.

13. On Roberts's architectural involvement with the Church of St. Asaph, see Roberts, *Our First One Hundred Years*, 5. On his involvement with Broad Street Station, constructed between 1880 and 1882, see Burgess and Kennedy, *Centennial History of the Pennsylvania Railroad Company*, 431–32.

14. George B. Roberts to Theophilus P. Chandler, 21 March 1888, asks for a sketch of the parsonage; Roberts to Karl Bitter, 11 May 1892, reveals Roberts's careful involvement with the design and architectural detail at St. Asaph's; and Roberts to Clayton & Bell Studios, London, 16 April 1895, addresses window design, all in GBRLB, LMHS. See also Spencer Ervin, *History of the Church of St. Asaph, 1888–1938*, Archives, Church of St. Asaph (Bala Cynwyd); and Roberts, *Our First One Hundred Years*, 8.

15. Bassett, "T. P. Chandler Jr., FAIA," 18; and Roberts, *Our First One Hundred Years*, 26.

16. Although members of the Roberts family were not the sole contributors to St. Asaph's, their contributions were by far the most numerous and influential. For a complete listing of early memorial gifts, see Ervin, *History of the Church of St. Asaph, 1888–1938*, supplement to Appendix V, Archives, Church of St. Asaph (Bala Cynwyd).

17. Patterns of class patronage were equally pronounced among residential commissions. See Thomas, "Architectural Patronage and Social Stratification in Philadelphia Between 1840 and 1920," 85–123.

18. See Woods, *From Craft to Profession*.

19. On Furness, see O'Gorman, *The Architecture of Frank Furness*, 15–19. On Evans, see Margaret Eleanor Evans, notes for the *National Cyclopedia of American Biography*, 099.36, Allen Evans Collection, Architecture Archives, University of Pennsylvania.

20. Yarnall, *Addison Hutton*, 21–58; and "Addison Hutton," in Tatman and Moss, *Biographical Dictionary of Philadelphia Architects*, 401–7.

21. Margaret Eleanor Evans, notes for the *National Cyclopedia of American Biography*, 099.36, Allen Evans Collection, Architecture Archives, University of Pennsylvania.

22. In Philadelphia, a handful of competing firms, notably those led by Edwin F. Durang, Henry D. Dagit, and George I. Lovatt, were responsible for a disproportionate number of diocesan projects executed in the late nineteenth and early twentieth centuries. See their respective entries in Tatman and Moss, *Biographical Dictionary of Philadelphia Architects*, 229–34, 181–84, and 489–92. For a sample of Durang's vast contribution to the institutional infrastructure of the archdiocese, with work on over 100 diocesan projects, see the listing in *Architectural Album of Edwin F. Durang & Son* (ca. 1920), PAHRC.

23. On Chandler's gift of the Christ Church chapel to the diocese, see Thomas J. Garland to Theophilus P. Chandler, 19 September 1919, TPCC, AthP.

24. See "Theophilus Parsons Chandler Jr.," in Tatman and Moss, *Biographical Dictionary of Philadelphia Architects*, 139–43; and George T. Tilden to Theophilus P. Chandler, 1 April 1870, TPCC, AthP.

25. Letter and receipt from Christ Church, [Christiana Hundred], Delaware to Theophilus P. Chandler, 12 March 1877, TPCC, AthP; Theophilus P. Chandler to Francis Gurney du Pont, 16 August 1888, Box 1, Francis Gurney du Pont Papers, Acc. 504, HML.

26. St. Thomas Church [New York City] to Mr. Samuel B. Brown, forwarded to Theophilus P. Chandler, 21 November 1905, TPCC, AthP.

27. Records compiled by the Philadelphia Athenaeum credit Chandler with 3,085 published references to drawings sent out during his professional career, which spanned nearly a half century (1872–1919). Among his projects, Chandler completed work on at least twenty-two

churches. Although other ecclesiastical architects working in Philadelphia at about the same time, such as Edwin F. Durang, may have had more churches to their names, Chandler acquired a greater reputation, distinguished by his gift for decorative detail. On this last point, see Bassett, "T. P. Chandler Jr., FAIA," 14–18.

28. For a sample of Chandler's professional schedule, with calls on members of the upper class, see Theophilus P. Chandler Jr., typed copy of diary entries of 2 February 1882 and 19 July 1882, TPCC, AthP.

29. See entries for Walter Cope, John Stewardson, and Addison Hutton in Tatman and Moss, *Biographical Dictionary of Philadelphia Architects*, 165–70; 761–62; 401–7.

30. Although Chandler headed the school for only one year, he selected his own successor, Warren P. Laird, and remained active in the city's architectural community. See Percy C. Stuart, "Architectural Schools in the United States, University of Pennsylvania— no. 2," *Architectural Record* (January 1901): 313–36; and Strong and Thomas, *The Book of the School*, 5–11.

31. Bassett, "T. P. Chandler Jr., FAIA," ii–iii.

32. "Theophilus P. Chandler," in Tatman and Moss, *Biographical Dictionary of Philadelphia Architects*, 139.

33. A partial database of projects completed by D'Ascenzo and Yellin is available through the Philadelphia Architects and Buildings Project, http://www.philadelphiabuildings.org/pab/. The Athenaeum of Philadelphia holds copies of Yellin's job cards, which reveal his extensive work, and an unprocessed collection of D'Ascenzo's studio records, which includes his equally extensive job files.

34. For an overview of Yellin Metalworks, see Davis, *Sketches in Iron*.

35. A copy of Yellin's lecture appears in Andrews, *Samuel Yellin, Metalworker*, 71–75. On ironwork in Philadelphia, see Magaziner, *The Golden Age of Ironwork*; and Wattenmaker, *Samuel Yellin in Context*.

36. Rider College Student Center Gallery, *D'Ascenzo: The Art of Stained Glass from the Collection of Stanley Switlik*, n.p.

37. On Cram's influence among the upper class, see Lears, *No Place of Grace*, 66–96, 203–9.

38. Cram, *Church Building*, 222, 224; and Clark, as quoted in Muccigrosso, *American Gothic*, 90.

39. See Gladish, *John Pitcairn: Uncommon Entrepreneur*; and "John Pitcairn," in Gladish and Glenn, *Pitcairn Patriarchs*, Bryn Athyn College Library.

40. On the development of Cairnwood and Bryn Athyn, see Gladish, *John Pitcairn: Uncommon Entrepreneur*, chaps. 12 and 13; John Pitcairn quotation on 311. On John Pitcairn's financial contributions to the New Church, see also Childs, *The Life and Times of John Pitcairn*, Bryn Athyn College Library.

41. Gladish, *John Pitcairn: Uncommon Entrepreneur*, 417–18.

42. Glenn, "The Pitcairn Brothers: Raymond, Theodore, Harold," 14. See also Jennie Gaskill, "Biography of Raymond Pitcairn" (1977), Bryn Athyn College Library.

43. Shand-Tucci, *Ralph Adams Cram*, 54–63.

44. Raymond Pitcairn, as quoted in Glenn, *Bryn Athyn Cathedral*, 23.

45. Ibid., 94.

46. The New Church claim that the structural imperfections of Bryn Athyn Cathedral were meant to represent "the unpredictable path of human growth" appears on the cathedral website, http://www.brynathynchurch.org/cathedral/history.html.

47. Architecture scholars generally distinguish three periods within the Gothic revival movement, which was not limited to ecclesiastical architecture: the early Gothic revival (ca. 1840–1870); Victorian Gothic (ca. 1870–1900); and the late Gothic revival (ca. 1900–1930). See Rifkind, *A Field Guide to American Architecture*; and Whiffen, *American Architecture Since 1780*. On further distinctions within the movement, see Loth and Sadler, *The Only Proper Style*.

48. On the appeal of the Gothic revival style to the upper class, see Lears, *No Place of Grace*, quotation on 198; and Stanton, *The Gothic Revival*, 332.

49. See Smith, *Gothic Arches, Latin Crosses*, 106–17.

50. Baltzell, *Puritan Boston and Quaker Philadelphia*, 450.

51. Kilde, *When Church Became Theatre*, quotation on 58.

52. Stanton, *The Gothic Revival*, xvii–xxiv; and Arthur Channing Downs, "America's First 'Medieval' Churches," *Historical Magazine of the Protestant Episcopal Church*, June 1976, 167–76. On the politics of the Gothic revival in England, see Reed, *Glorious Battle*.

53. See Pugin, *An Apology for the Revival of Christian Architecture in England*, esp. 22–33; Paley, *A Manual of Gothic Architecture*; and Duffy, *The Stripping of the Altars*.

54. On the politics of ecclesiological change within the Episcopal Church, see Chorley, *Men and Movements in the American Episcopal Church*.

55. Smith, *Gothic Arches, Latin Crosses*, 5.

56. Stanton, *The Gothic Revival*, 4.

57. Ibid., quotation on 91. See also Twelves, *A History of the Diocese of Pennsylvania*, 158–59; Moss, *Historic Sacred Places of Philadelphia*, 248–53; and "A Brief History and Guide to the Church of St. James the Less," St. Mark's Episcopal Church Archives.

58. Stanton, *The Gothic Revival*, 115–25; Moss, *Historic Sacred Places of Philadelphia*, 162–67; and Gilkyson, *St. Mark's*.

59. Stanton, *The Gothic Revival*, 28, 125.

60. Kilde, *When Church Became Theatre*, 72.

61. See, for instance, Hart, *Design for Parish Churches in the Three Styles of English Church Architecture*.

62. Representative churches include Church of St. Asaph, Bala Cynwyd (1888); Episcopal Church of the Redeemer, Bryn Mawr (1851, 1881); Christ Church, Ithan (1891, 1919); Church of St. John, Lower Merion (1863, 1900); St. Martin's Episcopal Church, Radnor (1881); Church of the Good Shepherd, Rosemont (1869, 1894); St. Mary's Episcopal Church, Wayne (1886); and All Saints' Church, Wynnewood (1911). The contrast in the style of these churches is evident when compared with the two established parishes of colonial origin in the area, St. David's Episcopal Church, Radnor (ca. 1700) and St. Peter's Church, Great Valley (ca. 1700). Examples of parish church architecture can also be found in other suburban communities, such as St. Paul's Episcopal Church, Elkins Park (1861) and St. Timothy's Church, Roxborough (1859). For brief parish histories, see Twelves, *History of the Episcopal Diocese of Pennsylvania*. (When two dates are given, the first indicates the year the parish was founded, and the second indicates the year its new and permanent church was built.)

63. For a good explanation of this upper-class mentality, see Morrison, *The Main Line*, 1–15.

64. On Montgomery, see Kathrens, *American Splendor*, 189; on Percival Roberts, see Phyllis Maier, "Rich Men and Their Castles," LMHS.

65. See Meigs, *An American Country House*. Meigs was a partner in the prestigious firm of Mellor, Meigs & Howe, which specialized in residential design. Included in the book is a reprint of Meigs's 1922 *Country Living* article, which describes how "an old-fashioned farm was brought into existence"(xxviii) at the Newbold estate.

66. For memoirs that speak to the importance of Main Line churches' upper-class community, see Townsend, *My Life and Heritage*; Thayer, *Muzzy*; and Brinton, *Their Lives and Mine*.

67. On the more intimate size of suburban parish churches, their reported seating capacity is revealing. Thus, in 1900, according to the *Journal of the Diocesan Convention*, the Church of St.Asaph, Bala Cynwyd, could seat 350, and the Church of the Redeemer, Bryn Mawr, one of the larger Main Line churches, 500. In contrast, the Church of the Holy Trinity, Rittenhouse Square, was able to accommodate 1,400.

68. Kilde, *When Church Became Theatre*, 84–111.

69. *St. Katharine of Siena, 1893–1993*, 10, Parish History Collection, PAHRC; and Ashmead, *History of Delaware County, Pennsylvania*, 682–84.

70. On the development of Bryn Mawr, see Lower Merion Historical Society, *The First 300*, 72–75.

71. Twelves, *A History of the Diocese of Pennsylvania*, 167–68; "Charles Marquedant Burns," in Tatman and Moss, *Biographical Dictionary of Philadelphia Architects*, 119–21; and Moss, *Historic Sacred Places in Philadelphia*, 248–53, 288–90.

72. Lower Merion Historical Society, *The First 300*, 182–83.

73. *A Century of Faith and Service, 1885–1985*, 9.

74. On the deed restriction for the Montgomery Avenue parcel, see ibid., 2–3, 9. On rules about development in Bryn Mawr imposed by the Pennsylvania Railroad, see Lower Merion Historical Society, *The First 300*, 73.

75. *A Century of Faith and Service*, 7–20.

76. "New Catholic Church: Corner-Stone of the Edifice at Bryn Mawr to be Laid on Sunday," *Philadelphia Inquirer*, 2 July 1896, 2.

77. See Oliveri, "Building a Baroque Catholicism"; and *E. F. Durang's Architectural Album* (Philadelphia, ca. 1900), PAHRC.

78. Contosta, *Villanova University, 1842–1992*, 49–50.

79. Kane, *Separatism and Subculture*, 114. On the newfound confidence of American Catholics in the early twentieth century, see Halsey, *The Survival of American Innocence*, 83; and Skerrett, Kantowicz, and Avella, *Catholicism, Chicago Style*, xxi.

80. Williams, "The Gospel of Wealth and the Gospel of Art," 220.

81. On party battles in the Episcopal Church, see Chorley, *Men and Movements*, esp. 264–69 and 336–49; and Guelzo, *For the Union of Evangelical Christendom*.

82. See Chorley, *Men and Movements*, 380–81.

83. Ibid., 390–92.

84. Vestry Minutes, 10 January 1854, St. Mark's Episcopal Church Archives.

85. Thus, several decades later at the Church of St. Asaph, the parish history records the following recollection of Mrs. David E. Williams: "When Dr. Watson was here we had a plain small wooden altar, a table cloth . . . a wooden cross, and two small glass vases. . . . Candles on the altar were not used till I think Mr. Bird's time [1921], and when my mother wanted to give a processional Cross as a memorial, it was turned down at once by the vestry as too high." See Ervin, *History of the Church of St. Asaph, 1888–1838*, 32, Archives, Church of St. Asaph (Bala Cynwyd). Another incident regarding a decision about floor candles in 1921 is recounted in All Saints' Church, *Prepared for Us to Walk In*, 28–29.

86. Efforts by members of the St. Clement's vestry (representing the pewholders) to remove the previous rector, Herman G. Batterson, led to a civil trial over whether they had the authority to dismiss their rector at will over the objection of other members of the congregation. See *St. Clement's Church Case* (1871). On the dispute at St. Clement's, see also Twelves, *A History of the Diocese of Pennsylvania*, 28–29; and Lilly, *The Story of St. Clement's Church, Philadelphia*.

87. On the 1874 schism in the Episcopal Church, see Guelzo, *For the Union of Evangelical Christendom*, chap. 5.

88. The clash between Bishop Stevens and Rev. Prescott was captured in a series of widely circulated tracts written by parties on both sides of the dispute. In particular, see Goodwin, *The New Ritualistic Divinity* (1879); and Prescott, "Is Fairness in Religious Controversy Impossible?" (1879).

89. Cecil Roberts, "Travels through the Prayer Book," *Church News*, October 1923, 10.

90. For an analysis of both the 1892 and the 1928 revisions to the Book of Common Prayer, see Sydnor, *The Real Prayer Book*, 59–83. See also Northrup, *The 1892 Book of Common Prayer*.

91. "Shrubbery," *Church News*, November 1928, 42; "The Latest Trends in Tombstones," *Church News*, April 1933, 238–39; and "Down with Concrete," *Church News*, December 1930, 110–11.

92. Jones, *Lantern Slides*, 106.

93. For the transcript of the proceedings and testimony of the St. Mark's chiming trial, see *Report of* [George L.] *Harrison et al. vs. St. Mark's Church, Philadelphia* (1877), quotations on 19, 41, 491. For the parish account, see Gilkyson, *St. Mark's*, 28–35. For a scholarly analysis of the case, see Weiner, "Religion Out Loud," 39–106.

94. "Sound Amplifier Augments Religious Services," *Popular Mechanics*, September 1921, 324; and advertisement for Sonora Phonographs, *Philadelphia Inquirer*, 5 December 1920, 16.

95. "An Awful Prospect," *Church News*, February 1930, 161. The Bok Carillon, regarded as one of the finest carillons in the world, was commissioned by Philadelphia publisher and music lover Edward William Bok for the grounds of his Florida estate, Pinewood. The carillon is housed not in a church, but in the "singing tower," an artistic masterpiece designed by Milton B. Medary Jr. and embellished with metalwork by Samuel Yellin, both fellow Philadelphians.

96. Borrowing from Willis, *Form Follows Finance*.

Chapter 4

1. Scull, *William Ellis Scull, Sometime Quaker*, quotation on 37. The term "meeting" had several usages among Quakers. It could refer to the physical structure where Quakers gathered for worship, the worship service itself, the community of faith, or to the administrative organization of the Society of Friends, in which individuals belonged to a monthly meeting, which then reported to a quarterly meeting, and through it, to the yearly meeting.

2. Ibid., 38–39.

3. Ibid., 39.

4. Baltzell, *Philadelphia Gentlemen*, 226.

5. For works suggesting that the industrial-era elite became Episcopalians merely for social reasons, see Wecter, *The Saga of American Society*; Konolige and Konolige, *The Power of Their Glory*; and Lears, *No Place of Grace*.

6. For a good survey of the theoretical literature on conversion, see Gooren, *Religious Conversion and Disaffiliation*, chap. 1.

7. For overviews of the Society of Friends, including discussion of membership decline, see Moore, *Friends in the Delaware Valley*; Benjamin, *The Philadelphia Quakers in the Industrial Age, 1865–1920*; and Hamm, *The Transformation of American Quakerism*.

8. Benjamin, *The Philadelphia Quakers in the Industrial Age, 1865–1920*, 4–5.

9. Joshua L. Baily to David Scull, 4 February 1907, Box 1, Joshua L. Baily Papers, Coll. 1032, QCHC.

10. Burt and Davies, "The Iron Age, 1876–1905," 494; and Benjamin, *The Philadelphia Quakers in the Industrial Age, 1865–1920*, 217–18.

11. Harris, "War in the Social Order," 182.

12. On factionalism and membership decline among the city's Quakers, see Benjamin, *The Philadelphia Quakers in the Industrial Age, 1865–1920*, 3–25.

13. Isabella P. Huston to Hannah Gibbons, 26 February 1858, 13 January 1856, 2 January 1855, and 29 June 1857, Box 104, HFP, Acc. 1174, HML.

14. Isabella P. Huston to Hannah Gibbons, 2 January 1855, 21 June 1858, and 20 January 1860, Box 104, HFP, Acc. 1174, HML.

15. Isabella Huston would speak of spiritual trials of varying severity for much of her life. For quotations, see Isabella P. Huston to Hannah Gibbons, 13 January 1856; and Helen Hotchkin to Isabella P. Huston, 28 November 1884, Box 104, HFP, Acc. 1174, HML.

16. Isabella P. Huston to Hannah Gibbons, 9 January 1859; and Elizabeth Evans to Isabella P. Huston, 15 June 1875, Box 104, HFP, Acc. 1174, HML.

17. Isabella P. Huston to Hannah Gibbons, 23 September 1864; and Morris Cope to Isabella P. Huston, 18 November 1879, Box 104, HFP, Acc. 1174, HML.

18. Joseph Potts to Isabella P. Huston, 5 March 1872, Box 104, HFP, Acc. 1174, HML; and Stokes, *Memoirs of John S. Stokes* (1893), 46.

19. See entry of 17 June 1883, in Stokes, *Memoirs of John S. Stokes*, 280.

20. Elizabeth Evans to Isabella P. Huston, 15 June 1875, Box 104, HFP, Acc. 1174, HML.

21. See Hamm, *The Transformation of American Quakerism*, chap. 4.

22. "Parents and Children" in *Christian Advices Issued by the Yearly Meeting of Friends* (Orthodox; 1879), 88.

23. Multiple references to George Roberts's drift from the Quaker faith appear in his letters to his family. See, in particular, those of 15 November 1848 and 5 August 1849, Box 4, RFP, Coll. 2087, HSP.

24. "Hireling Ministry," in *Christian Advices Issued by the Yearly Meeting of Friends* (Orthodox; 1879), 56–59.

25. Gainor Roberts to George B. Roberts, 20 April 1850, Box 5, RFP, Coll. 2087, HSP.

26. Rosalinda and Gainor Roberts to George B. Roberts, 25 April 1852, Box 5, RFP, Coll. 2087, HSP. For other mentions of their concern about George's interaction with proper society, see George B. Roberts to Rosalinda Roberts, 17 August 1853, Box 4; and Rosalinda Roberts to George B. Roberts, 2 September 1855, Box 5, RFP, Coll. 2087, HSP.

27. Of the five Roberts children who lived to adulthood, only Algernon (1828–1868) appeared to remain a member of the Society of Friends. On the Roberts family religious history, see Loth, *Pencoyd and the Roberts Family*, 35–54; and Roberts, *Our First One Hundred Years*, 4.

28. On the Jones family, see Lower Merion Historical Society, *The First* 300, 40–41; and Loth, *Pencoyd and the Roberts Family*, 37.

29. See Algernon Roberts to George B. Roberts, 15 August 1852, Box 5, RFP, Coll. 2087, HSP. For later references to the benefit fair, see Rosalinda Roberts, Diary, 17 June 1863 and 13 August 1867, Box 2, RFP, Coll. 2087, HSP.

30. See Loth, *Pencoyd and the Roberts Family*, 38–44; and A. & P. Roberts Company, *Pencoyd Iron Works* (1897).

31. "Joseph Wharton," *American National Biography*, 23:113–15.

32. Benjamin, *The Philadelphia Quakers in the Industrial Age, 1865–1920*, chap. 2; and Yates, *Joseph Wharton*, 206.

33. Tolles, as quoted in Benjamin, *The Philadelphia Quakers in the Industrial Age, 1865–1920*, 5. See also Tolles, *Meeting House and Counting House*.

34. Speakman, *Ritualism and Dogmatic Theology* (1891), 14.

35. See entries of 2 April 1871 and 7 February 1876 in Stokes, *Memoirs of John S. Stokes*, 46, 138.

36. Speakman, *Ritualism and Dogmatic Theology*, 12, 36.

37. Ibid., 10–14. Speakman's articles were originally published in the *Friends' Intelligencer* of Philadelphia and the *Manchester Friend* in 1872 and 1873. On Speakman, see also Kennedy, *British Quakerism, 1860–1920*, 90.

38. Speakman, *Ritualism and Dogmatic Theology*, 21.

39. Ibid., 45.

40. See Benjamin, *The Philadelphia Quakers in the Industrial Age, 1865–1920*, chap. 8.

41. *Discipline of the Yearly Meeting of Friends* (Orthodox; 1910), 121.

42. Germantown Monthly Meeting, Minutes, esp. 30 January 1916 and 23 January 1929, PYM Records, QCHC.

43. For a fuller discussion of the tension between luxury and simplicity among Quakers in regard to their homes and possessions, see Frost, "From Plainness to Simplicity: Changing Quaker Ideals for Material Culture," quotation on 23.

44. Stokes, *No Axe to Grind*, 17.

45. Scull, *William Ellis Scull, Sometime Quaker*, 4.

46. Yates, *Joseph Wharton*, 230. For other accounts of the Quaker colony at Jamestown, Rhode Island, see Stokes, *No Axe to Grind*, 39; and the diary entries of Wharton's daughter, Anna Wharton Morris, for 24 September 1893 and 5 September 1917, Box 53, Anna Wharton Morris Papers, RG 5/106, FHLSC.

47. See, for instance, "Plainness in Dress," *Friends' Intelligencer*, 11 April 1891; Emma Waln, "Plainness," *Friends' Intelligencer*, 11 March 1905; and "Christian Simplicity," *Friend*, 16 August 1923.

48. Francis Stokes to Katharine W. Stokes, 20 September 1865, Box 3, Stokes-Evans-Cope Family Papers, Coll. 1169, QCHC.

49. Anna Wharton Morris, Journal, 26 May 1904, Box 53, Anna Wharton Morris Papers, RG 5/106, FHLSC.

50. Morris E. Leeds, New Testament Study Scrapbook (1913), Box 9, MELP, Coll. 1127, QCHC.

51. See Forbes, "Quaker Tribalism," 145–73; and Benjamin, *The Philadelphia Quakers in the Industrial Age, 1865–1920*, 155–57.

52. Frost, "From Plainness to Simplicity," 32.

53. Benjamin, *The Philadelphia Quakers in the Industrial Age, 1865–1920*, 159–60, 236.

54. Frankford Monthly Meeting, Minutes, 1853–1906; and Germantown Monthly Meeting, Minutes, 1906–1924, PYM Records, QCHC.

55. Germantown Monthly Meeting, Minutes, 17 December 1908, PYM Records, QCHC.

56. Benjamin, *The Philadelphia Quakers in the Industrial Age, 1865–1920*, 156.

57. Hamm, *The Quakers in America*, 49–54.

58. Hein and Shattuck, *The Episcopalians*, 87.

59. Joseph Wharton to the Committee of the Yearly Meeting of Philadelphia upon the Revision of the Discipline, 9 March 1894, copy attached to the letter of Joseph Wharton to Anna Lovering Wharton, 9 March 1894, Box 20, Wharton Family Papers, RG 5/162, FHLSC. For more on Wharton's view on religious doctrines and creeds, see Wharton, "The Creed in the Discipline" (1892), Box 41; and Isaac H. Clothier to Joseph Wharton, 28 February 1896 and reply of 21 March 1896, Box 51, Wharton Family Papers, RG 5/162, FHLSC.

60. Scull, *William Ellis Scull, Sometime Quaker*, 39.

61. See "Hireling Ministry," in *Christian Advices Issued by the Yearly Meeting of Friends, Held in Philadelphia* (Orthodox; 1879), 56–59.

62. "Maintaining a Free Ministry," *Friends' Intelligencer*, 1 April 1905; and Jones, *The Later Periods of Quakerism* (1921), 2:917–18.

63. George B. Roberts to Rosalinda Roberts, 15 October 1854, Box 3, RFP, Coll. 2087, HSP.

64. Comfort, *The Quaker Way of Life*, 27. Quaker meetings for worship were conducted in two general manners: "unprogrammed" worship, the traditional mode, had no set order of service, relying instead on individuals to speak and share "vocal ministry" when so moved by the spirit; and "programmed" worship, a mode adopted by some Quakers during the mid-nineteenth century that included formal readings, hymns, sermons, or other elements in addition to the traditional silent worship and vocal ministry.

65. Ibid, chap. 2; and Jones, "The Sense of the Meeting."

66. On the spiritual beliefs that underlay meetinghouse design, see Catherine C. Lavoie, "Quaker Beliefs and Practices and the Eighteenth-Century Development of the Friends Meeting House in the Delaware Valley."

67. Brinton, *Their Lives and Mine*, 265. Another prie-dieu reference in a family memoir can be found in Thayer, *Muzzy*, 80.

68. Bispham, *A Quaker Singer's Recollection*, 28.

69. On Wistar Morris, see Overbrook Presbyterian Church, *The Place Where Thy Glory Dwells*; on Charles Lukens Huston, see HFP, Acc. 1174, HML; and on the Drexels and Wanamakers, see Baltzell, *Philadelphia Gentlemen*, 249, 256n.

70. See "Funeral of Mrs. Drexel," *Public Ledger*, 30 January 1912. Lucy Wharton Drexel's Catholicism is also mentioned in her daughter's memoirs: see Lehr, *King Lehr and the Gilded Age*, 23.

71. Harrison, *Annals of the Ancestry of Charles Custis Harrison and Ellen Waln Harrison*, 114.

72. Cooper, *A Living Faith*, 148.

73. *Friends' Library*, 16 vols. (1832–1838). For Quaker views on proper reading material, see "Books," in *Christian Advices Issued by the Yearly Meeting of Friends, Held in Philadelphia* (Orthodox; 1879), 9–15.

74. Esther [Evans] to Isabella P. Huston, 1 April 1860, Box 104, HFP, Acc. 1174, HML; Flexner, *A Quaker Childhood*, 324; and Quaker Fiction Collection, QCHC.

75. See Smith, *A Christian's Secret to a Happy Life*. For another autobiographical work, see Smith, *The Unselfishness of God and How I Discovered It*. For an analysis of Hannah Whitall Smith's influence among Quakers, see Abbott, *A Certain Kind of Perfection*, 63–64.

76. Smith, *John M. Whitall*, quotation on 192. On the Quaker biographical tradition, see Brinton, *Quaker Journals*.

77. Mary Berenson to Hannah Whitall Smith, 28 September 1891, reprinted in Strachey and Samuels, *Mary Berenson: A Self-Portrait*, 47–48.

78. Smith, *Unforgotten Years*, esp. 17, 30–35, 109, 150–52. See also Smith, *A Religious Rebel*.

79. In many ways, Logan Pearsall Smith and others of his generation share much in common with Catholics of a later period for whom the parochial world of pre–Vatican II Catholicism evoked similar feelings. On the Catholic experience, see Sewell, *Resurrecting Grace*.

80. Thayer, *Muzzy*, 24.

81. Pepper, *Philadelphia Lawyer*, 43. On patterns of intermarriage during this period, see Rose, *Beloved Strangers*.

82. For figures on Quaker disownment during the Revolution, see Tinkcom, "The Revolutionary City, 1765–1783," 131–32.

83. T. Williams Roberts to Mrs. Raymond Evans, 20 August 1956, R146, Roberts Family Collection, LMHS. T. Williams Roberts was the son of George B. Roberts and his second wife, Miriam Pyle Williams.

84. Loth, *Pencoyd and the Roberts Family*, 32.

85. Mitchell, *Hugh Wynne, Free Quaker*.

86. On Mitchell's family background, see Massey, *The Mitchells and Days of Philadelphia*; and Earnest, *S. Weir Mitchell*.

87. "Hugh Wynne," *Friends' Intelligencer*, 1 January 1898; and Burt, *The Perennial Philadelphians*, 381.

88. Brinton, *Their Lives and Mine*, 133–34.

89. Ibid., 51–57.

90. See Strachey, *A Quaker Grandmother*.

91. Annie Stewart Huston, "Romance of Charles L. and Annie S. Huston," typescript, n.d., 3, Box 106, HFP, Acc. 1174, HML.

92. See Welcome Society, *Twenty-Fifth Anniversary, Charter, By-Laws, Members, Annual Report, Activities*.

93. See Baltzell, *Puritan Boston and Quaker Philadelphia*, 92–106.

94. Lippincott, *A Narrative of Chestnut Hill*, 92.

95. Henry Seidel Canby, "The People Called Quakers," *Century Magazine*, June 1912, 278.

96. Burt and Davies, "The Iron Age, 1876–1905," 508.

97. The exact date the Quaker became the official mascot of the University of Pennsylvania is unclear, but it was not until the middle decades of the twentieth century. The university's athletes were called "the Quakers" in newspaper reports as early as the mid-1880s, however, and then more frequently from the 1890s on. See, for instance, "The Columbia Boys Win: A Hastily Arranged Race with the Quakers," *New York Times*, 25 June 1886, 1; and "Aimed at the Quakers: A New Rule of the Intercollegiate Football Association," *Washington Post*, 28 October 1893, 6.

98. Pennell, *Our Philadelphia*, 289.

99. For visions of Philadelphia's Quaker past, see Pennell, *Our Philadelphia* (1914); Faris, *The Romance of Old Philadelphia* (1918); and Lippincott, *Early Philadelphia* (1917).

Chapter 5

1. Diocesan Affairs Committee, Minutes, 28 May 1919, Episcopal Churchwomen Records, Coll. 2106, HSP.

2. For surveys of the history of the Episcopal Church and the Diocese of Pennsylvania, see Prichard, *A History of the Episcopal Church*; Hein and Shattuck, *The Episcopalians*; and Twelves, *A History of the Diocese of Pennsylvania*.

3. On nineteenth-century efforts to promote church unity, see Holmes, *A Brief History of the Episcopal Church*, 125–26. See also Huntington, *The Church Ideal*, and *A National Church*; and Woolverton, "William Reed Huntington and Church Unity."

4. In 1920, for instance, the Episcopal Church reported 1,096,895 members, or 0.93 percent of the total U.S. population of 117,823,165. For membership statistics, given in five-year increments, see *Living Church Annual* (2003), 20–21. Within the Diocese of Pennsylvania, the Episcopalian presence was somewhat stronger: Episcopalians constituted 2.69 percent of those residing in the diocese in 1920, as calculated from U.S. census figures and diocesan statistics reported in the *Living Church Annual*. For a fuller portrait of the nation's religious composition, see Gaustad and Barlow, *New Historical Atlas of Religion in America*.

5. Sociologist E. Digby Baltzell has been seen as popularizing the term "WASP," as noted above. On the history of the WASP religious establishment, see Baltzell, *The Protestant Establishment*; Hutchison, *Between the Times*; and Schrag, *The Decline of the WASP*, quotation on 15.

6. Episcopal Church statistics show that the Diocese of Pennsylvania was second only to the Diocese of New York in numerical size and financial strength throughout the early twentieth century. See, for instance, "General Table of Statistics," *Living Church Annual and Whittaker's Churchman's Almanac* (1911), 350–53; and "General Table of Statistics," *Living Church Annual* (1931), 504–9.

7. On immigration concerns, see Higham, *Strangers in the Land*; and Behdad, *A Forgetful Nation*. On the religious response to social change, see White and Hopkins, *The Social Gospel*; and Boyer, *Urban Masses and Moral Order in America, 1820–1920*.

8. See Lukacs, *Philadelphia Patricians and Philistines, 1900–1950*; and Sugeno, "The Establishmentarian Ideal and the Mission of the Episcopal Church."

9. Hein and Shattuck, *The Episcopalians*, 51–62.

10. See Gough, "The Roots of Episcopalian Authority Structures: The Church of England in Colonial Philadelphia."

11. *Living Church Annual* (1911), 350; and Twelves, *History of the Diocese of Pennsylvania*, 31.

12. See, in particular, the Bishop's Address, *Journal of the Diocesan Convention*, for 1881, 1885, and 1909.

13. Bishop's Address, *Journal of the Diocesan Convention* (1917); and "Report on the Nation-Wide Campaign," *Journal of the Diocesan Convention* (1921): 88–90.

14. See Chorley, *Men and Movements in the American Episcopal Church*; and Twelves, *History of the Diocese of Pennsylvania*, 25–26.

15. All Saints' Church, *Prepared for Us to Walk In*, 28–29.

16. The most famous dispute between the high and low church factions of the Episcopal Church involved the introduction of ritualist practices at St. Clement's Church during the 1870s, discussed in chapter 3.

17. For Bishop Whitaker's views, see Bishop's Address, *Journal of the Diocesan Convention*, for 1891, 1904, and 1905. On the schism, see Guelzo, *For the Union of Evangelical Christendom*.

18. The need to elect a new diocesan bishop arose unexpectedly when Alexander Mackay-Smith, Bishop Whitaker's coadjutor and appointed successor, died within one year of taking over the leadership of the diocese. On Bishop Rhinelander's background and election, see Twelves, *History of the Diocese of Pennsylvania*, 32–33; and Washburn, *Philip Mercer Rhinelander*.

19. Bishop's Address, *Journal of the Diocesan Convention* (1912).

20. Ibid. (1887).

21. Ibid. (1917).

22. "The 129th Convention of the Diocese," *Church News*, June 1913, 10; and "Report of the Commission on Church Building of the Diocese," Appendix T, *Journal of the Diocesan Convention* (1914): 286–91.

23. On Garland, see Twelves, *History of the Diocese of Pennsylvania*, 36–37. Within the Episcopal Church, a suffragan bishop serves as an auxiliary to the diocesan bishop, but, unlike a bishop coadjutor, does not possess a right of succession. There is no comprehensive study of the social composition of the lay representatives on the governing bodies of the Diocese of Pennsylvania, but their status is not difficult to surmise. In 1911, for instance, the laymen on the standing committee of the diocese—R. Francis Wood, William W. Frazier, John E. Baird, Samuel F. Houston, and Edward H. Bonsall—were powerful figures in industry, banking, and real estate. See "Officers of the Convention of the Diocese," *Journal of the Diocesan Convention* (1911): 3. For a discussion of the general class character of Protestant church boards in the early twentieth century, see Jerome Davis, "A Study of Protestant Church Boards of Control."

24. Bishop's Address, *Journal of the Diocesan Convention* (1923). Bishop Rhinelander's remarks were later reprinted as "The Creed: Its Place in the Life of the Church and in the Duty of the Church's Officers," *Church News*, May–June 1923, 263–64. "Higher criticism," also known as the "historical-critical method," referred to the practice of studying Scripture as a historical text reflective of its time, eliciting concern that eternal truths would be relativized or that the texts would no longer be seen as divinely inspired.

25. On Rhinelander's teaching career, see Washburn, *Philip Mercer Rhinelander*, chap. 6. On his involvement in the Philadelphia Divinity School, see Overseers and Joint Board, Minutes, 1912–1923, RG4, Philadelphia Divinity School Records, Episcopal Divinity School Archives (Cambridge, Massachusetts).

26. Rev. Nathanael Groton, Diary, 11 May 1914 and 6 April 1914. Privately held by Nathanael Groton Jr.

27. Bishop's Address, *Journal of the Diocesan Convention* (1919).

28. Rev. Nathanael Groton, Diary, 5 May 1914.

29. On the shift in emphasis from personal morality to civic responsibility among New York Episcopalians, see Bourgeois, *All Things Human*, 81–83.

30. Charles Custis Harrison, "Memoirs" (1925), Box 13, Folder 14, CCHP, UPA. See also, "Dr. C. C. Harrison Dies in 85th Year," *New York Times*, 13 February 1929, 23; and George L. Harrison, "Philadelphia as I Remember It, 1875–1950," 3 vols., Harrison Family Papers, Coll. 2048, HSP.

31. [Charles C. Harrison], "Report of the Provost of the U of Penn," *Church Standard*, 19 March 1898, 657. On the religious character of the University of Pennsylvania during the industrial era, see Baltzell, *Philadelphia Gentlemen*, 322.

32. Pepper, *Philadelphia Lawyer*, 290; and "Why the University," in Pepper, *Men and Issues*, 13–24. For a later editorial on public responsibility, see also "Churchmen in Public Service," *Church News*, January 1935, 114; and for an assessment of Pepper's character, see Lukacs, *Philadelphia Patricians and Philistines*, 219–39.

33. On the theme of public responsibility among the elite, see Baltzell, *The Protestant Establishment*.

34. Rev. Nathanael Groton, Diary, 27 March 1914.

35. Diocese of Pennsylvania, *Cathedral Church of Christ* [1922], HSP; and "The Bishop Announces Selection of Site for Cathedral," *Church News*, January 1927, 114–15.

36. Perry, *Memorial Sermon Preached at the Convention of the Diocese of Pennsylvania* (1911), 7. Whitaker's reluctance is also hinted at in "The Bishop Announces Selection of Site for Cathedral," 114–15.

37. Bishop's Address, *Journal of the Diocesan Convention* (1919); and *Church News*, April 1925, 253.

38. On the history of the founding of the Cathedral Chapter and its early work, see Scull, *William Ellis Scull, Sometime Quaker*, chap. 17. A reference to "The Evolution of a Cathedral" appears in "The Bishop's Address at Cathedral League Meeting," *Church News*, April 1920, 179.

39. Bishop's Address, *Journal of the Diocesan Convention* (1925). Advertisements encouraging support for the National Cathedral appeared in issues of *Church News* throughout 1927 and 1928.

40. "The Bishop Announces Selection of Site for Cathedral," 114–15; "The Bishop Breaks Ground for St. Mary's Chapel on the Cathedral Site in Upper Roxborough," *Church News*, October 1932, 22–23.

41. On the redevelopment of the 100-acre cathedral tract, see Shearer, *Cathedral Village*, n.p.

42. Though most often associated with the National Cathedral in Washington, D.C., the phrase "house of prayer for all God's people" was also used to describe the proposed Philadelphia Cathedral and other such projects. See "Parkway Cathedral will be P. E. Memorial," *Public Ledger*, 29 November 1918, 9; and the speech of Canon G. C. F. Bratenahl in Diocese of Pennsylvania, *Cathedral Church of Christ* [1922], HSP.

43. Diocesan Affairs Committee, Minutes, May 1918, Episcopal Churchwomen Records, Coll. 2106, HSP.

44. See, in particular, Williams, *Houses of God*; Kilde, *When Church Became Theatre*; and DeSanctis, *Building from Belief*.

45. For a narrative and visual depiction of the liturgical changes within the Episcopal Church, see Diocese of Pennsylvania, *Our Common Prayer*.

46. For a comprehensive history of the parish, see Gough, *Christ Church, Philadelphia*.

47. Ibid., 276. Though one of the first, Philadelphia's Christ Church was not alone in installing "historical windows." Examples can be found in other parishes in the Diocese of Pennsylvania, such as Christ Church, Ithan, established in 1919, whose rear central window depicts key figures in the history of the Anglican and Episcopal Churches.

48. The windows installed at Philadelphia's Christ Church in the 1890s were not the first stained glass to adorn its sanctuary. The large east window directly behind the altar had its clear glass replaced with stained glass in the 1850s to keep unsightly views of the outside world from disturbing worshippers. The memorial windows were removed and put in storage in the 1980s as part of the church's most recent restoration, which emphasized historical authenticity and returned the sanctuary to its original colonial appearance. See Gough, *Christ Church, Philadelphia*, 234–36, 260–62, 276–78, 307–8, 386; and photographic insert after p. 202.

49. Ibid., 316; "Old Christ Church is a Center of Interest to Sesqui Visitors," *Church News*, October 1926, 13; "Church Exhibit at the Sesqui-Centennial," *Church News*, October 1926, 12; and "Spiritual Sources from Which Signers Drew Their Inspiration," *Church News*, October 1926, 18–19.

50. On colonial-era political tensions over episcopal leadership, see Bridenbaugh, *Mitre and Sceptre*; and Woolverton, *Colonial Anglicanism in North America*.

51. W. Herbert Burk, "Washington the Churchman," sermon delivered 22 February 1903, Washington Memorial Chapel Archives, Valley Forge.

52. For a discussion of Washington's religious views, see Mapp, *The Faiths of Our Fathers*, 66–79.

53. Kammen, *Mystic Chords of Memory*, 196.

54. See Rev. W. Herbert Burk, "Washington Memorial Chapel, Valley Forge," *Church News*, October 1915, 27–28; and for Burk's explanation on how he came to hear the story of Washington at prayer, see Burk, *Valley Forge*, 63–65. On the popularity of the devotional story, which seems to have originated with Mason Locke Weems's *The Life of George Washington*, originally published in 1802, see Loewen, *Lies Across America*, 362–66.

55. See Burk, *In the Beginning at Valley Forge and the Washington Memorial Chapel*.

56. Treese, *Valley Forge*, 83–84.

57. Ibid., 82–89. For an example of Burk's funding solicitation advertisements, see *Church News*, February 1913, 35.

58. Treese, *Valley Forge*, 101.

59. Burk, "Washington Memorial Chapel, Valley Forge," 27.

60. Treese, *Valley Forge*, 98.

61. For evidence of the Harrison family's interest in history and genealogy, see Harrison, *Annals of the Ancestry of Charles Custis Harrison and Ellen Waln Harrison*.

62. Watson, *First Ladies of the United States*, 9–18.

63. Treese, *Valley Forge*, 99; and [Harrison], "Report of the Provost of the U of Penn.," 657.

64. On the character of elite education, see Cookson and Persell, *Preparing for Power*; and Jordan, "Between Heaven and Harvard." A glimpse of Harrison's own college-days views on social responsibility can be seen in an essay he wrote while a student at the University of Pennsylvania, "Respectability," 2 December 1858, Box 4, Folder 7, CCHP, UPA.

65. Burk, *Valley Forge*, 91.

66. Treese, *Valley Forge*, 215–18.

67. Gough, *Christ Church, Philadelphia*, 331–45.

68. For the official history of the National Cathedral, see Feller and Fishwick, *For Thy Great Glory*, esp. 3–8.

69. See Tweed, *America's Church: The National Shrine and Catholic Presence in the Nation's Capital*; and Bains, "A Capital Presence: The Presbyterian Quest for a 'National Church' in Washington, D.C."

70. Bellah, *Varieties of Civil Religion*, chap. 1.

Chapter 6

1. Richmond, *Sermons: Series II* (1915), quotation on 5; and Witmer, *The Nearing Case*.

2. For an account of the Social Order Committee, see Jones, *Quakers in Action*, 167–79; and Harris, "War in the Social Order," 191–96.

3. On the religious dimensions of progressive-era reform in Philadelphia, see Ken Fones-Wolf, *Trade Union Gospel*; and Benjamin, "Gentlemen Reformers in the Quaker City, 1870–1912." For other accounts of religious reform in the period, see Hopkins, *The Rise of the Social Gospel in American Protestantism*; May, *Protestant Churches and Industrial America*; Griffen, "Rich Laymen and Early Social Christianity"; Boyer, *Urban Masses and Moral Order*

in America, 1820–1920; Crunden, *Ministers of Reform*; Fox, "The Culture of Liberal Protestant Progressivism, 1875–1925"; Curtis, *A Consuming Faith*; and Zahniser, *Steel City Gospel.*

4. *Lloyd's Clerical Directory* (1910), 263.

5. Richmond, *Frederic Dan Huntington: An Appreciation* (1908), 5–7; "Rector Arraigns Negro's Lynchers," *Philadelphia Inquirer*, 21 August 1911, 5; and "Probe Will Do Good," *Philadelphia Inquirer*, 27 May 1912, 5.

6. Rainsford, *The Story of a Varied Life*, 203–31. Richmond mentioned Rainsford as a model for some of his actions on at least one occasion during the trial, referring to a time when they studied together. Richmond Trial, 27 November 1916, 693, GCRP, Coll. 550, HSP.

7. Richmond Trial, 11 December 1916, 1019, GCRP, Coll. 550, HSP. "Attacks Astor's Marriage," *New York Times*, 7 August 1911, 7; and Sinclair, *Dynasty*, 205–8.

8. Richmond, as quoted in Biel, *Down with the Old Canoe*, 68.

9. Richmond Trial, 27 November 1916, 763–64, GCRP, Coll. 550, HSP; and "Pulpits Subsidized Says Philadelphia Pastor" *New York Times*, 1 January 1912, 10.

10. "Talks to Business Men," *Official Journal* (Amalgamated Meat Cutters and Butcher Workmen of North America; February 1906): 41; "Astor Critic Long in the Limelight as Denunciator," *Lexington Herald*, 13 August 1911, 3; and "Militant Preacher," *Time*, 6 January 1930.

11. "Ministers Discuss Bishopric Candidates," *Philadelphia Inquirer*, 29 April 1911, 6; "Richmond Attacks Actions of Bishop," *Philadelphia Inquirer*, 6 January 1913, 14.

12. The official history of the Diocese of Pennsylvania devotes two paragraphs to the trial, but offers little in the way of explanation. See Twelves, *A History of the Diocese of Pennsylvania*, 35–36.

13. Richmond Trial, 7 December 1916, 936, GCRP, Coll. 550, HSP.

14. Richmond Trial, 21 December 1916, 1222, GCRP, Coll. 550, HSP.

15. Richmond Trial, 23 July 1917, 4728, GCRP, Coll. 550, HSP.

16. Richmond Trial, 23 July 1917, 4835, GCRP, Coll. 550, HSP.

17. Argo, "Opinion" (1917), 25. On Rhinelander's episcopal style, see Washburn, *Philip Mercer Rhinelander*, 133–39. On Richmond's opposition, see "Ministers Discuss Bishopric Candidates," 6.

18. Argo, "Opinion" (1917), 31.

19. See Canon 42, "On the Dissolution of the Pastoral Relation," in *Constitutions and Canons for the Government of the Protestant Episcopal Church in the United States of America* (1924), 696–719.

20. Budd, "The Charge to the Triers" (1917), 2.

21. Richmond Trial, 13 December 1916, 1153–1154, GCRP, Coll. 550, HSP.

22. Richmond Trial, 26 September 1915, 682, GCRP, Coll. 550, HSP.

23. Richmond Trial, 5 December 1916, 843, GCRP, Coll. 550, HSP; "Richmond Attacks Actions of Bishop," 14.

24. The St. Timothy's Workingmen's Club closed in 1912, after thirty-six years of operation. See Manton, *A Splendid Legacy*, 74–75.

25. *The Second Annual Report of the Free Church Association* (1877), 3–4.

26. For a tribute to J. Vaughan Merrick Sr., see "Pennsylvania," *Church Standard*, 14 April 1906, 806. On the Merrick family and their religious commitments, see Manton, *A Splendid Legacy*; and Brinton, *Their Lives and Mine*, which includes extracts from the memoirs of J. Vaughan Merrick Sr.

27. On George Wharton Pepper, see Lukacs, *Philadelphia Patricians and Philistines*, 219–39. On William Pepper, see Thorpe, *William Pepper, M.D., LL.D.* (1904).

28. Richmond Trial, 11 December 1916, 1000, GCRP, Coll. 550, HSP. Having died in 1914, Scarborough was unable to testify at the trial but was recorded as having lodged a complaint against Richmond.

29. Richmond Trial, 5 December 1916, 831, GCRP, Coll. 550, HSP. On the streetcarmen's strike, see Abernathy, "Progressivism, 1905–1919," 547–49.

30. Richmond Trial, 11 December 1916, 1020–21, GCRP, Coll. 550, HSP.

31. Richmond Trial, 27 November 1916, 763–64, GCRP, Coll. 550, HSP; and "Richmond Declares Money Power has Dominated Church," n.d, in Rhinelander Letters, Box 6, GCRP, Coll. 550, HSP.

32. The best documentary record of the public discussion surrounding the Nearing case is Witmer, *The Nearing Case* (1915), quotations on 15 and 30. See also Samuel Hughes, "An Affair to Remember"; and Cheyney, *History of the University of Pennsylvania, 1740–1940*, 367–71.

33. Saltmarsh, *Scott Nearing*, 10; and Nearing, *The Making of a Radical*, 4–19.

34. Saltmarsh, *Scott Nearing*, 10; and Steffens, *The Shame of Cities*, 193–229.

35. Nearing, *The Making of a Radical*, 36.

36. Saltmarsh, *Scott Nearing*, 15–16.

37. On Patten's place within the wider circle of progressive reformers, see McGerr, *A Fierce Discontent*, 93–95. On Patten's religious views, see Everett, *Religion in Economics*, 99; and Patten, *The Social Basis of Religion* (1914).

38. See DuBois, *The Philadelphia Negro* (1899); and Rowe, "The Municipality and the Gas Supply" (1898).

39. Saltmarsh, *Scott Nearing*, 18, Nearing quotation also on 18. On Nearing's admiration for Patten, see also Nearing, *Educational Frontiers* (1925).

40. Nearing, *The Solution of the Child Labor Problem* (1911), 125; and Sherman, *A Scott Nearing Reader*, 23.

41. Nearing, *Wages in the United States, 1908–1910* (1911), iv.

42. See Nearing, *Social Religion* (1913).

43. Witmer, *The Nearing Case*, 3–4.

44. On the university's precarious finances in the 1910s and 1920s, see Cheyney, *History of the University of Pennsylvania, 1740–1940*, 373; and the memoirs of provost Charles Custis Harrison (1894–1910), including "Some Amusing Incidents Relative to the Raising of Funds for the University During My Term of Provostship" and "The Organization of the University of Pennsylvania in 1876" (1925), Box 3, CCHP, UPA.

45. Sass, *The Pragmatic Imagination*, 121. Nearing also used such juxtapositions between rich and poor in his book *Poverty and Riches: A Study of the Industrial Regime* (1916), as in the photographs included between pages 204 and 205.

46. Although the wording varies from source to source, Nearing was reported to have told a student that "if I had a son, I would rather see him in hell than have him go to the Episcopal Academy." The student supposedly then related the incident to one of the deans. See Witmer, *The Nearing Case*, 31.

47. Nearing, *The Making of a Radical*, 58.

48. Saltmarsh, *Scott Nearing*, 84.

49. Rev. Augustus E. Barnett, as quoted in the *Public Ledger*, 21 June 1915. Rev. Barnett was a member of the clergy of the Reformed Episcopal Church in Philadelphia. Two days earlier in the *Public Ledger*, George Wharton Pepper, one of the university trustees, had admitted that the trustees were "sincere in their efforts to serve the best interests of the University." See Witmer, *The Nearing Case*, 8, 22.

50. On Morris's public comments, see Witmer, *The Nearing Case*, 1. Although the details of the conflict between Morris and Philadelphia's elite were never made entirely clear, it involved Morris's relationship with the members of the board of the Pennsylvania Academy of Fine Arts (PAFA). Even though Morris had served as managing director of the PAFA from 1892 to 1905, he was denied a place on the board. Given the interlocking nature of Philadelphia's many boards, events at the PAFA affected the relationship between members of the Wharton family and the trustees and alumni of the university. The PAFA board's snub of Morris was deemed

so grievous by Joseph Wharton that he rewrote his will to deny the Wharton School a planned $500,000 bequest. As Wharton's daughter, Anna Wharton Morris, would write shortly after her father's death: "I never heard a will read, and do not understand all the terms,—but it seemed simple, clear and fair. Only the codicil, revoking [the] $500,000. bequest to the University, seemed somewhat spectacular,—and caused tremendous comment in the papers. The *North American* presented the real explanation: C. C. Harrison's behaviour at the time of the Academy fight. The action proved Father's devotion to H. S. M. [Harrison S. Morris]—As for the $500,000, which is to come to me, my imagination cannot compass it." Anna Wharton Morris, Journal, 11 January 1909, Box 2, Anna Wharton Morris Papers, RG 5/106, FHLSC.

51. Witmer, *The Nearing Case*, 7.

52. For the early history of the university, see Cheyney, *History of the University of Pennsylvania, 1740–1940*, 32, 130–32. On the university's religious character, see Baltzell, *Philadelphia Gentlemen*, 322.

53. Harrison, "The Dormitory System" (1895), Box 3, CCHP, UPA.

54. The most vocal Catholic critic of Provost Smith's attempt to reinstate mandatory chapel attendance was Walter George Smith, a member of the Board of Trustees. See Walter George Smith, "Autobiography Notes," n.d, 81–85, Box 3, Walter George Smith Papers, MC 47, PAHRC. On the university's chapel attendance policy, see Charles Custis Harrison, "The Administration of Our University," in Box 3; and "Action of the Executive Committee Regarding Attendance at Chapel" (1904), Box 2, CCHP, UPA.

55. George Wharton Pepper to Harrison S. Morris, 24 June 1915, as quoted in Witmer, *The Nearing Case*, 35.

56. For university enrollment approximations, see Witmer, *The Nearing Case*, 101.

57. Scott Nearing to Billy Sunday, 1 February 1915, as published in the *North American*, 2 February 1915, and reprinted in Witmer, *The Nearing Case*, 54–55.

58. John Reed, "Back of Billy Sunday," *Metropolitan Magazine*, May 1915, reprinted in Lehman, *John Reed and the Writing of Revolution*, 244. See also Witmer, *The Nearing Case*, 52.

59. On Quaker business ethics, see Tolles, *Meeting House and Counting House*; Rhoads, "Business Ethics"; and Axelrod, "Quaker Education, Morality, and Business Practices in Philadelphia, Pennsylvania, 1850–1900."

60. "Deed of Trust" (1881), Box 52, Joseph Wharton Family Papers, RG 5/162, FHLSC. On the history of the Wharton School and its founder, see Sass, *The Pragmatic Imagination*; Yates, *Joseph Wharton*; and Khurana, *From Higher Aims to Hired Hands*. On Quaker teachings at the time, see *Rules of Discipline of the Yearly Meeting* (Hicksite; 1877); and *Christian Advices Issued by the Yearly Meeting of Friends* (Orthodox; 1879).

61. Smith, *Unforgotten Years*, 150.

62. For the first meeting of the Social Order Committee, see SOC Minutes, 9 April 1917, PYM Records, F4.18, QCHC. For an overview of the committee, see Jones, *Quakers in Action*, 167–79. The Hicksite community would form a Social Order Subcommittee in 1927, an outgrowth of their Committee on Philanthropic Labor. See Social Order Subcommittee Reports, Box 3, Committee on Philanthropic Labor Records, PYM Records, RG2/Phy/759, FHLSC.

63. Social Order Committee, "Statement of Principles," 11 February 1918, PYM Records, F4.18, QCHC.

64. SOC Minutes, 9 April 1917, PYM Records, F4.18, QCHC.

65. For early activities of the committee, see SOC Minutes, 1917–1920, PYM Records, F4.18, QCHC.

66. John Howell Harris offers two of the best studies of the Social Order Committee and its radical potential in *Bloodless Victories* and "War in the Social Order."

67. For Leeds's notes and a speech on Ernst Abbe and Carl Zeiss, see Box 9, MELP, Coll. 1127, QCHC. Leeds also recounted his visit to Germany in a talk to members of the Germantown Meeting. See Leeds, "Attitude of Friends Toward Industrial Conditions"

(ca. 1908–1909), Box 9, MELP, Coll. 1127, QCHC. On transatlantic reform more broadly, see Rodgers, *Atlantic Crossings*. For an overview of company unions and other corporate welfare practices in the early twentieth century, see Jacoby, *Modern Manors*, chap. 1.

68. Leeds, "Attitude of Friends Toward Industrial Conditions" (ca. 1908–1909), Box 9, MELP, Coll. 1127, QCHC.

69. Ibid.; and Leeds, "The Social Order—Why Should Friends Study It?" n.d., but preceding the formation of the Social Order Committee, Box 9, MELP, Coll. 1127, QCHC.

70. SOC Minutes, 9 June 1919, PYM Records, F4.18, QCHC.

71. Social Order Committee, Annual Report (1919), PYM Records, F4.13; and H. T. Brown, "Capitalism," 5 June 1917, PYM Records, F4.8, QCHC.

72. SOC Minutes, 24 April 1917, PYM Records, F4.18; and Annual Report (1920), PYM Records, F4.13, QCHC.

73. Social Order Committee, Annual Report (1918), PYM Records, F4.18, QCHC.

74. "Questionnaire for Members of the Social Order Committee," F4.8, PYM Records, QCHC.

75. Jones, *Quakers in Action*, 176.

76. SOC Minutes, 9 June 1919, PYM Records, F4.18, QCHC. For additional concerns about the committee's course of action, see also Jones, *Quakers in Action*, 178–79.

77. SOC Minutes, 10 January 1921, PYM Records, F4.17, QCHC. The composition of the larger Hicksite branch of the Society of Friends in Philadelphia tended to be slightly less affluent and more rural, but, in general, its members would have also been well represented in professional occupations and respectable trades. On the composition of the two branches, see Benjamin, *The Philadelphia Quakers in the Industrial Age, 1865–1920*, 49–72, and membership data tables on 217–37.

78. SOC Minutes, October 13–14, 1917, PYM Records, F4.18, QCHC.

79. SOC Minutes, 5 June 1922, PYM, F4.17, QCHC. As originally proposed by the subcommittee, the full text of the new social order query read: "Are you earnestly seeking to understand the social and industrial conditions of the day, and their causes, in the light of the religion of Jesus Christ, and are you endeavoring to build up an enlightened public opinion for the removal of those conditions which harmfully affect your fellow-men? Are you helping to make the service of others rather than self-advancement the controlling motive of all occupations? To what extent are your own standards of living, and opportunities, within the reach of your employees and the employees of others, with special reference to such matters as income, leisure, education and freedom to direct one's own life? And how far are you willing to surrender your own advantages in order that others may have greater opportunities to develop themselves for service?"

80. "Proposed Paragraph for the Advices and Revision of the Eighth Query," 4 December 1922, PYM Records, F4.17, QCHC.

81. *Faith and Practice* (Orthodox; 1926), 94.

82. Ibid., 52–58.

Chapter 7

1. "City Folk Urged to Purchase Autos," *Public Ledger*, 7 March 1927, 9; and Coale, "Influence of the Automobile on the City Church" (1924).

2. On the history of the congregation, see MacAfee, *The First Ninety Years of the Parish of the Holy Apostles, 1868–1958*.

3. For discussions of the religious culture wars of the early twentieth century, see Marsden, *Fundamentalism and American Culture*; Marty, *Modern American Religion*; Larson, *Summer of the Gods*; and Morone, *Hellfire Nation*.

4. Blumin, *The Emergence of the Middle Class*, 218–21.

5. See Rev. Fred Druckenmiller, "Be-Setting and Upsetting Sins of the Average Congregation," *Presbyterian*, 28 June 1928, 9; Bishop's Address, *Journal of the Diocesan Convention* (1921): 48; Elkinton, *Selections from the Diary and Correspondence of Joseph S. Elkinton, 1830–1905*, 263; Russell H. Conwell, "Shall the Rich Divide the Poor?" *Temple Review*, 5 May 1922, 5; and Untitled Speech Fragment, n.d., in Unpublished Addresses/Lectures, 1888–1913, Box 33, JKP, TUUA.

6. See, for example, Rainsford, *The Story of a Varied Life* (1922); Sears, *The Redemption of the City* (1911); Plantz, *The Church and the Social Problem* (1906); and Coale, "Protestantism and the Masses" (1921), quotation on 84.

7. Niebuhr, *The Social Sources of Denominationalism*, quotation on vii.

8. Russell H. Conwell, "Duty to Succeed," *Temple Review*, 11 March 1921. For Conwell in his larger context, see Hilkey, *Character Is Capital*.

9. On the number of times Conwell delivered the "Acres of Diamonds" sermon, see Russell H. Conwell to Rabbi Joseph Krauskopf, 7 November 1921, Box 6, JKP, TUUA.

10. Burr, *Russell H. Conwell and His Work*, 212.

11. Russell H. Conwell, "American Aristocracy," *Temple Review*, 23 September 1910.

12. See Conwell, *Praying for Money*, and *The Key to Success*. The claim that the Grace Baptist Temple was the largest Protestant church in America appeared on the masthead of the church's weekly newsletter, the *Temple Review*.

13. On Baldwin, see Russell H. Conwell, "Baldwin Locomotive," *Temple Review*, 14 February 1908. On Wanamaker, see Conwell, *The Romantic Rise of a Great American*. Conwell also penned the introduction to Wanamaker, *Maxims of Life in Business*.

14. Conwell, "American Aristocracy."

15. Hilty, *Temple University*, 1–21.

16. Conwell, "Shall the Rich Divide the Poor?"

17. Russell H. Conwell, "The History of the Fifty-Seven Cents," *Temple Review*, 19 December 1912.

18. The various sources of financial support for the Grace Baptist Temple are chronicled in Elliott, *Tent to Temple*, esp. 9–21, 52–75.

19. On Drexel, see J. Douglas Perry, "Money Is the Root," AR11–3, Box 2, Conwellana-Templana Collection, Temple University Archives.

20. John D. Rockefeller to Russell H. Conwell, 7 July 1920, Conwellana-Templana Collection, Temple University Archives; and Conwell, *Acres of Diamonds*, 109.

21. Burr, *Russell H. Conwell and His Work*, 193, 204–6.

22. On the history of Keneseth Israel, see *Reform Congregation Keneseth Israel: Its First 100 Years, 1847–1947*.

23. For a sense of Conwell's and Krauskopf's mutual affection, see Russell Conwell, "A Godly Rabbi," *Temple Review*, 7 September 1923; and Joseph Krauskopf, "Toast on Dr. Russell H. Conwell: A Liberalist and Neighbor," 13 February 1913, Box 33, JKP, TUUA.

24. Joseph Krauskopf to Milton J. Flarsheim, 13 March 1919, Box 3, JKP, TUUA.

25. Pennell, *Our Philadelphia*, 461, 472–73.

26. See Blood, *Apostle of Reason*; Joseph Krauskopf, "Out of the Ghettos—Into the Public Life," 26 September 1889, Box 33, and, for the quotation, "The Future of Hebrew Union College," 28 June 1908, Box 28, JKP, TUUA.

27. See *Reform Congregation Keneseth Israel: Its First 100 Years, 1847-1947*; and Rosenberg, *Reform Congregation Keneseth Israel, 150 Years*. On the social composition of the Jewish community, see Baltzell, *Philadelphia Gentlemen*, 280–91, and Friedman, *Jewish Life in Philadelphia, 1830–1940*.

28. Joseph Krauskopf to Ellis Gimbel, 20 October 1920, Box 4, JKP, TUUA.

29. Program from the "Reform Congregation Keneseth Israel Dinner Dance," 31 October 1922, Box 36, JKP, TUUA.

30. Joseph Krauskopf, Diary (1891), 214, Box 35, JKP, TUUA.

31. Joseph Krauskopf, "The Year's Review," 9 September 1907, in Unpublished Addresses/Lectures, 1888–1913, Box 33, JKP, TUUA.

32. Joseph Krauskopf, "Godless Jews and Christless Christians: I. Godless Jews," 19 November 1922, in Pamphlets, Box 34, JKP, TUUA. See also Krauskopf, *Prejudice*.

33. For comments about manners and refinement, see Joseph Krauskopf, Diary (1891), 94 and 185, Box 35, JKP, TUUA.

34. See Allman, *A Unique Institution*.

35. Krauskopf, Diary (1891), 146–47, Box 35, JKP, TUUA.

36. Krauskopf, "Godless Jews and Christless Christians: I. Godless Jews," 19 November 1922.

37. Joseph Krauskopf, "Hear, O Israel," 12 October 1913, in Unpublished Addresses/Lectures, 1888–1913, Box 33, JKP, TUUA.

38. Krauskopf, Diary (1891), 94, Box 35, JKP, TUUA.

39. Ibid., 199–200.

40. Krauskopf, "Hear, O Israel," 12 October 1913.

41. "Against the Pew System," *Philadelphia Inquirer*, 15 October 1887, 2.

42. Ogden, *Pew Rents and the New Testament*, quotations on 19, 24, 26. For Ogden's biography, see Young, *Memorial History of the City of Philadelphia*, 2:427–28.

43. Budd, as quoted in "Against the Pew System," 2.

44. Pepper, *A Voice from the Crowd*, 121.

45. W. B. B., "A Parson's Outlook," *Church Standard*, 29 January 1898; and Riley, *The Perennial Revival*, 154.

46. Ogden, *Pew Rents and the New Testament*, 28.

47. Fones-Wolf, *Trade Union Gospel*, 94.

48. Chestnut Hill Presbyterian Church, Trustees' and Congregational Records, vol. I (1852–1886) and vol. II (1886–1917), PHS. See also St. Peter's Church, "Plan of Endowment Trust for Accumulation" (Philadelphia, 1872), Pamphlets, Philadelphia Churches, vol. 10, HSP.

49. Trustee Minutes, 13 May 1886, Chestnut Hill Presbyterian Church Records, PHS.

50. Joseph Krauskopf to Russell Conwell, 13 November 1918, Box 3; and Floyd W. Tomkins to Joseph Krauskopf, 18 November 1918, Box 27, JKP, TUUA. For an overview of the history of seating fees within the Jewish community, see Sarna, "Seating and the American Synagogue."

51. For an overview of Protestant church funding practices during the industrial era, see Hudnut-Beumler, *In Pursuit of the Almighty's Dollar*, 47–75.

52. "The Financial System," in Handbook of Southwestern Presbyterian Church (Philadelphia, 1885), 31–33, PHS; and Nathanael Groton, Diary, 24 April 1914, privately held by Nathanael Groton Jr.

53. Rector's Letter, *Church of the Holy Trinity Parish Handbook (1895–1896)*, 85–86, Church of the Holy Trinity Archives (Philadelphia).

54. "The Incorporated Free and Open Church Association," in *Official Year-Book of the Church of England* (London, 1897), quotation on 127. A collection of sermons and other primary sources related to the Free Church Movement dating from 1844 to 1892 has been compiled and made available online by Project Canterbury, http://www.anglicanhistory.org/misc/freechurch. Among these, see "Free and Open Churches: A Sermon Preached at St. Paul's Cathedral on the 23rd of June, 1876, the Tenth Anniversary of the London Free and Open Church Association" (London, 1876).

55. *Second Annual Report of the Free Church Association, 1876–7* (Philadelphia, 1877), 5.

56. See, for example, Henry Adams Neely, "The Church of Christ a Free Church Freely Maintained: A Sermon Delivered Before the Free Church Association on the Occasion of Their

First Annual Meeting, in St. Mark's Church, Philadelphia, May 28th, 1876," available at http://www.anglicanhistory.org/misc/freechurch.

57. See Neale, *The History of Pews* (1841).

58. The Free Church Association's U.S. headquarters were in Philadelphia and all thirteen of the association's original life members were from the Diocese of Pennsylvania. See *The Second Annual Report of the Free Church Association, 1876-7* (Philadelphia, 1877); and "Free and Open Church Association," in *Living Church Annual* (1931), 227.

59. Rev. G. Woolsey Hodge, "The Anglican Position: A Sermon Preached at the Consecration of the Church of the Ascension, Philadelphia, February 8, 1906," *Church Standard*, 24 February 1906, 570.

60. See "Rev. G. Woolsey Hodge," in Morris, *Makers of Philadelphia*, 299. See also Gough, *Christ Church, Philadelphia*.

61. Hodge, "The Anglican Position," 571.

62. Excerpts from the memoirs of J. Vaughan Merrick Sr. appear in Brinton, *Their Lives and Mine*, quotation on 46.

63. Manton, *A Splendid Legacy*, 36. For a parallel story of an Episcopal church abandoning and then reinstating pew rents, also in 1873, see MacAfee, *The First Ninety Years of the Parish of the Holy Apostles*, chap. 1.

64. Brinton, *Their Lives and Mine*, 46; and Manton, *A Splendid Legacy*, 46.

65. Offerings for St. Timothy's Church rose from $44,308.74 to $128,964.81; baptisms, from 243 to 701. Manton, *A Splendid Legacy*, 46. Manton does not specify how these figures were derived, but they do not seem to match those in the parish report printed in the *Journal of the Diocesan Convention* for the same years. He may, however, have employed a different accounting method or aggregated figures from several years before and after rents were abolished. In the parish's 1872 convention report, total contributions were listed as only $10,852.79. In 1874, after rents were abolished, contributions had risen to only $12,639.70. Yet the latter figure also included a note that there had been a "gift of an addition to the parish, the gift of a single member of the parish," presumably Merrick. In terms of parish growth reported for those years, the gains were substantial, with a nearly 50 percent increase after pew rents were abolished, from 84 members in 1872 to 120 in 1874.

66. Brinton, *Their Lives and Mine*, 45.

67. "Free and Open Church Association," *Church News*, February 1925, 157.

68. As part of its annual report, printed in the *Journal of the Diocesan Convention*, each Episcopal parish was required to state the number of seats in its church and identify how many of those were free. A rough sampling of the parish reports from 1880 to 1930 shows the practice of pew rents in decline, with many parishes that once had them eliminating or significantly curtailing them by the 1910s. For representative examples, see listings for St. David's Episcopal Church, Radnor; Episcopal Church of the Saviour, Philadelphia; Episcopal Church of the Redeemer, Bryn Mawr; and St. Paul's Episcopal Church, Chestnut Hill.

69. Manton, *A Splendid Legacy*, 74–75.

70. On social stratification in Philadelphia, see Cutler and Gillette, *The Divided Metropolis*, esp. William W. Cutler III, "The Persistent Dualism: Centralization and Decentralization in Philadelphia."

71. The reasoning that the prosperity and privatist logic that spurred the growth of congregations and denominations would also lead to their undoing was informed by scholars who applied Joseph Schumpeter's notion of "creative destruction" to the study of urban development. See esp. Page, *The Creative Destruction of Manhattan, 1900-1940*.

72. On the history and mission of the Institute for Social and Religious Research, see Douglass, *The Church in the Changing City*, ii. On Douglass's background, see Hadden, "H. Paul Douglass."

73. Douglass's principal works include *The St. Louis Church Survey* (1924), *1,000 City Churches* (1926), and *The City's Church* (1929). For a review that places Douglass's work in context, see Holman "Are City Churches Effectively Organized." On Douglass's lasting influence and criticism of his work, see the introduction to Cross, *The Church and the City, 1865–1910*.

74. Douglass, *The St. Louis Church Survey*, 55–94.

75. On Douglass's ecumenical work, see "Harlan Paul Douglass," in *American National Biography*, 6:819–20. On the support he received from interdenominational agencies in St. Louis, see Douglass, *The St. Louis Church Survey*, 271–75.

76. Hadden, "H. Paul Douglass," 75.

77. Douglass, *The St. Louis Church Survey*, 76.

78. Ibid., 55–77, quotations on 71 and 77.

79. The trend toward removal of congregations cut across denominational lines. On removal of Episcopal congregations, see the maps of downtown church locations for 1860 and 1914 in Gough, *Christ Church, Philadelphia*, 245, 303; and Twelves, *A History of the Diocese of Pennsylvania*, 96. For statistical information on removal of Presbyterian congregations, see the tables compiled in Hammonds, *Historical Directory of Presbyterian Churches and Presbyteries of Greater Philadelphia*, 5–7. On removal of Quaker assemblies, see D. Robert Yarnall, "Philadelphia City Meetings—What of the Future?" *Friend*, 21 July 1927. See also Gamm, *Urban Exodus*.

80. See MacAfee, *The First Ninety Years of the Parish of the Holy Apostles, 1868–1958*, 24–27; Twelves, *History of the Diocese of Pennsylvania*, 164; Rector's Letter, St. Mark Church, *Yearbook* (1916), St. Mark's Episcopal Church Archives; "Philadelphia," *Church Standard*, 20 April 1905; "Philadelphia," *Church Standard*, 24 June 1905; and "A Great Missionary Opportunity: Proposed Memorial to George C. Thomas" (1915), Pamphlets, Philadelphia Churches, HSP.

81. See Young, *The Down-Town Church*. Though none of Douglass's books refers to Young or his work, notice of it did appear in the local press and denominational publications, including "Downtown Church Decadence," *Philadelphia Inquirer*, 30 June 1912, 8; and "Record of New Publications," *Journal of Presbyterian History* (March 1913): 61.

82. Young, *The Down-Town Church*, 36.

83. Ibid., 45–49; 51.

84. Ibid., 78, 81. Records indicate only one instance of Catholic parish closure in Philadelphia in the years prior to World War II: St. Brendan's parish (1925–1934). See Catholic Standard and Times, *The Catholic Directory* (1997), 166; and Rev. Francis P. McDonald to Cardinal Dougherty, n.d, 80.7054, Cardinal Dougherty Papers, PAHRC.

85. "Most Blessed Sacrament Church Cornerstone Laid," *Catholic Standard and Times*, 23 September 1922, 1, 9. See also "Church of Transfiguration Dedicated by His Eminence," *Catholic Standard and Times*, 2 June 1928, 5.

86. "Select New Site for High School," *Catholic Standard and Times*, 12 February 1927, 1; "The Episcopal Academy," *Pennsylvania Gazette*, 22 October 1920, 98; and Latham, *The Episcopal Academy, 1785–1984*, 127–39.

87. "The Religious Problem in Cities," *Presbyterian*, 6 November 1901.

88. Young, *The Down-Town Church*, 51, 132.

89. Rector's Letter, *Church of the Holy Trinity Parish Yearbook* (1894), Church of the Holy Trinity Archives (Philadelphia).

90. "St. James P.E. Church," *Philadelphia Inquirer*, 17 October 1871, 2.

91. See, in particular, the rector's letters that appear in the parish yearbooks of 1895–1896, 1900, 1910, and 1924, as well as the financial reports in them for the years between 1919 through 1929, Church of the Holy Trinity Archives (Philadelphia).

92. See the financial report (1928) and rector's letter (1923) in the *St. Mark's Church Parish Yearbook*, St. Mark's Episcopal Church Archives.

93. Leach, "The Weakness of Protestantism in American Cities," 620.

94. William P. Shriver, *The Presbyterian Church in Metropolitan Philadelphia* (January 1930), PHS, quotation on 8. On the history of the merger of First Presbyterian and Calvary Presbyterian Churches, see Hammonds, *Historical Directory of Presbyterian Churches and Presbyteries of Greater Philadelphia*, 35–38; and Moss, *Historic Sacred Places in Philadelphia*, 196–98.

95. Shriver, *The Presbyterian Church in Metropolitan Philadelphia* (January 1930), 40–41.

96. Rev. Henry Davies, "The Suburban Missionary and His Problems," part II, *Church News*, March 1925, 192; "The Bishop's Message," *Church News*, November 1926; and "For the Glory of God in the Diocese of Pennsylvania" (published for the Diocese's Campaign for Missions and Institutions), 26 November–December 6, 1926, Pamphlets, Philadelphia Churches, HSP.

97. "Changing Philadelphia," *Church News*, December 1928, 90.

98. Rev. David M. Steele, "The Problem of the Central City Church," *Church News*, March 1933, 213.

99. Twelves, *A History of the Diocese of Pennsylvania*, 145, 149–50, 225–26; Charles Robert Ritchie, "The Church of St. Luke and the Epiphany," in Pamphlets, Philadelphia Churches, vol. 14, HSP; "Dr. Steele's Resignation," *Church News*, March 1933, 202; and Rev. David M. Steele, "The Problem of the Central City Church," *Church News*, March 1933, 213.

100. "Report of the Committee on Problems of City Churches," *Journal of the Diocesan Convention* (1934).

101. Douglass, *The St. Louis Church Survey*, 77.

Conclusion

1. Lower Merion Historical Society, *The First 300*, 248–49.

2. Ibid., 242–43.

3. Schultz, *Tri-Faith America*, 7.

4. Rodgers, *Age of Fracture*, quotations on 3.

5. See Lemann, "No Man's Town."

6. Stephen Salisbury, "Gross Clinic to Stay in City," *Philadelphia Inquirer*, 22 December 2006, 1.

7. For good examples of the transformation of benefactions from endowments or bequests to grants, see records related to the establishment of the Glenmede Trust Company and the Pew Charitable Trusts, Box 187, J. Howard Pew Papers, Acc. 1634, HML.

8. Donna Gordon Blankinship, "Lenfest Makes Giving Pledge," *Philadelphia Inquirer*, 5 August 2010, 1; and http://www.givingpledge.org.

9. Ian Lovett, "California: Crystal Cathedral Will Be Sold to Catholic Diocese," *New York Times*, 18 November 2011, 13.

10. Kristin A. Graham and David O'Reilly, "Philly Catholic High Schools to Be Managed by a Private Foundation," *Philadelphia Inquirer*, 22 August 2012, 1.

BIBLIOGRAPHY

Manuscript and Archival Collections

Architecture Archives, University of Pennsylvania
 Allen Evans Collection
Archives, Sisters of the Blessed Sacrament (ASBS)
 Drexel Family Collection
 Katharine Drexel Papers
Athenaeum of Philadelphia (AthP)
 Theophilus P. Chandler Collection (TPCC)
 Philadelphia Architects and Buildings Project
Bryn Athyn College Library
 Bryn Athyn History Holdings
Drexel University Archives
 Drexel Family Collection
Episcopal Divinity School
 Philadelphia Divinity School Records
Free Library of Philadelphia
 Clipping Files, Social Science and History Department
Friends Historical Library, Swarthmore College (FHLSC)
 Elkinton Family Papers, RG 5/037
 Hadassah Moore Leeds Holcombe Papers, RG 5/063
 Anna Wharton Morris Papers, RG 5/106
 Philadelphia Yearly Meeting Records (Hicksite)
 Joseph Wharton Family Papers, RG 5/162
Hagley Museum and Library (HML)
 Francis Gurney du Pont Papers, Acc. 504
 Huston Family Papers, Acc. 1174, Acc. 1441
 Leeds & Northrup Company Records, Acc. 1110
 Lukens Steel Company Records, Acc. 50
 Pew Family Papers, Acc. 1862
 J. Howard Pew Papers, Acc. 1634
 Philadelphia Quartz Company Records, Acc. 1865
 Provident Mutual Life Insurance Company Records, Acc. 1930
Historical Society of Pennsylvania (HSP)
 Episcopal Churchwomen Records, Coll. 2106
 Family History Collection
 Albert M. Greenfield Papers, Coll. 1959
 Harrison Family Papers, Coll. 2048
 George L. Harrison Papers, Coll. 1464
 Horstmann-Lippincott Family Papers, Coll. 1899
 Morris Family Papers, Coll. 2000
 Religious Institutions Collection
 George Chalmers Richmond Papers (GCRP), Acc. 550
 Roberts Family Papers, Coll. 2087

St. Andrew's Church Records, Coll. 1517
John Wanamaker Collection, Coll. 2188
Lower Merion Historical Society (LMHS)
    Roberts Family Collection
    George B. Roberts Letterpress Books
Philadelphia Archdiocese Historical Research Center (PAHRC)
    Cardinal Dennis J. Dougherty Papers
    Parish History Collection
    Archbishop Edmond F. Prendergast Papers
    Archbishop Patrick J. Ryan Papers
    Walter George Smith Papers
    Archbishop James F. Wood Papers
    Federation of Jewish Charities Records
Presbyterian Historical Society (PHS)
    Bethany Presbyterian Church (Philadelphia) Records
    Chestnut Hill Presbyterian Church Records
    Church of the Covenant (Bala-Cynwyd) Records
    Disston Memorial Presbyterian Church (Philadelphia) Records
    Overbrook Presbyterian Church Records
Philadelphia Jewish Archives Center
Private Church Records
    Bryn Mawr Presbyterian Church (Bryn Mawr)
    Church of St. Asaph (Bala Cynwyd)
    Church of the Holy Trinity (Philadelphia)
    Reform Congregation Keneseth Israel (Elkins Park)
    St. Mark's Episcopal Church Archives (Philadelphia)
    St. Thomas's Episcopal Church (Whitemarsh)
Quaker Collections, Haverford College (QCHC)
    Joshua Longstreth Baily Papers, Ms. Coll. 975A, Ms. Coll. 1032
    Germantown Monthly Meeting Records
    Addison Hutton Papers, Ms. Coll. 1122
    Morris Evans Leeds Papers, Ms. Coll. 1127
    Morris-Sansom Collection, Ms. Coll. 1008
    Philadelphia Yearly Meeting (PYM) Records (Orthodox)
    Stokes-Evans-Cope Family Papers, Ms. Coll. 1169
    Edward Morris Wistar Papers, Ms. Coll. 1137
    Morris Wistar Wood Collection, Ms. Coll. 1140
Temple University Archives
    Conwellana-Templana Collection
Temple University Urban Archives (TUUA)
    Evening Bulletin Newsclipping Collection
    Joseph Krauskopf Papers (JKP)
University of Pennsylvania Archives (UPA)
    E. Digby Baltzell Papers
    Charles Custis Harrison Papers (CCHP)
Washington Memorial Chapel Archives (Valley Forge)

Select Periodicals

Catholic Directory (Archdiocese of Philadelphia)
Catholic Standard and Times

Church News of the Diocese of Pennsylvania (*Church News*)
Church Standard
Friend
Friends' Intelligencer
Journal of the Annual Convention of the Diocese of Pennsylvania (*Journal of the Diocesan Convention*)
Living Church Annual/Episcopal Church Annual
Lloyd's Clerical Directory
Philadelphia Inquirer
Philadelphia Public Ledger
Presbyterian
Temple Magazine
Temple Review

Published Sources, Theses, and Dissertations

A. & P. Roberts Company. *Pencoyd Iron Works*. Philadelphia, 1897.

Abbott, Margery Post. *A Certain Kind of Perfection: An Anthology of Evangelical and Liberal Quaker Writers*. Wallingford, PA: Pendle Hill, 1997.

Abernathy, Lloyd M. "Progressivism, 1905–1919." In Russell F. Weigley, ed., *Philadelphia: A 300-Year History*. New York: Norton, 1982.

Acts and Debates of the General Assembly of the Presbyterian Church. Philadelphia: Joseph M. Wilson, 1856.

Adam, Thomas, ed. *Philanthropy, Patronage, and Civil Society*. Bloomington: Indiana University Press, 2004.

Addison, Daniel Dulany. "The Growth of the Layman's Power in the Episcopal Church." In *Papers of the American Society of Church History*. 2nd ser. New York: Putnam, 1912.

Aldrich, Nelson W. *Old Money: The Mythology of America's Upper Class*. New York: Knopf, 1988.

Allinson, Edward P., and Boies Penrose. *Ground Rents in Philadelphia*. Philadelphia, 1888.

Allman, Herbert D. *A Unique Institution: The Story of the National Farm School*. Philadelphia: Jewish Publication Society, 1935.

All Saints' Church. *Prepared for Us to Walk In: The History of All Saints' Church, Wynnewood, Pennsylvania, 1911–1986*. Wynnewood, 1986.

American National Biography. 24 vols. New York: Oxford University Press, 1999.

Amory, Cleveland. *Who Killed Society?* New York: Harper, 1960.

Anderson, James D. *The Education of Blacks in the South*. Chapel Hill: University of North Carolina Press, 1988.

Andrews, Jack. *Samuel Yellin, Metalworker*. Ocean Pines, MD: SkipJack Press, 1992.

Andrews, Wayne. *American Gothic: Its Origins, Its Trials, Its Triumphs*. New York: Random House, 1975.

———. *Architecture, Ambition, and Americans*. 1947. Rev. ed. New York: Free Press, 1978.

Anonymous. *Philadelphia: Or, Glances at Lawyers, Physicians, First-Circle, Wistar-Parties, &c. &c*. Philadelphia: R. H. Small, 1826.

———. *Philadelphia Scrapple: Whimsical Bits Anent Eccentrics and the City's Oddities*. Richmond, VA: Dietz Press, 1956.

Appel, Joseph Herbert. *The Business Biography of John Wanamaker*. New York: Macmillan, 1930.

Argo, Rev. Fordyce H. "Opinion." In Henry Budd, Esq., and Rev. Fordyce H. Argo, *The Richmond Ecclesiastical Trial*. Philadelphia, 1917.

Aronowitz, Stanley. *How Class Works: Power and Social Movement.* New Haven: Yale University Press, 2003.

Ashbrook, William S. *Fifty Years: The Provident Life and Trust Company of Philadelphia, 1865–1915.* Philadelphia: Holmes Press, 1915.

Ashmead, Graham. *History of Delaware County, Pennsylvania.* Philadelphia: L. H. Everts, 1884.

Aslet, Clive. *The American Country House.* New Haven: Yale University Press, 1990.

Aspinwall, Marguerite. *A Hundred Years in His House: The Story of the Church of the Holy Trinity on Rittenhouse Square, Philadelphia, 1857–1957.* Philadelphia: Church of the Holy Trinity, 1956.

Avella, Steven M. *This Confident Church: Catholic Leadership and Life in Chicago, 1940–1965.* Notre Dame: University of Notre Dame Press, 1992.

Axelrod, Barzilai K. "Quaker Education, Morality, and Business Practices in Philadelphia, Pennsylvania, 1850–1900: The Legacy of Joseph Elkinton (1794–1868) and the Philadelphia Quartz Company." Bachelor's thesis, Haverford College, 2004.

Bains, David R. "A Capital Presence: The Presbyterian Quest for a 'National Church' in Washington, D.C." Annual Meeting of the American Academy of Religion, Washington, DC, November 21, 2006.

Balch, Thomas Willing. *The Philadelphia Assemblies.* Philadelphia: Allen, Lane & Scott, 1916.

Baldwin, Lou. *Saint Katharine Drexel: Apostle to the Oppressed.* Philadelphia: Catholic Standard and Times, 2000.

Balmer, Randall, and John R. Fitzmier. *The Presbyterians.* Westport, CT: Greenwood Press, 1993.

Baltzell, E. Digby. *Philadelphia Gentlemen: The Making of a National Upper Class.* Glencoe, IL: Free Press, 1958.

———. *The Protestant Establishment: Aristocracy and Caste in America.* New York: Random House, 1964.

———. *The Protestant Establishment Revisited.* New Brunswick, NJ: Transaction, 1991.

———. *Puritan Boston and Quaker Philadelphia: Two Protestant Ethics and the Spirit of Class Authority and Leadership.* New York: Free Press, 1979.

Bancroft, Joseph, with Robert Barclay. *A Persuasive to Unity.* Philadelphia: Thomas William Stuckey, 1874.

Barry, Philip. *The Philadelphia Story: A Comedy in Three Acts.* New York: Coward-McCann, 1939.

Bassett, William B. "T. P. Chandler Jr., FAIA: An Introduction." Bachelor's thesis, University of Pennsylvania, 1967.

Bean, Theodore W. *History of Montgomery County, Pennsylvania.* 2 vols. Philadelphia: Everts & Peck, 1884.

Beckert, Sven. "Comments on 'Studying the Middle Class in the Modern City.'" *Journal of Urban History* 31 (March 2005): 393–99.

———. *The Monied Metropolis: New York City and the Consolidation of the American Bourgeoisie, 1850–1896.* New York: Cambridge University Press, 2001.

Behdad, Ali. *A Forgetful Nation: On Immigration and Cultural Identity in the United States.* Durham: Duke University Press, 2005.

Bellah, Robert N. *Varieties of Civil Religion.* New York: Harper & Row, 1980.

Benjamin, Philip S. "Gentlemen Reformers in the Quaker City, 1870–1912." *Political Science Quarterly* 85 (March 1970): 61–79.

———. *The Philadelphia Quakers in the Industrial Age, 1865–1920.* Philadelphia: Temple University Press, 1976.

Biddle, Cordelia Drexel. *My Philadelphia Father.* Garden City, NY: Doubleday, 1955.

Biddle, Francis. *The Llanfear Pattern.* New York: Scribner, 1927.

Biel, Steven. *Down with the Old Canoe: A Cultural History of the Titanic Disaster.* New York: Norton, 1996.

Birmingham, Stephen. *The Grandes Dames.* New York: Simon & Schuster, 1982.

———. *Real Lace: America's Irish Rich.* New York: Harper and Row, 1973.

———. *"The Rest of Us": The Rise of America's Eastern European Jews.* Boston: Little, Brown, 1984.

———. *The Right People: A Portrait of the American Social Establishment.* Boston: Little, Brown, 1958.

Bispham, David. *A Quaker Singer's Recollection.* New York: Macmillan, 1921.

Blood, William W. *Apostle of Reason: A Biography of Joseph Krauskopf.* Philadelphia: Dorrance, 1973.

Blumin, Stuart M. *The Emergence of the Middle Class: Social Experience in the American City, 1760–1900.* New York: Cambridge University Press, 1989.

Bok, Edward. *The Americanization of Edward Bok: The Autobiography of a Dutch Boy Fifty Years After.* 1920. Reprint, New York: Scribner, 1922.

———. *Why I Believe in Poverty as the Richest Experience That Can Come to a Boy.* Boston and New York: Houghton Mifflin, 1915.

———. *The Young Man and the Church.* Philadelphia: Henry Altemus, 1896.

Bond, Mary Wickham. *Ninety Years "At Home" in Philadelphia.* Privately printed, 1988.

Bonner, Edwin B. "Quaker Voluntary Organizations in Three Centuries." In Jean Barth Toll and Mildred S. Gillam, eds., *Invisible Philadelphia: Community Through Voluntary Organizations.* Philadelphia: Atwater Kent Museum, 1995.

Bourdieu, Pierre. *Distinction: A Social Critique of the Judgement of Taste.* Translated by Richard Nice. Cambridge, MA: Harvard University Press, 1984.

———. *The Field of Cultural Production: Essays on Art and Literature.* Edited by Randal Johnson. New York: Columbia University Press, 1993.

Bourgeois, Michael. *All Things Human: Henry Codman Potter and the Social Gospel in the Episcopal Church.* Urbana: University of Illinois Press, 2004.

Bowden, Robert Douglas. *Boies Penrose: Symbol of an Era.* New York: Greenberg, 1937.

Boyer, Paul S. *Urban Masses and Moral Order in America, 1820–1920.* New York: Cambridge University Press, 1978.

Bratt, James D. "The Reorientation of American Protestantism, 1835–1845." *Church History* (March 1998): 52–82.

Bremner, Robert H. *American Philanthropy.* 1960. 2nd ed. Chicago: University of Chicago Press, 1988.

Bridenbaugh, Carl. *Mitre and Sceptre: Transatlantic Faiths, Ideas, Personalities, and Politics, 1689–1775.* New York: Oxford University Press, 1962.

Brinton, Howard H. *Quaker Journals: Varieties of Religious Experience Among Friends.* Wallingford, PA: Pendle Hill Publications, 1972.

Brinton, Mary Williams. *My Cap and My Cape.* Philadelphia: Dorrance, 1950.

———. *Their Lives and Mine.* Philadelphia: privately printed, 1972.

Brookhiser, Richard. *The Way of the WASP: How It Made America, and How It Can Save It, So to Speak.* New York: Free Press, 1991.

Brooks, David. *Bobos in Paradise: The New Upper Class and How They Got There.* New York: Simon & Schuster, 2000.

Brown, Callum G. "The Costs of Pew-Renting: Church Management, Church-Going and Social Class in Nineteenth-Century Glasgow." *Journal of Ecclesiastical History* 38 (July 1987): 347–61.

Brown, Dorothy M., and Elizabeth McKeown. *The Poor Belong to Us: Catholic Charities and American Welfare.* Cambridge, MA: Harvard University Press, 1997.

Brown, John K. *The Baldwin Locomotive Works, 1831–1915.* Baltimore: Johns Hopkins University Press, 1995.

Bryson, Thomas A. *Walter George Smith.* Washington, DC: Catholic University of America Press, 1977.

Budd, Henry, Esq. "The Charge to the Triers." In Henry Budd, Esq., and Rev. Fordyce H. Argo, *The Richmond Ecclesiastical Trial*. Philadelphia, 1917.

Burgess, George H., and Miles C. Kennedy. *Centennial History of the Pennsylvania Railroad Company, 1846–1946*. Philadelphia: Pennsylvania Railroad Company, 1949.

Burk, Eleanor H. S. *In the Beginning at Valley Forge and the Washington Memorial Chapel*. North Wales, PA: Norman B. Nuss, 1938.

Burk, Rev. W. Herbert. *Good News for the Home Lovers of Valley Forge. A Sermon Preached in the Washington Memorial Chapel, Sunday, December 22, 1918*. [Valley Forge, 1918].

———. *Making a Museum: The Confessions of a Curator*. [Philadelphia, 1926].

———. *Valley Forge: What It Is, Where It Is, and What to See There*. North Wales, PA: Norman B. Nuss, 1928.

Burr, Agnes Rush. *Russell H. Conwell and His Work: One Man's Interpretation of Life*. Philadelphia: John C. Winston, 1917.

Burt, Maxwell. *Philadelphia, Holy Experiment*. New York: Rich & Gowan, 1947.

Burt, Nathaniel. *First Families: The Making of an American Aristocracy*. Boston: Little, Brown, 1970.

———. *The Perennial Philadelphians: The Anatomy of an American Aristocracy*. 1963. Reprint, Philadelphia: University of Pennsylvania Press, 1999.

Burt, Nathaniel, and Wallace E. Davies. "The Iron Age, 1876–1905." In Russell F. Weigley, ed., *Philadelphia: A 300-Year History*. New York: Norton, 1982.

Burton, Katherine. *The Golden Door: The Life of Katharine Drexel*. New York: Kenedy, 1957.

Bushman, Richard L. *The Refinement of America: Persons, Houses, Cities*. New York: Knopf, 1992.

Butler, Jon. "Religion in New York City: Faith That Could Not Be." *U.S. Catholic Historian* 22 (Spring 2004): 51–61.

Butler, Jon, and Harry S. Stout, eds. *Religion and American History: A Reader*. New York: Oxford University Press, 1997.

Cable, Mary. *Top Drawer: American High Society from the Gilded Age to the Roaring Twenties*. New York: Atheneum, 1984.

Carey, Henry C. *A Memoir of Stephen Colwell: Read Before the American Philosophical Society, Friday, November 17, 1871*. Philadelphia: Collins, 1871.

Carey, Patrick W. *People, Priests, and Prelates: Ecclesiastical Democracy and the Tensions of Trusteeism*. Notre Dame: University of Notre Dame Press, 1987.

Carnegie, Andrew. *The Gospel of Wealth and Other Timely Essays*. 1889. Reprint, New York: Century, 1900.

Carr, William. *The du Ponts of Delaware*. New York: Dodd, Mead, 1964.

Carroll, Jackson W., and Wade Clark Roof, eds. *Beyond Establishment: Protestant Identity in a Post-Protestant Age*. Louisville: Westminster John Knox Press, 1993.

Carter, Paul A. *The Decline and Revival of the Social Gospel: Social and Political Liberalism in American Protestant Churches, 1920–1940*. Ithaca: Cornell University Press, 1954.

———. *The Spiritual Crisis of the Gilded Age*. De Kalb: Northern Illinois University Press, 1971.

Catholic Encyclopedia. 18 vols. New York: Universal Knowledge Foundation, 1913.

Catholic Standard and Times. The Catholic Directory. Philadelphia, 1997.

———. *Official Jubilee Volume: Life and Work of His Eminence D. Cardinal Dougherty and History of St. Charles Seminary, June 10th, 1928*. Philadelphia, 1928.

A Century of Faith and Service, 1885–1985: A Centennial History of the Church of Our Mother of Good Counsel, Pennswood Road, Bryn Mawr, PA. Devon, PA: Cooke, [1985].

Chambers, Thomas A. *Drinking the Waters: Creating an American Leisure Class at Nineteenth-Century Mineral Springs*. Washington, DC: Smithsonian Institution Press, 2002.

Chandler, Alfred D., Jr. *The Invisible Hand: The Managerial Revolution in American Business*. Cambridge, MA: Belknap Press, 1977.

Chaves, Mark, and John R. Sutton. "Organizational Consolidation in American Protestant Denominations, 1890–1900." *Journal for the Scientific Study of Religion* 43 (March 2004): 51–66.

Chernow, Ron. *Titan: The Life of John D. Rockefeller Sr.* New York: Random House, 1998.

Chesebrough, David B. *Philips Brooks: Pulpit Eloquence.* Westport, CT: Greenwood Press, 2001.

Cheyney, Edward Potts. *History of the University of Pennsylvania, 1740–1940.* Philadelphia: University of Pennsylvania Press, 1940.

Childs, George W. *Recollections.* Philadelphia: J. B. Lippincott, 1892.

Childs, Walter C., II, comp. *The Life and Times of John Pitcairn: Captured in Original Correspondence and Photographs from the John Pitcairn Archives.* Bryn Athyn: Academy of the New Church, 1999.

Chorley, E. Clowes. *Men and Movements in the American Episcopal Church.* New York: Scribner, 1946.

Christian Advices Issued by the Yearly Meeting of Friends, Held in Philadelphia (Orthodox). Philadelphia: Friends Bookstore, 1879.

Christopher, Robert C. *Crashing the Gates: The De-WASPing of America's Power Elite.* New York: Simon & Schuster, 1989.

Civic Club Digest of the Educational and Charitable Institutions and Societies in Philadelphia. Philadelphia, 1895.

Clark, Dennis. *The Irish in Philadelphia: Ten Generations of Urban Experience.* Philadelphia: Temple University Press, 1973.

———. "A Pattern of Urban Growth: Residential Development and Church Location in Philadelphia." *Records of the American Catholic Historical Society* (September 1971): 159–70.

Clark, Michael D. *The American Discovery of Tradition, 1865–1942.* Baton Rouge: Louisiana State University Press, 2005.

Coale, James J. "Influence of the Automobile on the City Church." *Annals of the American Academy of Political and Social Science* (November 1924): 80–82.

———. "Protestantism and the Masses." *Yale Review* (October 1921): 78–88.

Coates, E. Osborne. *An Historical Sketch of the Church of the Good Shepherd, Rosemont, Pennsylvania, 1869–1934.* [Rosemont, PA: Church of the Good Shepherd, 1934].

Coburn, Carol, and Martha Smith. *Spirited Lives: How Nuns Shaped Catholic Culture and American Life, 1836–1920.* Chapel Hill: University of North Carolina Press, 1999.

Cocke, Stephanie Hetos. "The Gilded Age Estates of Lower Merion Township, Pennsylvania: A History and Preservation Plan." Master's thesis, University of Pennsylvania, 1987.

Coffin, Elizabeth W. *A Girl's Life in Germantown.* Boston: Sherman, French, 1916.

Cohen, Lizabeth. *Making a New Deal: Industrial Workers in Chicago, 1919–1939.* New York: Cambridge University Press, 1990.

Colwell, Stephen. *New Themes for Protestant Clergy.* 1851. Reprint, New York: Arno Press, 1969.

———. *The Ways and Means of Payment.* 1859. Reprint, New York: Augustus M. Kelley, 1965.

Comfort, William Wistar. *Just Among Friends: The Quaker Way of Life.* 1941. Reprint, Philadelphia: Blakiston, 1945.

Conger, A. B. *An Historical Sermon Delivered in the Memorial Church of the Good Shepherd.* Rosemont: Church of the Good Shepherd, 1910.

Connelly, James F., ed. *The History of the Archdiocese of Philadelphia.* Philadelphia: Archdiocese of Philadelphia, 1976.

———. *St. Charles Seminary, Philadelphia: A History of the Theological Seminary of Saint Charles Borromeo, Overbrook, Philadelphia, Pennsylvania, 1832–1979.* Philadelphia: St. Charles Seminary, 1979.

——. "The Visit of Archbishop Gaetano Bedini to the United States of America (June, 1853–February, 1854)." *Analecta Gregoriana* (Rome), 1960.

Constitution of the Presbyterian Church in the United States of America. Philadelphia: Presbyterian Board of Publication, 1892.

Constitutions and Canons for the Government of the Protestant Episcopal Church in the Diocese of Pennsylvania, Ordered Printed by the Convention of the Diocese, Held in May, A.D. 1923. Philadelphia: John C. Winston, 1923.

Constitutions and Canons for the Government of the Protestant Episcopal Church in the United States of America, Adopted in General Conventions 1789–1922. New York: Edwin S. Gorham by order of the House of Deputies, 1924.

Consuelo, Sister Mary, IHM. "The Church of Philadelphia, 1884–1918." In James F. Connelly, ed., *The History of the Archdiocese of Philadelphia*. Philadelphia: Archdiocese of Philadelphia, 1976.

Contosta, David R. *A Philadelphia Family: The Houstons and Woodwards of Chestnut Hill*. Philadelphia: University of Pennsylvania Press, 1988.

——. *Suburb in the City: Chestnut Hill, Philadelphia, 1850–1990*. Columbus: Ohio State University Press, 1992.

——. *A Venture in Faith: The Church of St. Martin-in-the-Fields, 1889–1989*. Philadelphia: Church of St. Martin-in-the Fields, 1988.

——. *Villanova University, 1842–1992: American—Catholic—Augustinian*. University Park: Pennsylvania State University Press, 1995.

Conwell, Russell H. *Acres of Diamonds*. New York: Harper, 1915.

——. *Health, Healing, and Faith*. New York: National Extension University, 1921.

——. *Praying for Money*. New York: National Extension University, 1921.

——. *The Romantic Rise of a Great American*. New York: Harper, 1924.

Cookson, Peter W., and Caroline Hodges Persell. *Preparing for Power: America's Elite Boarding Schools*. New York: Basic Books, 1985.

Cooper, Wilmer A. *A Living Faith: An Historical Study of Quaker Beliefs*. 1990. Reprint, Richmond, IN: Friends United Press, 2001.

Cram, Ralph Adams. *Church Building: A Study of the Principles of Architecture in Their Relation to the Church*. 1901. 3rd ed. Boston: Marshall Jones, 1924.

——. *The Gothic Quest*. 1907. 2nd and rev. ed. Garden City, NY: Doubleday, Page, 1918.

Crapsey, Algernon Sidney. *The Last of the Heretics*. New York: Knopf, 1924.

Cross, Robert D. *The Church and the City, 1865–1910*. Indianapolis: Bobbs-Merrill, 1967.

Crunden, Robert. *Ministers of Reform: The Progressives' Achievement in American Civilization, 1889–1920*. New York: Basic Books, 1982.

Curtis, Susan. *A Consuming Faith: The Social Gospel and Modern American Culture*. Baltimore: Johns Hopkins University Press, 1991.

Cutler, William W., III, and Howard Gillette Jr., eds. *The Divided Metropolis: Social and Spatial Dimensions in Philadelphia, 1800–1975*. Westport, CT: Greenwood Press, 1980.

Dator, James Allen, and Jan Nunley. *Many Parts, One Body: How the Episcopal Church Works*. New York: Church Publishing, 2010.

Davenport, Stewart. *Friends of Unrighteous Mammon: Northern Christians and Market Capitalism, 1815–1860*. Chicago: University of Chicago Press, 2008.

Davidoff, Leonore, and Catherine Hall. *Family Fortunes: Men and Women of the English Middle Class, 1780–1850*. Chicago: University of Chicago Press, 1987.

Davis, Allen F., and Mark H. Haller, eds. *The Peoples of Philadelphia: A History of Ethnic Groups and Lower-Class Life, 1790–1940*. Philadelphia: Temple University Press, 1973.

Davis, Rev. Bradford. "Presbyterian Organizations in Philadelphia." In Jean Barth Toll and Mildred S. Gillam, eds., *Invisible Philadelphia: Community Through Voluntary Organizations*. Philadelphia: Atwater Kent Museum, 1995.

Davis, Jerome. "A Study of Protestant Church Boards of Control." *American Journal of Sociology* 38 (November 1932): 418–31.

Davis, Myra Tolmach. *Sketches in Iron: Samuel Yellin, American Master of Wrought Iron, 1885–1940.* Washington, DC, 1971.

Davis, Patricia Talbot. *End of the Line: Alexander J. Cassatt and the Pennsylvania Railroad.* New York: Neale Watson Academic, 1978.

Dawley, Powel Mills. *The Story of the General Theological Seminary: A Sesquicentennial History, 1817–1967.* New York: Oxford University Press, 1969.

Demerath, N. J. *Social Class in American Protestantism.* Chicago: Rand McNally, 1965.

DeSanctis, Michael. *Building from Belief: Advance, Retreat, and Compromise in the Remaking of Catholic Church Architecture.* Collegeville, MN: Liturgical Press, 2002.

Dianteill, Erwan. "Pierre Bourdieu and the Sociology of Religion: A Central and Peripheral Concern." In David L. Swartz and Vera L. Zolberg, eds., *After Bourdieu: Influence, Critique, Elaboration.* Dordrecht: Kluwer Academic, 2004.

Dignan, Patrick J. *A History of the Legal Incorporation of Catholic Church Property in the United States (1784–1932).* Washington, DC: Catholic University of America, 1933.

Dilworth, Richardson, ed. *Social Capital in the City: Community and Civic Life in Philadelphia.* Philadelphia: Temple University Press, 2006.

Dinner of the Trustees of the University of Pennsylvania to Provost Charles Custis Harrison. The Bellevue-Stratford, Philadelphia, May 23, 1906. [Philadelphia, 1906].

Diocese of Pennsylvania. *Cathedral Church of Christ of the Diocese of Pennsylvania.* Philadelphia, [1922].

———. *Our Common Prayer: A Bicentennial Book Celebrating the History of the Diocese of Pennsylvania, 1784–1984.* Philadelphia, 1984.

Discipline of the Yearly Meeting of Friends (Orthodox). Philadelphia: Friends' Book Store, 1910.

Doherty, Robert W. *The Hicksite Separation: A Sociological Analysis of Religious Schism in Early Nineteenth Century America.* New Brunswick: Rutgers University Press, 1967.

———. "Social Basis for the Presbyterian Schism of 1837–1838: The Philadelphia Case." *Journal of Social History* (Fall 1968): 69–79.

Dolan, Jay P. *The American Catholic Experience: A History from Colonial Times to the Present.* Garden City, NY: Doubleday, 1985.

———. *The American Catholic Parish.* 2 vols. New York: Paulist Press, 1987.

———. *The Immigrant Church: New York's Irish and German Catholics, 1815–1865.* Notre Dame: University of Notre Dame Press, 1975.

Domhoff, G. William. *The Higher Circles: The Governing Class in America.* New York: Random House, 1970.

Douglass, H. Paul. *Church Comity: A Study of Cooperative Church Extension in American Cities.* Garden City, NY: Doubleday, Doran, 1929.

———. *The Church in the Changing City: Case Studies Illustrating Adaptation.* New York: George H. Doran, 1927.

———. *The City's Church.* New York: Friendship Press, 1929.

———. *1,000 City Churches.* New York: George H. Doran, 1926.

———. *The St. Louis Church Survey: A Religious Investigation with a Social Background.* New York: George H. Doran, 1924.

Dreiser, Theodore. *The Bulwark.* New York: Book Find Club, 1946.

———. *The Financier.* New York: Boni & Liveright, 1927.

Du Bois, W. E. B. *The Philadelphia Negro: A Social Study.* 1899. Reprint, New York: Benjamin Books, 1967.

Dudden, Arthur P. "The City Embraces 'Normalcy,' 1919–1929." In Russell F. Weigley, ed., *Philadelphia: A 300-Year History.* New York: Norton, 1982.

Duffy, Sister Consuela Marie, SBS. *Katharine Drexel: A Biography.* Cornwells Heights, PA: Sisters of the Blessed Sacrament, 1966.

Durandus, William. *The Symbolism of Churches and Church Ornaments.* 1843. 3rd ed. London: Gibbings, 1906.

Earnest, Ernest. S. *Weir Mitchell: Novelist and Physician*. Philadelphia: University of Pennsylvania Press, 1950.

Eckert, Jack, comp. *Guide to the Records of Philadelphia Yearly Meeting*. Philadelphia: Philadelphia Yearly Meeting, 1989.

Einhorn, Robyn. *Property Rules: Political Economy in Chicago, 1833–1939*. Chicago: University of Chicago Press, 1991.

Eleanor, Sister Mary, SHCJ. *Mother Mary Ignatius of the Society of the Holy Child Jesus, President of Rosemont College, 1924–1939*. Philadelphia: Peter Reilly, 1949.

Elfenbein, Jessica I. *The Making of a Modern City: Philanthropy, Civic Culture, and the Baltimore YMCA*. Gainesville: University Press of Florida, 2001.

Elkinton, David Cope. *Family Footprints: The Lives, Ancestry, and Descendants of Joseph Scotton Elkinton and Malinda Patterson Elkinton*. 4 vols. Kennett Square, PA: KNA Press, 1992.

Elkinton, Joseph, ed. *Selections from the Diary and Correspondence of Joseph S. Elkinton, 1830–1905*. Philadelphia: Press of Leeds and Biddle, 1913.

Elkinton, J. Russell, and David C. Elkinton, eds. *Joseph Elkinton, 1859–1920: His Life, Travels and Ministry*. Media, PA: Baker's Print Shop, 1981.

Elliott, Edward O. *Tent to Temple: A History of the Grace Baptist Church, Philadelphia, Pa., 1870–1895, and of the Founding by Russell H. Conwell of The Baptist Temple the College—Samaritan Hospital (now) Temple University*. [Jenkintown, PA: Times Chronicle, 1946].

Encyclical Letter of His Holiness Pope Leo XIII on the Condition of the Working Classes: Rerum Novarum. 1891. Boston: Pauline Books and Media, 1999.

Ennis, Arthur J., OSA. "The New Diocese of Philadelphia." In James F. Connelly, ed., *The History of the Archdiocese of Philadelphia*. Philadelphia: Archdiocese of Philadelphia, 1976.

Ershkowitz, Herbert. *John Wanamaker, Philadelphia Merchant*. Conshohocken, PA: Combined, 1999.

Evensen, Bruce J. *God's Man for the Gilded Age: D. L. Moody and the Rise of Modern Mass Evangelicalism*. New York: Oxford University Press, 2003.

Everett, John Rutherford. *Religion in Economics: A Study of John Bates Clark, Richard T. Ely, Simon N. Patten*. New York: King's Crown Press, 1946.

Faith and Practice. Philadelphia: Philadelphia Yearly Meeting [Orthodox], 1926.

Faris, John Thomson. *The Romance of Old Philadelphia*. Philadelphia: J. B. Lippincott, 1918.

Farnsworth, Jean M., Carmen R. Croce, and Joseph F. Chorpenning, eds. *Stained Glass in Catholic Philadelphia*. Philadelphia: Saint Joseph's University Press, 2002.

Farraday, Clayton L. *Friends' Central School, 1845–1984*. Philadelphia: Friends' Central School, 1984.

Farrell, Betty. *Elite Families: Class and Power in Nineteenth-Century Boston*. Albany: State University of New York Press, 1993.

Faught, C. Brad. *The Oxford Movement: A Thematic History of the Tractarians and Their Times*. University Park: Pennsylvania State University Press, 2003.

Feller, Richard T., and Marshall W. Fishwick. *For Thy Great Glory*. 1965. 2nd ed. Culpeper, VA: Community Press, 1979.

Finke, Roger, and Rodney Stark. *The Churching of America, 1776–1990: Winners and Losers in Our Religious Economy*. New Brunswick: Rutgers University Press, 1992.

Fischer, David Hackett. *Albion's Seed: Four British Folkways in America*. New York: Oxford University Press, 1989.

Fisher, Joshua Francis. *Recollections of Joshua Francis Fisher, Written in 1864*. Arr. Sophia Cadwalader. Boston: privately printed, 1929.

Fitzgerald, Maureen. *Habits of Compassion: Irish-Catholic Nuns and the Origins of New York's Welfare System, 1830–1920*. Urbana: University of Illinois Press, 2005.

Flexner, Helen Thomas. *A Quaker Childhood*. New Haven: Yale University Press, 1940.

Fones-Wolf, Ken. *Trade Union Gospel: Christianity and Labor in Industrial Philadelphia, 1865–1915*. Philadelphia: Temple University Press, 1989.

Forbes, Susan S. "Quaker Tribalism." In Michael Zuckerman, ed., *Friends and Neighbors: Group Life in America's First Plural Society*. Philadelphia: Temple University Press, 1982.

Fox, Richard Wightman. "The Culture of Liberal Protestant Progressivism, 1875–1925." *Journal of Interdisciplinary History* 23 (Winter 1993): 639–60.

Franchot, Jenny. *Roads to Rome: The Antebellum Protestant Encounter with Catholicism*. Berkeley: University of California Press, 1994.

Fraser, Steve, and Gary Gerstle, eds. *Ruling America: A History of Wealth and Power in a Democracy*. Cambridge, MA: Harvard University Press, 2005.

Friedman, Lawrence J., and Mark D. McGarvie, eds. *Charity, Philanthropy, and Civility in American History*. New York: Cambridge University Press, 2003.

Friedman, Murray, ed. *Jewish Life in Philadelphia, 1830–1940*. Philadelphia: ISHI, 1983.

———. *When Philadelphia Was the Capital of Jewish America*. Philadelphia: Balch Institute Press, 1993.

Friends' Library, Consisting Principally of Journals and Extracts from Journals and Other Writings of Members of the Society of Friends. 16 vols. Linfield, England: Longman, 1832–1838.

Frost, J. William. "From Plainness to Simplicity: Changing Quaker Ideals for Material Culture." In Emma Jones Lapsansky and Anne A. Verplanck, eds., *Quaker Aesthetics: Reflections on a Quaker Ethic in American Design and Consumption*. Philadelphia: University of Pennsylvania Press, 2003.

Gamm, Gerald. *Urban Exodus: Why the Jews Left Boston and the Catholics Stayed*. Cambridge, MA: Harvard University Press, 1999.

Garrigan, Kristine Ottesen. *Ruskin on Architecture: His Thought and Influence*. Madison: University of Wisconsin Press, 1973.

Gaustad, Edwin Scott, and Philip L. Barlow. *New Historical Atlas of Religion in America*. New York: Oxford University Press, 2001.

Gerstle, Gary. *Working-Class Americanism: The Politics of Labor in a Textile City, 1914–1960*. New York: Cambridge University Press, 1989.

Gibbons, Herbert Adams. *John Wanamaker*. New York: Harper, 1926.

Giles, Richard. *Re-Pitching the Tent: Re-Ordering the Church Building for Worship and Mission*. 1996. Rev. and expanded ed. Collegeville, MN: Liturgical Press, 1997.

Gilkyson, Claude. *St. Mark's: One Hundred Years on Locust Street*. Philadelphia: St. Mark's Church, 1948.

Gillespie, Mrs. E. D. *A Book of Remembrance*. Philadelphia: J. B. Lippincott, 1901.

Gladish, Richard R. *John Pitcairn: Uncommon Entrepreneur*. Bryn Athyn: Academy of the New Church, 1989.

Gladish, Richard R., and E. Bruce Glenn, eds. *Pitcairn Patriarchs*. Bryn Athyn: General Church of the New Jerusalem, 1985.

Glenn, E. Bruce. *Bryn Athyn Cathedral: The Building of a Church*. New York: C. Harrison Conroy, 1971.

———. "The Pitcairn Brothers: Raymond, Theodore, Harold." In Richard R. Gladish and E. Bruce Glenn, eds., *Pitcairn Patriarchs*. Bryn Athyn: General Church of the New Jerusalem, 1985.

Goodwin, Daniel R. *The New Ritualistic Divinity: Neither the Religion of the Bible and Prayer-Book nor of the Holy Catholic Church; Being a Defense of the Protestant Episcopal Church in Pennsylvania, Against the Attack of Henry Flanders, Esq., of the Philadelphia Bar*. 2nd ed. Philadelphia, 1879.

Gooren, Henri. *Religious Conversion and Disaffiliation: Tracing Patterns of Change in Faith Practice*. New York: Palgrave Macmillan, 2010.

Gordon, Elizabeth G. B. *Days of Now and Then*. Philadelphia: Dorrance, 1945.

Gough, Deborah Mathias. *Christ Church, Philadelphia: The Nation's Church in a Changing City*. Philadelphia: University of Pennsylvania Press, 1995.

———. "The Roots of Episcopalian Authority Structures: The Church of England in Colonial Philadelphia." In Michael Zuckerman, ed., *Friends and Neighbors: Group Life in America's First Plural Society*. Philadelphia: Temple University Press, 1982.

Green, Constance McLaughlin. *The Church on Lafayette Square: A History of St. John's Church, Washington, D.C., 1815–1970*. Washington, DC: Potomac Books, 1970.

Greiff, Constance M. *John Notman, Architect, 1810–1865*. Philadelphia: Athenaeum of Philadelphia, 1979.

Griffen, Clyde C. "Rich Laymen and Early Social Christianity." *Church History* (March 1967): 45–65.

Griffis, Rev. Wm. Elliot. *John Chambers: Servant of Christ and Master of Hearts and His Ministry in Philadelphia*. Ithaca, NY: Andrus & Church, 1903.

Grossman, James R. *Land of Hope: Chicago, Black Southerners, and the Great Migration*. Chicago: University of Chicago Press, 1989.

The Ground of the Testimony of the Religious Society of Friends Against Removing the Hat and Using Complimentary Forms of Speech as Tokens of Respect. Philadelphia: Friends' Book Store, 1884.

Guelzo, Allen C. *For the Union of Evangelical Christendom: The Irony of the Reformed Episcopalians*. University Park: Pennsylvania State University Press, 1994.

Gunther, John. *Inside U.S.A.* New York: Harper, 1947.

Hackett, David, Laurie Maffly-Kipp, R. Laurence Moore, and Leslie Tentler. "Forum: American Religion and Class." *Religion and American Culture* 15 (Winter 2005): 1–29.

Hadden, Jeffrey K. "H. Paul Douglass: His Perspective and His Work." *Review of Religious Research* (September 1980): 66–88.

Halsey, William M. *The Survival of American Innocence: Catholicism in an Age of Disillusionment, 1920–1940*. Notre Dame: University of Notre Dame Press, 1980.

Hamer, John H. *America, Philanthropy, and the Moral Order*. Lewiston, NY: Edwin Mellen Press, 2002.

Hamm, Thomas D. *The Quakers in America*. New York: Columbia University Press, 2003.

———. *The Transformation of American Quakerism: Orthodox Friends, 1800–1907*. Bloomington: Indiana University Press, 1988.

Hammack, David C. *Making the Nonprofit Sector in the United States: A Reader*. Bloomington: Indiana University Press, 1998.

Hammonds, Kenneth A. *Historical Directory of Presbyterian Churches and Presbyteries of Greater Philadelphia: Related to the Presbyterian Church (U.S.A.) and Its Antecedents, 1690–1990*. Philadelphia: Presbyterian Historical Society, 1993.

Hanby, Victor Dure. *A Short History of St. John's Church, Wilmington, Delaware*. [Wilmington], 1947.

Handlin, Oscar. *The Uprooted: The Epic Story of the Great Migrations That Made the American People*. Boston: Little, Brown, 1951.

Harper, John C. *A Symbol of a Nation Praying: A Brief History of St. John's Episcopal Church, Lafayette Square, Washington, D.C., 1815–1965*. Washington, DC: St. John's Church, 1965.

Harris, Howell John. *Bloodless Victories: The Rise and Fall of the Open Shop in the Philadelphia Metal Trades, 1890–1940*. New York: Cambridge University Press, 2004.

———. "War in the Social Order: The Great War and the Liberalization of American Quakerism." In David K. Adams and Cornelis A. van Minnen, eds., *Religious and Secular Reform in America: Ideas, Belief, and Social Change*. New York: New York University Press, 1999.

Harrison, Mary. *Annals of the Ancestry of Charles Custis Harrison and Ellen Waln Harrison*. Philadelphia: printed for private circulation by J. B. Lippincott, 1932.

Hart, J. Coleman. *Design for Parish Churches in the Three Styles of English Church Architecture*. New York: Dana, 1857.

Hatch, Nathan O. *The Democratization of American Christianity*. New Haven: Yale University Press, 1989.

Hawks, Edward. *William McGarvey and the Open Pulpit: An Intimate History of a Celibate Movement in the Episcopal Church and of Its Collapse, 1870–1908*. Philadelphia: Dolphin Press, 1935.

Heales, Alfred. *The History and Law of Church Seats or Pews*. Book 1: *History*. London, 1872.

Hein, David. *Noble Powell and the Episcopal Establishment in the Twentieth Century*. Urbana: University of Illinois Press, 2001.

Hein, David, and Gardiner H. Shattuck Jr. *The Episcopalians*. Westport, CT: Praeger, 2004.

Henry, Allan J., ed. *Francis Gurney du Pont: A Memoir*. 2 vols. Philadelphia: William F. Fell, 1951.

Hepp, John Henry. *The Middle-Class City: Transforming Space and Time in Philadelphia, 1876–1926*. Philadelphia: University of Pennsylvania Press, 2003.

Hershberg, Theodore, ed. *Philadelphia: Work Space, Family, and Group Experience in the Nineteenth Century; Essays Toward an Interdisciplinary History of the City*. New York: Oxford University Press, 1981.

Heyrman, Christine Leigh. *Southern Cross: The Beginnings of the Bible Belt*. New York: Knopf, 1997.

Higham, John. *Send These to Me: Jews and Other Immigrants in Urban America*. New York: Athenaeum, 1975.

———. *Strangers in the Land: Patterns of American Nativism, 1860–1925*. 1955. 2nd ed. New Brunswick: Rutgers University Press, 1988.

Higley, Stephen Richard. *Privilege, Power, and Place: The Geography of the American Upper Class*. Lanham, MD: Rowman & Littlefield, 1995.

Hilkey, Judy. *Character Is Capital: Success Manuals and Manhood in Gilded Age America*. Chapel Hill: University of North Carolina Press, 1997.

Hilty, James W. *Temple University: 125 Years of Service to Philadelphia, the Nation, and the World*. Philadelphia: Temple University Press, 2010.

Hinshaw, David. *Rufus Jones: Master Quaker*. 1951. Reprint, Freeport, NY: Books for Libraries Press, 1970.

The History of Old St. David's Church, Radnor, in Delaware County, Pennsylvania. Philadelphia: John C. Winston, 1907.

Hodges, George, and John Reichert. *The Administration of an Institutional Church: A Detailed Account of the Operation of St. George's Parish in the City of New York*. New York: Harper, 1906.

Holman, Charles T. "Are City Churches Effectively Organized?" *Journal of Religion* 7 (March 1927): 209–12.

Holmes, David L. *A Brief History of the Episcopal Church*. Valley Forge: Trinity Press, 1993.

———. *The Faiths of the Founding Fathers*. New York: Oxford University Press, 2006.

Hopkins, Charles Howard. *The Rise of the Social Gospel in American Protestantism, 1865–1915*. New Haven: Yale University Press, 1940.

Hopkins, Samuel Miles. *Manual of Church Polity*. Auburn, NY: Wm. J. Moses, 1878.

Horowitz, Helen Lefkowitz. *The Power and Passion of M. Carey Thomas*. New York: Knopf, 1994.

Horstman, Allen. *Victorian Divorce*. New York: St. Martin's Press, 1985.

Howe, Jeffrey W. *Houses of Worship: An Identification Guide to the History and Styles of American Religious Architecture*. San Diego: Thunder Bay Press, 2003.

Hudnut-Beumler, James. *In Pursuit of the Almighty's Dollar: A History of Money and American Protestantism*. Chapel Hill: University of North Carolina Press, 2007.

Hughes, Samuel. "An Affair to Remember: The Dismissal of Economics Professor Scott Nearing Taught the University a Valuable Lesson—the Hard Way." *Pennsylvania Gazette: Alumni Magazine of the University of Pennsylvania* (March/April 2002).

Huntington, William Reed. *The Church Ideal: An Essay Toward Unity*. New York: E. P. Dutton, 1870.

———. *A National Church*. New York: Scribner, 1898.

Huston, I[sabella] P[ennock]. *Superficial Glimpses of Travel*. Philadelphia: Porter & Coates, 1888.
Hutchison, William R., ed. *Between the Times: The Travail of the Protestant Establishment in America, 1900–1960*. New York: Cambridge University Press, 1989.
——. *Religious Pluralism in America: The Contentious History of a Founding Ideal*. New Haven: Yale University Press, 2003.
Hutton, C. Osborne, comp. *Descendants of the Quaker Huttons of Pennsylvania*. Mentor, OH: privately printed, 1965.
Ingersoll, R. Sturgis. *Our Parents: A Family Chronicle*. [Boyertown, PA]: privately printed, 1973.
——. *Recollections of a Philadelphian at Eighty*. Philadelphia: National, 1971.
——. *Sketch of the Ingersoll Family of Philadelphia*. Privately printed, 1966.
Ingham, John N. *The Iron Barons: A Social Analysis of an American Urban Elite, 1874–1965*. Westport, CT: Greenwood Press, 1978.
Ingle, H. Larry. *Quakers in Conflict: The Hicksite Reformation*. Knoxville: University of Tennessee Press, 1986.
Jacoby, Sanford M. *Modern Manors: Welfare Capitalism Since the New Deal*. Princeton: Princeton University Press, 1997.
Jaher, Frederic Cople. *The Urban Establishment: Upper Strata in Boston, New York, Charleston, Chicago, and Los Angeles*. Urbana: University of Illinois Press, 1982.
Jenkins, Edward Corbin. *Philanthropy in America*. New York: Associated Press, 1950.
Johnson, Allan G. *The Blackwell Dictionary of Sociology: A User's Guide to Sociological Language*. Malden, MA: Blackwell, 2000.
Johnson, E. R. Fenimore. *The Taste of A Silver Spoon*. Privately printed, 1928.
Johnson, Paul E. *A Shopkeeper's Millennium: Society and Revivals in Upstate New York, 1815–1837*. New York: Hill & Wang, 1978.
Johnston, Robert D. *The Radical Middle Class: Populist Democracy and the Question of Capitalism in Progressive Era Portland, Oregon*. Princeton: Princeton University Press, 2003.
Jones, Lester M. *Quakers in Action: Recent Humanitarian and Reform Activities of the American Quakers*. New York: Macmillan, 1929.
Jones, Mary Cadwalader. *Lantern Slides*. Philadelphia: privately printed, 1937.
Jones, Rufus M. *Haverford College: A History and Interpretation*. New York: Macmillan, 1933.
——. *The Later Periods of Quakerism*. 2 vols. London: Macmillan, 1921.
——. "The Sense of the Meeting." In Jessamyn West, ed., *The Quaker Reader*. New York: Viking Press: 1962.
Jordan, Frederick W. "Between Heaven and Harvard: Protestant Faith and the American Boarding School Experience, 1778–1940." Ph.D. diss., University of Notre Dame, 2004.
Jordan, John W. *A History of Delaware County, Pennsylvania, and Its People*. 3 vols. New York: Lewis Historical, 1914.
Josephson, Matthew. *The Robber Barons: The Great American Capitalists, 1861–1901*. New York: Harcourt, Brace, 1934.
Joyce, Patrick, ed. *Class*. New York: Oxford University Press, 1995.
Kane, Paula M. *Separatism and Subculture: Boston Catholicism, 1900–1920*. Chapel Hill: University of North Carolina Press, 1994.
Kannerstein, Gregory, ed. *The Spirit and the Intellect: Haverford College, 1833–1983*. Haverford: Haverford College, 1983.
Kantowicz, Edward R. *Corporation Sole: Cardinal Mundelein and Chicago Catholicism*. Notre Dame: University of Notre Dame Press, 1983.
Kashatus, William C., III. "Images of William Penn: An Evolving Portrait of Pennsylvania's Founding Father." In *An Image of Peace: The Penn Treaty Collection of Mr. and Mrs. Meyer P. Potamkin*. Harrisburg: Pennsylvania Historical and Museum Commission, 1996.

Kasson, John F. *Rudeness and Civility: Manners in Nineteenth-Century Urban America.* New York: Hill & Wang, 1990.

Kathrens, Michael C. *American Splendor: The Residential Architecture of Horace Trumbauer.* New York: Acanthus Press, 2002.

Katznelson, Ira. "Levels of Class Formation." In Patrick Joyce, ed., *Class.* New York: Oxford University Press, 1995.

Kaufmann, Eric P. *The Rise and Fall of Anglo-America.* Cambridge, MA: Harvard University Press, 2004.

Keating, Ann Durkin. *Building Chicago: Suburban Developers and the Creation of a Divided Metropolis.* Urbana: University of Illinois Press, 2002.

Kendall, Diana. *The Power of Good Deeds: Privileged Women and the Social Reproduction of the Upper Class.* Lanham, MD: Rowman & Littlefield, 2002.

Kennedy, Thomas C. *British Quakerism, 1860–1920: The Transformation of a Religious Community.* New York: Oxford University Press, 2001.

Kessner, Thomas. *Capital City: New York City and the Men Behind America's Rise to Economic Dominance, 1860–1900.* New York: Simon & Schuster, 2003.

Khurana, Rakesh. *From Higher Aims to Hired Hands: The Social Transformation of American Business Schools and the Unfulfilled Promise of Management as a Profession.* Princeton: Princeton University Press, 2010.

Kilde, Jeanne Halgren. *When Church Became Theatre: The Transformation of Evangelical Architecture and Worship in Nineteenth-Century America.* New York: Oxford University Press, 2002.

King, Moses. *Philadelphia and Notable Philadelphians.* New York, 1902.

Klein, Esther M. *A Guidebook to Jewish Philadelphia.* Philadelphia: Philadelphia Jewish Times Institute, 1965.

Klein, Maury. *The Life and Legend of Jay Gould.* Baltimore: Johns Hopkins University Press, 1986.

Klein, Philip S., and Ari Hoogenboom, eds. *A History of Pennsylvania.* 1973. 2nd ed. University Park: Pennsylvania State University Press, 1980.

Knowles, Archibald Campbell. *Fifty Years: The Picture of a Priest and His People as They Played Their Part on the Stage of Life.* Philadelphia: Saint Alban Church, 1949.

———. *Reminiscences of a Parish Priest.* New York: Morehouse, 1935.

Konolige, Kit, and Frederica Konolige. *The Power of Their Glory: America's Ruling Class, The Episcopalians.* New York: Wyden Books, 1978.

Krass, Peter. *Carnegie.* New York: Wiley, 2002.

Krauskopf, Joseph. *Prejudice: Its Genesis and Exodus.* New York: Block, 1909.

Krefetz, Gerald. *Jews and Money: The Myths and the Reality.* New Haven: Ticknor & Fields, 1982.

Lafferty, James P. *Religious Unrest: The Way Out. Comments on Lectures of Rev. Alfred G. Mortimer, D.D., Rector of St. Mark's P.E. Church, Philadelphia.* Philadelphia: Catholic Standard and Times, 1908.

Lagemann, Ellen Clondliffe, ed. *Philanthropic Foundations: New Scholarship, New Possibilities.* Bloomington: Indiana University Press, 2001.

Lapham, Lewis. *Money and Class in America: Notes and Observations on Our Civil Religion.* New York: Weidenfeld & Nicolson, 1988.

Lapsansky, Emma Jones, and Anne A. Verplanck, eds. *Quaker Aesthetics: Reflections on a Quaker Ethic in American Design and Consumption.* Philadelphia: University of Pennsylvania Press, 2003.

Larson, Edward J. *Summer of the Gods: The Scopes Trial and America's Continuing Debate over Science and Religion.* New York: Basic Books, 1997.

Larson, Henrietta Melia. *Jay Cooke: Private Banker.* Cambridge, MA: Harvard University Press, 1936.

Lasch, Christopher. *The Revolt of the Elites and the Betrayal of Democracy.* New York: Norton, 1995.

Latham, Charles. *The Episcopal Academy, 1785–1984*. Devon, PA: Cooke, 1984.

Lavoie, Catherine C. "Quaker Beliefs and Practices and the Eighteenth-Century Development of the Friends Meeting House in the Delaware Valley." In Emma Jones Lapsansky and Anne A. Verplanck, eds., *Quaker Aesthetics: Reflections on a Quaker Ethic in American Design and Consumption*. Philadelphia: University of Pennsylvania Press, 2003.

Leach, William H. *Protestant Church Building: Planning, Financing, Designing*. New York: Abingdon-Cokesbury Press, 1948.

———. "The Weakness of Protestantism in American Cities." *Journal of Religion* (November 1922): 616–23.

Lears, T. J. Jackson. *No Place of Grace: Antimodernism and the Transformation of American Culture, 1880–1920*. New York: Pantheon Books, 1981.

Ledwith, William L. "The Record of Fifty Years, 1852–1902: Historical Sketch of the Presbyterian Historical Society." *Journal of the Presbyterian Historical Society* 1 (1902): 370–408.

Leeds, Morris E. "Democratic Organization in the Leeds & Northrup Company, Inc." *Annals of the American Academy of Political and Social Science* (July 1920): 13–17.

Lehman, Daniel W. *John Reed and the Writing of Revolution*. Athens: Ohio University Press, 2002.

Lehr, Elizabeth Drexel. *King Lehr and the Gilded Age*. Philadelphia: J. B. Lippincott, 1935.

Lemann, Nicholas. *The Big Test: The Secret History of the American Meritocracy*. New York: Farrar, Straus & Giroux, 1999.

———. "No Man's Town." In David Remnick, ed., *The New Gilded Age: "The New Yorker" Looks at the Culture of Affluence*. New York: Random House, 2000.

Letterhouse, Sister Dolores Marie. *The Francis A. Drexel Family*. Cornwells Heights, PA: Sisters of the Blessed Sacrament, 1939.

Lewis, Arthur H. *The Worlds of Chippy Patterson*. New York: Harcourt, Brace, 1960.

Lewis, Michael J. *Frank Furness: Architecture and the Violent Mind*. New York: Norton, 2001.

Licht, Walter. *Getting Work: Philadelphia, 1840–1950*. Cambridge, MA: Harvard University Press, 1992.

Lief, Alfred. *Family Business: A Century in the Life and Times of Strawbridge and Clothier*. New York: McGraw-Hill, 1968.

Light, Dale B. *Rome and the New Republic: Conflict and Community in Philadelphia Catholicism Between the Revolution and the Civil War*. Notre Dame: University of Notre Dame Press, 1996.

Lilly, May. *The Story of St. Clement's Church, Philadelphia, 1864–1964*. Philadelphia: St. Clement's Church, 1964.

Lippincott, Horace Mather. *An Account of the People Called Quakers in Germantown, Pennsylvania*. Burlington, NJ: Enterprise, 1923.

———. *Early Philadelphia: Its People, Life, and Progress*. Philadelphia: J. B. Lippincott, 1917.

———. *A Narrative of Chestnut Hill, Philadelphia with Some Account of Springfield, Whitemarsh and Cheltenham Townships in Montgomery County, Pennsylvania*. Jenkintown: Old York Road, 1948.

———, ed. *Through a Quaker Archway*. New York: Thomas Yoseloff, 1959.

———. *University of Pennsylvania, Class of 1897, College, University of Pennsylvania, June, 1907*. [Philadelphia, 1907].

Loetscher, Lefferts A. *A Brief History of the Presbyterians*. Philadelphia: Westminster Press, 1978.

Loewen, James W. *Lies Across America: What Our Historic Sites Get Wrong*. New York: New Press, 1999.

Logan, Algernon Sydney. *Vistas from the Stream*. 2 vols. Philadelphia: National, 1934.

Longstreth, Thacher. *Main Line Wasp: The Education of Thacher Longstreth*. New York: Norton, 1990.

Lord, Ruth. *Henry F. du Pont and Winterthur: A Daughter's Portrait*. New Haven: Yale University Press, 1999.

Loth, Calder, and Julius Trousdale Sadler Jr. *The Only Proper Style: Gothic Architecture in America*. Boston: New York Graphic Society, 1975.

Loth, David. *Pencoyd and the Roberts Family*. New York: privately printed, 1985.

Lower Merion Historical Society. *The First 300: The Amazing and Rich History of Lower Merion*. Ardmore, PA, 2000.

Lukacs, John. *Philadelphia Patricians and Philistines, 1900–1950*. New York: Farrar, Straus & Giroux, 1981.

Lundberg, Ferdinand. *America's 60 Families*. New York: Vanguard Press, 1937.

Lynch, Patricia, SBS. *Sharing the Bread in Service: Sisters of the Blessed Sacrament, 1891–1991*. 2 vols. Bensalem, PA: Sisters of the Blessed Sacrament, 1998.

MacAfee, John Curtin. *The First Ninety Years of the Parish of the Holy Apostles, 1868–1958*. Philadelphia: Parish of the Holy Apostles, 1958.

Magat, Richard, ed. *Philanthropic Giving: Studies in Varieties and Goals*. New York: Oxford University Press, 1989.

Magaziner, Henry Jonas. *The Golden Age of Ironwork*. Ocean Pines, MD: SkipJack Press, 2000.

Manross, William Wilson. *A History of the American Episcopal Church*. New York: Morehouse-Gorham, 1959.

Manton, John C. *A Splendid Legacy: St. Timothy's, Roxborough, 1859–1984*. Philadelphia: St. Timothy's Church, 1984.

Mapp, Alf J., Jr. *The Faiths of Our Fathers: What America's Founders Really Believed*. Lanham, MD: Rowman & Littlefield, 2003.

Marcosson, Isaac F. "The Millionaire Yield of Philadelphia." *Munsey's Magazine*, July 1912, 483–505.

Marsden, George M. *Fundamentalism and American Culture*. New York: Oxford University Press, 1980.

———. *The Soul of the American University: From Protestant Establishment to Established Non-Belief*. New York: Oxford University Press, 1994.

Martin, Frederick Townsend. *The Passing of the Idle Rich*. 1911. Reprint, New York: Arno Press, 1975.

Martino, Joseph F. *Catharinae Mariae Drexel*. 3 vols. Rome: Congregatio pro Causis Sanctorum, 1986.

Marty, Martin E. *Modern American Religion: The Irony of It All, 1893–1919*. Chicago: University of Chicago Press, 1986.

Massa, Mark S. *Catholics and American Culture: Fulton Sheen, Dorothy Day, and the Notre Dame Football Team*. New York: Crossroad, 1999.

Massey, George Valentine, II. *The Mitchells and Days of Philadelphia*. New York: Irene A. Hermann Lithography, 1968.

Mathews, Shailer. *The Social Gospel*. Philadelphia: Griffith & Rowland Press, 1910.

May, Henry F. *Protestant Churches and Industrial America*. 1949. Reprint, New York: Harper & Row, 1967.

McCarthy, Kathleen D. *American Creed: Philanthropy and the Rise of Civil Society*. Chicago: University of Chicago Press, 2003.

———. *Noblesse Oblige: Charity and Cultural Philanthropy in Chicago, 1849–1929*. Chicago: University of Chicago Press, 1982.

McCloud, Sean. *Divine Hierarchies: Class in American Religion and Religious Studies*. Chapel Hill: University of North Carolina Press, 2007.

McCloud, Sean, and William A. Mirola, eds. *Religion and Class in America: Culture, History and Politics*. Boston: Brill Academic, 2008.

McDannell, Colleen. *Material Christianity: Religion and Popular Culture in America*. New Haven: Yale University Press, 1995.

McDonald, Edward D., and Edward M. Hinton. *Drexel Institute of Technology, 1891–1941: A Memorial History*. Philadelphia: Drexel Institute, 1942.

McGerr, Michael. *A Fierce Discontent: The Rise and Fall of the Progressive Movement in America, 1870–1920*. New York: Free Press, 2003.

McGreevy, John T. *Catholicism and American Freedom: A History*. New York: Norton, 2003.

———. *Parish Boundaries: The Catholic Encounter with Race in the Twentieth-Century Urban North*. Chicago: University of Chicago Press, 1996.

McWilliams, Carey. *A Mask for Privilege: Anti-Semitism in America*. Boston: Little, Brown, 1948.

Meigs, Arthur J. *An American Country House: The Property of Arthur E. Newbold Jr., Esq., Laverock, PA*. New York: Architectural Book, 1925.

Mellor, Walter, Arthur I. Meigs, and George Howe. *A Monograph of the Work of Mellor, Meigs, and Howe*. 1923. 2nd ed. New York: Architectural Book, 2000.

Memorial of Charles Wheeler. Philadelphia: privately printed, 1884.

Memorial Sermon and Addresses Delivered on the Occasion of the Twenty-fifth Anniversary of the Consecration to the Episcopate of the Right Reverend O. W. Whitaker, DD, Bishop of Pennsylvania, Together with Letters of Congratulation. Philadelphia: George W. Jacobs, 1895.

Meyer, Michael A. *Response to Modernity: A History of the Reform Movement in Judaism*. New York: Oxford University Press, 1988.

Middleton, Rev. Thomas C. *Historical Sketch of the Augustinian Monastery, College and Mission of St. Thomas of Villanova, Delaware County, PA During the First Half Century of Their Existence, 1842–1892*. Villanova, PA: Villanova College, 1893.

Miller, Thomas P. "Magnificent Obsession: Bishop Manning's Campaign to Build the Cathedral of St. John the Divine." Master's thesis, General Theological Seminary, 1997.

Mills, C. Wright. *The Power Elite*. New York: Oxford University Press, 1956.

Minnigerode, Meade. *Certain Rich Men: Stephen Girard—John Jacob Astor—Jay Cooke —Daniel Drew—Cornelius Vanderbilt—Jay Gould—Jim Fisk*. New York: Putnam, 1927.

Mitchell, S. Weir. *Hugh Wynne, Free Quaker*. New York: Century, 1896.

Montgomery, Maureen. *Gilded Prostitution: Status, Money, and Transatlantic Marriages, 1870–1914*. London: Routledge, 1989.

Moore, John M., ed. *Friends in the Delaware Valley: Philadelphia Yearly Meeting, 1681–1981*. Haverford: Friends Historical Association, 1981.

Moore, R. Laurence. *Selling God: American Religion in the Marketplace of Culture*. New York: Oxford University Press, 1994.

Morgan, David, and Sally M. Promey. *The Visual Culture of American Religions*. Berkeley: University of California Press, 2001.

Morley, Christopher. *Kitty Foyle*. Philadelphia: J. B. Lippincott, 1939.

Morone, James A. *Hellfire Nation: The Politics of Sin in American History*. New Haven: Yale University Press, 2004.

Morris, Charles, ed. *Makers of Philadelphia: An Historic Work*. Philadelphia: R. L. Hamersly, 1894.

Morris, Charles R. *American Catholic: The Saints and Sinners Who Built America's Most Powerful Church*. New York: Times Books, 1997.

Morrison, William. *The Main Line: Country Houses of Philadelphia's Storied Suburb, 1870–1930*. New York: Acanthus Press, 2002.

Mortimer, Rev. Alfred G. *Catholic Faith and Practice: A Manual of Theological Instruction for Confirmation and First Communion*. New York: Longmans, Green, 1897.

———. *It Ringeth to Evensong: Thoughts for Advancing Years on the Trials and the Blessings of Old Age*. London: Skeffington, 1906.

———. *S. Mark's Church, Philadelphia and its Lady Chapel with an Account of its History and Treasures*. New York: privately printed, 1909.

Moss, Roger W. *Historic Sacred Places of Philadelphia*. Philadelphia: University of Pennsylvania Press, 2005.

Muccigrosso, Robert. *American Gothic: The Mind and Art of Ralph Adams Cram*. Washington, DC: University Press of America, 1979.

Mullin, Robert Bruce. *Episcopal Vision/American Reality: High Church Theology and Social Thought in Evangelical America*. New Haven: Yale University Press, 1986.

Murphy, Thomas. *Duties of the Church Member to the Church*. Philadelphia: Presbyterian Board of Publication, 1878.

Mutchmore, Samuel A. *Mites Against Millions: Or, Childhood Against the World: How a Church Was Built and Paid for Through a Bequest of $4.41*. Philadelphia: Presbyterian, 1883.

Myers, Gustavus. *History of the Great American Fortunes*. Chicago: C. H. Kerr, 1909.

Nasaw, David. *Andrew Carnegie*. New York: Penguin Press, 2006.

Neale, J[ohn] M[ason]. *The History of Pews: A Paper Read Before the Cambridge Camden Society on Monday, November 22, 1841*. 2nd ed. Cambridge, 1842.

Nearing, Scott. *Educational Frontiers: A Book About Simon Nelson Patten and Other Teachers*. New York: T. Seltzer, 1925.

———. *The Making of a Radical: A Political Autobiography*. New York: Harper & Row, 1972.

———. *Poverty and Riches: A Study of the Industrial Regime*. Philadelphia: John C. Winston, 1916.

———. *Social Religion: An Interpretation of Christianity in Terms of Modern Life*. New York: Macmillan, 1913.

———. *The Solution of the Child Labor Problem*. New York: Moffat, Yard, 1911.

———. *Wages in the United States, 1908–1910*. New York: Macmillan, 1911.

Nelson, Timothy J. "At Ease with Our Own Kind: Worship Practices and Class Segregation in American Religion." In Sean McCloud and William A. Mirola, eds. *Religion and Class in America: Culture, History, and Politics*. Boston: Brill Academic, 2008.

Newman, Daisy. *A Procession of Friends: Quakers in America*. Garden City, NY: Doubleday, 1972.

Newton, Joseph Fort. *River of Years: An Autobiography*. Philadelphia: J. B. Lippincott, 1946.

Niebuhr, H. Richard. *The Social Sources of Denominationalism*. New York: Henry Holt, 1929.

Noll, Mark A. *America's God: From Jonathan Edwards to Abraham Lincoln*. New York: Oxford University Press, 2002.

———, ed. *God and Mammon: Protestants, Money, and the Market, 1790–1860*. New York: Oxford University Press, 2002.

Northup, Lesley Armstrong. *The 1892 Book of Common Prayer*. Lewiston, NY: Edwin Mellen Press, 1993.

Oates, Mary J. *The Catholic Philanthropic Tradition in America*. Bloomington: Indiana University Press, 1995.

———. *Saint Katharine Drexel: Salvation, Education, and Philanthropy*. Indianapolis: Center on Philanthropy at Indiana University, 2001.

Oberholtzer, Ellis Paxson. *Philadelphia: A History of the City and Its People*. 3 vols. Philadelphia: S. J. Clarke, 1912.

Official Year-Book of the Church of England. London: Society for Promoting Christian Knowledge, 1897.

Ogden, Robert C. *Pew Rents and the New Testament: Can They Be Reconciled?* New York: Fleming H. Revell, 1892.

O'Gorman, James F. *The Architecture of Frank Furness*. Philadelphia: Philadelphia Museum of Art, 1973.

———, ed. *The Makers of Trinity Church in the City of Boston*. Amherst: University of Massachusetts Press, 2004.

O'Hara, Constance. *Heaven Was Not Enough*. Philadelphia: J. B. Lippincott, 1955.

Olds, Kelly. "Privatizing the Church: Disestablishment in Connecticut and Massachusetts." *The Journal of Political Economy* 102 (April 1994): 277–97.

Oliveri, Gregory William. "Building a Baroque Catholicism: The Philadelphia Churches of Edwin Forrest Durang." Master's thesis, University of Delaware, 1999.

Orsi, Robert A. *The Madonna of 115th Street: Faith and Community in Italian Harlem, 1880–1950*. New Haven: Yale University Press, 1985.

Ostrander, Susan A. *Women of the Upper Class*. Philadelphia: Temple University Press, 1984.

Ostrower, Francie. "Donor Control and Perpetual Trusts: Does Anything Last Forever?" In Richard Magat, ed. *Philanthropic Giving: Studies in Varieties and Goals*. New York: Oxford University Press, 1989.

———. *Why the Wealthy Give: The Culture of Elite Philanthropy*. Princeton: Princeton University Press, 1995.

O'Toole, Patricia. *Money and Morals in America: A History*. New York: Clarkson Potter, 1998.

Overbrook Presbyterian Church. *The Place Where Thy Glory Dwells: The Story of Overbrook Presbyterian Church, 1890–1958*. Philadelphia, 1958.

Page, Max. *The Creative Destruction of Manhattan, 1900–1940*. Chicago: University of Chicago Press, 2001.

Paley, F. A. *A Manual of Gothic Architecture*. London: J. Van Voorst, 1846.

Paret, William. *Reminiscences*. Philadelphia: George W. Jacobs, 1911.

Patten, Simon N. *The Social Basis of Religion*. New York: Macmillan, 1914.

Pennell, Elizabeth Robins. *Our Philadelphia*. Philadelphia: J. B. Lippincott, 1914.

Penn Mutual Life Insurance Company. *Seventy-Fifth Anniversary*. Philadelphia, 1922.

Pepper, George Wharton. *By What Authority?* Cambridge: Episcopal Evangelical Fellowship, 1934.

———. *Men and Issues: A Selection of Speeches and Articles*. Compiled by Horace Green. New York: Duffield, 1924.

———. *Philadelphia Lawyer: An Autobiography*. Philadelphia: J. B. Lippincott, 1944.

———. *A Voice from the Crowd*. New Haven: Yale University Press, 1915.

———. *The Way: A Devotional Book for Boys*. New York: Longmans, Green, 1912.

Perry, Rev. J. DeWolf. *Memorial Sermon Preached at the Convention of the Diocese of Pennsylvania, May 9, 1911 in Memory of the Rt. Rev. O. W. Whitaker, DD, LLD*. [Philadelphia, 1911].

Philadelphia and Popular Philadelphians. Philadelphia: North American, 1891.

Philadelphia War History Committee. *Philadelphia in the World War, 1914–1919*. New York: Wynkoop Hallenbeck Crawford, 1922.

Phillips, Kevin P. *Wealth and Democracy: A Political History of the American Rich*. New York: Broadway Books, 2002.

Phillips, Roderick. *Untying the Knot: A Short History of Divorce*. New York: Cambridge University Press, 1991.

Plantz, Samuel. *The Church and the Social Problem: A Study in Applied Christianity*. Cincinnati: Jennings & Graham, 1906.

Pointer, Richard W. "Philadelphia Presbyterians, Capitalism, and the Morality of Economic Success." In Mark A. Noll, ed., *God and Mammon: Protestants, Money, and the Market, 1790–1860*. New York: Oxford University Press, 2002.

Potter, Henry Codman, D.D., LL.D. *The Scholar and the State and Other Orations and Addresses*. New York: Century, 1897.

PQ Corporation. *A Proper Concern: A History of the PQ Corporation; 150th Anniversary, 1831–1981*. [Valley Forge,] 1981.

Prescott, Oliver S. "Is Fairness in Religious Controversy Impossible? A Letter to Rev. Daniel R. Goodwin, DD, LLD." Philadelphia, 1879.

Prichard, Robert W. *A History of the Episcopal Church*. Harrisburg: Morehouse, 1991.

Provident Life Insurance and Trust Company. "Charter and By-laws of the Provident Life and Trust Company of Philadelphia: Incorporated by the State of Pennsylvania, Third Month 22, 1865; Organized, Sixth Month 28, 1865; Capital, $1,000,000.00; Insures Lives, Grants Annuities, and Executes Trusts." Philadelphia, 1865.

Provident Mutual Life Insurance Company. "75 Years of Provident Protection." Philadelphia, 1940.

Pugin, A. Welby. *An Apology for the Revival of Christian Architecture in England.* 1843. Reprint, London: Butler & Tanner, 1969.

Putnam, Robert D. *Bowling Alone: The Collapse and Revival of American Community.* New York: Simon & Schuster, 2000.

Pyle, Ralph E. *Persistence and Change in the Protestant Establishment.* Westport, CT: Praeger, 1996.

Rainsford, W. S. *The Story of a Varied Life: An Autobiography.* 1922. Reprint, Freeport, NY: Books for Libraries Press, 1970.

Rauschenbusch, Walter. *Christianity and the Social Crisis.* 1907. Reprint, New York: Harper & Row, 1964.

Reed, John Shelton. *Glorious Battle: The Cultural Politics of Victorian Anglo-Catholicism.* Nashville: Vanderbilt University Press, 1996.

Reed, Pat Bringhurst, ed. *Westtown in Word and Deed, 1799–1999: An Anthology.* Westtown, PA: Westtown School, 1998.

Reeve, J. Stanley. *Radnor Reminiscences: A Foxhunting Journal.* Boston: Houghton Mifflin, 1921.

Reform Congregation Keneseth Israel: Its First 100 Years, 1847–1947. Philadelphia: Drake Press, 1950.

Remnick, David, ed. *The New Gilded Age: "The New Yorker" Looks at the Culture of Affluence.* New York: Random House, 2000.

Report of [George L.] Harrison et al. vs. St. Mark's Church, Philadelphia: A Bill to Restrain the Ringing of Bells so as to Cause a Nuisance to the Occupants of the Dwellings in the Immediate Vicinity of the Church: In the Court of Common Pleas, no. 2. In Equity. Before Hare, PJ, and Mitchell, Associate J. Philadelphia, 1877.

Repplier, Agnes. *Agnes Irwin: A Biography.* Garden City, NY: Doubleday, Doran, 1934.

———. *Eight Decades.* 1904. Reprint, Boston: Houghton Mifflin, 1937.

———. *In Our Convent Days.* Boston: Houghton Mifflin, 1905.

———. *Philadelphia: The Place and the People.* New York: Macmillan, 1898.

Resek, Carl, ed. *The Progressives.* Indianapolis: Bobbs-Merrill, 1967.

Rhinelander, Philip Mercer. *The Faith of the Cross: Being the Bishop Paddock Lectures Delivered at the General Theological Seminary New York in February 1914.* New York: Longmans, Green, 1916.

Rhodes, Harrison. "Who Is a Philadelphian?" *Harper's Magazine* (June 1916): 1–13.

Richards, F. Lee. "The Episcopalians." In Jean Barth Toll and Mildred S. Gillam, eds., *Invisible Philadelphia: Community Through Voluntary Organizations.* Philadelphia: Atwater Kent Museum, 1995.

Richey, Russell E. "Denominations and Denominationalism: An American Morphology." In Robert Bruce Mullin and Russell E. Richey, eds., *Re-Imagining Denominationalism: Interpretive Essays.* New York: Oxford University Press, 1994.

Richmond, George Chalmers. *Frederic Dan Huntington, First Bishop of Central New York, 1869–1894: An Appreciation.* Rochester, NY, 1908.

———. *Sermons: Series II* ["Case of Scott Nearing"—"Pepperism"—"The Curse of Philadelphia's Educational, Political and Religious Life"— "A Reply to J. William White's Defense of the University Trustees"—"Christianity and Grundyism"]. Philadelphia, 1915.

Rider College Student Center Gallery. *D'Ascenzo: The Art of Stained Glass from the Collection of Stanley Switlik.* Trenton: Rider College, 1973.

Rifkind, Carole. *A Field Guide to American Architecture.* New York: New American Library, 1980.

Rights and Duties of Sessions and Trustees in Presbyterian Churches. Philadelphia: Presbyterian Board of Publication, [1883].

Riley, Glenda. *Divorce: An American Tradition.* New York: Oxford University Press, 1991.

Riley, William B. *The Perennial Revival: A Plea for Evangelization.* 1904. Rev. ed. Philadelphia: American Baptist Publication Society, 1916.

Rilling, Donna J. *Making Houses, Crafting Capitalism: Builders in Philadelphia, 1790–1850.* Philadelphia: University of Pennsylvania Press, 2001.

Rittler, Rev. John Marlin. *One Man and His God: An Historical Memento of John Wanamaker and Bethany Presbyterian Church of Philadelphia, Pa.* [Philadelphia]: 1969.

Roberts, Joan Church. *Our First One Hundred Years, 1888–1988.* Bala Cynwyd: Church of St. Asaph, 1992.

Rodgers, Daniel T. *Age of Fracture.* Cambridge, MA: Belknap Press, 2011.

———. *Atlantic Crossings: Social Politics in a Progressive Age.* Cambridge, MA: Belknap Press, 1998.

Rose, Anne C. *Beloved Strangers: Interfaith Families in Nineteenth-Century America.* Cambridge, MA: Harvard University Press, 2001.

Rosen, Evelyn Bodek. *The Philadelphia Fels, 1880–1920: A Social Portrait.* Madison, NJ: Fairleigh Dickinson University Press, 2000.

Rosen, Philip. "German Jews vs. Russian Jews in Philadelphia Philanthropy." In Murray Friedman, ed., *Jewish Life in Philadelphia, 1830–1940.* Philadelphia: ISHI, 1983.

Rosenberg, Shelley Kapnek. *Reform Congregation Keneseth Israel, 150 Years.* Elkins Park: Reform Congregation Keneseth Israel, 1997.

Roth, Anthony, comp. *The Episcopal Churches of Philadelphia: A Series of Articles that Appeared in the Church Standard, 1899–1900.* Philadelphia, 1973.

Roth, Leland M. *American Architecture: A History.* Boulder, CO: Icon Editions/Westview Press, 2001.

Rottenberg, Dan. *The Man Who Made Wall Street: Anthony J. Drexel and the Rise of Modern Finance.* Philadelphia: University of Pennsylvania Press, 2001.

———. *The Shared Vision of Saint Katharine Drexel and Anthony J. Drexel.* Philadelphia: Drexel University, 2000.

Rowe, L. S. "The Municipality and the Gas Supply, as Illustrated by the Experience of Philadelphia." *Annals of the American Academy of Political and Social Science* 11 (May 1898): 301–23.

Rowntree, B. Seebohm. *The Human Factor in Business: Further Experiments in Industrial Democracy.* 1921. 3rd ed. London: Longmans, Green, 1938.

Rugoff, Milton. *America's Gilded Age: Intimate Portraits from an Era of Extravagance and Change, 1850–1890.* New York: Holt, 1989.

Rules of Discipline of the Yearly Meeting of Friends for Pennsylvania, New Jersey, Delaware, and the Eastern Parts of Maryland (Orthodox). Philadelphia: Friends' Book Store, 1890.

Rules of Discipline of the Yearly Meeting of Men and Women Friends (Hicksite). Philadelphia: Philadelphia Yearly Meeting, 1877.

Rush, Cary H. *All Saints' Church: A 225 Year History of a Parish, 1772–1997.* Philadelphia: All Saints' Church, 1996.

Ryan, Mary P. *Cradle of the Middle Class: The Family in Oneida County, New York, 1790–1865.* New York: Cambridge University Press, 1981.

Rzeznik, Thomas F. "The Parochial Enterprise: Financing Institutional Growth in the Brick-and-Mortar Era." *American Catholic Studies* (Fall 2010): 1–24.

St. Clement's Church Case: A Complete Account of the Proceedings in the Court of Common Pleas for the County of Philadelphia in Equity Before the Honorable James R. Ludlow, one of the Judges of said court, to restrain the vestry of St. Clement's Church from dismissing the Rector and Assistant Minister without a trial and against the protest of the congregation of said church, together with an appendix containing statements of similar cases in New Jersey, Michigan, Massachusetts, and Maryland. Philadelphia: Bourquin & Welsh, 1871.

Saltmarsh, John A. *Scott Nearing: An Intellectual Biography.* Philadelphia: Temple University Press, 1991.

Sarna, Jonathan. "Seating and the American Synagogue." In Jon Butler and Harry S. Stout, eds., *Religion and American History: A Reader.* New York: Oxford University Press, 1997.

Sass, Steven A. *The Pragmatic Imagination: A History of the Wharton School, 1881–1991.* Philadelphia: University of Pennsylvania Press, 1982.

Schama, Simon. *The Embarrassment of Riches: An Interpretation of Dutch Culture in the Golden Age.* New York: Knopf, 1987.

Schantz, Mark S. *Piety in Providence: Class Dimensions of Religious Experience in Antebellum Rhode Island.* Ithaca: Cornell University Press, 2000.

Scharf, J. Thomas. *History of Philadelphia, 1609–1884.* 3 vols. Philadelphia: L. H. Everts, 1884.

Schmidt, Corwin, ed. *Religion as Social Capital: Producing the Common Good.* Waco: Baylor University Press, 2004.

Schmidt, Eric Leigh. *Consumer Rites: The Buying and Selling of American Holidays.* Princeton: Princeton University Press, 1995.

Schrag, Peter. *The Decline of the WASP.* New York: Touchstone Press, 1970.

Schultz, Kevin M. *Tri-Faith America: How Catholics and Jews Held Postwar America to Its Protestant Promise.* New York: Oxford University Press, 2011.

Scranton, Philip. *Endless Novelty: Specialty Production and American Industrialization, 1865–1925.* Princeton: Princeton University Press, 1997.

———. *Figured Tapestry: Production, Markets, and Power in Philadelphia Textiles, 1885–1941.* New York: Cambridge University Press, 1989.

———. "Large Firms and Industrial Restructuring: The Philadelphia Region, 1900–1980." *Pennsylvania Magazine of History and Biography* 116 (October 1992): 419–65.

———. *Proprietary Capitalism: The Textile Manufacture at Philadelphia, 1800–1885.* New York: Cambridge University Press, 1983.

Scull, William Ellis. *William Ellis Scull, Sometime Quaker: An Autobiography.* Philadelphia: John C. Winston, 1939.

Sealander, Judith. *Private Wealth and Public Life: Foundation Philanthropy and the Reshaping of American Social Policy from the Progressive Era to the New Deal.* Baltimore: Johns Hopkins University Press, 1997.

Sears, Charles Hatch. *The Redemption of the City.* Philadelphia: Griffith & Rowland Press, 1911.

Seasoltz, R. Kevin. *A Sense of the Sacred: Theological Foundations of Sacred Architecture and Art.* New York: Continuum, 2005.

Second Annual Report of the Free Church Association. Philadelphia: Free Church Association, 1877.

Sellers, Horace Wells. "The Architectural Spirit of Christ Church." *Pennsylvania Magazine of History and Biography* 54 (1930): 315–19.

Sewell, Marilyn, ed. *Resurrecting Grace: Remembering Catholic Childhoods.* Boston: Beacon Press, 2001.

Shackelford, Geoff. *The Captain: George C. Thomas Jr. and His Golf Architecture.* Chelsea, MI: Sleeping Bear Press, 1996.

Shand-Tucci, Douglass. *Ralph Adams Cram: Life and Architecture.* Amherst: University of Massachusetts Press, 1995.

Sharpless, Isaac. *The Story of A Small College.* Philadelphia: John C. Winston, 1918.

Shearer, Francis A., ed. *Cathedral Village: The First Decade, 1979–1989.* [Philadelphia, 1989].

Shelton, Cynthia J. *The Mills of Manayunk: Industrialization and Social Conflict in the Philadelphia Region, 1787–1873.* Baltimore: Johns Hopkins University Press, 1986.

Shepherd, Samuel C., Jr. *Avenues of Faith: Shaping the Urban Religious Culture of Richmond, Virginia, 1900–1929.* Tuscaloosa: University of Alabama Press, 2001.

Sherman, Steve, ed. *A Scott Nearing Reader: The Good Life in Bad Times.* Metuchen, NJ: Scarecrow Press, 1989.

Shinn, George Wolfe. *King's Handbook of Notable Episcopal Churches in the United States.* Boston: Moses King, 1889.

Silcox, Harry C. *A Place to Live and Work: The Henry Disston Saw Works and the Tacony Community of Philadelphia.* University Park: Pennsylvania State University Press, 1994.

Silk, Leonard, and Mark Silk. *The American Establishment*. New York: Basic Books, 1978.

Silliman, Charles A. *The Episcopal Church in Delaware, 1785–1954*. Wilmington: Diocese of Delaware, 1982.

———. *The Story of Christ Church Christiana Hundred and Its People*. Wilmington, 1960.

Sinclair, David. *Dynasty: The Astors and Their Times*. New York: Beaufort Books, 1984.

Sisters of the Blessed Sacrament. *Century Book*. Bensalem, PA, 1990.

Skerrett, Ellen, Edward R. Kantowicz, and Steven M. Avella. *Catholicism, Chicago Style*. Chicago: Loyola University Press, 1993.

Smith, Chris. *Reshaping Work: The Cadbury Experience*. New York: Cambridge University Press, 1990.

Smith, Gary Scott. *The Search for Social Salvation: Social Christianity and America, 1880–1925*. Lanham, MD: Lexington Books, 2000.

Smith, Hannah Whitall. *A Christian's Secret to a Happy Life*. 1875. Reprint, New York: Garland, 1984.

———. *John M. Whitall: The Story of His Life*. Philadelphia: privately printed, 1879.

———. *The Unselfishness of God and How I Discovered It: A Spiritual Autobiography*. New York: Fleming H. Revell, 1903.

Smith, Logan Pearsall. *A Religious Rebel: The Letters of "HWS" (Mrs. Pearsall Smith)*. London: Nisbet, 1949.

———. *Unforgotten Years*. 1937. Reprint, Boston: Little, Brown, 1939.

Smylie, James H. *A Brief History of the Presbyterians*. Louisville: Geneva Press, 1996.

Spanning Four Centuries: Pages of Parish Histories of the Episcopal Diocese of Pennsylvania. Philadelphia: Diocese of Pennsylvania, 1997.

Speakman, Thomas H. *Ritualism and Dogmatic Theology: A Series of Essays on the Causes of the Declension in the Society of Friends*. Philadelphia: Friends Book Association, 1891.

Stanton, Phoebe B. *The Gothic Revival and American Church Architecture: An Episode in Taste, 1840–1856*. Baltimore: Johns Hopkins Press, 1968.

Steffens, Lincoln. *The Shame of the Cities*. New York: McClure, Phillips, 1904.

Stern, Robert A. M. *George Howe: Toward a Modern American Architecture*. New Haven: Yale University Press, 1975.

Sterne, Evelyn Savidge. *Ballots and Bibles: Ethnic Politics and the Catholic Church in Providence*. Ithaca: Cornell University Press, 2004.

Stevick, Philip. *Imagining Philadelphia: Travelers' Views of the City from 1800 to the Present*. Philadelphia: University of Pennsylvania Press, 1996.

Stokes, John S. *Memoirs of John S. Stokes: A Minister of the Gospel in the Society of Friends*. Edited by Joseph Walton. Philadelphia: Friends' Book Store, 1893.

Stokes, Tyson. *No Axe to Grind*. Wayne, PA: Haverford House, 1982.

Story, Ronald. *The Forging of an Aristocracy: Harvard and the Boston Upper Class, 1800–1870*. Middletown, CT: Wesleyan University Press, 1980.

Stout, Harry S., and D. G. Hart, eds. *New Directions in American Religious History*. New York: Oxford University Press, 1997.

Strachey, Barbara, and Jane Samuels, eds. *Mary Berenson: A Self-Portrait from Her Letters and Diaries*. New York: Norton, 1983.

Strachey, Ray. *A Quaker Grandmother: Hannah Whitall Smith*. New York: Fleming H. Revell, 1914.

Strong, Ann L., and George E. Thomas. *The Book of the School, 100 Years: The Graduate School of Fine Arts of the University of Pennsylvania*. Philadelphia: Graduate School of Fine Arts, 1990.

Strong, Josiah. *Our Country*. 1891. Reprint, Cambridge, MA: Belknap Press, 1963.

Strouse, Jean. *Morgan: American Financier*. New York: Random House, 1999.

Stuart, Percy C. "Architectural Schools in the United States, University of Pennsylvania—no. 2." *Architectural Record* (January 1901): 313–36.

Sugeno, Frank. "The Establishmentarian Ideal and the Mission of the Episcopal Church."
    Historical Magazine of the Protestant Episcopal Church (December 1984): 285–92.

Sydnor, William. *The Story of the Real Prayer Book, 1549–1979*. Wilton, CT: Morehouse, 1989.

Tatman, Sandra L. and Roger W. Moss, eds. *Biographical Dictionary of Philadelphia Architects,
    1700–1930*. Boston: G. K. Hall, 1985.

T[aylor], R[ebecca] N[icholson]. *Memoir of Mary Whitall*. Philadelphia: privately printed, 1885.

Teaford, Jon. *The Unheralded Triumph: City Government in America, 1870–1900*. Baltimore:
    Johns Hopkins University Press, 1984.

Thayer, Charles W. *Muzzy*. New York: Harper & Row, 1966.

Thomas, George C. *Books, Autographs and Manuscripts in the Library of George C. Thomas*.
    Philadelphia: privately printed, 1907.

———. *Letters to the Officers, Teachers, and Scholars of the Sunday-School of the Church of the
    Holy Apostles, Philadelphia, by George C. Thomas While Abroad in 1904*. Philadelphia:
    privately printed, 1904.

Thomas, George E. "Architectural Patronage and Social Stratification in Philadelphia Between
    1840 and 1920." In William W. Cutler, III, and Howard Gillette, Jr., eds., *The Divided
    Metropolis: Social and Spatial Dimensions in Philadelphia, 1800–1975*. Westport, CT:
    Greenwood Press, 1980.

Thomas, Kathleen H. *The History and Significance of Quaker Symbols in Sect Formation*.
    Lewiston, NY: Edwin Mellen Press, 2002.

Thorpe, Francis Newton. *William Pepper, M.D., LL.D. (1843–1898), Provost of the University of
    Pennsylvania*. Philadelphia: J. B. Lippincott, 1904.

Tinkcom, Harry M. "The Revolutionary City, 1765–1783." In Russell F. Weigley, ed.,
    Philadelphia: A 300-Year History. New York: Norton, 1982.

Toll, Jean Barth, and Mildred S. Gillam, eds. *Invisible Philadelphia: Community Through
    Voluntary Organizations*. Philadelphia: Atwater Kent Museum, 1995.

Toll, Jean Barth, and Michael J. Schwanger, eds. *Montgomery County: The Second Hundred
    Years*. 2 vols. Norristown, PA: Montgomery County Federation of Historical
    Societies, 1983.

Tolles, Frederick B. *Meeting House and Counting House: The Quaker Merchants of Colonial
    Philadelphia, 1682–1763*. Chapel Hill: University of North Carolina Press, 1948.

Toop, George Herbert. *History of the Parish of the Holy Apostles, Philadelphia, 1868–1918*.
    Philadelphia: Parish of the Holy Apostles, 1918.

*To Prohibit the Use of the Name of Any Religious Denomination, Society, or Association for the
    Purposes of Trade and Commerce*. H. R. 435, Serial 30, February 3, 1916. Washington,
    DC: Government Printing Office, 1916.

Townsend, John W. *The Old Main Line*. [Philadelphia], 1922.

Townsend, Thomas. *My Life and Heritage*. Mystic, CT: privately printed, 1998.

Tralle, Henry Edward. *Planning Church Buildings*. Philadelphia: Judson Press, 1921.

Treese, Lorett. *Valley Forge: Making and Remaking a National Symbol*. University Park:
    Pennsylvania State University Press, 1995.

Tucker, Gregory W. *America's Church: The Basilica of the National Shrine of the Immaculate
    Conception*. Huntington, IN: Our Sunday Visitor Publications, 2000.

Tweed, Thomas A. *America's Church: The National Shrine and Catholic Presence in the Nation's
    Capital*. Oxford University Press, 2011.

Twelves, J. Wesley. *A History of the Diocese of Pennsylvania of the Protestant Episcopal Church
    in the USA, 1784–1968*. Philadelphia: Diocese of Pennsylvania, 1969.

Van Rensselaer, Mrs. John King. *Newport: Our Social Capital*. Philadelphia: J. B. Lippincott, 1905.

Van Rensselaer, Mrs. John King, with Frederic Van de Water. *The Social Ladder*. New York:
    Henry Holt, 1924.

Varter, Bradford. "Spiritual Capital: Theorizing Religion with Bourdieu Against Bourdieu."
    Sociological Theory (June 2003): 150–74.

Vauclain, Samuel M., with Earl Chapin May. *Steaming Up! The Autobiography of Samuel M. Vauclain*. New York: Brewer & Warren, 1930.

Veblen, Thorstein. *The Theory of the Leisure Class*. 1899. Reprint, New York: Modern Library, 2001.

Vogel, William P., Jr. *Precision, People, and Progress: A Business Philosophy at Work*. Philadelphia: Leeds & Northrup, 1949.

Wagner, Rev. Harold Ezra. *The Episcopal Church in Wisconsin, 1847–1947: A History of the Diocese of Milwaukee*. Milwaukee: Diocese of Milwaukee, 1947.

Wainwright, Nicholas B. *History of the Church of the Messiah, Gwynedd: Its First Hundred Years, 1866–1966*. Gwynedd: Church of the Messiah, 1966.

Wall, Joseph Frazier. *Alfred I. du Pont: The Man and His Family*. New York: Oxford University Press, 1990.

———. *Andrew Carnegie*. New York: Oxford University Press, 1970.

Wallace, Anthony F. C. *Rockdale: The Growth of an American Village in the Early Industrial Revolution*. New York: Knopf, 1978.

Walton, Joseph, ed. *Memoirs of John S. Stokes: A Minister of the Gospel in the Society of Friends*. Philadelphia: Friends' Book Store, 1893.

Wanamaker, John. *Maxims of Life in Business*. New York: Harper, 1923.

———. *Prayers at Bethany Chapel*. Edited by A. Gordon MacLennan. New York: Fleming H. Revell, 1925.

Ward, Harry F. *The New Social Order: Principles and Programs*. New York: Macmillan, 1923.

Ward, James A. *J. Edgar Thomson: Master of the Pennsylvania*. Westport, CT: Greenwood Press, 1980.

Warner, Sam Bass, Jr. *The Private City: Philadelphia in Three Periods of Its Growth*. Philadelphia: University of Pennsylvania Press, 1968.

Warren, Richard A. "Displaced 'Pan-Americans' and the Transformation of the Catholic Church in Philadelphia." *Pennsylvania Magazine of History and Biography* (October 2004): 343–66.

Washburn, Henry Bradford. *Philip Mercer Rhinelander: Seventh Bishop of Pennsylvania, First Warden of the College of Preachers*. New York: Morehouse-Gorham, 1950.

Watson, Frank R. "The Cathedral Vision for Philadelphia." *Cathedral Age* (Easter 1933): 13–21.

Watson, Robert C. *First Ladies of the United States: A Biographical Dictionary*. Boulder, CO: Lynne Rienner, 2001.

Wattenmaker, Richard J. *Samuel Yellin in Context*. Flint: Flint Institute of Arts, 1985.

Wecter, Dixon. *The Saga of American Society: A Record of Social Aspiration, 1607–1937*. New York: Scribner, 1937.

Weigley, Russell F., ed. *Philadelphia: A 300-Year History*. New York: Norton, 1982.

Weiner, Isaac A. "Religion Out Loud: Religious Sound, Public Space, and American Pluralism." Ph.D. diss., University of North Carolina at Chapel Hill, 2009.

Welcome Society. *Twenty-Fifth Anniversary, Charter, By-Laws, Members, Annual Report, Activities: 250th Anniversary of Pennsylvania*. Philadelphia, 1931.

Werner, M. R. *Julius Rosenwald: The Life of a Practical Humanitarian*. New York: Harper, 1939.

West, Stanley R. *Centennial History of the Philadelphia Divinity School: The Divinity School of the Protestant Episcopal Church in Philadelphia, 1857–1957*. Philadelphia, 1971.

Whiffen, Marcus. *American Architecture Since 1780: A Guide to Styles*. 1969. Rev. ed. Cambridge, MA: MIT Press, 1992.

White, Ronald C., Jr., and Howard C., Hopkins, eds. *The Social Gospel: Religion and Reform in Changing America*. Philadelphia: Temple University Press, 1976.

White, Tretwell M. *Famous Leaders of Industry*. 3rd series: *The Life Stories of Boys Who Have Succeeded*. 1931. Reprint, Freeport, NY: Books for Libraries Press, 1971.

White, William P., and William H. Scott, eds. *The Presbyterian Church in Philadelphia*. Philadelphia: Allen, Lane & Scott, 1893.

Whiteman, Maxwell. *Gentlemen in Crisis: The First Century of the Union League of Philadelphia, 1862–1962*. Philadelphia: The Union League, 1975.

Wiebe, Robert H. *Businessmen and Reform: A Study of the Progressive Movement.* Cambridge, MA: Harvard University Press, 1962.

———. *The Search for Order, 1877–1920.* New York: Hill and Wang, 1967.

Williams, Peter W. "The Gospel of Wealth and the Gospel of Art: Episcopalians and Cultural Philanthropy from the Gilded Age to the Depression." *Anglican and Episcopal History* (June 2006): 170–223.

———. *Houses of God: Region, Religion, and Architecture in the United States.* Urbana: University of Illinois Press, 1997.

Willis, Carol. *Form Follows Finance: Skyscrapers and Skylines in New York and Chicago.* New York: Princeton Architectural Press, 1995.

Willits, Joseph H., ed. *Unemployment: Some Points of Attack in Lessening It in the Future.* Philadelphia: Friends' General Conference, 1935.

Willson, Joseph. *The Elite of Our People: Joseph Willson's Sketches of Upper-Class Life in Antebellum Philadelphia.* 1841. Reprint, University Park: Pennsylvania State University Press, 2000.

Wilson, William Bender. *History of the Pennsylvania Railroad Company.* 2 vols. Philadelphia: Henry T. Coates, 1895.

Wing, Asa. *Mortality Experience of the Provident Life & Trust Company of Philadelphia, 1866 to 1885.* Philadelphia: Provident Life & Trust, 1886.

Wistar, Isaac Jones. *The Autobiography of Isaac Jones Wistar.* 2 vols. Philadelphia: Wistar Institute of Anatomy and Biology, 1914.

Wister, Jones. *Jones Wister's Reminiscences.* Philadelphia: J. B. Lippincott, 1920.

Wister, Owen. *Romney, and Other New Works About Philadelphia.* Edited by James A. Butler. University Park: Pennsylvania State University Press, 2001.

Witmer, Lightner. *The Nearing Case: The Limitation of Academic Freedom at the University of Pennsylvania by Act of the Board of Trustees, June 14, 1915.* New York: B. W. Huebsch, 1915.

Wolf, Edwin, II. "The German-Jewish Influence in Philadelphia's Jewish Charities." In Murray Friedman, ed., *Jewish Life in Philadelphia, 1830–1940.* Philadelphia: ISHI, 1983.

Woodruff, Clinton Rogers, ed. *City Government by Commission.* New York: D. Appleton, 1911.

———. *A New Municipal Program.* New York: D. Appleton, 1919.

Woods, Mary N. *From Craft to Profession: The Practice of Architecture in Nineteenth-Century America.* Berkeley: University of California Press, 1999.

Woods, Thomas E., Jr. *The Church Confronts Modernity: Catholic Intellectuals and the Progressive Era.* New York: Columbia University Press, 2004.

Woodward, George. *Memoirs of a Mediocre Man.* Philadelphia: Harris, 1935.

Woolverton, John Frederick. *Colonial Anglicanism in North America.* Detroit: Wayne State University Press, 1984.

———. "William Reed Huntington and Church Unity: The Historical and Theological Background of the Chicago-Lambeth Quadrilateral." Ph.D. diss., Columbia University, 1963.

Worcester, J. H., Jr. *The Power and Weakness of Money.* Philadelphia: Presbyterian Board of Publication and Sabbath-School Work, 1889.

Wright, Carroll D. *The Battles of Labor: Being the William Levi Bull Lectures for the Year 1906.* Philadelphia: George W. Jacobs, 1906.

———. *The Slums of Baltimore, Chicago, New York, and Philadelphia.* 1894. Reprint, New York: Arno Press, 1970.

Wright, J. Robert. *Saint Thomas Church Fifth Avenue.* Grand Rapids, MI: Eerdmans; New York: Saint Thomas Church Fifth Avenue, 2001.

Wuthnow, Robert. *All in Sync: How Music and Art Are Revitalizing American Religion.* Berkeley: University of California Press, 2003.

———. *The Restructuring of American Religion: Society and Faith Since World War II.* Princeton: Princeton University Press, 1988.

Yanagihara, Hikaru. "Some Educational Attitudes of the Protestant Episcopal Church in America: A Historical Study of the Attitudes of the Church and Churchmen Toward the Founding and Maintaining of Colleges and Schools Under Their Influence Before 1900." Ph.D. diss., Columbia University, 1958.

Yarnall, Elizabeth Biddle. *Addison Hutton: Quaker Architect, 1834–1916*. Philadelphia: Art Alliance Press, 1974.

Yates, W. Ross. *Joseph Wharton: Quaker Industrial Pioneer*. Bethlehem: Lehigh University Press, 1987.

Yerkes, Rev. Royden Keith. *The History of Saint Luke's Church, Germantown, Pennsylvania*. Philadelphia, 1912.

Young, Clarence Andrew. *The Down-Town Church: A Study of a Social Institution in Transition*. Lancaster, PA: Intelligencer Printing, 1912.

Young, John Russell, ed. *Memorial History of the City of Philadelphia*. 2 vols. New York: New York History, 1898.

Zahniser, Keith. *Steel City Gospel: Protestant Laity and Reform in Progressive-Era Pittsburgh*. New York: Routledge, 2005.

Zelizer, Viviana A. Rotman. *Morals and Markets: The Development of Life Insurance in the United States*. New York: Columbia University Press, 1979.

Zuckerman, Michael, ed. *Friends and Neighbors: Group Life in America's First Plural Society*. Philadelphia: Temple University Press, 1982.

Zunz, Oliver. *Philanthropy in America: A History*. Princeton: Princeton University Press, 2011.

INDEX

Page numbers in italics refer to illustrations.

CPSIA information can be obtained
at www.ICGtesting.com
Printed in the USA
LVHW041555130619
621125LV00002B/356

9 780271 059686